OECD/G20 Base Erosion and Profit Shifting Project

Country-by-Country Reporting – Compilation of Peer Review Reports (Phase 3)

INCLUSIVE FRAMEWORK ON BEPS: ACTION 13

OECD
BETTER POLICIES FOR BETTER LIVES

Please cite this publication as:
OECD (2020), *Country-by-Country Reporting – Compilation of Peer Review Reports (Phase 3) : Inclusive Framework on BEPS: Action 13* , OECD/G20 Base Erosion and Profit Shifting Project, OECD Publishing, Paris, *https://doi.org/10.1787/fa6d31d7-en*.

ISBN 978-92-64-87254-7 (print)
ISBN 978-92-64-78206-8 (pdf)

OECD/G20 Base Erosion and Profit Shifting Project
ISSN 2313-2604 (print)
ISSN 2313-2612 (online)

Photo credits: Cover © ninog - Fotolia.com.

Corrigenda to publications may be found on line at: *www.oecd.org/about/publishing/corrigenda.htm*.

Foreword

The integration of national economies and markets has increased substantially in recent years, putting a strain on the international tax rules, which were designed more than a century ago. Weaknesses in the current rules create opportunities for base erosion and profit shifting (BEPS), requiring bold moves by policy makers to restore confidence in the system and ensure that profits are taxed where economic activities take place and value is created.

Following the release of the report Addressing Base Erosion and Profit Shifting in February 2013, OECD and G20 countries adopted a 15-point Action Plan to address BEPS in September 2013. The Action Plan identified 15 actions along three key pillars: introducing coherence in the domestic rules that affect cross-border activities, reinforcing substance requirements in the existing international standards, and improving transparency as well as certainty.

After two years of work, measures in response to the 15 actions were delivered to G20 Leaders in Antalya in November 2015. All the different outputs, including those delivered in an interim form in 2014, were consolidated into a comprehensive package. The BEPS package of measures represents the first substantial renovation of the international tax rules in almost a century. Once the new measures become applicable, it is expected that profits will be reported where the economic activities that generate them are carried out and where value is created. BEPS planning strategies that rely on outdated rules or on poorly co-ordinated domestic measures will be rendered ineffective.

Implementation is now the focus of this work. The BEPS package is designed to be implemented via changes in domestic law and practices, and in tax treaties. With the negotiation of a multilateral instrument (MLI) having been finalised in 2016 to facilitate the implementation of the treaty related BEPS measures, over 90 jurisdictions are covered by the MLI. The entry into force of the MLI on 1 July 2018 paves the way for swift implementation of the treaty related measures. OECD and G20 countries also agreed to continue to work together to ensure a consistent and co-ordinated implementation of the BEPS recommendations and to make the project more inclusive. Globalisation requires that global solutions and a global dialogue be established which go beyond OECD and G20 countries.

A better understanding of how the BEPS recommendations are implemented in practice could reduce misunderstandings and disputes between governments. Greater focus on implementation and tax administration should therefore be mutually beneficial to governments and business. Proposed improvements to data and analysis will help support ongoing evaluation of the quantitative impact of BEPS, as well as evaluating the impact of the countermeasures developed under the BEPS Project.

As a result, the OECD established the OECD/G20 Inclusive Framework on BEPS (Inclusive Framework), bringing all interested and committed countries and jurisdictions on an equal footing in the Committee on Fiscal Affairs and all its subsidiary bodies. The Inclusive Framework, which already has 137 members, is monitoring and peer reviewing the implementation of the minimum standards as well as completing the work on standard setting to address BEPS issues. In addition to BEPS members, other international organisations and regional tax bodies are involved in the work of the Inclusive Framework, which also consults business and the civil society on its different work streams.

This report was approved by the Inclusive Framework on 8 September 2020 and prepared for publication by the OECD Secretariat.

Table of contents

Abbreviations and acronyms

AEOI	Automatic Exchange of Information
BEPS	Base Erosion and Profit Shifting
CAA	Competent Authority Agreement
CbC	Country-by-Country
CbCR	Country-by-Country Reporting
CTS	Common Transmission System
DTC	Double Tax Convention
EOI	Exchange of Information
EU	European Union
MAAC	Convention on Mutual Administrative Assistance in Tax Matters
MCAA	Multilateral Competent Authority Agreement
MNE	Multinational Enterprise
OECD	Organisation for Economic Co-operation and Development
PE	Permanent Establishment
QCAA	Qualifying Competent Authority Agreement
SPE	Surrogate Parent Entity
TIEA	Tax Information Exchange Agreement
TP	Transfer Pricing
UPE	Ultimate Parent Entity
XML	Extensible Mark-up Language

Executive summary

Context of Country-by-Country Reporting

A key component of the transparency pillar of the Base Erosion and Profit Shifting (BEPS) minimum standards is the obligation for all large multinational enterprise groups (MNE Groups) to file a Country-by-Country (CbC) report. The Action 13 Report (*Transfer Pricing Documentation and Country-by-Country Reporting*) provides a template for these MNE Groups to report annually, and for each tax jurisdiction in which they do business, the amount of revenue, profit before income tax and income tax paid and accrued, as well as the number of employees, stated capital, retained earnings and tangible assets. MNE Groups should also identify each entity within the group doing business in a particular jurisdiction and provide an indication of the business activities each entity engages in. In 2018, for the first time, tax authorities around the world received information on large foreign-headed MNE Groups which was not previously available, enabling them to grasp the structure of the businesses while enhancing their risk assessment capacity.

In general, the Ultimate Parent Entity (UPE) of an MNE Group will prepare and file its CbC report with the tax administration in its jurisdiction of tax residence. That tax administration will automatically exchange the CbC report with the tax administration in each jurisdiction listed in the CbC report as being a place in which the MNE Group has a Constituent Entity resident for tax purposes. This will be carried out under an International Agreement (such as the Multilateral Convention on Mutual Administrative Assistance in Tax Matters (MAAC), a Double Tax Convention (DTC) or a Tax Information Exchange Agreement (TIEA) permitting automatic exchange of information (AEOI). A Qualifying Competent Authority Agreement (QCAA) that sets out the operational details of the exchange of CbC reports will also need to be in place.

As one of the four BEPS minimum standards, the Country-by-Country reporting (CbCR) requirements contained in the 2015 Action 13 Report are subject to peer review in order to ensure timely and accurate implementation and thus safeguard the level playing field. All members of the Inclusive Framework on BEPS commit to implementing the Action 13 minimum standard and to participating in the peer review, on an equal footing. The peer review process focuses on three key elements of the minimum standard: (i) the domestic legal and administrative framework, (ii) the exchange of information (EOI) framework and (iii) the confidentiality and appropriate use of CbC reports.

Implementation of CbC Reporting is well underway as the peer review process evidences: over 90 jurisdictions have now introduced an obligation for relevant MNE Groups to file a CbC report in their domestic legal framework.

Scope of this review

This is the third annual peer review for the Action 13 minimum standard. It covers 131 jurisdictions which provided legislation and /or information relating to the implementation of CbC Reporting.

For each jurisdiction, the review covered the domestic legal and administrative framework, the exchange of information framework and measures in place to ensure the confidentiality and appropriate use of CbC reports.

Key findings

The key findings of the third annual peer review are as follows:

- ***Domestic legal and administrative framework***: Over 90 jurisdictions have a domestic legal framework for CbC reporting in place. In addition, a number of jurisdictions have final legislation approved that is awaiting official publication. In this peer review report, 41 jurisdictions have received a general recommendation to put in place or finalise their domestic legal or administrative framework and 34 jurisdictions received one or more recommendations for improvements to specific areas of their framework.
- ***Exchange of information framework:*** In total 76 jurisdictions have multilateral or bilateral competent authority agreements in place.
- ***Confidentiality:*** Of the jurisdictions included in this review, 78 have undergone an assessment by the Global Forum on Transparency and Exchange of Information for Tax Purposes (the Global Forum) concerning confidentiality and data safeguards in the context of implementing the AEOI standard and did not receive any action plan. In contrast, 10 jurisdictions are currently working on an action plan issued by the Global Forum as a consequence of its review.
- ***Appropriate use:*** 82 jurisdictions have provided detailed information, enabling the Inclusive Framework to obtain sufficient assurance that measures are in place to ensure the appropriate use of CbC reports.

A number of Inclusive Framework members are not included in this peer review report, either because they joined the Inclusive Framework after 1 December 2019 (at which point it was too late to incorporate them into the current peer review process) or they opted out of the peer review in accordance with the peer review terms of reference. Jurisdictions opting out of the peer review are required to confirm that they do not have any resident entities that are the UPE of an MNE group above the consolidated revenue threshold and that they will not require local filing of CbC reports. Members of the Inclusive Framework that are not included in this peer review report are:

- Albania
- Burkina Faso
- Cook Islands
- Honduras
- Montenegro
- Saint Kitts and Nevis.

Next steps

The peer review of the Action 13 minimum standard is an annual process. Work will continue to monitor the implementation and operation of CbC reporting by members of the Inclusive Framework and to highlight progress made by jurisdictions to address recommendations that have been made.

1 The peer review of the BEPS Action 13 minimum standard on Country-by-Country Reporting

Background

1. The Country-by-Country (CbC) reporting requirements contained in the 2015 Action 13 Report form one of the four BEPS minimum standards. Each of the four BEPS minimum standards is subject to peer review in order to ensure timely and accurate implementation and thus safeguard the level playing field. All members of the Inclusive Framework on BEPS commit to implementing the Action 13 minimum standard and to participating in the peer review, on an equal footing.

2. The purpose of a peer review is to ensure the effective and consistent implementation of an agreed standard and to recognise progress made by jurisdictions in this regard.

3. The peer review is a review of the legal and administrative framework put in place by a jurisdiction to implement the CbC reporting standard. This peer review is a separate exercise to the ongoing review of the Action 13 minimum standard to evaluate whether modifications to the CbC reporting standard should be made (the 2020 review).

Outline of the key aspects assessed in the annual report

4. This peer review report contains the findings of the third annual peer review process ("phase three"), undertaken by an Ad Hoc Joint Working Party 6 / Working Party 10 sub-group referred to as the "CbC Reporting Group". This focuses on each jurisdiction's domestic legal and administrative framework, its exchange of information network, and its measures to ensure the confidentiality and appropriate use of CbC reports.

5. The structure of each section relating to a specific reviewed jurisdiction is as follows:

- summary of key findings
- domestic legal and administrative framework
- exchange of information
- confidentiality and appropriate use
- a table summarising any recommendations issued.

6. Jurisdictions which joined the Inclusive Framework after 1 December 2019 have not been reviewed as part of this third annual peer review process. These jurisdictions will be included in the next peer review process.

7. This peer review evaluates an Inclusive Framework member's implementation of the Action 13 minimum standard against an agreed set of criteria.[1] These criteria are set out in terms of reference, which include each of the elements that a jurisdiction needs to demonstrate it has fulfilled in order to show proper implementation of the standard. These terms of reference are supplemented by additional questions

concerning measures implemented by a jurisdiction to ensure the appropriate use of CbC reporting information. The Action 13 Report recommended that the first CbC reports be required to be filed for fiscal years beginning on or after 1 January 2016. It was however acknowledged that some jurisdictions may need time to follow their particular domestic legislative process in order to make necessary adjustments to the law. In this respect, the peer review takes account of the specific timeline followed by certain jurisdictions, and the review will focus on the efforts taken by these jurisdictions in order to meet their commitment to implement the minimum standard.

8. The manner in which the peer review is undertaken is set out in an agreed methodology. The methodology sets out the procedural mechanisms by which jurisdictions will complete the peer review, including the process for collecting the relevant data, the preparation and approval of reports, the outputs of the review and the follow up process.

9. The methodology recognised that the three key aspects of CbC reporting would be implemented and become operational over a number of years, starting with the domestic legal and administrative framework being put in place generally from 2016, followed by the international exchanges of CbC reports to occur for the first time by mid-2018, and the work to ensure that CbC reports are kept confidential and used appropriately in any subsequent tax compliance actions.

10. Given the fact not all of these three key aspects were being implemented at the same time, these three key aspects have been reviewed according to a staged approach. A staged review enabled the review of aspects of CbC reporting to occur as they were implemented, starting in 2017 and allowing for the early detection of inconsistencies in implementing the minimum standard as well as providing an opportunity for early remedial action to be taken by jurisdictions, if necessary.

11. There have been three phases for the peer review structured into annual reviews, starting respectively in 2017, 2018 and 2019. Each phase has focused on different key aspects of jurisdictions' implementation so as to mirror the staged introduction of the different elements that make up the CbC reporting and exchange of information framework.

12. An annual review process allows the CbC Reporting Group to report each year to the Inclusive Framework, taking into account any updates since the previous review, as well as any follow-up actions by reviewed jurisdictions to address any recommendations made by the Inclusive Framework.

13. The Global Forum has conducted preliminary expert assessments of confidentiality and data safeguards with respect to the standard on automatic exchange of information. Given its expertise in this area, the CbC Reporting Group has relied on the work and conclusions of the Global Forum. As it contains non-public information on jurisdictions' internal systems and procedures, the outcomes of that work are not published and no further details of the review of confidentiality are provided in this compilation of peer review reports.

14. The terms of reference and methodology do not alter the Action 13 minimum standard. Any terms used in the terms of reference or methodology take their meaning from the language and context of the 2015 Action 13 Report and the references therein. Capitalised terms in this report take their meaning from the language and context of the 2015 Action 13 Report and the references therein.

15. The jurisdictions' individual sections in this report generally reflect the status of implementation as of 31 March 2020, with the exception of information on the exchange of CbC reports which reflects the position as of 31 December 2019.

Note

1 www.oecd.org/tax/beps/beps-action-13-on-country-by-country-reporting-peer-review-documents.pdf (approved by the Inclusive Framework on 20 January 2017).

2 Peer review reports

Andorra

1. Andorra was reviewed as part of the 2017/2018 and the 2018/2019 peer reviews. This report is supplementary to those previous reports (OECD, 2019[1]) (OECD, 2018[2])

2. The first filing obligation for a CbC report in Andorra applies to reporting fiscal years commencing on or after 1 January 2018.

Summary of key findings

3. Andorra's implementation of the Action 13 minimum standard meets all applicable terms of reference (OECD, 2017[3]), except for the following:

- It is recommended that Andorra take steps to implement processes or written procedures to ensure that the exchange of information is conducted in a manner consistent with the terms of reference relating to the exchange of information framework ahead of its first exchanges of information. This recommendation remains unchanged since the 2018/2019-peer review.
- It is recommended that Andorra take steps to ensure that the appropriate use condition is met ahead of the first exchanges of information. This recommendation remains unchanged since the 2017/2018 peer review.

Part A: The domestic legal and administrative framework

4. Andorra has law in place which implements the BEPS Action 13 minimum standard, establishing the necessary requirements.

(a) Parent entity filing obligation

5. No changes were identified

(b) Scope and timing of parent entity filing

6. No changes were identified.

(c) Limitation on local filing obligation

7. No changes were identified.

(d) Limitation on local filing in case of surrogate filing

8. No changes were identified.

(e) Effective implementation

9. No changes were identified.

Conclusion

10. Andorra meets all the terms of reference relating to the domestic legal and administrative framework.

Part B: The exchange of information framework

(a) Exchange of information framework

11. As of 31 March 2020 Andorra has 63 bilateral relationships in place for the exchange of CbC reports, activated under the CbC MCAA. Within the context of its international exchange of information agreements that allow automatic exchange of tax information, Andorra has taken steps to have qualifying competent authority agreements in effect with jurisdictions of the Inclusive Framework that currently meet the confidentiality, consistency and appropriate use conditions. Regarding Andorra's exchange of information framework, no inconsistencies with the terms of reference were identified.[1]

(b) Content of information exchanged

12. Andorra does not have processes or written procedures in place that are intended to ensure that each of the mandatory fields of information as required in the CbC template is present in the information exchanged.

(c) Completeness of exchanges

13. Andorra does not have processes or written procedures in place that are intended to ensure that CbC reports are exchanged with all tax jurisdictions listed in Table 1 of a CbC reporting template with which it should exchange information as per the relevant QCAAs.

(d) Timeliness of exchanges

14. Andorra does not have processes or written procedures in place that are intended to ensure that the information to be exchanged is transmitted to the relevant jurisdictions in accordance with the timelines provided for in the relevant QCAAs and terms of reference.

(e) Temporary suspension of exchange or termination of QCAA

15. Andorra does not have processes or written procedures in place that are intended to ensure that a temporary suspension of the exchange of information or termination of a relevant QCAA be carried out only as per the conditions set out in the QCAA.

(f) Consultation with other Competent Authority before determining systemic failure or significant non-compliance

16. Andorra does not have processes or written procedures in place that are intended to ensure that the Competent Authority consults with the other Competent Authority prior to making a determination that there is or has been significant non-compliance with the terms of the relevant QCAA or that the other Competent Authority has caused a systemic failure.

(g) Format for information exchange

17. Andorra indicates that it will use the OECD XML Schema and User Guide for the international exchange of CbC reports (OECD, 2017[4]).

(h) Method for transmission

18. Andorra indicates that it will use the Common Transmission System to exchange CbC reports.

Conclusion

19. It is recommended that Andorra take steps to implement processes or written procedures to ensure that the exchange of information is conducted in a manner consistent with the terms of reference relating

to the exchange of information framework ahead of its first exchanges of information. This recommendation remains unchanged since the 2018/2019 review.

Part C: Appropriate use

Appropriate use

20. No changes were identified in respect of appropriate use. The recommendation in the 2017/2018 peer review for Andorra to take steps to have measures in place relating to appropriate use remains in place.

Conclusion

21. The recommendation for Andorra take steps to ensure that the appropriate use condition is met ahead of its first exchanges of information remain in place.

Summary of recommendations on the implementation of country-by-country reporting

Aspect of the implementation that should be improved		Recommendation for improvement
Part A	Domestic legal and administrative framework	-
Part B	Exchange of information framework	It is recommended that Andorra take steps to implement processes or written procedures to ensure that the exchange of information is conducted in a manner consistent with the terms of reference relating to the exchange of information framework ahead of its first exchanges of information.
Part C	Appropriate use	It is recommended that Andorra take steps to ensure that the appropriate use condition is met ahead of the first exchanges of information.

References

OECD (2019), *Country-by-Country Reporting – Compilation of Peer Review Reports (Phase 2): Inclusive Framework on BEPS: Action 13*, OECD/G20 Base Erosion and Profit Shifting Project, OECD Publishing, Paris, https://dx.doi.org/10.1787/f9bf1157-en. [1]

OECD (2018), *Country-by-Country Reporting – Compilation of Peer Review Reports (Phase 1): Inclusive Framework on BEPS: Action 13*, OECD/G20 Base Erosion and Profit Shifting Project, OECD Publishing, Paris, https://dx.doi.org/10.1787/9789264300057-en. [2]

OECD (2017), *Terms of reference for the conduct of peer review of the Action 13 minimum standard on country-by-country reporting*, OECD Publishing, https://www.oecd.org/tax/beps/beps-action-13-on-country-by-country-reporting-peer-review-documents.pdf. [3]

Note

[1] No inconsistency with the terms of reference will be identified where a QCAA is not in effect with one or more jurisdictions of the Inclusive Framework that meet the confidentiality, consistency and appropriate use conditions, but this is due to circumstances that are not under the control of the reviewed jurisdiction. This may include, for example, where the other jurisdiction intends to exchange CbC reports using the MCAA but it does not have the Convention in effect for the relevant fiscal period, or where the other jurisdiction has declined to have a QCAA in effect with the reviewed jurisdiction.

Angola

1. Angola was reviewed as part of the 2017/2018 and the 2018/2019 peer reviews. This report is supplementary to those previous reports (OECD, 2019[1]) (OECD, 2018[2]).

2. There is no filing obligation for a CbC report in Angola yet.

Summary of key findings

3. Angola does not yet have legislation in place for implementing the BEPS Action 13 minimum standard. It is recommended that Angola take steps to implement a domestic legal and administrative framework to impose and enforce CbC reporting requirements as soon as possible. This recommendation remains unchanged since the 2017/2018 peer review.

4. It is recommended that Angola take steps to have QCAAs in effect with jurisdictions of the Inclusive Framework which meet the confidentiality, consistency and appropriate use prerequisites and with which Angola has an international exchange of information agreement in effect that allows for the automatic exchange of tax information. This recommendation remains unchanged since the 2017/2018 peer review.

5. It is recommended that Angola take steps to implement processes or written procedures to ensure that the exchange of information is conducted in a manner consistent with the terms of reference (OECD, 2017[3]) relating to the exchange of information framework ahead of the first exchanges of information. This recommendation remains unchanged since the 2018/2019 peer review.

6. It is recommended that Angola take steps to ensure that the appropriate use condition is met ahead of the first exchanges of information. This recommendation remains unchanged since the 2017/2018 peer review.

Part A: The domestic legal and administrative framework

7. Angola does not yet have legislation in place for implementing the BEPS Action 13 minimum standard although we note that drafting is taking place.

(a) Parent entity filing obligation

(b) Scope and timing of parent entity filing

(c) Limitation on local filing obligation

(d) Limitation on local filing in case of surrogate filing

(e) Effective implementation

Conclusion

8. There is no change in relation to the domestic legal and administration framework for Angola since the previous peer review. The recommendation in the 2017/18 peer review, that Angola take steps to implement a domestic legal and administrative framework to impose and enforce CbC reporting requirements as soon as possible, remains in place.

Part B: The exchange of information framework

(a) Exchange of information framework

9. As of 31 March 2020, Angola has no bilateral relationships in place for the exchange of CbC reports. It is recommended that Angola take steps to have qualifying competent authority agreements in effect with jurisdictions of the Inclusive Framework that meet the confidentiality, consistency and appropriate use conditions and with which Angola has an international exchange of information agreement in effect that allows for the automatic exchange of tax information. This recommendation remains unchanged since the 2018/2019 peer review.

(b) Content of information exchanged

10. No changes were identified.

(c) Completeness of exchanges

11. No changes were identified.

(d) Timeliness of exchanges

12. No changes were identified.

(e) Temporary suspension of exchange or termination of QCAA

13. No changes were identified.

(f) Consultation with other Competent Authority before determining systemic failure or significant non-compliance

14. No changes were identified.

(g) Format for information exchange

15. No changes were identified.

(h) Method for transmission

16. No changes were identified.

Conclusion

17. It is recommended that Angola take steps to have QCAAs in effect with jurisdictions of the Inclusive Framework which meet the confidentiality, consistency and appropriate use prerequisites and with which Angola has an international exchange of information agreement in effect that allows for the automatic exchange of tax information. This recommendation remains unchanged since the 2018/2019 peer review.

18. It is recommended that Angola take steps to implement processes or written procedures to ensure that the exchange of information is conducted in a manner consistent with the terms of reference relating to the exchange of information framework ahead of its first exchanges of information. This recommendation remains unchanged since the 2018/2019 peer review.

Part C: Appropriate use

Appropriate use

19. No changes were identified in respect of appropriate use. The recommendation in the 2017/2018 peer review for Angola to take steps to have measures in place relating to appropriate use ahead of the first exchanges of information remains in place.

Conclusion

20. The recommendation in the 2017/2018 peer review for Angola to take steps to ensure that the appropriate use condition is met ahead of its first exchanges of information remains in place.

Summary of recommendations on the implementation of Country-by-Country Reporting

Aspect of the implementation that should be improved		Recommendation for improvement
Part A	Domestic legal and administrative framework	It is recommended that Angola take steps to implement a domestic legal and administrative framework to impose and enforce CbC requirements as soon as possible.
Part B	Exchange of information framework	It is recommended that Angola take steps to have qualifying competent authority agreements in effect with jurisdictions of the Inclusive Framework that meet the confidentiality, consistency and appropriate use conditions and with which Angola has an international exchange of information agreement in effect that allows for the automatic exchange of tax information.
Part B	Exchange of information framework	It is recommended that Angola take steps to implement the necessary processes or written procedures to ensure that the exchange of information is conducted in a manner consistent with the terms of reference relating to the exchange of information framework.
Part C	Appropriate use	It is recommended that Angola take steps to ensure that the appropriate use condition is met ahead of the first exchanges of information.

References

OECD (2019), *Country-by-Country Reporting – Compilation of Peer Review Reports (Phase 2): Inclusive Framework on BEPS: Action 13*, OECD/G20 Base Erosion and Profit Shifting Project, OECD Publishing, Paris, https://dx.doi.org/10.1787/f9bf1157-en. [1]

OECD (2018), *Country-by-Country Reporting – Compilation of Peer Review Reports (Phase 1): Inclusive Framework on BEPS: Action 13*, OECD/G20 Base Erosion and Profit Shifting Project, OECD Publishing, Paris, https://dx.doi.org/10.1787/9789264300057-en. [2]

OECD (2017), *Terms of reference for the conduct of peer review of the Action 13 minimum standard on country-by-country reporting*, OECD Publishing, https://www.oecd.org/tax/beps/beps-action-13-on-country-by-country-reporting-peer-review-documents.pdf. [3]

Anguilla

1. Anguilla was first reviewed during the 2018/2019 peer review. This report is supplementary to that previous report (OECD, 2018[2]).

2. The first filing obligation for a CbC report in Anguilla commences on or after the 1 January 2019.

Summary of key findings

3. Anguilla's implementation of the Action 13 minimum standard meets all applicable terms of reference (OECD, 2017[3]).

Part A: The domestic legal and administrative framework

4. Anguilla has primary law in place to implement the BEPS Action 13 minimum standard, establishing the necessary requirements including the filing and reporting obligations.

(a) Parent entity filing obligation

5. No changes were identified.

(b) Scope and timing of parent entity filing

6. No changes were identified.

(c) Limitation on local filing obligation

7. No changes were identified.

(d) Limitation on local filing in case of surrogate filing

8. No changes were identified.

(e) Effective implementation

9. No changes were identified.

Conclusion

10. Anguilla meets all the terms of reference with regard to its domestic and legal framework.

Part B: The exchange of information framework

(a) Exchange of information framework

11. As of 31 March 2020, Anguilla has 34 bilateral relationships in place for the exchange of CbC reports including those activated under the CbC MCAA. Within the context of its international exchange of information agreements that allow automatic exchange of information, Anguilla has taken steps to have Qualifying Competent Authority agreements in effect with jurisdictions of the Inclusive Framework that meet the confidentiality, consistency and appropriate use condition.[1] Regarding Anguilla's exchange of information framework, no inconsistencies with the terms of reference were identified.

(b) Content of information exchanged

12. No changes were identified.

(c) Completeness of exchanges

13. No changes were identified.

(d) Timeliness of exchanges

14. No changes were identified.

(e) Temporary suspension of exchange or termination of QCAA

15. No changes were identified.

(f) Consultation with other Competent Authority before determining systemic failure or significant non-compliance

16. No changes were identified.

(g) Format for information exchange

17. Anguilla confirms that it uses the OECD XML Schema and User Guide (OECD, 2017[4]) for the international exchange of CbC reports.

(h) Method for transmission

18. Anguilla indicates that it will use the Common Transmission System to exchange CbC reports.

Conclusion

19. Anguilla meets all the terms of reference regarding the exchange of information.

Part C: Appropriate use

Appropriate use

20. Anguilla is a non-reciprocal jurisdiction and, as such, will not receive CbC reports submitted to tax authorities in other jurisdictions, and will not apply local filing. It is therefore not necessary for this peer review evaluation to reach any conclusions with respect to appropriate use of the reports.

Conclusion

21. Anguilla is a non-reciprocal jurisdiction and, as such, will not receive CbC reports submitted to tax authorities in other jurisdictions, and will not apply local filing. It is therefore not necessary for this peer review evaluation to reach any conclusions with respect to Anguilla's compliance with paragraphs 11(a), (b), (c) and (d) and paragraph 12(a) of the terms of reference on appropriate use.

Summary of recommendations on the implementation of Country-by-Country Reporting

Aspect of the implementation that should be improved		Recommendation for improvement
Part A	Domestic legal and administrative framework	-
Part B	Exchange of information framework	-
Part C	Appropriate use	-

References

OECD (2018), *Country-by-Country Reporting – Compilation of Peer Review Reports (Phase 1): Inclusive Framework on BEPS: Action 13*, OECD/G20 Base Erosion and Profit Shifting Project, OECD Publishing, Paris, https://dx.doi.org/10.1787/9789264300057-en. [2]

OECD (2017), *Country-by-Country Reporting XML Schema: User Guide for Tax Administrations*, OECD Publishing, http://www.oecd.org/tax/country-by-country-reporting-xmlschema-user-guide-for-tax-administrations.pdf. [4]

OECD (2017), *Terms of reference for the conduct of peer review of the Action 13 minimum standard on country-by-country reporting*, OECD Publishing, https://www.oecd.org/tax/beps/beps-action-13-on-country-by-country-reporting-peer-review-documents.pdf. [3]

Note

[1] No inconsistency with the terms of reference will be identified where a QCAA is not in effect with one or more jurisdictions of the Inclusive Framework that meet the confidentiality, consistency and appropriate use conditions, but this is due to circumstances that are not under the control of the reviewed jurisdiction. This may include, for example, where the other jurisdiction intends to exchange CbC reports using the MCAA but it does not have the Convention in effect for the relevant fiscal period, or where the other jurisdiction has declined to have a QCAA in effect with the reviewed jurisdiction.

Antigua and Barbuda

1. This report is Antigua and Barbuda's first annual peer review report. Consistent with the agreed methodology this report covers: (i) the domestic legal and administrative framework, (ii) the exchange of information framework as well as (iii) the appropriate use of CbC reports.

2. There is no filing obligation for a CbC report in Antigua and Barbuda yet.

Summary of key findings

3. Antigua and Barbuda does not yet have legislation in place for implementing the BEPS Action 13 minimum standard.

4. It is recommended that Antigua and Barbuda take steps to implement a domestic legal and administrative framework to impose and enforce CbC reporting requirements as soon as possible.

5. It is recommended that Antigua and Barbuda take steps to put in place an exchange of information framework that allows automatic exchange of information and have QCAAs in effect with jurisdictions of the Inclusive Framework which meet the confidentiality, consistency and appropriate use prerequisites and with which Antigua and Barbuda has an international exchange of information agreement in effect that allows for the automatic exchange of tax information.

6. It is recommended that Antigua and Barbuda take steps to implement processes or written procedures to ensure that the exchange of information is conducted in a manner consistent with the terms of reference (OECD, 2017[3]) relating to the exchange of information framework ahead of the first exchanges of information.

7. It is recommended that Antigua and Barbuda take steps to ensure that the appropriate use condition is met ahead of the first exchanges of information.

Part A: The domestic legal and administrative framework

8. Antigua and Barbuda does not yet have legislation in place for implementing the BEPS Action 13 minimum standard.

(a) Parent entity filing obligation

(b) Scope and timing of parent entity filing

(c) Limitation on local filing obligation

(d) Limitation on local filing in case of surrogate filing

(e) Effective implementation

Conclusion

9. It is recommended that Antigua and Barbuda take steps to implement a domestic legal and administrative framework to impose and enforce CbC reporting requirements as soon as possible.

Part B: The exchange of information framework

(a) Exchange of information framework

10. As of 31 March 2020, Antigua and Barbuda has no bilateral relationships in place for the exchange of CbC reports. It is recommended that Antigua and Barbuda take steps to have qualifying competent authority agreements in effect with jurisdictions of the Inclusive Framework that meet the confidentiality, consistency and appropriate use conditions and with which Antigua and Barbuda has an international exchange of information agreement in effect that allows for the automatic exchange of tax information.

(b) Content of information exchanged

11. Antigua and Barbuda does not have processes or written procedures in place that are intended to ensure that each of the mandatory fields of information required in the CbC reporting template are present in the information exchanged.

(c) Completeness of exchanges

12. Antigua and Barbuda does not have processes or written procedures in place that are intended to ensure that CbC reports are exchanged with all tax jurisdictions listed in Table 1 of a CbC report with which it should exchange information as per the relevant QCAA.

(d) Timeliness of exchanges

13. Antigua and Barbuda does not have processes or written procedures in place that are intended to ensure that the information to be exchanged is transmitted to the relevant jurisdictions in accordance with the timelines provided for in the relevant QCAAs.

(e) Temporary suspension of exchange or termination of QCAA

14. Antigua and Barbuda does not have processes or written procedures in place that are intended to ensure that a temporary suspension of the exchange of information or termination of a relevant QCAA would be carried out only as per the conditions set out in the relevant QCAA.

(f) Consultation with other Competent Authority before determining systemic failure or significant non-compliance

15. Antigua and Barbuda does not have processes or written procedures in place that are intended to ensure that its Competent Authority consults with the other Competent Authority before making a determination of systemic failure or significant non-compliance with the terms of the relevant QCAA by that other Competent Authority.

(g) Format for information exchange

16. Antigua and Barbuda has not confirmed the format that will be used for the international exchange of CbC reports.

(h) Method for transmission

17. Antigua and Barbuda has not indicated confirmed the mechanism that it will use to exchange CbC reports.

Conclusion

18. It is recommended that Antigua and Barbuda take steps to have qualifying competent authority agreements in effect with jurisdictions of the Inclusive Framework that meet the confidentiality, consistency

and appropriate use conditions and with which Antigua and Barbuda has an international exchange of information agreement in effect that allows for the automatic exchange of tax information.

19. It is recommended that Antigua and Barbuda take steps to implement processes or written procedures to ensure that the exchange of information is conducted in a manner consistent with the terms of reference (OECD, 2017[3]) relating to the exchange of information framework ahead of its first exchanges of information.

Part C: Appropriate use

Appropriate use

20. Antigua and Barbuda does not yet have measures in place relating to appropriate use.

Conclusion

21. It is recommended that Antigua and Barbuda take steps to ensure that the appropriate use condition is met ahead of its first exchanges of information.

Summary of recommendations on the implementation of Country-by-Country Reporting

Aspect of the implementation that should be improved		Recommendation for improvement
Part A	Domestic legal and administrative framework	It is recommended that Antigua and Barbuda take steps to implement a domestic legal and administrative framework to impose and enforce CbC requirements as soon as possible.
Part B	Exchange of information framework	It is recommended that Antigua and Barbuda take steps to put in place an exchange of information framework that allows Automatic Exchange of Information and have QCAAs in effect with jurisdictions of the Inclusive Framework which meet the confidentiality, consistency and appropriate use prerequisites and with which Antigua and Barbuda has an international exchange of information agreement in effect that allows for the automatic exchange of tax information.
Part B	Exchange of information framework	It is recommended that Antigua and Barbuda take steps to implement the necessary processes or written procedures to ensure that the exchange of information is conducted in a manner consistent with the terms of reference relating to the exchange of information framework.
Part C	Appropriate use	It is recommended that Antigua and Barbuda take steps to ensure that the appropriate use condition is met ahead of the first exchanges of information.

References

OECD (2017), *Terms of reference for the conduct of peer review of the Action 13 minimum standard on country-by-country reporting*, OECD Publishing, https://www.oecd.org/tax/beps/beps-action-13-on-country-by-country-reporting-peer-review-documents.pdf. [3]

Argentina

1. Argentina was reviewed as part of the 2017/2018 and the 2018/2019 peer reviews. This report is supplementary to those previous reports (OECD, 2019[1]) (OECD, 2018[2]).

2. The first filing obligation for a CbC report in Argentina commences on or after the 1 January 2017.

Summary of key findings

3. Argentina's implementation of the Action 13 minimum standard meets all applicable terms of reference (OECD, 2017[3]).

Part A: The domestic legal and administrative framework

4. Argentina meets all the terms of reference relating to the domestic legal and administrative framework.

(a) Parent entity filing obligation

5. No changes were identified.

(b) Scope and timing of parent entity filing

6. No changes were identified.

(c) Limitation on local filing obligation

7. No changes were identified.

(d) Limitation on local filing in case of surrogate filing

8. No changes were identified.

(e) Effective implementation

9. No changes were identified.

Conclusion

10. There is no change to the conclusion in relation to the domestic legal and administration framework for Argentina since the previous peer review. Argentina meets all the terms of reference relating to the domestic legal and administrative framework.

Part B: The exchange of information framework

(a) Exchange of information framework

11. As of 31 March 2020, Argentina has [64] bilateral relationships, including those activated under the CbC MCAA and under bilateral CAAs. Within the context of its international exchange of information agreements that allow automatic exchange of information, Argentina has taken steps to have Qualifying

Competent Authority agreements in effect with jurisdictions of the Inclusive Framework that meet the confidentiality, consistency and appropriate use conditions.[1] Regarding Argentina's exchange of information framework, no inconsistencies with the terms of reference were identified.

(b) Content of information exchanged

12. No changes were identified.

(c) Completeness of exchanges

13. No changes were identified.

(d) Timeliness of exchanges

14. No changes were identified.

(e) Temporary suspension of exchange or termination of QCAA

15. No changes were identified.

(f) Consultation with other Competent Authority before determining systemic failure or significant non-compliance

16. No changes were identified.

(g) Format for information exchange

17. Argentina confirms that it uses the OECD XML Schema and User Guide (OECD, 2017[4]) for the international exchange of CbC reports.

(h) Method for transmission

18. Argentina indicates that it uses the Common Transmission System to exchange CbC reports.

Conclusion

19. Argentina has in place the necessary processes and written procedures to ensure that the exchange of information is conducted in a manner consistent with the terms of reference relating to the exchange of information framework. Argentina meets all the terms of reference regarding the exchange of information.

Part C: Appropriate use

Appropriate use

20. No changes were identified.

Conclusion

21. Argentina meets all the terms of reference relating to appropriate use of CbC reports.

Summary of recommendations on the implementation of country-by-country reporting

Aspect of the implementation that should be improved		Recommendation for improvement
Part A	Domestic legal and administrative framework	-
Part B	Exchange of information framework	-
Part C	Appropriate use	-

References

OECD (2019), *Country-by-Country Reporting – Compilation of Peer Review Reports (Phase 2): Inclusive Framework on BEPS: Action 13*, OECD/G20 Base Erosion and Profit Shifting Project, OECD Publishing, Paris, https://dx.doi.org/10.1787/f9bf1157-en. [1]

OECD (2018), *Country-by-Country Reporting – Compilation of Peer Review Reports (Phase 1): Inclusive Framework on BEPS: Action 13*, OECD/G20 Base Erosion and Profit Shifting Project, OECD Publishing, Paris, https://dx.doi.org/10.1787/9789264300057-en. [2]

OECD (2017), *Country-by-Country Reporting XML Schema: User Guide for Tax Administrations*, OECD Publishing, http://www.oecd.org/tax/country-by-country-reporting-xmlschema-user-guide-for-tax-administrations.pdf. [4]

OECD (2017), *Terms of reference for the conduct of peer review of the Action 13 minimum standard on country-by-country reporting*, OECD Publishing, https://www.oecd.org/tax/beps/beps-action-13-on-country-by-country-reporting-peer-review-documents.pdf. [3]

Note

[1] No inconsistency with the terms of reference will be identified where a QCAA is not in effect with one or more jurisdictions of the Inclusive Framework that meet the confidentiality, consistency and appropriate use conditions, but this is due to circumstances that are not under the control of the reviewed jurisdiction. This may include, for example, where the other jurisdiction intends to exchange CbC reports using the MCAA but it does not have the Convention in effect for the relevant fiscal period, or where the other jurisdiction has declined to have a QCAA in effect with the reviewed jurisdiction.

Armenia

1. This report is Armenia's first annual peer review report. Consistent with the agreed methodology this report covers: (i) the domestic legal and administrative framework, (ii) the exchange of information framework as well as (iii) the appropriate use of CbC reports.

2. There is no filing obligation for a CbC report in Armenia yet.

Summary of key findings

3. Armenia does not yet have legislation in place for implementing the BEPS Action 13 minimum standard.

4. It is recommended that Armenia take steps to implement a domestic legal and administrative framework to impose and enforce CbC reporting requirements as soon as possible.

5. It is recommended that Armenia take steps to put in place an exchange of information framework that allows automatic exchange of information and have QCAAs in effect with jurisdictions of the Inclusive Framework which meet the confidentiality, consistency and appropriate use prerequisites and with which Armenia has an international exchange of information agreement in effect that allows for the automatic exchange of tax information.

6. It is recommended that Armenia take steps to implement processes or written procedures to ensure that the exchange of information is conducted in a manner consistent with the terms of reference (OECD, 2017[3]) relating to the exchange of information framework ahead of the first exchanges of information.

7. It is recommended that Armenia take steps to ensure that the appropriate use conditions is met ahead of the first exchanges of information.

Part A: The domestic legal and administrative framework

8. Armenia does not yet have legislation in place for implementing the BEPS Action 13 minimum standard.

(a) Parent entity filing obligation

(b) Scope and timing of parent entity filing

(c) Limitation on local filing obligation

(d) Limitation on local filing in case of surrogate filing

(e) Effective implementation

Conclusion

9. It is recommended that Armenia take steps to implement a domestic legal and administrative framework to impose and enforce CbC reporting requirements as soon as possible.

Part B: The exchange of information framework

(a) Exchange of information framework

10. As of 31 March 2020, Armenia has no bilateral relationships in place for the exchange of CbC reports. It is recommended that Armenia take steps to have qualifying competent authority agreements in effect with jurisdictions of the Inclusive Framework that meet the confidentiality, consistency and appropriate use conditions and with which Armenia has an international exchange of information agreement in effect that allows for the automatic exchange of tax information.

(b) Content of information exchanged

11. Armenia does not have processes or written procedures in place that are intended to ensure that each of the mandatory fields of information required in the CbC reporting template are present in the information exchanged.

(c) Completeness of exchanges

12. Armenia does not have processes or written procedures in place that are intended to ensure that CbC reports are exchanged with all tax jurisdictions listed in Table 1 of a CbC report with which it should exchange information as per the relevant QCAA.

(d) Timeliness of exchanges

13. Armenia does not have processes or written procedures in place that are intended to ensure that the information to be exchanged is transmitted to the relevant jurisdictions in accordance with the timelines provided for in the relevant QCAAs.

(e) Temporary suspension of exchange or termination of QCAA

14. Armenia does not have processes or written procedures in place that are intended to ensure that a temporary suspension of the exchange of information or termination of a relevant QCAA would be carried out only as per the conditions set out in the relevant QCAA.

(f) Consultation with other Competent Authority before determining systemic failure or significant non-compliance

15. Armenia does not have processes or written procedures in place that are intended to ensure that its Competent Authority consults with the other Competent Authority before making a determination of systemic failure or significant non-compliance with the terms of the relevant QCAA by that other Competent Authority.

(g) Format for information exchange

16. Armenia has not confirmed the format that will be used for the international exchange of CbC reports.

(h) Method for transmission

17. Armenia has not confirmed the mechanism that it will use to exchange CbC reports.

Conclusion

18. It is recommended that Armenia take steps to have qualifying competent authority agreements in effect with jurisdictions of the Inclusive Framework that meet the confidentiality, consistency and

appropriate use conditions and with which Armenia has an international exchange of information agreement in effect that allows for the automatic exchange of tax information.

19. It is recommended that Armenia take steps to implement processes or written procedures to ensure that the exchange of information is conducted in a manner consistent with the terms of reference (OECD, 2017[3]) relating to the exchange of information framework ahead of its first exchanges of information.

Part C: Appropriate use

Appropriate use

20. Armenia does not yet have measures in place relating to appropriate use.

21. It is recommended that Armenia take steps to have measures in place relating to appropriate use ahead of the first exchanges of information.

Conclusion

22. It is recommended that Armenia take steps to ensure that the appropriate use condition is met ahead of its first exchanges of information.

Summary of recommendations on the implementation of Country-by-Country Reporting

Aspect of the implementation that should be improved		Recommendation for improvement
Part A	Domestic legal and administrative framework	It is recommended that Armenia take steps to implement a domestic legal and administrative framework to impose and enforce CbC requirements as soon as possible.
Part B	Exchange of information framework	It is recommended that Armenia take steps to put in place an exchange of information framework that allows Automatic Exchange of Information and have QCAAs in effect with jurisdictions of the Inclusive Framework which meet the confidentiality, consistency and appropriate use prerequisites and with which Armenia has an international exchange of information agreement in effect that allows for the automatic exchange of tax information.
Part B	Exchange of information framework	It is recommended that Armenia take steps to implement the necessary processes or written procedures to ensure that the exchange of information is conducted in a manner consistent with the terms of reference relating to the exchange of information framework.
Part C	Appropriate use	It is recommended that Armenia take steps to ensure that the appropriate use condition is met ahead of the first exchanges of information.

References

OECD (2017), *Terms of reference for the conduct of peer review of the Action 13 minimum standard on country-by-country reporting*, OECD Publishing, https://www.oecd.org/tax/beps/beps-action-13-on-country-by-country-reporting-peer-review-documents.pdf. [3]

Aruba

1. Aruba was first reviewed during the 2018/2019 peer review. This report is supplementary to that previous report (OECD, 2018[2]).

2. There is no filing obligation for a CbC report in Aruba yet.

Summary of key findings

3. Aruba does not yet have legislation in place for implementing the BEPS Action 13 minimum standard. It is recommended that Aruba take steps to implement a domestic legal and administrative framework to impose and enforce CbC reporting requirements as soon as possible. This recommendation remains unchanged since the 2018/2019 peer review.

4. It is recommended that Aruba take steps to have qualifying competent authority agreements in effect with jurisdictions of the Inclusive Framework that meet the confidentiality, consistency and appropriate use conditions and with which Aruba has an international exchange of information agreement in effect that allows for the automatic exchange of tax information. This recommendation remains unchanged since the 2018/2019 peer review.

5. It is recommended that Aruba take steps to implement processes or written procedures to ensure that the exchange of information is conducted in a manner consistent with the terms of reference (OECD, 2017[3]) relating to the exchange of information framework ahead of the first exchanges of information. This recommendation remains unchanged since the 2018/2019 peer review.

6. It is recommended that Aruba take steps to ensure that the appropriate use condition is met ahead of the first exchanges of information. This recommendation remains unchanged since the 2018/2019 peer review.

Part A: The domestic legal and administrative framework

7. Aruba does not yet have legislation in place for implementing the BEPS Action 13 minimum standard.

(a) Parent entity filing obligation

(b) Scope and timing of parent entity filing

(c) Limitation on local filing obligation

(d) Limitation on local filing in case of surrogate filing

(e) Effective implementation

Conclusion

8. It is recommended that Aruba take steps to implement a domestic legal and administrative framework to impose and enforce CbC reporting requirements as soon as possible.

Part B: The exchange of information framework

(a) Exchange of information framework

9. As of 31 March 2020, Aruba has no bilateral relationships in place for the exchange of CbC reports. It is recommended that Aruba take steps to have qualifying competent authority agreements in effect with jurisdictions of the Inclusive Framework that meet the confidentiality, consistency and appropriate use conditions and with which Aruba has an international exchange of information agreement in effect that allows for the automatic exchange of tax information.

(b) Content of information exchanged

10. No changes were identified.

(c) Completeness of exchanges

11. No changes were identified.

(d) Timeliness of exchanges

12. No changes were identified.

(e) Temporary suspension of exchange or termination of QCAA

13. No changes were identified.

(f) Consultation with other Competent Authority before determining systemic failure or significant non-compliance

14. No changes were identified.

(g) Format for information exchange

15. No changes were identified.

(h) Method for transmission

16. No changes were identified.

Conclusion

17. It is recommended that Aruba take steps to have qualifying competent authority agreements in effect with jurisdictions of the Inclusive Framework that meet the confidentiality, consistency and appropriate use conditions and with which Aruba has an international exchange of information agreement in effect that allows for the automatic exchange of tax information. This recommendation remains unchanged since the 2018/2019 peer review.

18. It is recommended that Aruba take steps to implement processes or written procedures to ensure that the exchange of information is conducted in a manner consistent with the terms of reference relating to the exchange of information framework ahead of its first exchanges of information. This recommendation remains unchanged since the 2018/2019 peer review.

Part C: Appropriate use

Appropriate use

19. No changes were identified.

Conclusion

20. It is recommended that Aruba take steps to ensure that the appropriate use condition is met ahead of its first exchanges of information. This recommendation remains unchanged since the 2018/2019 peer review.

Summary of recommendations on the implementation of Country-by-Country Reporting

Aspect of the implementation that should be improved		**Recommendation for improvement**
Part A	Domestic legal and administrative framework	It is recommended that Aruba take steps to implement a domestic legal and administrative framework to impose and enforce CbC requirements as soon as possible.
Part B	Exchange of information framework	It is recommended that Aruba take steps to have qualifying competent authority agreements in effect with jurisdictions of the Inclusive Framework that meet the confidentiality, consistency and appropriate use conditions and with which Aruba has an international exchange of information agreement in effect that allows for the automatic exchange of tax information.
Part B	Exchange of information framework	It is recommended that Aruba take steps to implement processes or written procedures to ensure that the exchange of information is conducted in a manner consistent with the terms of reference relating to the exchange of information framework ahead of its first exchanges of information.
Part C	Appropriate use	It is recommended that Aruba take steps to ensure that the appropriate use condition is met ahead of the first exchanges of information.

References

OECD (2018), *Country-by-Country Reporting – Compilation of Peer Review Reports (Phase 1): Inclusive Framework on BEPS: Action 13*, OECD/G20 Base Erosion and Profit Shifting Project, OECD Publishing, Paris, https://dx.doi.org/10.1787/9789264300057-en. [2]

OECD (2017), *Terms of reference for the conduct of peer review of the Action 13 minimum standard on country-by-country reporting*, OECD Publishing, https://www.oecd.org/tax/beps/beps-action-13-on-country-by-country-reporting-peer-review-documents.pdf. [3]

Australia

1. Australia was reviewed as part of the 2017/2018 and the 2018/2019 peer reviews. This report is supplementary to those previous reports (OECD, 2019[1]) (OECD, 2018[2]).

2. The first filing obligation for a CbC report in Australia applies to reporting fiscal years commencing on or after 1 January 2016.

Summary of key findings

3. Australia's implementation of the Action 13 minimum standard meets all applicable terms of reference (OECD, 2017[3]).

Part A: The domestic legal and administrative framework

4. Australia has primary law in place to implement the BEPS Action 13 minimum standard, establishing the necessary requirements including the filing and reporting obligations.

(a) Parent entity filing obligation

5. No changes were identified.[1]

(b) Scope and timing of parent entity filing

6. No changes were identified.

(c) Limitation on local filing obligation

7. No changes were identified.

(d) Limitation on local filing in case of surrogate filing

8. No changes were identified.

(e) Effective implementation

9. No changes were identified.

Conclusion

10. Australia meets all the terms of reference with regard to its domestic and legal framework.

Part B: The exchange of information framework

(a) Exchange of information framework

11. As of 31 March 2020, Australia has 65 bilateral relationships in place, including those activated under the CbC MCAA and under a bilateral CAA. Within the context of its international exchange of information agreements that allow automatic exchange of information, Australia has taken steps to have qualifying competent authority agreements in effect with jurisdictions of the Inclusive Framework that

meet the confidentiality, consistency and appropriate use conditions. Regarding Australia's exchange of information framework, no inconsistencies with the terms of reference identified.[2]

(b) Content of information exchanged

12. No changes were identified.

(c) Completeness of exchanges

13. No changes were identified.

(d) Timeliness of exchanges

14. No changes were identified.

(e) Temporary suspension of exchange or termination of QCAA

15. No changes were identified.

(f) Consultation with other Competent Authority before determining systemic failure or significant non-compliance

16. No changes were identified.

(g) Format for information exchange

17. No changes were identified.

(h) Method for transmission

18. No changes were identified.

Conclusion

19. Australia meets all the terms of reference regarding the exchange of information.

Part C: Appropriate use

Appropriate use

20. No changes were identified.

Conclusion

21. Australia meets all the terms of reference relating to appropriate use of CbC reports.

Summary of recommendations on the implementation of country-by-country reporting

Aspect of the implementation that should be improved		Recommendation for improvement
Part A	Domestic legal and administrative framework	-
Part B	Exchange of information framework	-
Part C	Appropriate use	-

References

OECD (2019), *Country-by-Country Reporting – Compilation of Peer Review Reports (Phase 2): Inclusive Framework on BEPS: Action 13*, OECD/G20 Base Erosion and Profit Shifting Project, OECD Publishing, Paris, https://dx.doi.org/10.1787/f9bf1157-en. [1]

OECD (2018), *Country-by-Country Reporting – Compilation of Peer Review Reports (Phase 1): Inclusive Framework on BEPS: Action 13*, OECD/G20 Base Erosion and Profit Shifting Project, OECD Publishing, Paris, https://dx.doi.org/10.1787/9789264300057-en. [2]

OECD (2017), *Terms of reference for the conduct of peer review of the Action 13 minimum standard on country-by-country reporting*, OECD Publishing, https://www.oecd.org/tax/beps/beps-action-13-on-country-by-country-reporting-peer-review-documents.pdf. [3]

Notes

[1] Australia's 2017/2018 peer review included a monitoring point in relation to the fact that its legislation did not include the situation of an Ultimate Parent Entity that does not prepare Consolidated Financial Statements, but would be required to do so if its equity interests were traded on a public securities exchange in its jurisdiction of tax residence (i.e. the "deemed listing provision"). Legislation has now been enacted to address this and can be viewed here: https://www.legislation.gov.au/Details/C2020B00007 (accessed 11 September 2020).

[2] No inconsistency with the terms of reference will be identified where a QCAA is not in effect with one or more jurisdictions of the Inclusive Framework that meet the confidentiality, consistency and appropriate use conditions, but this is due to circumstances that are not under the control of the reviewed jurisdiction. This may include, for example, where the other jurisdiction intends to exchange CbC reports using the MCAA but it does not have the Convention in effect for the relevant fiscal period, or where the other jurisdiction has declined to have a QCAA in effect with the reviewed jurisdiction.

Austria

1. Austria was first reviewed during the 2017/2018 and 2018/2019 peer review. This report is supplementary to those previous reports (OECD, 2019[1]) (OECD, 2018[2]).

2. The first filing obligation for a CbC report in Austria applies to reporting fiscal years commencing on or after 1 January 2016.

Summary of key findings

3. Austria's implementation of the Action 13 minimum standard meets all applicable terms of reference (OECD, 2017[3]).

Part A: The domestic legal and administrative framework

4. Austria has primary law in place that implements the BEPS Action 13 minimum standard, establishing the necessary requirements, including the filing and reporting obligations.

(a) Parent entity filing obligation

5. No changes were identified.

(b) Scope and timing of parent entity filing

6. No changes were identified.

(c) Limitation on local filing obligation

7. No changes were identified.

(d) Limitation on local filing in case of surrogate filing

8. No changes were identified.

(e) Effective implementation

9. No changes were identified.[1]

Conclusion

10. Austria meets all the terms of reference relating to the domestic legal and administrative framework.

Part B: The exchange of information framework

11. As of 31 March 2020, Austria has 67 bilateral relationships in place, including those activated under the CbC MCAA, under bilateral QCAAs, and under the EU Council Directive (2016/881/EU). Within the context of its international exchange of information agreements that allow automatic exchange of information, Austria has taken steps to have qualifying competent authority agreements in effect with jurisdictions of the Inclusive Framework that currently meet the confidentiality, consistency

and appropriate use conditions. Regarding Austria's exchange of information framework, no inconsistencies with the terms of reference identified.[2]

(b) Content of information exchanged

12. No changes were identified.

(c) Completeness of exchanges

13. No changes were identified.

(d) Timeliness of exchanges

14. No changes were identified.

(e) Temporary suspension of exchange or termination of QCAA

15. No changes were identified.

(f) Consultation with other Competent Authority before determining systemic failure or significant non-compliance

16. No changes were identified.

(g) Format for information exchange

17. No changes were identified.

(h) Method for transmission

18. No changes were identified.

Conclusion

19. Austria meets all the terms of reference regarding the exchange of information.

Part C: Appropriate use

Appropriate use

20. No changes were identified.

Conclusion

21. Austria meets all the terms of reference relating to appropriate use of CbC reports.

Summary of recommendations on the implementation of Country-by-Country Reporting

Aspect of the implementation that should be improved		Recommendation for improvement
Part A	Domestic legal and administrative framework	-
Part B	Exchange of information framework	-
Part C	Appropriate Use	-

References

OECD (2019), *Country-by-Country Reporting – Compilation of Peer Review Reports (Phase 2): Inclusive Framework on BEPS: Action 13*, OECD/G20 Base Erosion and Profit Shifting Project, OECD Publishing, Paris, https://dx.doi.org/10.1787/f9bf1157-en. [1]

OECD (2018), *Country-by-Country Reporting – Compilation of Peer Review Reports (Phase 1): Inclusive Framework on BEPS: Action 13*, OECD/G20 Base Erosion and Profit Shifting Project, OECD Publishing, Paris, https://dx.doi.org/10.1787/9789264300057-en. [2]

OECD (2017), *Terms of reference for the conduct of peer review of the Action 13 minimum standard on country-by-country reporting*, OECD Publishing, https://www.oecd.org/tax/beps/beps-action-13-on-country-by-country-reporting-peer-review-documents.pdf. [3]

Notes

[1] Austria's 2017/2018 peer review included a general monitoring point relating to the absence of a specific process that would allow Austria to take appropriate measures in case it is notified by another jurisdiction that such other jurisdiction has reason to believe that an error may have led to incorrect or incomplete information reporting by a Reporting Entity or that there is non-compliance of a Reporting Entity with respect to its obligation to file a CbC report. Austria indicates that audit processes would apply in cases where no CbC Report was transmitted. This monitoring point remains in place.

[2] No inconsistency with the terms of reference will be identified where a QCAA is not in effect with one or more jurisdictions of the Inclusive Framework that meet the confidentiality, consistency and appropriate use conditions, but this is due to circumstances that are not under the control of the reviewed jurisdiction. This may include, for example, where the other jurisdiction intends to exchange CbC reports using the MCAA but it does not have the Convention in effect for the relevant fiscal period, or where the other jurisdiction has declined to have a QCAA in effect with the reviewed jurisdiction.

The Bahamas

1. The Bahamas was first reviewed during the 2018/2019 peer review. This report is supplementary to that previous report (OECD, 2018[2]).

2. The first filing obligation for a CbC report in the Bahamas applies to reporting fiscal years commencing on or after 1 January 2018.

Summary of key findings

3. The Bahamas meets all the terms of reference relating to the domestic legal and administrative framework (OECD, 2017[3]).

4. It is recommended that the Bahamas take steps to implement processes or written procedures to ensure that the exchange of information is conducted in a manner consistent with the terms of reference relating to the exchange of information framework ahead of its first exchanges of information. This recommendation remains in place since the 2018/2019 peer review. It is noted that steps to address this recommendation by the Bahamas have been delayed as a result of the effects of hurricane Dorian.

5. The Bahamas' 2018/2019 peer review report included a recommendation that the Bahamas amend the deadline for filing a CbC report with respect to the specific filing deadline relating to the reporting fiscal years that began on or before 31 May 2018. The Bahamas made a legislative amendment in April 2019 to make this amendment and the recommendation is therefore removed.

6. The Bahamas' previous peer review included a recommendation that it take steps to have QCAAs in effect with jurisdictions of the Inclusive Framework which meet the confidentiality, consistency and appropriate use prerequisites and with which the Bahamas has international agreements which allow for the automatic exchange of tax information. Bilateral relationships are now in place so the recommendation is removed.

Part A: The domestic legal and administrative framework

7. The Bahamas meets all the terms of reference relating to the domestic legal and administrative framework.

(a) Parent entity filing obligation

8. No changes were identified.

(b) Scope and timing of parent entity filing

9. The Bahamas' 2018/2019 peer review report included a recommendation that the Bahamas amend the deadline for filing a CbC report with respect to the specific filing deadline relating to the reporting fiscal years that began on or before 31 May 2018 The Bahamas made a legislative amendment in April 2019 to make this amendment and the recommendation is therefore removed.

(c) Limitation on local filing obligation

10. No changes were identified[1].

(d) Limitation on local filing in case of surrogate filing

11. No changes were identified.

(e) Effective implementation

12. No changes were identified[2].

Conclusion

13. The Bahamas meets all the terms of reference relating to the domestic legal and administrative framework.

Part B: The exchange of information framework

(a) Exchange of information framework

14. The Bahamas' previous peer review included a recommendation that it take steps to have QCAAs in effect with jurisdictions of the Inclusive Framework which meet the confidentiality, consistency and appropriate use prerequisites and with which the Bahamas has international agreements which allow for the automatic exchange of tax information. Bilateral relationships are now in place so the recommendation is removed.

15. As of 31 March 2020, the Bahamas has 41 bilateral relationships in place for the exchange of CbC reports, activated under the CbC MCAA. Within the context of its international exchange of information agreements that allow automatic exchange of tax information, the Bahamas has taken steps to have qualifying competent authority agreements in effect with jurisdictions of the Inclusive Framework that currently meet the confidentiality, consistency and appropriate use conditions. Regarding the Bahamas' exchange of information framework, no inconsistencies with the terms of reference were identified.[3]

(b) Content of information exchanged

16. No changes were identified.

(c) Completeness of exchanges

17. No changes were identified.

(d) Timeliness of exchanges

18. No changes were identified.

(e) Temporary suspension of exchange or termination of QCAA

19. No changes were identified.

(f) Consultation with other Competent Authority before determining systemic failure or significant non-compliance

20. No changes were identified.

(g) Format for information exchange

21. No changes were identified.

(h) Method for transmission

22. No changes were identified.

Conclusion

23. It is recommended that the Bahamas take steps to implement processes or written procedures to ensure that the exchange of information is conducted in a manner consistent with the terms of reference relating to the exchange of information framework ahead of its first exchanges of information. This recommendation remains unchanged since the 2018/2019 peer review. It is noted that steps to address this recommendation by the Bahamas have been delayed as a result of the effects of hurricane Dorian

Part C: Appropriate use

Appropriate use

24. No changes were identified.

Conclusion

25. The Bahamas is a non-reciprocal jurisdiction and, as such, will not receive CbC reports submitted to tax authorities in other jurisdictions, and will not apply local filing. It is not necessary for this peer review evaluation to reach any conclusion with respect to appropriate use.

Summary of recommendations on the implementation of country-by-country reporting

Aspect of the implementation that should be improved		Recommendation for improvement
Part A	Domestic legal and administrative framework	-
Part B	Exchange of information framework	It is recommended that the Bahamas take steps to implement processes or written procedures to ensure that the exchange of information in conducted in a manner consistent with the terms of reference relating to the exchange of information framework ahead of its first exchanges of information.
Part C	Appropriate use	

References

OECD (2018), *Country-by-Country Reporting – Compilation of Peer Review Reports (Phase 1): Inclusive Framework on BEPS: Action 13*, OECD/G20 Base Erosion and Profit Shifting Project, OECD Publishing, Paris, https://dx.doi.org/10.1787/9789264300057-en. [2]

OECD (2017), *Terms of reference for the conduct of peer review of the Action 13 minimum standard on country-by-country reporting*, OECD Publishing, https://www.oecd.org/tax/beps/beps-action-13-on-country-by-country-reporting-peer-review-documents.pdf. [3]

Notes

[1] The Bahamas 2018/2019 peer review included a monitoring point which remains in place. It was noted that the Bahamas' legislation includes provisions relating to (i) the deactivation of local filing in case of surrogate filing (see Section 3(4) of The Bahamas CbC Act) and (ii) the fact that a single Constituent Entity could file a CbC report that satisfies the filing requirement of all Constituent Entities of such MNE Group that are resident in the Bahamas (see Section 3(3) of The Bahamas CbC Act). While these provisions do not seem to create a filing obligation on Constituent Entities in the Bahamas (being noted that according to Section 3(1) and 3(2), only Ultimate Parent Entities and Surrogate Parent Entities shall file a CbC report in the Bahamas), they may introduce uncertainty for taxpayers. This will be monitored to ensure that no local filing obligations arise from Section 3 of the act.

[2] The Bahamas 2018/2019 peer review included a monitoring point which remains in place. There are no specific processes in place that would allow the Bahamas to take appropriate measures in case it is notified by another jurisdiction that such other jurisdiction has reason to believe that an error may have led to incorrect or incomplete information reporting by a Reporting Entity or that there is non-compliance of a Reporting Entity with respect to its obligation to file a CbC report. However, the Bahamas indicates that the penalties will be applied to any person providing inaccurate information under Section 19 of the CbC Act. As no exchange of CbC reports has yet occurred, no recommendation is made but this respect will be further monitored.

[3] No inconsistency with the terms of reference will be identified where a QCAA is not in effect with one or more jurisdictions of the Inclusive Framework that meet the confidentiality, consistency and appropriate use conditions, but this is due to circumstances that are not under the control of the reviewed jurisdiction. This may include, for example, where the other jurisdiction intends to exchange CbC reports using the MCAA but it does not have the Convention in effect for the relevant fiscal period, or where the other jurisdiction has declined to have a QCAA in effect with the reviewed jurisdiction.

Bahrain

1. Bahrain was first reviewed during the 2018/2019 peer review. This report is supplementary to that previous report (OECD, 2018[2]).

2. There is no filing obligation for a CbC report in Bahrain yet.

Summary of key findings

3. It is recommended that Bahrain take steps to implement a domestic legal and administrative framework to impose and enforce CbC reporting requirements as soon as possible. This recommendation remains unchanged since the 2018/2019 peer review.

4. It is recommended that Bahrain take steps to have qualifying competent authority agreements in effect with jurisdictions of the Inclusive Framework that meet the confidentiality, consistency and appropriate use conditions and with which Bahrain has an international exchange of information agreement in effect that allows for the automatic exchange of tax information. This recommendation remains unchanged since the 2018/2019 peer review.

5. It is recommended that Bahrain take steps to implement processes or written procedures to ensure that the exchange of information is conducted in a manner consistent with the terms of reference (OECD, 2017[3]) relating to the exchange of information framework ahead of the first exchanges of information. This recommendation remains unchanged since the 2018/2019 peer review.

Part A: The domestic legal and administrative framework

6. Bahrain does not yet have legislation in place for implementing the BEPS Action 13 minimum standard. Bahrain reports that it is in the preliminary stages of drafting legislation.

(a) Parent entity filing obligation

(b) Scope and timing of parent entity filing

(c) Limitation on local filing obligation

(d) Limitation on local filing in case of surrogate filing

(e) Effective implementation

Conclusion

7. It is recommended that Bahrain take steps to implement a domestic legal and administrative framework to impose and enforce CbC reporting requirements as soon as possible. This recommendation remains unchanged since the 2018/2019 peer review.

Part B: The exchange of information framework

(a) Exchange of information framework

8. As of 31 March 2020, Bahrain has no bilateral relationships in place for the exchange of CbC reports. It is recommended that Bahrain take steps to have qualifying competent authority agreements in effect with jurisdictions of the Inclusive Framework that meet the confidentiality, consistency and appropriate use conditions and with which Bahrain has an international exchange of information agreement in effect that allows for the automatic exchange of tax information. This recommendation remains unchanged since the 2018/2019 peer review.

(b) Content of information exchanged

9. No changes were identified.

(c) Completeness of exchanges

10. No changes were identified.

(d) Timeliness of exchanges

11. No changes were identified.

(e) Temporary suspension of exchange or termination of QCAA

12. No changes were identified.

(f) Consultation with other Competent Authority before determining systemic failure or significant non-compliance

13. No changes were identified.

(g) Format for information exchange

14. No changes were identified.

(h) Method for transmission

15. No changes were identified.

Conclusion

16. It is recommended that Bahrain take steps to have qualifying competent authority agreements in effect with jurisdictions of the Inclusive Framework that meet the confidentiality, consistency and appropriate use conditions and with which Bahrain has an international exchange of information agreement in effect that allows for the automatic exchange of tax information. This recommendation remains unchanged since the 2018/2019 peer review.

17. It is recommended that Bahrain take steps to implement processes or written procedures to ensure that the exchange of information is conducted in a manner consistent with the terms of reference relating (OECD, 2017[3]) to the exchange of information framework ahead of its first exchanges of information. This recommendation remains unchanged since the 2018/2019 peer review.

Part C: Appropriate use

Appropriate use

18. No changes were identified.

Conclusion

19. Bahrain is a non-reciprocal jurisdiction and, as such, will not receive CbC reports submitted to tax authorities in other jurisdictions, and will not apply local filing. It is not necessary for this peer review evaluation to reach any conclusion with respect to appropriate use.

Summary of recommendations on the implementation of Country-by-Country Reporting

Aspect of the implementation that should be improved		Recommendation for improvement
Part A	Domestic legal and administrative framework	It is recommended that Bahrain take steps to implement a domestic legal and administrative framework to impose and enforce CbC requirements as soon as possible.
Part B	Exchange of information framework	It is recommended that Bahrain take steps to have qualifying competent authority agreements in effect with jurisdictions of the Inclusive Framework that meet the confidentiality, consistency and appropriate use conditions and with which Bahrain has an international exchange of information agreement in effect that allows for the automatic exchange of tax information.
Part B	Exchange of information framework	It is recommended that Bahrain take steps to implement processes or written procedures to ensure that the exchange of information is conducted in a manner consistent with the terms of reference relating to the exchange of information framework.
Part C	Appropriate use	-

References

OECD (2018), *Country-by-Country Reporting – Compilation of Peer Review Reports (Phase 1): Inclusive Framework on BEPS: Action 13*, OECD/G20 Base Erosion and Profit Shifting Project, OECD Publishing, Paris, https://dx.doi.org/10.1787/9789264300057-en. [2]

OECD (2017), *Terms of reference for the conduct of peer review of the Action 13 minimum standard on country-by-country reporting*, OECD Publishing, https://www.oecd.org/tax/beps/beps-action-13-on-country-by-country-reporting-peer-review-documents.pdf. [3]

Barbados

1. Barbados was reviewed as part of the 2017/2018 and the 2018/2019 peer reviews. This report is supplementary to those previous reports (OECD, 2019[1]) (OECD, 2018[2]).

2. There is no filing obligation for a CbC report in Barbados yet.

Summary of key findings

3. Barbados does not yet have legislation in place for implementing the BEPS Action 13 minimum standard. It is recommended that Barbados take steps to implement a domestic legal and administrative framework to impose and enforce CbC reporting requirements as soon as possible. This recommendation remains unchanged since the 2017/2018 peer review.

4. It is recommended that Barbados take steps to have QCAAs in effect with jurisdictions of the Inclusive Framework which meet the confidentiality, consistency and appropriate use prerequisites and with which it has an international agreement in place which allows for the automatic exchange of information. This recommendation remains unchanged since the 2017/2018 peer review.

5. It is recommended that Barbados take steps to implement processes or written procedures to ensure that the exchange of information is conducted in a manner consistent with the terms of reference (OECD, 2017[3]) relating to the exchange of information framework ahead of the first exchanges of information. This recommendation remains unchanged since the 2018/2019 peer review.

6. It is recommended that Barbados take steps to ensure that the appropriate use condition is met ahead of the first exchanges of information. This recommendation remains unchanged since the 2017/2018 peer review.

Part A: The domestic legal and administrative framework

7. Barbados does not yet have legislation in place for implementing the BEPS Action 13 minimum standard.

(a) Parent entity filing obligation

(b) Scope and timing of parent entity filing

(c) Limitation on local filing obligation

(d) Limitation on local filing in case of surrogate filing

(e) Effective implementation

Conclusion

8. The recommendation in the 2017/18 peer review, that Barbados take steps to implement a domestic legal and administrative framework to impose and enforce CbC reporting requirements as soon as possible, remains in place.

Part B: The exchange of information framework

(a) Exchange of information framework

9. As of 31 March 2020, Barbados has no bilateral relationships in place for the exchange of CbC reports. It is recommended that Barbados take steps to have qualifying competent authority agreements in effect with jurisdictions of the Inclusive Framework that meet the confidentiality, consistency and appropriate use conditions and with which Barbados has an international exchange of information agreement in effect that allows for the automatic exchange of tax information.

(b) Content of information exchanged

10. No changes were identified.

(c) Completeness of exchanges

11. No changes were identified.

(d) Timeliness of exchanges

12. No changes were identified.

(e) Temporary suspension of exchange or termination of QCAA

13. No changes were identified.

(f) Consultation with other Competent Authority before determining systemic failure or significant non-compliance

14. No changes were identified.

(g) Format for information exchange

15. No changes were identified.

(h) Method for transmission

16. No changes were identified.

Conclusion

17. It is recommended that Barbados take steps to have QCAAs in effect with jurisdictions of the Inclusive Framework which meet the confidentiality, consistency and appropriate use prerequisites and with which Barbados has an international exchange of information agreement in effect that allows for the automatic exchange of tax information. This recommendation remains unchanged since the 2018/2019 peer review.

18. It is recommended that Barbados take steps to implement processes or written procedures to ensure that the exchange of information is conducted in a manner consistent with the terms of reference relating to the exchange of information framework ahead of its first exchanges of information. This recommendation remains unchanged since the 2018/2019 peer review.

Part C: Appropriate use

Appropriate use

19. No changes were identified.

Conclusion

20. It is recommended that Barbados take steps to ensure that the appropriate use condition is met ahead of its first exchanges of information remains in place. This recommendation remains unchanged since the 2017/2018 peer review.

Summary of recommendations on the implementation of Country-by-Country Reporting

Aspect of the implementation that should be improved		Recommendation for improvement
Part A	Domestic legal and administrative framework	It is recommended that Barbados take steps to implement a domestic legal and administrative framework to impose and enforce CbC requirements as soon as possible.
Part B	Exchange of information framework	It is recommended that Barbados take steps to have QCAAs in effect with jurisdictions of the Inclusive Framework which meet the confidentiality, consistency and appropriate use prerequisites and with which Barbados has an international exchange of information agreement in effect that allows for the automatic exchange of tax information.
Part B	Exchange of information framework	It is recommended that Barbados take steps to implement the necessary processes or written procedures to ensure that the exchange of information is conducted in a manner consistent with the terms of reference relating to the exchange of information framework.
Part C	Appropriate use	It is recommended that Barbados take steps to ensure that the appropriate use condition is met ahead of the first exchanges of information.

References

OECD (2019), *Country-by-Country Reporting – Compilation of Peer Review Reports (Phase 2): Inclusive Framework on BEPS: Action 13*, OECD/G20 Base Erosion and Profit Shifting Project, OECD Publishing, Paris, https://dx.doi.org/10.1787/f9bf1157-en. [1]

OECD (2018), *Country-by-Country Reporting – Compilation of Peer Review Reports (Phase 1): Inclusive Framework on BEPS: Action 13*, OECD/G20 Base Erosion and Profit Shifting Project, OECD Publishing, Paris, https://dx.doi.org/10.1787/9789264300057-en. [2]

OECD (2017), *Terms of reference for the conduct of peer review of the Action 13 minimum standard on country-by-country reporting*, OECD Publishing, https://www.oecd.org/tax/beps/beps-action-13-on-country-by-country-reporting-peer-review-documents.pdf. [3]

Belgium

1. Belgium was reviewed as part of the 2017/2018 and the 2018/2019 peer reviews. This report is supplementary to those previous reports (OECD, 2019[1]) (OECD, 2018[2]).

2. The first filing obligation for a CbC report in Belgium commenced in respect of reporting fiscal years commencing on or after 1 January 2016.

Summary of key findings

3. Belgium's implementation of the Action 13 minimum standard meets all applicable terms of reference (OECD, 2017[3]).

Part A: The domestic legal and administrative framework

4. Belgium meets all the terms of reference relating to the domestic legal and administrative framework.

(a) Parent entity filing obligation

5. No changes were identified.

(b) Scope and timing of parent entity filing

6. No changes were identified.

(c) Limitation on local filing obligation

7. No changes were identified.[1]

(d) Limitation on local filing in case of surrogate filing

8. No changes were identified.

(e) Effective implementation

9. No changes were identified.

Conclusion

10. Belgium meets all the terms of reference relating to the domestic legal and administrative framework.

Part B: The exchange of information framework

(a) Exchange of information framework

11. As of 31 March 2020, Belgium has 67 bilateral relationships in place for the exchange of CbC reports, including those activated under the CbC MCAA, under bilateral CAAs and under the EU Council Directive (2016/881/EU). Within the context of its international exchange of information agreements that allow automatic exchange of tax information, Belgium has taken steps to have qualifying competent

authority agreements in effect with jurisdictions of the Inclusive Framework that currently meet the confidentiality, consistency and appropriate use conditions. Regarding Belgium's exchange of information framework, no inconsistencies with the terms of reference were identified.[2]

(b) Content of information exchanged

12. No changes were identified.

(c) Completeness of exchanges

13. No changes were identified.

(d) Timeliness of exchanges

14. No changes were identified.

(e) Temporary suspension of exchange or termination of QCAA

15. No changes were identified.

(f) Consultation with other Competent Authority before determining systemic failure or significant non-compliance

16. No changes were identified.

(g) Format for information exchange

17. No changes were identified.

(h) Method for transmission

18. No changes were identified

Conclusion

19. Belgium meets all the terms of reference regarding the exchange of information.

Part C: Appropriate use

Appropriate use

20. No changes were identified.

Conclusion

21. Belgium meets all the terms of reference relating to appropriate use of CbC reports.

Summary of recommendations on the implementation of country-by-country reporting

Aspect of the implementation that should be improved		Recommendation for improvement
Part A	Domestic legal and administrative framework	-
Part B	Exchange of information framework	-
Part C	Appropriate use	-

References

OECD (2019), *Country-by-Country Reporting – Compilation of Peer Review Reports (Phase 2): Inclusive Framework on BEPS: Action 13*, OECD/G20 Base Erosion and Profit Shifting Project, OECD Publishing, Paris, https://dx.doi.org/10.1787/f9bf1157-en. [1]

OECD (2018), *Country-by-Country Reporting – Compilation of Peer Review Reports (Phase 1): Inclusive Framework on BEPS: Action 13*, OECD/G20 Base Erosion and Profit Shifting Project, OECD Publishing, Paris, https://dx.doi.org/10.1787/9789264300057-en. [2]

OECD (2017), *Terms of reference for the conduct of peer review of the Action 13 minimum standard on country-by-country reporting*, OECD Publishing, https://www.oecd.org/tax/beps/beps-action-13-on-country-by-country-reporting-peer-review-documents.pdf. [3]

Notes

1 Belgium's 2017/2018 review included a monitoring point relating to the rule according to which where there are more than one Constituent Entities of the same MNE Group that are resident for tax purposes in the EU, the MNE Group may designate one of such Constituent Entities to file the country-by-country report conforming to the requirements that would satisfy the filing requirement of all the Constituent Entities of such MNE Group that are resident for tax purposes in the EU. This monitoring point remains in place.

2 No inconsistency with the terms of reference will be identified where a QCAA is not in effect with one or more jurisdictions of the Inclusive Framework that meet the confidentiality, consistency and appropriate use conditions, but this is due to circumstances that are not under the control of the reviewed jurisdiction. This may include, for example, where the other jurisdiction intends to exchange CbC reports using the MCAA but it does not have the Convention in effect for the relevant fiscal period, or where the other jurisdiction has declined to have a QCAA in effect with the reviewed jurisdiction.

Belize

1. Belize was reviewed as part of the 2017/2018 and the 2018/2019 peer reviews. This report is supplementary to those previous reports (OECD, 2019[1]) (OECD, 2018[2]).

2. The filing obligation for a CbC report in Belize applies to reporting fiscal years commencing on or after 1 January 2019.

Summary of key findings

3. The 2017/2018 peer review recommended that Belize take steps to implement a domestic legal and administrative framework to impose and enforce CbC reporting requirements as soon as possible. Legislation is now in force and the recommendation is removed.

4. It is recommended that Belize take steps to qualifying competent authority agreements in effect with jurisdictions of the Inclusive Framework that meet the confidentiality, consistency and appropriate use conditions and with which Belize has an international exchange of information agreement in effect that allows for the automatic exchange of tax information. This recommendation remains unchanged since the 2017/2018 peer review.

5. It is recommended that Belize take steps to implement processes or written procedures to ensure that the exchange of information is conducted in a manner consistent with the terms of reference (OECD, 2017[3]) relating to the exchange of information framework ahead of the first exchanges of information.

6. It is recommended that Belize take steps to ensure that the appropriate use condition is met ahead of the first exchanges of information. This recommendation remains unchanged since the 2017/2018 peer review.

Part A: The domestic legal and administrative framework

7. Belize has legislation in place for implementing the BEPS Action 13 minimum standard, requiring filing of CbC reports for fiscal years commencing on or after 1 January 2019.[1]

(a) Parent entity filing obligation

8. Belize has introduced a filing requirement which applies to all Ultimate Parent Entities of MNE Groups above a certain threshold and which requires inclusion of all constituent entities.

9. No inconsistencies were identified.

(b) Scope and timing of parent entity filing

10. The first filing requirements for MNE Groups in Belize enforce a CbC filing requirement for fiscal years commencing on or after 1 January 2019 and filing is required 12 months after the reporting year end.

11. No inconsistencies were identified.

(c) Limitation on local filing obligation

12. Belize has a local filing requirement which applies to reporting fiscal periods beginning on or after 1 January 2019.

13. No inconsistencies were identified.

(d) Limitation on local filing in case of surrogate filing

14. Belize's local filing requirements will not apply if there is surrogate filing in another jurisdiction.

15. No inconsistencies were identified.

(e) Effective implementation

16. Belize has systems to ensure effective implementation of the CbC filing requirement which include a notification requirement and an audit function with a penalty regime in the case of non-cooperation with an audit or failure to provide relevant documents.

Conclusion

17. The 2017/2018 peer review recommended that Belize take steps to implement a domestic legal and administrative framework to impose and enforce CbC reporting requirements as soon as possible. Legislation is now in force and the recommendation is removed.

18. Belize's legal framework meets all of the terms of reference.

Part B: The exchange of information framework

(a) Exchange of information framework

19. As of 31 March 2020, Belize has no bilateral relationships in place for the exchange of CbC reports. It is recommended that Belize take steps to have qualifying competent authority agreements in effect with jurisdictions of the Inclusive Framework that meet the confidentiality, consistency and appropriate use conditions and with which Belize has an international exchange of information agreement in effect that allows for the automatic exchange of tax information.

(b) Content of information exchanged

20. No changes were identified.

(c) Completeness of exchanges

21. No changes were identified.

(d) Timeliness of exchanges

22. No changes were identified.

(e) Temporary suspension of exchange or termination of QCAA

23. No changes were identified.

(f) Consultation with other Competent Authority before determining systemic failure or significant non-compliance

24. No changes were identified.

(g) Format for information exchange

25. No changes were identified.

(h) Method for transmission

26. No changes were identified.

Conclusion

27. It is recommended that Belize take steps to have QCAAs in effect with jurisdictions of the Inclusive Framework which meet the confidentiality, consistency and appropriate use prerequisites remains in place. This recommendation remains unchanged since the 2017/2018 peer review.

28. It is recommended that Belize take steps to implement processes or written procedures to ensure that the exchange of information is conducted in a manner consistent with the terms of reference relating to the exchange of information framework ahead of its first exchanges of information. This recommendation remains unchanged since the 2018/2019 peer review.

Part C: Appropriate use

Appropriate use

29. No changes were identified.

Conclusion

30. The recommendation for Belize to take steps to ensure that the appropriate use condition is met ahead of its first exchanges of information remains in place.

Summary of recommendations on the implementation of Country-by-Country Reporting

Aspect of the implementation that should be improved		Recommendation for improvement
Part A	Domestic legal and administrative framework	-
Part B	Exchange of information framework	It is recommended that Belize take steps to have qualifying competent authority agreements in effect with jurisdictions of the Inclusive Framework that meet the confidentiality, consistency and appropriate use conditions and with which Belize has an international exchange of information agreement in effect that allows for the automatic exchange of tax information.
Part B	Exchange of information framework	It is recommended that Belize take steps to implement processes or written procedures to ensure that the exchange of information is conducted in a manner consistent with the terms of reference relating to the exchange of information framework ahead of its first exchanges of information.
Part C	Appropriate use	It is recommended that Belize take steps to ensure that the appropriate use condition is met ahead of the first exchanges of information.

References

OECD (2019), *Country-by-Country Reporting – Compilation of Peer Review Reports (Phase 2): Inclusive Framework on BEPS: Action 13*, OECD/G20 Base Erosion and Profit Shifting Project, OECD Publishing, Paris, https://dx.doi.org/10.1787/f9bf1157-en. [1]

OECD (2018), *Country-by-Country Reporting – Compilation of Peer Review Reports (Phase 1): Inclusive Framework on BEPS: Action 13*, OECD/G20 Base Erosion and Profit Shifting Project, OECD Publishing, Paris, https://dx.doi.org/10.1787/9789264300057-en. [2]

OECD (2017), *Terms of reference for the conduct of peer review of the Action 13 minimum standard on country-by-country reporting*, OECD Publishing, https://www.oecd.org/tax/beps/beps-action-13-on-country-by-country-reporting-peer-review-documents.pdf. [3]

Note

[1] http://incometaxbelize.gov.bz/ (accessed on 24 August 2020).

Benin

1. Benin was reviewed as part of the 2017/2018 and the 2018/2019 peer reviews. This report is supplementary to those previous reports (OECD, 2019[1]) (OECD, 2018[2]).

2. There is no filing obligation for a CbC report in Benin yet.

Summary of key findings

3. Benin does not yet have legislation in place for implementing the BEPS Action 13 minimum standard.[1] It is recommended that Benin take steps to implement a domestic legal and administrative framework to impose and enforce CbC reporting requirements as soon as possible. This recommendation remains unchanged since the 2017/2018 peer review.

4. It is recommended that Benin take steps to have QCAAs in effect with jurisdictions of the Inclusive Framework which meet the confidentiality, consistency and appropriate use prerequisites and with which Benin has an international exchange of information agreement in effect that allows for the automatic exchange of tax information. This recommendation remains unchanged since the 2017/2018 peer review.

5. It is recommended that Benin take steps to implement processes or written procedures to ensure that the exchange of information is conducted in a manner consistent with the terms of reference (OECD, 2017[3]) relating to the exchange of information framework ahead of the first exchanges of information. This recommendation remains unchanged since the 2018/2019 peer review.

6. It is recommended that Benin take steps to ensure that the appropriate use condition is met ahead of the first exchanges of information. This recommendation remains unchanged since the 2017/2018 peer review.

Part A: The domestic legal and administrative framework

7. Benin does not yet have legislation in place for implementing the BEPS Action 13 minimum standard.

(a) Parent entity filing obligation

(b) Scope and timing of parent entity filing

(c) Limitation on local filing obligation

(d) Limitation on local filing in case of surrogate filing

(e) Effective implementation

Conclusion

8. The recommendation in the 2017/18 peer review, that Benin take steps to implement a domestic legal and administrative framework to impose and enforce CbC reporting requirements as soon as possible, remains in place.

Part B: The exchange of information framework

(a) Exchange of information framework

9. As of 31 March 2020, Benin has no bilateral relationships in place for the exchange of CbC reports. It is recommended that Benin take steps to have qualifying competent authority agreements in effect with jurisdictions of the Inclusive Framework that meet the confidentiality, consistency and appropriate use conditions and with which Benin has an international exchange of information agreement in effect that allows for the automatic exchange of tax information

(b) Content of information exchanged

10. No changes were identified.

(c) Completeness of exchanges

11. No changes were identified.

(d) Timeliness of exchanges

12. No changes were identified.

(e) Temporary suspension of exchange or termination of QCAA

13. No changes were identified.

(f) Consultation with other Competent Authority before determining systemic failure or significant non-compliance

14. No changes were identified.

(g) Format for information exchange

15. No changes were identified.

(h) Method for transmission

16. No changes were identified.

Conclusion

17. It is recommended that Benin take steps to have QCAAs in effect with jurisdictions of the Inclusive Framework which meet the confidentiality, consistency and appropriate use prerequisites and with which Benin has an international exchange of information agreement in effect that allows for the automatic exchange of tax information. This recommendation remains unchanged since the 2017/2018 peer review.

18. It is recommended that Benin take steps to implement processes or written procedures to ensure that the exchange of information is conducted in a manner consistent with the terms of reference relating to the exchange of information framework ahead of its first exchanges of information. This recommendation remains unchanged since the 2018/2019 peer review.

Part C: Appropriate use

Appropriate use

19. No changes were identified.

Conclusion

20. It is recommended that Benin take steps to ensure that the appropriate use condition is met ahead of its first exchanges of information. This recommendation remains unchanged since the 2017/2018 peer review.

Summary of recommendations on the implementation of Country-by-Country Reporting

Aspect of the implementation that should be improved		Recommendation for improvement
Part A	Domestic legal and administrative framework	It is recommended that Benin take steps to implement a domestic legal and administrative framework to impose and enforce CbC requirements as soon as possible.
Part B	Exchange of information framework	It is recommended that Benin take steps to have QCAAs in effect with jurisdictions of the Inclusive Framework which meet the confidentiality, consistency and appropriate use prerequisites and with which Benin has an international exchange of information agreement in effect that allows for the automatic exchange of tax information.
Part B	Exchange of information framework	It is recommended that Benin take steps to implement processes or written procedures to ensure that the exchange of information is conducted in a manner consistent with the terms of reference relating to the exchange of information framework ahead of its first exchanges of information.
Part C	Appropriate use	It is recommended that Benin take steps to ensure that the appropriate use condition is met ahead of the first exchanges of information.

References

OECD (2019), *Country-by-Country Reporting – Compilation of Peer Review Reports (Phase 2): Inclusive Framework on BEPS: Action 13*, OECD/G20 Base Erosion and Profit Shifting Project, OECD Publishing, Paris, https://dx.doi.org/10.1787/f9bf1157-en. [1]

OECD (2018), *Country-by-Country Reporting – Compilation of Peer Review Reports (Phase 1): Inclusive Framework on BEPS: Action 13*, OECD/G20 Base Erosion and Profit Shifting Project, OECD Publishing, Paris, https://dx.doi.org/10.1787/9789264300057-en. [2]

OECD (2017), *Terms of reference for the conduct of peer review of the Action 13 minimum standard on country-by-country reporting*, OECD Publishing, https://www.oecd.org/tax/beps/beps-action-13-on-country-by-country-reporting-peer-review-documents.pdf. [3]

Note

[1] CbC requirements may first apply for taxable years commencing on or after 1 January 2019 if they are included in the Finance Bill for 2019. According to the latest information provided, the draft legislation was submitted to the parliamentary budgetary session.

Bermuda

1. Bermuda was reviewed as part of the 2017/2018 and the 2018/2019 peer reviews. This report is supplementary to those previous reports (OECD, 2019[1]) (OECD, 2018[2]).

2. The first filing obligation for a CbC report in Bermuda applies to reporting fiscal years commencing on or after 1 January 2016.

Summary of key findings

3. Bermuda's implementation of the Action 13 minimum standard meets all applicable terms of reference (OECD, 2017[3]).

Part A: The domestic legal and administrative framework

4. Bermuda meets all the terms of reference relating to the domestic legal and administrative framework.

(a) Parent entity filing obligation

5. No changes were identified.

(b) Scope and timing of parent entity filing

6. No changes were identified.[1]

(c) Limitation on local filing obligation

7. No changes were identified.

(d) Limitation on local filing in case of surrogate filing

8. No changes were identified.

(e) Effective implementation

9. No changes were identified.

Conclusion

10. Bermuda meets all the terms of reference relating to the domestic legal and administrative framework.

Part B: The exchange of information framework

(a) Exchange of information framework

11. As of 31 March 2020, Bermuda has 53 bilateral relationships in place, including those activated under the CbC MCAA and under bilateral CAAs. Within the context of its international exchange of information agreements that allow automatic exchange of information, Bermuda has taken steps to have

qualifying competent authority agreements in effect with jurisdictions of the Inclusive Framework that meet the confidentiality, consistency and appropriate use conditions.[2] Regarding Bermuda's exchange of information framework, no inconsistencies with the terms of reference were identified.

(b) Content of information exchanged

12. No changes were identified.

(c) Completeness of exchanges

13. No changes were identified.

(d) Timeliness of exchanges

14. No changes were identified.

(e) Temporary suspension of exchange or termination of QCAA

15. No changes were identified.

(f) Consultation with other Competent Authority before determining systemic failure or significant non-compliance

16. No changes were identified.

(g) Format for information exchange

17. No changes were identified.

(h) Method for transmission

18. No changes were identified.

Conclusion

19. Bermuda meets all the terms of reference regarding the exchange of information.

Part C: Appropriate use

Appropriate use

20. No changes were identified.

Conclusion

21. Bermuda is a non-reciprocal jurisdiction and, as such, will not receive CbC reports submitted to tax authorities in other jurisdictions, and will not apply local filing. It is not necessary for this peer review evaluation to reach any conclusion with respect to these paragraphs of the terms of reference.

Summary of recommendations on the implementation of country-by-country reporting

Aspect of the implementation that should be improved		Recommendation for improvement
Part A	Domestic legal and administrative framework	-
Part B	Exchange of information framework	-
Part C	Appropriate use	-

References

OECD (2019), *Country-by-Country Reporting – Compilation of Peer Review Reports (Phase 2): Inclusive Framework on BEPS: Action 13*, OECD/G20 Base Erosion and Profit Shifting Project, OECD Publishing, Paris, https://dx.doi.org/10.1787/f9bf1157-en. [1]

OECD (2018), *Country-by-Country Reporting – Compilation of Peer Review Reports (Phase 1): Inclusive Framework on BEPS: Action 13*, OECD/G20 Base Erosion and Profit Shifting Project, OECD Publishing, Paris, https://dx.doi.org/10.1787/9789264300057-en. [2]

OECD (2017), *Terms of reference for the conduct of peer review of the Action 13 minimum standard on country-by-country reporting*, OECD Publishing, https://www.oecd.org/tax/beps/beps-action-13-on-country-by-country-reporting-peer-review-documents.pdf. [3]

Notes

[1] Bermuda's 2017/2018 peer review included a monitoring point relating to the interpretation of the definition of "Revenue – Unrelated Party" and "Revenue – Related Party". This monitoring point remains in place.

[2] No inconsistency with the terms of reference will be identified where a QCAA is not in effect with one or more jurisdictions of the Inclusive Framework that meet the confidentiality, consistency and appropriate use conditions, but this is due to circumstances that are not under the control of the reviewed jurisdiction. This may include, for example, where the other jurisdiction intends to exchange CbC reports using the MCAA but it does not have the Convention in effect for the relevant fiscal period, or where the other jurisdiction has declined to have a QCAA in effect with the reviewed jurisdiction.

Bosnia and Herzegovina

1. This report is Bosnia and Herzegovina's first annual peer review report. Consistent with the agreed methodology this report covers: (i) the domestic legal and administrative framework, (ii) the exchange of information framework as well as (iii) the appropriate use of CbC reports.

2. The filing obligation for a CbC report in Bosnia and Herzegovina applies to reporting fiscal years commencing on or after 1 January 2018.

Summary of key findings

3. Bosnia and Herzegovina has legislation requiring the filing of CbC reports which meets all of the requirement with the exception that:

- It is recommended that Bosnia and Herzegovina take steps to ensure that the filing requirement for CbC applies equally to all relevant entities with no exemptions.
- It is recommended that Bosnia and Herzegovina take steps to amend legislation or otherwise clarify that the threshold requirement timing applies in line with the standard.
- It is recommended that Bosnia and Herzegovina take steps to amend legislation or otherwise ensure that the filing deadline is not more than 12 months from the end of the reporting fiscal year.
- It is recommended that Bosnia and Herzegovina take steps to implement procedures to ensure compliance with their filing requirement.

4. It is recommended that Bosnia and Herzegovina take steps to have qualifying competent authority agreements in effect with jurisdictions of the Inclusive Framework that meet the confidentiality, consistency and appropriate use conditions and with which Bosnia and Herzegovina has an international exchange of information agreement in effect that allows for the automatic exchange of tax information.

5. It is recommended that Bosnia and Herzegovina take steps to implement processes or written procedures to ensure that the exchange of information is conducted in a manner consistent with the terms of reference (OECD, 2017[3]) relating to the exchange of information framework ahead of the first exchanges of information.

6. It is recommended that Bosnia and Herzegovina take steps to ensure that the appropriate use condition is met ahead of the first exchanges of information.

Part A: The domestic legal and administrative framework

7. Bosnia and Herzegovina has legislation in place for implementing the BEPS Action 13 minimum standard.

(a) Parent entity filing obligation

8. Bosnia and Herzegovina has legislation that imposes a filing obligation on Ultimate Parent Entities of MNE Groups, which have a consolidated group revenue over a certain threshold, whereby all required Constituent Entities of the MNE Group are included in the CbC report.

9. Bosnia and Herzegovina has three tax administrations covering three jurisdictions for CbC reporting. Only one of these jurisdictions has a full set of reporting requirements. This lack of reporting requirements in two of the tax jurisdictions means that there is an effective exemption form filing for MNE groups which would otherwise have to file in Bosnia and Herzegovina if they are resident for tax in those regions. Additionally one other region of Bosnia and Herzegovina has a filing requirement with a threshold set at 750m Euro rather than the local equivalent. This different threshold may further result in MNE groups falling into the filing requirement in one tax administration and not in the other result in a further effective exemption.

10. It is recommended that Bosnia and Herzegovina take steps to ensure that the filing requirement for CbC applies to all relevant entities in Bosnia and Herzegovina equally with no exemptions.

11. Bosnia and Herzegovina apply a threshold requirement, which is at a level in line with the standard, but is measured against the MNE group turnover in the reporting year rather than the year before the reporting year in order to assess whether filing is required.

12. It is recommended that Bosnia and Herzegovina take steps to amend legislation or otherwise clarify that the threshold requirement timing applies in line with the standard.

(b) Scope and timing of parent entity filing

13. Bosnia and Herzegovina has a filing requirement commencing from fiscal years beginning on or after 1 January 2018 requiring all and only all of the information contained in the CbC reporting template in the Action 13 report. The filing deadline for this report in Bosnia and Herzegovina is 31 March of the year following the end of the reporting year. Where a reporting year ends between 1 January and 31 March this will mean that the filing deadline is more than 12 months after that reporting year end.

14. It is recommended that Bosnia and Herzegovina take steps to amend legislation or otherwise ensure that the filing deadline is not more than 12 months from the end of the reporting fiscal year

(c) Limitation on local filing obligation

15. Bosnia and Herzegovina do not have a local filing requirement.

(d) Limitation on local filing in case of surrogate filing

16. Bosnia and Herzegovina do not have a local filing requirement.

(e) Effective implementation

17. Bosnia and Herzegovina have a penalty regime for MNE Groups who fail to file or make an inaccurate filing of a CbC report but do not have a process for ensure that all MNE groups who should file do so.

18. It is recommended that Bosnia and Herzegovina take steps to implement procedures to ensure compliance with their filing requirement

Conclusion

19. Bosnia and Herzegovina has legislation requiring the filing of CbC reports which meets all of the requirement with the exception that:

- It is recommended that Bosnia and Herzegovina take steps to ensure that the filing requirement for CbC applies equally to all relevant entities with no exemptions.
- It is recommended that Bosnia and Herzegovina take steps to amend legislation or otherwise clarify that the threshold requirement timing applies in line with the standard.

- It is recommended that Bosnia and Herzegovina take steps to amend legislation or otherwise ensure that the filing deadline is not more than 12 months from the end of the reporting fiscal year.
- It is recommended that Bosnia and Herzegovina take steps to implement procedures to ensure compliance with their filing requirement.

Part B: The exchange of information framework

(a) Exchange of information framework

20. As of 31 March 2020, Bosnia and Herzegovina has no bilateral relationships in place for the exchange of CbC reports. It is recommended that Bosnia and Herzegovina take steps to have qualifying competent authority agreements in effect with jurisdictions of the Inclusive Framework that meet the confidentiality, consistency and appropriate use conditions and with which Bosnia and Herzegovina has an international exchange of information agreement in effect that allows for the automatic exchange of tax information.

(b) Content of information exchanged

21. Bosnia and Herzegovina does not have processes or written procedures in place that are intended to ensure that each of the mandatory fields of information required in the CbC reporting template are present in the information exchanged.

(c) Completeness of exchanges

22. Bosnia and Herzegovina does not have processes or written procedures in place that are intended to ensure that CbC reports are exchanged with all tax jurisdictions listed in Table 1 of a CbC report with which it should exchange information as per the relevant QCAA.

(d) Timeliness of exchanges

23. Bosnia and Herzegovina does not have processes or written procedures in place that are intended to ensure that the information to be exchanged is transmitted to the relevant jurisdictions in accordance with the timelines provided for in the relevant QCAAs.

(e) Temporary suspension of exchange or termination of QCAA

24. Bosnia and Herzegovina does not have processes or written procedures in place that are intended to ensure that a temporary suspension of the exchange of information or termination of a relevant QCAA would be carried out only as per the conditions set out in the relevant QCAA.

(f) Consultation with other Competent Authority before determining systemic failure or significant non-compliance

25. Bosnia and Herzegovina does not have processes or written procedures in place that are intended to ensure that its Competent Authority consults with the other Competent Authority before making a determination of systemic failure or significant non-compliance with the terms of the relevant QCAA by that other Competent Authority.

(g) Format for information exchange

26. Bosnia and Herzegovina has not confirmed the format that will be used for the international exchange of CbC reports.

(h) Method for transmission

27. Bosnia and Herzegovina has not indicated confirmed the mechanism that it will use to exchange CbC reports.

Conclusion

28. It is recommended that Bosnia and Herzegovina take steps to have qualifying competent authority agreements in effect with jurisdictions of the Inclusive Framework that meet the confidentiality, consistency and appropriate use conditions and with which Bosnia and Herzegovina has an international exchange of information agreement in effect that allows for the automatic exchange of tax information.

29. It is recommended that Bosnia and Herzegovina take steps to implement processes or written procedures to ensure that the exchange of information is conducted in a manner consistent with the terms of reference (OECD, 2017[3]) relating to the exchange of information framework ahead of its first exchanges of information.

Part C: Appropriate use

Appropriate use

30. Bosnia and Herzegovina does not yet have measures in place relating to appropriate use.

31. It is recommended that Bosnia and Herzegovina take steps to have measures in place relating to appropriate use ahead of the first exchanges of information remains in place.

Conclusion

32. It is recommended that Bosnia and Herzegovina take steps to ensure that the appropriate use condition is met ahead of its first exchanges of information.

Summary of recommendations on the implementation of Country-by-Country Reporting

Aspect of the implementation that should be improved		Recommendation for improvement
Part A	Domestic legal and administrative framework	It is recommended that Bosnia and Herzegovina take steps to ensure that the filing requirement for CbC applies equally to all relevant entities with no exemptions. It is recommended that Bosnia and Herzegovina take steps to amend legislation or otherwise clarify that the threshold requirement timing applies in line with the standard. It is recommended that Bosnia and Herzegovina take steps to amend legislation or otherwise ensure that the filing deadline is not more than 12 months from the end of the reporting fiscal year. It is recommended that Bosnia and Herzegovina take steps to implement procedures to ensure compliance with their filing requirement. .
Part B	Exchange of information framework	It is recommended that Bosnia and Herzegovina take steps to put in place an exchange of information framework that allows Automatic Exchange of Information and have QCAAs in effect with jurisdictions of the Inclusive Framework which meet the confidentiality, consistency and appropriate use prerequisites and with which Bosnia and Herzegovina has an international exchange of information agreement in effect that allows for the automatic exchange of tax information.
Part B	Exchange of information framework	It is recommended that Bosnia and Herzegovina take steps to implement the necessary processes or written procedures to ensure that the exchange of information is conducted in a manner consistent with the terms of reference relating to the exchange of information framework.
Part C	Appropriate use	It is recommended that Bosnia and Herzegovina take steps to ensure that the appropriate use condition is met ahead of the first exchanges of information.

References

OECD (2017), *Terms of reference for the conduct of peer review of the Action 13 minimum standard on country-by-country reporting*, OECD Publishing, https://www.oecd.org/tax/beps/beps-action-13-on-country-by-country-reporting-peer-review-documents.pdf. [3]

Botswana

1. Botswana was first reviewed during the 2018/2019 peer review. This report is supplementary to that previous report (OECD, 2018[2]).

2. There is no filing obligation for a CbC report in Botswana yet.

Summary of key findings

3. Botswana does not yet have legislation in place for implementing the BEPS Action 13 minimum standard. It is recommended that Botswana take steps to implement a domestic legal and administrative framework to impose and enforce CbC reporting requirements as soon as possible. This recommendation remains unchanged since the 2018/2019 peer review.

4. It is recommended that Botswana take steps to put in place an exchange of information framework that allows Automatic Exchange of Information and have QCAAs in effect with jurisdictions of the Inclusive Framework which meet the confidentiality, consistency and appropriate use prerequisites and with which Botswana has an international exchange of information agreement in effect that allows for the automatic exchange of tax information. This recommendation remains unchanged since the 2018/2019 peer review.

5. It is recommended that Botswana take steps to implement processes or written procedures to ensure that the exchange of information is conducted in a manner consistent with the terms of reference (OECD, 2017[3]) relating to the exchange of information framework ahead of the first exchanges of information. This recommendation remains unchanged since the 2018/2019 peer review.

6. It is recommended that Botswana take steps to ensure that the appropriate use condition is met ahead of the first exchanges of information. This recommendation remains unchanged since the 2018/2019 peer review.

Part A: The domestic legal and administrative framework

7. Botswana does not yet have legislation in place for implementing the BEPS Action 13 minimum standard.

(a) Parent entity filing obligation

(b) Scope and timing of parent entity filing

(c) Limitation on local filing obligation

(d) Limitation on local filing in case of surrogate filing

(e) Effective implementation

Conclusion

8. It is recommended that Botswana take steps to implement a domestic legal and administrative framework to impose and enforce CbC reporting requirements as soon as possible.

Part B: The exchange of information framework

(a) Exchange of information framework

9. As of 31 March 2020, Botswana has no bilateral relationships in place for the exchange of CbC reports. It is recommended that Botswana take steps to have qualifying competent authority agreements in effect with jurisdictions of the Inclusive Framework that meet the confidentiality, consistency and appropriate use conditions and with which Botswana has an international exchange of information agreement in effect that allows for the automatic exchange of tax information.

(b) Content of information exchanged

10. No changes were identified.

(c) Completeness of exchanges

11. No changes were identified.

(d) Timeliness of exchanges

12. No changes were identified.

(e) Temporary suspension of exchange or termination of QCAA

13. No changes were identified.

(f) Consultation with other Competent Authority before determining systemic failure or significant non-compliance

14. No changes were identified.

(g) Format for information exchange

15. No changes were identified.

(h) Method for transmission

16. No changes were identified.

Conclusion

17. It is recommended that Botswana take steps to have qualifying competent authority agreements in effect with jurisdictions of the Inclusive Framework that meet the confidentiality, consistency and appropriate use conditions and with which Botswana has an international exchange of information agreement in effect that allows for the automatic exchange of tax information. This recommendation remains unchanged since the 2018/2019 peer review.

18. It is recommended that Botswana take steps to implement processes or written procedures to ensure that the exchange of information is conducted in a manner consistent with the terms of reference (OECD, 2017[3]) relating to the exchange of information framework ahead of its first exchanges of information. This recommendation remains unchanged since the 2018/2019 peer review.

Part C: Appropriate use

Appropriate use

19. No changes were identified.

Conclusion

20. It is recommended that Botswana take steps to ensure that the appropriate use condition is met ahead of its first exchanges of information. This recommendation remains unchanged since the 2018/2019 peer review.

Summary of recommendations on the implementation of Country-by-Country Reporting

Aspect of the implementation that should be improved		Recommendation for improvement
Part A	Domestic legal and administrative framework	It is recommended that Botswana take steps to implement a domestic legal and administrative framework to impose and enforce CbC requirements as soon as possible.
Part B	Exchange of information framework	It is recommended that Botswana take steps to put in place an exchange of information framework that allows Automatic Exchange of Information and have QCAAs in effect with jurisdictions of the Inclusive Framework which meet the confidentiality, consistency and appropriate use prerequisites and with which Botswana has an international exchange of information agreement in effect that allows for the automatic exchange of tax information.
Part B	Exchange of information framework	It is recommended that Botswana take steps to implement the necessary processes or written procedures to ensure that the exchange of information is conducted in a manner consistent with the terms of reference relating to the exchange of information framework.
Part C	Appropriate use	It is recommended that Botswana take steps to ensure that the appropriate use condition is met ahead of the first exchanges of information.

References

OECD (2018), *Country-by-Country Reporting – Compilation of Peer Review Reports (Phase 1): Inclusive Framework on BEPS: Action 13*, OECD/G20 Base Erosion and Profit Shifting Project, OECD Publishing, Paris, https://dx.doi.org/10.1787/9789264300057-en. [2]

OECD (2017), *Terms of reference for the conduct of peer review of the Action 13 minimum standard on country-by-country reporting*, OECD Publishing, https://www.oecd.org/tax/beps/beps-action-13-on-country-by-country-reporting-peer-review-documents.pdf. [3]

Brazil

1. Brazil was reviewed as part of the 2017/2018 and the 2018/2019 peer reviews. This report is supplementary to those previous reports (OECD, 2019[1]) (OECD, 2018[2]).

2. The first filing obligation for a CbC report in Brazil commences in respect of periods commencing on or after 1 January 2016.

Summary of key findings

3. Brazil's implementation of the Action 13 minimum standard meets all applicable terms of reference (OECD, 2017[3]).

Part A: The domestic legal and administrative framework

4. Brazil meets all the terms of reference relating to the domestic legal and administrative framework.

(a) Parent entity filing obligation

5. No changes were identified.

(b) Scope and timing of parent entity filing

6. No changes were identified.

(c) Limitation on local filing obligation

7. No changes were identified.

(d) Limitation on local filing in case of surrogate filing

8. No changes were identified.

(e) Effective implementation

9. No changes were identified with respect to the effective implementation.[1]

Conclusion

10. Brazil meets all the terms of reference relating to the domestic legal and administrative framework.

Part B: The exchange of information framework

(a) Exchange of information framework

11. As of 31 March 2020, Brazil has 73 bilateral relationships, including those activated under the CbC MCAA and under bilateral CAAs. Within the context of its international exchange of information agreements that allow automatic exchange of information, Brazil has taken steps to have qualifying competent authority agreements in effect with jurisdictions of the Inclusive Framework that meet the

confidentiality, consistency and appropriate use conditions.[2] Regarding Brazil's exchange of information framework, no inconsistencies with the terms of reference were identified.

(b) Content of information exchanged

12. No changes were identified.

(c) Completeness of exchanges

13. No changes were identified.

(d) Timeliness of exchanges

14. Peer input was received indicating that Brazil made some late exchanges of CbC reports. Brazil reports that these exchanges were late because of a delay resending reports after receipt of an error status message. Brazil has changed their procedures to ensure that these status messages are picked up and dealt with more quickly so that the delay will not occur and therefore no recommendation is required.

(e) Temporary suspension of exchange or termination of QCAA

15. No changes were identified.

(f) Consultation with other Competent Authority before determining systemic failure or significant non-compliance

16. No changes were identified.

(g) Format for information exchange

17. No changes were identified.

(h) Method for transmission

18. No changes were identified.

Conclusion

19. Brazil meets all the terms of reference regarding the exchange of information.

Part C: Appropriate use

Appropriate use

20. No changes were identified.

Conclusion

21. Brazil meets all the terms of reference relating to appropriate use of CbC reports.

Summary of recommendations on the implementation of country-by-country reporting

Aspect of the implementation that should be improved		Recommendation for improvement
Part A	Domestic legal and administrative framework	-
Part B	Exchange of information framework	-
Part C	Appropriate use	-

References

OECD (2019), *Country-by-Country Reporting – Compilation of Peer Review Reports (Phase 2): Inclusive Framework on BEPS: Action 13*, OECD/G20 Base Erosion and Profit Shifting Project, OECD Publishing, Paris, https://dx.doi.org/10.1787/f9bf1157-en. [1]

OECD (2018), *Country-by-Country Reporting – Compilation of Peer Review Reports (Phase 1): Inclusive Framework on BEPS: Action 13*, OECD/G20 Base Erosion and Profit Shifting Project, OECD Publishing, Paris, https://dx.doi.org/10.1787/9789264300057-en. [2]

OECD (2017), *Terms of reference for the conduct of peer review of the Action 13 minimum standard on country-by-country reporting*, OECD Publishing, https://www.oecd.org/tax/beps/beps-action-13-on-country-by-country-reporting-peer-review-documents.pdf. [3]

Notes

[1] Brazil's 2017/2018 peer review included a general monitoring point relating to a specific process to that would allow to take appropriate measures in case Brazil is notified by another jurisdiction that such other jurisdiction has reason to believe that an error may have led to incorrect or incomplete information reporting by a Reporting Entity or that there is non-compliance of a Reporting Entity with respect to its obligation to file a CbC report. This monitoring point remains in place.

[2] No inconsistency with the terms of reference will be identified where a QCAA is not in effect with one or more jurisdictions of the Inclusive Framework that meet the confidentiality, consistency and appropriate use conditions, but this is due to circumstances that are not under the control of the reviewed jurisdiction. This may include, for example, where the other jurisdiction intends to exchange CbC reports using the MCAA but it does not have the Convention in effect for the relevant fiscal period, or where the other jurisdiction has declined to have a QCAA in effect with the reviewed jurisdiction.

British Virgin Islands

1. The British Virgin Islands was reviewed as part of the 2017/2018 and the 2018/2019 peer reviews. This report is supplementary to those previous reports (OECD, 2019[1]) (OECD, 2018[2]).

2. The filing obligation for a CbC report in the British Virgin Islands applies to reporting fiscal years commencing on or after 1 January 2018.

Summary of key findings

3. The British Virgin Islands' legislative implementation of the Action 13 minimum standard meets all applicable terms of reference (OECD, 2017[3]).

4. The British Virgin Islands' previous peer reviews included a recommendation that it take steps to have QCAAs in effect with jurisdictions of the Inclusive Framework which will meet the confidentiality, consistency and appropriate use prerequisites and with which the British Virgin Islands has international agreements which allow for the automatic exchange of tax information. Bilateral relationships are now in place so the recommendation is removed.

5. It is recommended that the British Virgin Islands take steps to implement processes or written procedures to ensure that the exchange of information is conducted in a manner consistent with the terms of reference relating to the exchange of information framework ahead of its first exchanges of information. This recommendation remains unchanged since the 2018/2019 peer review.

Part A: The domestic legal and administrative framework

6. The British Virgin Islands meets all the terms of reference relating to the domestic legal and administrative framework.

(a) Parent entity filing obligation

7. No changes were identified.

(b) Scope and timing of parent entity filing

8. No changes were identified.

(c) Limitation on local filing obligation

9. No changes were identified.

(d) Limitation on local filing in case of surrogate filing

10. No changes were identified.

(e) Effective implementation

11. No changes were identified[1]

Conclusion

12. The British Virgin Islands meets all the terms of reference relating to the domestic legal and administrative framework.

Part B: The exchange of information framework

(a) Exchange of information framework

13. The British Virgin Islands' previous peer reviews included a recommendation that it take steps to have QCAAs in effect with jurisdictions of the Inclusive Framework which will meet the confidentiality, consistency and appropriate use prerequisites and with which the British Virgin Islands has international agreements which allow for the automatic exchange of tax information. Bilateral relationships are now in place so the recommendation is removed.

14. As of 31 March 2020 the British Virgin Islands has 46 bilateral relationships in place for the exchange of CbC reports, activated under the CbC MCAA. Within the context of its international exchange of information agreements that allow automatic exchange of tax information, the British Virgin Islands has taken steps to have qualifying competent authority agreements in effect with jurisdictions of the Inclusive Framework that currently meet the confidentiality, consistency and appropriate use conditions. Regarding the British Virgin Island's exchange of information framework, no inconsistencies with the terms of reference were identified.[2]

(b) Content of information exchanged

15. No changes were identified.

(c) Completeness of exchanges

16. No changes were identified.

(d) Timeliness of exchanges

17. No changes were identified.

(e) Temporary suspension of exchange or termination of QCAA

18. No changes were identified.

(f) Consultation with other Competent Authority before determining systemic failure or significant non-compliance

19. No changes were identified.

(g) Format for information exchange

20. No changes were identified.

(h) Method for transmission

21. No changes were identified.

Conclusion

22. The British Virgin Islands' previous peer reviews included a recommendation that it take steps to have QCAAs in effect with jurisdictions of the Inclusive Framework which will meet the confidentiality, consistency and appropriate use prerequisites and with which the British Virgin Islands has international

agreements which allow for the automatic exchange of tax information. Bilateral relationships are now in place so the recommendation is removed.

23. It is recommended that the British Virgin Islands take steps to implement processes or written procedures to ensure that the exchange of information is conducted in a manner consistent with the terms of reference relating to the exchange of information framework ahead of its first exchanges of information. This recommendation remains unchanged since the 2018/2019 peer review.

Part C: Appropriate use

Appropriate use

24. No changes were identified.

Conclusion

25. The British Virgin Islands is a non-reciprocal jurisdiction and, as such, will not receive CbC reports submitted to tax authorities in other jurisdictions, and will not apply local filing. It is not necessary for this peer review evaluation to reach any conclusion with respect to these paragraphs of the terms of reference.

Summary of recommendations on the implementation of Country-by-Country Reporting

Aspect of the implementation that should be improved		Recommendation for improvement
Part A	Domestic legal and administrative framework	-
Part B	Exchange of information framework	It is recommended that the British Virgin Islands take steps to implement processes or written procedures to ensure that the exchange of information is conducted in a manner consistent with the terms of reference relating to the exchange of information framework ahead of the first exchanges of information.
Part C	Appropriate use	-

References

OECD (2019), *Country-by-Country Reporting – Compilation of Peer Review Reports (Phase 2): Inclusive Framework on BEPS: Action 13*, OECD/G20 Base Erosion and Profit Shifting Project, OECD Publishing, Paris, https://dx.doi.org/10.1787/f9bf1157-en. [1]

OECD (2018), *Country-by-Country Reporting – Compilation of Peer Review Reports (Phase 1): Inclusive Framework on BEPS: Action 13*, OECD/G20 Base Erosion and Profit Shifting Project, OECD Publishing, Paris, https://dx.doi.org/10.1787/9789264300057-en. [2]

OECD (2017), *Terms of reference for the conduct of peer review of the Action 13 minimum standard on country-by-country reporting*, OECD Publishing, https://www.oecd.org/tax/beps/beps-action-13-on-country-by-country-reporting-peer-review-documents.pdf. [3]

Notes

[1] There are no specific process in place to take appropriate measures in case the British Virgin Islands is notified by another jurisdiction that such other jurisdiction has reason to believe that an error may have led to incorrect or incomplete information reporting by a Reporting Entity or that there is non-compliance of a Reporting Entity with respect to its obligation to file a CbC report. This aspect will be further monitored.

[2] No inconsistency with the terms of reference will be identified where a QCAA is not in effect with one or more jurisdictions of the Inclusive Framework that meet the confidentiality, consistency and appropriate use conditions, but this is due to circumstances that are not under the control of the reviewed jurisdiction. This may include, for example, where the other jurisdiction intends to exchange CbC reports using the MCAA but it does not have the Convention in effect for the relevant fiscal period, or where the other jurisdiction has declined to have a QCAA in effect with the reviewed jurisdiction.

Brunei Darussalam

1. Brunei Darussalam was reviewed as part of the 2017/2018 and the 2018/2019 peer reviews. This report is supplementary to those previous reports (OECD, 2019[1]) (OECD, 2018[2]).

2. There is no filing obligation for a CbC report in Brunei Darussalam yet.

Summary of key findings

3. It is recommended that Brunei Darussalam take steps to implement a domestic legal and administrative framework to impose and enforce CbC reporting requirements as soon as possible. This recommendation remains unchanged since the 2017/2018 peer review.

4. It is recommended that Brunei take steps to have QCAAs in effect with jurisdictions of the Inclusive Framework which meet the confidentiality, consistency and appropriate use prerequisites and with which Brunei Darussalam has an international exchange of information agreement in effect that allows for the automatic exchange of tax information. This recommendation remains unchanged since the 2017/2018 peer review.

5. It is recommended that Brunei Darussalam have in place the necessary processes or written procedures to ensure that the exchange of information is conducted in a manner consistent with the terms of reference (OECD, 2017[3]) relating to the exchange of information framework. This recommendation remains unchanged since the 2018/2019 peer review.

6. It is recommended that Brunei Darussalam take steps to ensure that the appropriate use condition is met ahead of the first exchanges of information. This recommendation remains unchanged since the 2017/2018 peer review.

Part A: The domestic legal and administrative framework

7. Brunei Darussalam does not yet have a legal and administrative framework in place to implement CbC Reporting.

(a) Parent entity filing obligation

(b) Scope and timing of parent entity filing

(c) Limitation on local filing obligation

(d) Limitation on local filing in case of surrogate filing

(e) Effective implementation

Conclusion

8. It is recommended that Brunei Darussalam take steps to implement a domestic legal and administrative framework to impose and enforce CbC requirements as soon as possible. This recommendation remains unchanged since the 2017/2018 peer review.

Part B: The exchange of information framework

(a) Exchange of information framework

9. As of 31 March 2020, Brunei Darussalam has no bilateral relationships in place for the exchange of CbC reports. It is recommended that Brunei Darussalam take steps to have qualifying competent authority agreements in effect with jurisdictions of the Inclusive Framework that meet the confidentiality, consistency and appropriate use conditions and with which Brunei Darussalam has an international exchange of information agreement in effect that allows for the automatic exchange of tax information.

(b) Content of information exchanged

10. No changes were identified.

(c) Completeness of exchanges

11. No changes were identified.

(d) Timeliness of exchanges

12. No changes were identified.

(e) Temporary suspension of exchange or termination of QCAA

13. No changes were identified.

(f) Consultation with other Competent Authority before determining systemic failure or significant non-compliance

14. No changes were identified.

(g) Format for information exchange

15. No changes were identified.

(h) Method for transmission

16. No changes were identified.

Conclusion

17. It is recommended that Brunei Darussalam take steps to have qualifying competent authority agreements in effect with jurisdictions of the Inclusive Framework that meet the confidentiality, consistency and appropriate use conditions and with which Brunei Darussalam has an international exchange of information agreement in effect that allows for the automatic exchange of tax information. This recommendation remains unchanged since the 2017/2018 peer review.

18. It is recommended that Brunei Darussalam take steps to implement processes or written procedures to ensure that the exchange of information is conducted in a manner consistent with the terms of reference relating to the exchange of information framework ahead of its first exchanges of information. This recommendation remains unchanged since the 2018/2019 peer review.

Part C: Appropriate use

Appropriate use

19. No changes were identified.

Conclusion

20. It is recommended that Brunei Darussalam take steps to ensure that the appropriate use condition is met ahead of its first exchanges of information. This recommendation remains unchanged since the 2017/2018 peer review.

Summary of recommendations on the implementation of country-by-country reporting

Aspect of the implementation that should be improved		Recommendation for improvement
Part A	Domestic legal and administrative framework	It is recommended that Brunei Darussalam take steps to implement a domestic legal and administrative framework to impose and enforce CbC requirements as soon as possible, taking into account its particular domestic legislative process.
Part B	Exchange of information framework	It is recommended that Brunei Darussalam take steps to have qualifying competent authority agreements in effect with jurisdictions of the Inclusive Framework that meet the confidentiality, consistency and appropriate use conditions and with which Brunei Darussalam has an international exchange of information agreement in effect that allows for the automatic exchange of tax information
Part B	Exchange of information framework	It is recommended that Brunei Darussalam have in place the necessary processes or written procedures to ensure that the exchange of information is conducted in a manner consistent with the terms of reference relating to the exchange of information framework.
Part C	Appropriate use	It is recommended that Brunei Darussalam take steps to ensure that the appropriate use condition is met ahead of the first exchanges of information.

References

OECD (2019), *Country-by-Country Reporting – Compilation of Peer Review Reports (Phase 2): Inclusive Framework on BEPS: Action 13*, OECD/G20 Base Erosion and Profit Shifting Project, OECD Publishing, Paris, https://dx.doi.org/10.1787/f9bf1157-en. [1]

OECD (2018), *Country-by-Country Reporting – Compilation of Peer Review Reports (Phase 1): Inclusive Framework on BEPS: Action 13*, OECD/G20 Base Erosion and Profit Shifting Project, OECD Publishing, Paris, https://dx.doi.org/10.1787/9789264300057-en. [2]

OECD (2017), *Terms of reference for the conduct of peer review of the Action 13 minimum standard on country-by-country reporting*, OECD Publishing, https://www.oecd.org/tax/beps/beps-action-13-on-country-by-country-reporting-peer-review-documents.pdf. [3]

Bulgaria

1. Bulgaria was reviewed as part of the 2017/2018 and the 2018/2019 peer reviews. This report is supplementary to those previous reports (OECD, 2019[1]) (OECD, 2018[2]).

2. The first filing obligation for a CbC report in Bulgaria applies to reporting fiscal years commencing on or after 1 January 2016.

Summary of key findings

3. Bulgaria's implementation of the Action 13 minimum standard meets all applicable terms of reference (OECD, 2017[3]) except for the following:

- It is recommended that Bulgaria take steps to align its local filing implementation with that required by the Action 13 minimum standard.

Part A: The domestic legal and administrative framework

4. Bulgaria meets all the terms of reference relating to the domestic legal and administrative framework.

(a) Parent entity filing obligation

5. No changes were identified.

(b) Scope and timing of parent entity filing

6. No changes were identified.

(c) Limitation on local filing obligation

7. Bulgaria has notified as a non-reciprocal jurisdiction and is therefore applying a local filing requirement more widely than is allowed by the standard. It is recommended that Bulgaria take steps to align its local filing implementation with that required by the Action 13 minimum standard.

(d) Limitation on local filing in case of surrogate filing

8. No changes were identified.

(e) Effective implementation

9. No changes were identified.

Conclusion

10. Bulgaria meets all the terms of reference relating to the domestic legal and administrative framework except for the following:

- It is recommended that Bulgaria take steps to align its local filing implementation with that required by the Action 13 minimum standard.

Part B: The exchange of information framework

(a) Exchange of information framework

11. As of 31 March 2020, Bulgaria has 62 bilateral relationships in place, including those activated under the CbC MCAA and under the EU Council Directive (2016/881/EU). Within the context of its international exchange of information agreements that allow automatic exchange of information, Bulgaria has taken steps to have qualifying competent authority agreements in effect with jurisdictions of the Inclusive Framework that meet the confidentiality, consistency and appropriate use conditions.[1] Regarding Bulgaria's exchange of information framework, no inconsistencies with the terms of reference were identified.

(b) Content of information exchanged

12. No changes were identified.

(c) Completeness of exchanges

13. No changes were identified.

(d) Timeliness of exchanges

14. No changes were identified.

(e) Temporary suspension of exchange or termination of QCAA

15. No changes were identified.

(f) Consultation with other Competent Authority before determining systemic failure or significant non-compliance

16. No changes were identified.

(g) Format for information exchange

17. No changes were identified.

(h) Method for transmission

18. No changes were identified.

Conclusion

19. Bulgaria meets all the terms of reference regarding the exchange of information.

Part C: Appropriate use

Appropriate use

20. In August 2019 Bulgaria notified as a non-reciprocal jurisdiction for the exchange of CbC reports under the Multilateral Competent Authority Agreement for CbC.

Conclusion

21. Bulgaria is a non-reciprocal jurisdiction and, as such, will not receive CbC reports submitted to tax authorities in other jurisdictions under the CbC MCAA, and will not apply local filing. It is not necessary for this peer review evaluation to reach any conclusion with respect to these paragraphs of the terms of reference.

Summary of recommendations on the implementation of country-by-country reporting

Aspect of the implementation that should be improved		Recommendation for improvement
Part A	Domestic legal and administrative framework	It is recommended that Bulgaria take steps to align its local filing implementation with that required by the Action 13 minimum standard
Part B	Exchange of information framework	-
Part C	Appropriate use	-

References

OECD (2019), *Country-by-Country Reporting – Compilation of Peer Review Reports (Phase 2): Inclusive Framework on BEPS: Action 13*, OECD/G20 Base Erosion and Profit Shifting Project, OECD Publishing, Paris, https://dx.doi.org/10.1787/f9bf1157-en. [1]

OECD (2018), *Country-by-Country Reporting – Compilation of Peer Review Reports (Phase 1): Inclusive Framework on BEPS: Action 13*, OECD/G20 Base Erosion and Profit Shifting Project, OECD Publishing, Paris, https://dx.doi.org/10.1787/9789264300057-en. [2]

OECD (2017), *Terms of reference for the conduct of peer review of the Action 13 minimum standard on country-by-country reporting*, OECD Publishing, https://www.oecd.org/tax/beps/beps-action-13-on-country-by-country-reporting-peer-review-documents.pdf. [3]

Note

[1] No inconsistency with the terms of reference will be identified where a QCAA is not in effect with one or more jurisdictions of the Inclusive Framework that meet the confidentiality, consistency and appropriate use conditions, but this is due to circumstances that are not under the control of the reviewed jurisdiction. This may include, for example, where the other jurisdiction intends to exchange CbC reports using the MCAA but it does not have the Convention in effect for the relevant fiscal period, or where the other jurisdiction has declined to have a QCAA in effect with the reviewed jurisdiction.

Cabo Verde

1. This report is Cabo Verde's first annual peer review report. Consistent with the agreed methodology this report covers: (i) the domestic legal and administrative framework, (ii) the exchange of information framework as well as (iii) the appropriate use of CbC reports.

2. There is no filing obligation for a CbC report in Cabo Verde yet.

Summary of key findings

3. Cabo Verde does not yet have legislation in place for implementing the BEPS Action 13 minimum standard.

4. It is recommended that Cabo Verde take steps to implement a domestic legal and administrative framework to impose and enforce CbC reporting requirements as soon as possible.

5. It is recommended that Cabo Verde take steps to put in place an exchange of information framework that allows automatic exchange of information and have QCAAs in effect with jurisdictions of the Inclusive Framework which meet the confidentiality, consistency and appropriate use prerequisites and with which Cabo Verde has an international exchange of information agreement in effect that allows for the automatic exchange of tax information.

6. It is recommended that Cabo Verde take steps to implement processes or written procedures to ensure that the exchange of information is conducted in a manner consistent with the terms of reference (OECD, 2017[3]) relating to the exchange of information framework ahead of the first exchanges of information.

7. It is recommended that Cabo Verde take steps to ensure that the appropriate use condition is met ahead of the first exchanges of information.

Part A: The domestic legal and administrative framework

8. Cabo Verde does not yet have legislation in place for implementing the BEPS Action 13 minimum standard.

(a) Parent entity filing obligation

(b) Scope and timing of parent entity filing

(c) Limitation on local filing obligation

(d) Limitation on local filing in case of surrogate filing

(e) Effective implementation

Conclusion

9. It is recommended that Cabo Verde take steps to implement a domestic legal and administrative framework to impose and enforce CbC reporting requirements as soon as possible.

Part B: The exchange of information framework

(a) Exchange of information framework

10. As of 31 March 2020, Cabo Verde has no bilateral relationships in place for the exchange of CbC reports. It is recommended that Cabo Verde take steps to have qualifying competent authority agreements in effect with jurisdictions of the Inclusive Framework that meet the confidentiality, consistency and appropriate use conditions and with which Cabo Verde has an international exchange of information agreement in effect that allows for the automatic exchange of tax information.

(b) Content of information exchanged

11. Cabo Verde does not have processes or written procedures in place that are intended to ensure that each of the mandatory fields of information required in the CbC reporting template are present in the information exchanged.

(c) Completeness of exchanges

12. Cabo Verde does not have processes or written procedures in place that are intended to ensure that CbC reports are exchanged with all tax jurisdictions listed in Table 1 of a CbC report with which it should exchange information as per the relevant QCAA.

(d) Timeliness of exchanges

13. Cabo Verde does not have processes or written procedures in place that are intended to ensure that the information to be exchanged is transmitted to the relevant jurisdictions in accordance with the timelines provided for in the relevant QCAAs.

(e) Temporary suspension of exchange or termination of QCAA

14. Cabo Verde does not have processes or written procedures in place that are intended to ensure that a temporary suspension of the exchange of information or termination of a relevant QCAA would be carried out only as per the conditions set out in the relevant QCAA.

(f) Consultation with other Competent Authority before determining systemic failure or significant non-compliance

15. Cabo Verde does not have processes or written procedures in place that are intended to ensure that its Competent Authority consults with the other Competent Authority before making a determination of systemic failure or significant non-compliance with the terms of the relevant QCAA by that other Competent Authority.

(g) Format for information exchange

16. Cabo Verde has not confirmed the format that will be used for the international exchange of CbC reports.

(h) Method for transmission

17. Cabo Verde has not indicated confirmed the mechanism that it will use to exchange CbC reports.

Conclusion

18. It is recommended that Cabo Verde take steps to have qualifying competent authority agreements in effect with jurisdictions of the Inclusive Framework that meet the confidentiality,

consistency and appropriate use conditions and with which Cabo Verde has an international exchange of information agreement in effect that allows for the automatic exchange of tax information.

19. It is recommended that Cabo Verde take steps to implement processes or written procedures to ensure that the exchange of information is conducted in a manner consistent with the terms of reference (OECD, 2017[3]) relating to the exchange of information framework ahead of its first exchanges of information.

Part C: Appropriate use

Appropriate use

20. Cabo Verde does not yet have measures in place relating to appropriate use.

21. It is recommended that Cabo Verde take steps to have measures in place relating to appropriate use ahead of the first exchanges of information remains in place.

Conclusion

22. It is recommended that Cabo Verde take steps to ensure that the appropriate use condition is met ahead of its first exchanges of information.

Summary of recommendations on the implementation of Country-by-Country Reporting

Aspect of the implementation that should be improved		Recommendation for improvement
Part A	Domestic legal and administrative framework	It is recommended that Cabo Verde take steps to implement a domestic legal and administrative framework to impose and enforce CbC requirements as soon as possible.
Part B	Exchange of information framework	It is recommended that Cabo Verde take steps to put in place an exchange of information framework that allows Automatic Exchange of Information and have QCAAs in effect with jurisdictions of the Inclusive Framework which meet the confidentiality, consistency and appropriate use prerequisites and with which Cabo Verde has an international exchange of information agreement in effect that allows for the automatic exchange of tax information.
Part B	Exchange of information framework	It is recommended that Cabo Verde take steps to implement the necessary processes or written procedures to ensure that the exchange of information is conducted in a manner consistent with the terms of reference relating to the exchange of information framework.
Part C	Appropriate use	It is recommended that Cabo Verde take steps to ensure that the appropriate use condition is met ahead of the first exchanges of information.

References

OECD (2017), *Terms of reference for the conduct of peer review of the Action 13 minimum standard on country-by-country reporting*, OECD Publishing, https://www.oecd.org/tax/beps/beps-action-13-on-country-by-country-reporting-peer-review-documents.pdf. [3]

Cameroon

1. Cameroon was reviewed as part of the 2017/2018 and the 2018/2019 peer reviews. This report is supplementary to those previous reports (OECD, 2019[1]) (OECD, 2018[2]).

2. There is no filing obligation for a CbC report in Cameroon yet.

Summary of key findings

3. Cameroon does not yet have legislation in place for implementing the BEPS Action 13 minimum standard. It is recommended that Cameroon take steps to implement a domestic legal and administrative framework to impose and enforce CbC reporting requirements as soon as possible. This recommendation remains unchanged since the 2017/2018 peer review.

4. It is recommended that Cameroon take steps to have QCAAs in effect with jurisdictions of the Inclusive Framework which meet the confidentiality, consistency and appropriate use prerequisites and with which Cameroon has an international exchange of information agreement in effect that allows for the automatic exchange of tax information. This recommendation remains unchanged since the 2017/2018 peer review.

5. It is recommended that Cameroon take steps to implement processes or written procedures to ensure that the exchange of information is conducted in a manner consistent with the terms of reference (OECD, 2017[3]) relating to the exchange of information framework ahead of the first exchanges of information. This recommendation remains unchanged since the 2018/2019 peer review.

6. It is recommended that Cameroon take steps to ensure that the appropriate use condition is met ahead of the first exchanges of information. This recommendation remains unchanged since the 2017/2018 peer review.

Part A: The domestic legal and administrative framework

7. Cameroon does not yet have legislation in place for implementing the BEPS Action 13 minimum standard.

(a) Parent entity filing obligation

(b) Scope and timing of parent entity filing

(c) Limitation on local filing obligation

(d) Limitation on local filing in case of surrogate filing

(e) Effective implementation

Conclusion

8. It is recommended that Cameroon take steps to implement a domestic legal and administrative framework to impose and enforce CbC reporting requirements as soon as possible. This recommendation remains unchanged since the 2017/2018 peer review.

Part B: The exchange of information framework

(a) Exchange of information framework

9. As of 31 March 2020, Cameroon has no bilateral relationships in place for the exchange of CbC reports. It is recommended that Cameroon take steps to have qualifying competent authority agreements in effect with jurisdictions of the Inclusive Framework that meet the confidentiality, consistency and appropriate use conditions and with which Cameroon has an international exchange of information agreement in effect that allows for the automatic exchange of tax information.

(b) Content of information exchanged

10. No changes were identified.

(c) Completeness of exchanges

11. No changes were identified.

(d) Timeliness of exchanges

12. No changes were identified.

(e) Temporary suspension of exchange or termination of QCAA

13. No changes were identified.

(f) Consultation with other Competent Authority before determining systemic failure or significant non-compliance

14. No changes were identified.

(g) Format for information exchange

15. No changes were identified.

(h) Method for transmission

16. No changes were identified.

Conclusion

17. It is recommended that Cameroon to take steps to have QCAAs in effect with jurisdictions of the Inclusive Framework which meet the confidentiality, consistency and appropriate use prerequisites and with which Cameroon has an international exchange of information agreement in effect that allows for the automatic exchange of tax information. This recommendation remains unchanged since the 2017/2018 peer review.

18. It is recommended that Cameroon take steps to implement processes or written procedures to ensure that the exchange of information is conducted in a manner consistent with the terms of reference relating to the exchange of information framework ahead of its first exchanges of information. This recommendation remains unchanged since the 2018/2019 peer review.

Part C: Appropriate use

Appropriate use

19. No changes were identified.

Conclusion

20. It is recommended that Cameroon to take steps to ensure that the appropriate use condition is met ahead of its first exchanges of information. This recommendation remains unchanged since the 2017/2018 peer review.

Summary of recommendations on the implementation of Country-by-Country Reporting

Aspect of the implementation that should be improved		Recommendation for improvement
Part A	Domestic legal and administrative framework	It is recommended that Cameroon take steps to implement a domestic legal and administrative framework to impose and enforce CbC requirements as soon as possible.
Part B	Exchange of information framework	It is recommended that Cameroon take steps to have QCAAs in effect with jurisdictions of the Inclusive Framework which meet the confidentiality, consistency and appropriate use prerequisites and with which it has international agreements which provide for the automatic exchange of information.
Part B	Exchange of information framework	It is recommended that Cameroon take steps to implement the necessary processes or written procedures to ensure that the exchange of information is conducted in a manner consistent with the terms of reference relating to the exchange of information framework.
Part C	Appropriate use	It is recommended that Cameroon take steps to ensure that the appropriate use condition is met ahead of the first exchanges of information.

References

OECD (2019), *Country-by-Country Reporting – Compilation of Peer Review Reports (Phase 2): Inclusive Framework on BEPS: Action 13*, OECD/G20 Base Erosion and Profit Shifting Project, OECD Publishing, Paris, https://dx.doi.org/10.1787/f9bf1157-en. [1]

OECD (2018), *Country-by-Country Reporting – Compilation of Peer Review Reports (Phase 1): Inclusive Framework on BEPS: Action 13*, OECD/G20 Base Erosion and Profit Shifting Project, OECD Publishing, Paris, https://dx.doi.org/10.1787/9789264300057-en. [2]

OECD (2017), *Terms of reference for the conduct of peer review of the Action 13 minimum standard on country-by-country reporting*, OECD Publishing, https://www.oecd.org/tax/beps/beps-action-13-on-country-by-country-reporting-peer-review-documents.pdf. [3]

Canada

1. Canada was reviewed as part of the 2017/2018 and the 2018/2019 peer reviews. This report is supplementary to those previous reports (OECD, 2019[1]) (OECD, 2018[2]).

2. The first filing obligation for a CbC report in Canada applies to reporting fiscal years commencing on or after 1 January 2016.

Summary of key findings

3. Canada's implementation of the Action 13 minimum standard meets all applicable terms of reference (OECD, 2017[3]).

Part A: The domestic legal and administrative framework

4. Canada meets all the terms of reference relating to the domestic legal and administrative framework.

(a) Parent entity filing obligation

5. No changes were identified.

(b) Scope and timing of parent entity filing

6. No changes were identified.

(c) Limitation on local filing obligation

7. No changes were identified.

(d) Limitation on local filing in case of surrogate filing

8. No changes were identified.

(e) Effective implementation

9. No changes were identified.

Conclusion

10. Canada meets all the terms of reference relating to the domestic legal and administrative framework.

Part B: The exchange of information framework

(a) Exchange of information framework

11. As of 31 March 2020, Canada has 65 bilateral relationships in place, including those activated under the CbC MCAA and under bilateral QCAAs. Within the context of its international exchange of information agreements that allow automatic exchange of information, Canada has taken steps to have qualifying competent authority agreements in effect with jurisdictions of the Inclusive Framework that

meet the confidentiality, consistency, and appropriate use conditions.[1] Regarding Canada's exchange of information framework, no inconsistencies with the terms of reference were identified.

(b) Content of information exchanged

12. No changes were identified.

(c) Completeness of exchanges

13. No changes were identified.

(d) Timeliness of exchanges

14. No changes were identified.

(e) Temporary suspension of exchange or termination of QCAA

15. No changes were identified.

(f) Consultation with other Competent Authority before determining systemic failure or significant non-compliance

16. No changes were identified.

(g) Format for information exchange

17. No changes were identified.

(h) Method for transmission

18. No changes were identified.

Conclusion

19. Canada meets all the terms of reference regarding the exchange of information.

Part C: Appropriate use

Appropriate use

20. No changes were identified.

Conclusion

21. Canada meets all the terms of reference relating to the appropriate use of CbC reports.

Summary of recommendations on the implementation of country-by-country reporting

Aspect of the implementation that should be improved		Recommendation for improvement
Part A	Domestic legal and administrative framework	-
Part B	Exchange of information framework	-
Part C	Appropriate use	-

References

OECD (2019), *Country-by-Country Reporting – Compilation of Peer Review Reports (Phase 2): Inclusive Framework on BEPS: Action 13*, OECD/G20 Base Erosion and Profit Shifting Project, OECD Publishing, Paris, https://dx.doi.org/10.1787/f9bf1157-en. [1]

OECD (2018), *Country-by-Country Reporting – Compilation of Peer Review Reports (Phase 1): Inclusive Framework on BEPS: Action 13*, OECD/G20 Base Erosion and Profit Shifting Project, OECD Publishing, Paris, https://dx.doi.org/10.1787/9789264300057-en. [2]

OECD (2017), *Terms of reference for the conduct of peer review of the Action 13 minimum standard on country-by-country reporting*, OECD Publishing, https://www.oecd.org/tax/beps/beps-action-13-on-country-by-country-reporting-peer-review-documents.pdf. [3]

Note

[1] No inconsistency with the terms of reference will be identified where a QCAA is not in effect with one or more jurisdictions of the Inclusive Framework that meet the confidentiality, consistency and appropriate use conditions, but this is due to circumstances that are not under the control of the reviewed jurisdiction. This may include, for example, where the other jurisdiction intends to exchange CbC reports using the MCAA but it does not have the Convention in effect for the relevant fiscal period, or where the other jurisdiction has declined to have a QCAA in effect with the reviewed jurisdiction.

Cayman Islands

1. The Cayman Islands was reviewed as part of the 2017/2018 and the 2018/2019 peer reviews. This report is supplementary to those previous reports (OECD, 2019[1]) (OECD, 2018[2]).

2. The first filing obligation for a CbC report in the Cayman Islands applies to reporting fiscal years commencing on or after 1 January 2016.

Summary of key findings

3. The Cayman Islands' implementation of the Action 13 minimum standard meets all applicable terms of reference (OECD, 2017[3]).

Part A: The domestic legal and administrative framework

4. The Cayman Islands meets all the terms of reference relating to the domestic legal and administrative framework.

(a) Parent entity filing obligation

5. No changes were identified.

(b) Scope and timing of parent entity filing

6. No changes were identified.

(c) Limitation on local filing obligation

7. No changes were identified.

(d) Limitation on local filing in case of surrogate filing

8. No changes were identified.

(e) Effective implementation

9. No changes were identified.

Conclusion

10. The Cayman Islands meets all the terms of reference relating to the domestic legal and administrative framework.

Part B: The exchange of information framework

(a) Exchange of information framework

11. As of 31 March 2020, the Cayman Islands has 56 bilateral relationships in place, including those activated under the CbC MCAA and under bilateral CAAs. Within the context of its international exchange of information agreements that allow automatic exchange of information, the Cayman Islands has taken steps to have qualifying competent authority agreements in effect with jurisdictions of the

Inclusive Framework that meet the confidentiality, consistency and appropriate use conditions.[1] Regarding the Cayman Islands' exchange of information framework, no inconsistencies with the terms of reference were identified.

(b) Content of information exchanged

12. No changes were identified.

(c) Completeness of exchanges

13. No changes were identified.

(d) Timeliness of exchanges

14. No changes were identified.

(e) Temporary suspension of exchange or termination of QCAA

15. No changes were identified.

(f) Consultation with other Competent Authority before determining systemic failure or significant non-compliance

16. No changes were identified.

(g) Format for information exchange

17. No changes were identified.

(h) Method for transmission

18. No changes were identified.

Conclusion

19. The Cayman Islands meets all the terms of reference regarding the exchange of information.

Part C: Appropriate use

Appropriate use

20. No changes were identified.

Conclusion

21. The Cayman Islands is a non-reciprocal jurisdiction and, as such, will not receive CbC reports submitted to tax authorities in other jurisdictions, and will not apply local filing. As such, it is not necessary for this peer review evaluation to reach any conclusion with respect to these paragraphs of the terms of reference.

Summary of recommendations on the implementation of country-by-country reporting

Aspect of the implementation that should be improved		Recommendation for improvement
Part A	Domestic legal and administrative framework	-
Part B	Exchange of information framework	-
Part C	Appropriate use	-

References

OECD (2019), *Country-by-Country Reporting – Compilation of Peer Review Reports (Phase 2): Inclusive Framework on BEPS: Action 13*, OECD/G20 Base Erosion and Profit Shifting Project, OECD Publishing, Paris, https://dx.doi.org/10.1787/f9bf1157-en. [1]

OECD (2018), *Country-by-Country Reporting – Compilation of Peer Review Reports (Phase 1): Inclusive Framework on BEPS: Action 13*, OECD/G20 Base Erosion and Profit Shifting Project, OECD Publishing, Paris, https://dx.doi.org/10.1787/9789264300057-en. [2]

OECD (2017), *Terms of reference for the conduct of peer review of the Action 13 minimum standard on country-by-country reporting*, OECD Publishing, https://www.oecd.org/tax/beps/beps-action-13-on-country-by-country-reporting-peer-review-documents.pdf. [3]

Note

[1] No inconsistency with the terms of reference will be identified where a QCAA is not in effect with one or more jurisdictions of the Inclusive Framework that meet the confidentiality, consistency and appropriate use conditions, but this is due to circumstances that are not under the control of the reviewed jurisdiction. This may include, for example, where the other jurisdiction intends to exchange CbC reports using the MCAA but it does not have the Convention in effect for the relevant fiscal period, or where the other jurisdiction has declined to have a QCAA in effect with the reviewed jurisdiction

Chile

1. Chile was reviewed as part of the 2017/2018 and the 2018/2019 peer reviews. This report is supplementary to those previous reports (OECD, 2019[1]) (OECD, 2018[2]).

2. The first filing obligation for a CbC report in Chile commences in respect of fiscal years commencing on or after 1 January 2016.

Summary of key findings

3. Chile's domestic and administrative framework to implement the Action 13 minimum standard meets all applicable terms of reference (OECD, 2017[3]), except that:

- It is recommended that Chile introduce enforcement measures applicable to Surrogate Parent Entities. This recommendation is unchanged since the 2017/2018 peer review.

4. It is recommended that Chile take steps to implement processes or written procedures to ensure that the exchange of information is conducted in a manner consistent with the terms of reference (OECD, 2017[3]) relating to the exchange of information framework as soon as possible. This recommendation remains unchanged since the 2018/2019 peer review.

5. it is recommended the Chile take steps to ensure that reports are exchanged by the required date.

6. It is recommended that Chile take steps to ensure that the appropriate use condition is met ahead of the first exchanges of information. This recommendation remains unchanged since the 2017/2018 peer review.

Part A: The domestic legal and administrative framework

7. Chile meets all the terms of reference relating to the domestic legal and administrative framework, with the exception of the absence of enforcement measures on Surrogate Parent Entities.

(a) Parent entity filing obligation

8. No changes were identified.

(b) Scope and timing of parent entity filing

9. No changes were identified.

(c) Limitation on local filing obligation

10. No changes were identified.

(d) Limitation on local filing in case of surrogate filing

11. No changes were identified.

(e) Effective implementation

12. It is recommended that Chile take steps to introduce enforcement measures applicable to Surrogate Parent Entities, as the current penalties only apply to Ultimate Parent Entities. This recommendation remains unchanged since the 2017/2018 peer review.

Conclusion

13. Chile meets all the terms of reference relating to the domestic legal and administrative framework, with the exception of the absence of enforcement measures on Surrogate Parent Entities.

Part B: The exchange of information framework

(a) Exchange of information framework

14. As of 31 March 2020, Chile has 71 bilateral relationships in place for the exchange of CbC reports activated under the CbC MCAA. Within the context of its international exchange of information agreements that allow automatic exchange of tax information, Chile has taken steps to have qualifying competent authority agreements in effect with jurisdictions of the Inclusive Framework that currently meet the confidentiality, consistency and appropriate use conditions. Regarding Chile's exchange of information framework, no inconsistencies with the terms of reference were identified.[1]

(b) Content of information exchanged

15. No changes were identified.

(c) Completeness of exchanges

16. No changes were identified.

(d) Timeliness of exchanges

17. Peer input was received that Chile exchanged some reports relating to the 2017 reporting periods after the required date.

18. As Chile have not provided any information in relation to these late exchanges it is recommended the Chile take steps to ensure that reports are exchanged by the required date.

(e) Temporary suspension of exchange or termination of QCAA

19. No changes were identified.

(f) Consultation with other Competent Authority before determining systemic failure or significant non-compliance

20. No changes were identified.

(g) Format for information exchange

21. No changes were identified.

(h) Method for transmission

22. No changes were identified.

Conclusion

23. It is recommended that Chile take steps to implement processes or written procedures to ensure that the exchange of information is conducted in a manner consistent with the terms of reference relating to the exchange of information framework as soon as possible. This recommendation remains unchanged since the 2018/2019 peer review.

24. It is recommended the Chile take steps to ensure that reports are exchanged by the required date

Part C: Appropriate use

Appropriate use

25. No changes were identified.

Conclusion

26. Chile is recommended to take steps to ensure that appropriate use condition is met as soon as possible.

Summary of recommendations on the implementation of country-by-country reporting

Aspect of the implementation that should be improved		Recommendation for improvement
Part A	Domestic legal and administrative framework	It is recommended that Chile introduce enforcement measures applicable to Surrogate Parent Entities.
Part B	Exchange of information framework	It is recommended that Chile take steps to implement the necessary processes or written procedures to ensure that the exchange of information is conducted in a manner consistent with the terms of reference relating to the exchange of information framework.
Part B	Exchange of information framework	It is recommended that Chile take steps to ensure that reports are exchanged by the required date.
Part C	Appropriate use	It is recommended that Chile take steps to ensure that the appropriate use condition is met as soon as possible.

References

OECD (2019), *Country-by-Country Reporting – Compilation of Peer Review Reports (Phase 2): Inclusive Framework on BEPS: Action 13*, OECD/G20 Base Erosion and Profit Shifting Project, OECD Publishing, Paris, https://dx.doi.org/10.1787/f9bf1157-en. [1]

OECD (2018), *Country-by-Country Reporting – Compilation of Peer Review Reports (Phase 1): Inclusive Framework on BEPS: Action 13*, OECD/G20 Base Erosion and Profit Shifting Project, OECD Publishing, Paris, https://dx.doi.org/10.1787/9789264300057-en. [2]

OECD (2017), *Terms of reference for the conduct of peer review of the Action 13 minimum standard on country-by-country reporting*, OECD Publishing, https://www.oecd.org/tax/beps/beps-action-13-on-country-by-country-reporting-peer-review-documents.pdf. [3]

Note

[1] No inconsistency with the terms of reference will be identified where a QCAA is not in effect with one or more jurisdictions of the Inclusive Framework that meet the confidentiality, consistency and appropriate use conditions, but this is due to circumstances that are not under the control of the reviewed jurisdiction. This may include, for example, where the other jurisdiction intends to exchange CbC reports using the MCAA but it does not have the Convention in effect for the relevant fiscal period, or where the other jurisdiction has declined to have a QCAA in effect with the reviewed jurisdiction.

China (People's Republic of)

1. China was reviewed as part of the 2017/2018 and the 2018/2019 peer reviews. This report is supplementary to those previous reports (OECD, 2019[1]) (OECD, 2018[2]).

2. The first filing obligation for a CbC report in China commences in respect of financial years beginning on or after 1 January 2016.

Summary of key findings

3. China's implementation of the Action 13 minimum standard meets all applicable terms of reference (OECD, 2017[3]) relating to the domestic legal and administrative framework, except for the following:

- China's 2017/2018 peer review included a recommendation that China clarify the exact scope, conditions and legal basis under the minimum standard and/or the exchange of information framework for the filing exemption in relation to information relating to National Security. This recommendation remains in place.
- China's 2017/2018 peer review included a recommendation that China amend its legislation or otherwise takes steps to ensure that local filing is only required in the circumstances contained in the terms of reference. This recommendation remains in place.

4. It is recommended that China should continue to work actively towards putting in place qualifying competent authority arrangements with jurisdictions of the Inclusive Framework that meet the confidentiality, consistency and appropriate use conditions and with which China has an international exchange of information agreement in effect that allows for the automatic exchange of tax information. This recommendation remains unchanged since the 2018/2019 peer review.

5. It is recommended that China take steps to implement processes or written procedures to ensure that the exchange of information is conducted in a manner consistent with the terms of reference relating to the exchange of information framework ahead of its first exchanges of information. This recommendation remains unchanged since the 2018/2019 peer review.

Part A: The domestic legal and administrative framework

6. China has primary and secondary laws in place to implement the BEPS Action 13 minimum standard, establishing the necessary requirements, including the filing and reporting obligations.

(a) Parent entity filing obligation

7. China's 2017/2018 peer review included a recommendation that China clarify the exact scope, conditions and legal basis under the minimum standard and/or the exchange of information framework for the filing exemption in relation to information relating to National Security. This recommendation remains in place. China confirm that, as at 31 March 2020, no MNEs have been exempted from filing under this provision.

(b) Scope and timing of parent entity filing

8. No changes were identified.

(c) Limitation on local filing obligation

9. China's 2017/2018 peer review included a recommendation that China amend its legislation or otherwise takes steps to ensure that local filing is only required in the circumstances contained in the terms of reference. This recommendation remains in place. China confirm that, as at 31 March 2020, no foreign MNEs have been required to comply with local filing rules.

(d) Limitation on local filing in case of surrogate filing

10. No changes were identified.

(e) Effective implementation

11. No changes were identified.

Conclusion

12. It is recommended that China clarify the exact scope, conditions and legal basis under the minimum standard and/or the exchange of information framework for the filing exemption in relation to information relating to National Security. This recommendation remains in place since the 2017/2018 peer review.

13. It is recommended that China amend its legislation or otherwise takes steps to ensure that local filing is only required in the circumstances contained in the terms of reference. This recommendation remains in place since the 2017/2018 peer review.

Part B: The exchange of information framework

(a) Exchange of information framework

14. As at 31 March 2020, China has 45 bilateral relationships activated under the CbC MCAA and under bilateral agreements. Within the context of its international exchange of information agreements that allow automatic exchange of information, China should continue to take steps to have qualifying competent authority agreements in effect with jurisdictions of the Inclusive Framework that meet the confidentiality, consistency and appropriate use conditions.

(b) Content of information exchanged

15. No changes were identified.

(c) Completeness of exchanges

16. No changes were identified.

(d) Timeliness of exchanges

17. No changes were identified.

(e) Temporary suspension of exchange or termination of QCAA

18. No changes were identified.

(f) Consultation with other Competent Authority before determining systemic failure or significant non-compliance

19. No changes were identified.

(g) Format for information exchange

20. No changes were identified.

(h) Method for transmission

21. No changes were identified.

Conclusion

22. It is recommended that China should continue to work actively towards putting in place qualifying competent authority arrangements with jurisdictions of the Inclusive Framework that meet the confidentiality, consistency and appropriate use conditions and with which China has an international exchange of information agreement in effect that allows for the automatic exchange of tax information. This recommendation remains unchanged since the 2018/2019 peer review.

23. It is recommended that China implement a process to ensure that each of the mandatory fields of information required in the CbC reporting template are present in the information exchanged. This recommendation remains unchanged since the 2017/2018 peer review.

Part C: Appropriate use

Appropriate use

24. No changes were identified.

Conclusion

25. China meets all the terms of reference in relation to appropriate use.

Summary of recommendations on the implementation of Country-by-Country Reporting

Aspect of the implementation that should be improved		Recommendation for improvement
Part A	Domestic legal and administrative framework	It is recommended that China clarify the exact scope and legal basis under the minimum standard and/or the exchange of information framework for the filing exemption in relation to national security.
Part A	Domestic legal and administrative framework	It is recommended that China amend its legislation or otherwise take steps to ensure that local filing is only required in the circumstances contained in the terms of reference.
Part B	Exchange of information framework	It is recommended that China should continue to work actively towards putting in place qualifying competent authority arrangements with jurisdictions of the Inclusive Framework that meet the confidentiality, consistency and appropriate use conditions and with which China has an international exchange of information agreement in effect that allows for the automatic exchange of tax information.
Part B	Exchange of information framework	It is recommended that China implement a process to ensure that each of the mandatory fields of information required in the CbC reporting template are present in the information exchanged.
Part C	Appropriate Use	-

References

OECD (2019), *Country-by-Country Reporting – Compilation of Peer Review Reports (Phase 2): Inclusive Framework on BEPS: Action 13*, OECD/G20 Base Erosion and Profit Shifting Project, OECD Publishing, Paris, https://dx.doi.org/10.1787/f9bf1157-en. [1]

OECD (2018), *Country-by-Country Reporting – Compilation of Peer Review Reports (Phase 1): Inclusive Framework on BEPS: Action 13*, OECD/G20 Base Erosion and Profit Shifting Project, OECD Publishing, Paris, https://dx.doi.org/10.1787/9789264300057-en. [2]

OECD (2017), *Terms of reference for the conduct of peer review of the Action 13 minimum standard on country-by-country reporting*, OECD Publishing, https://www.oecd.org/tax/beps/beps-action-13-on-country-by-country-reporting-peer-review-documents.pdf. [3]

Colombia

1. Colombia was reviewed as part of the 2017/2018 and the 2018/2019 peer reviews. This report is supplementary to those previous reports (OECD, 2019[1]) (OECD, 2018[2]).

2. The first filing obligation for a CbC report in Colombia commences in respect of periods commencing on or after 1 January 2016.

Summary of key findings

3. Colombia's implementation of the Action 13 minimum standard meets all applicable terms of reference (OECD, 2017[3]).

Part A: The domestic legal and administrative framework

4. No changes were identified.

(a) Parent entity filing obligation

5. No changes were identified.

(b) Scope and timing of parent entity filing

6. No changes were identified.

(c) Limitation on local filing obligation

7. No changes were identified.

(d) Limitation on local filing in case of surrogate filing

8. No changes were identified.

(e) Effective implementation

9. No changes were identified.

Conclusion

10. Colombia meets all the terms of reference relating to the domestic legal and administrative framework.

Part B: The exchange of information framework

(a) Exchange of information framework

11. As of 31 March 2020, Colombia has 72 bilateral relationships in place, including those activated under the CbC MCAA and under bilateral CAAs. Within the context of its international exchange of information agreements that allow automatic exchange of information, Colombia has taken steps to have qualifying competent authority agreements in effect with jurisdictions of the Inclusive Framework

that meet the confidentiality, consistency and appropriate use conditions.[1] Regarding Colombia's exchange of information framework, no inconsistencies with the terms of reference were identified.

(b) Content of information exchanged

12. No changes were identified.

(c) Completeness of exchanges

13. No changes were identified.

(d) Timeliness of exchanges

14. No changes were identified.

(e) Temporary suspension of exchange or termination of QCAA

15. No changes were identified.

(f) Consultation with other Competent Authority before determining systemic failure or significant non-compliance

16. No changes were identified.

(g) Format for information exchange

17. No changes were identified.

(h) Method for transmission

18. No changes were identified.

Conclusion

19. Colombia meets all the terms of reference regarding the exchange of information.

Part C: Appropriate use

Appropriate use

20. No changes were identified.

Conclusion

21. Colombia meets all the terms of reference relating to appropriate use of CbC reports.

Summary of recommendations on the implementation of country-by-country reporting

Aspect of the implementation that should be improved		Recommendation for improvement
Part A	Domestic legal and administrative framework	-
Part B	Exchange of information framework	-
Part C	Appropriate use	-

References

OECD (2019), *Country-by-Country Reporting – Compilation of Peer Review Reports (Phase 2): Inclusive Framework on BEPS: Action 13*, OECD/G20 Base Erosion and Profit Shifting Project, OECD Publishing, Paris, https://dx.doi.org/10.1787/f9bf1157-en. [1]

OECD (2018), *Country-by-Country Reporting – Compilation of Peer Review Reports (Phase 1): Inclusive Framework on BEPS: Action 13*, OECD/G20 Base Erosion and Profit Shifting Project, OECD Publishing, Paris, https://dx.doi.org/10.1787/9789264300057-en. [2]

OECD (2017), *Terms of reference for the conduct of peer review of the Action 13 minimum standard on country-by-country reporting*, OECD Publishing, https://www.oecd.org/tax/beps/beps-action-13-on-country-by-country-reporting-peer-review-documents.pdf. [3]

Note

[1] No inconsistency with the terms of reference will be identified where a QCAA is not in effect with one or more jurisdictions of the Inclusive Framework that meet the confidentiality, consistency and appropriate use conditions, but this is due to circumstances that are not under the control of the reviewed jurisdiction. This may include, for example, where the other jurisdiction intends to exchange CbC reports using the MCAA but it does not have the Convention in effect for the relevant fiscal period, or where the other jurisdiction has declined to have a QCAA in effect with the reviewed jurisdiction.

Congo

1. Congo was first reviewed during the 2018/2019 peer review. This report is supplementary to that previous report (OECD, 2018[2]).

2. There is no filing obligation for a CbC report in Congo yet.

Summary of key findings

3. Congo does not yet have legislation in place for implementing the BEPS Action 13 minimum standard. It is recommended that Congo take steps to implement a domestic legal and administrative framework to impose and enforce CbC reporting requirements as soon as possible. This recommendation remains unchanged since the 2018/2019 peer review.

4. It is recommended that Congo take steps to have qualifying competent authority agreements in effect with jurisdictions of the Inclusive Framework that meet the confidentiality, consistency and appropriate use conditions and with which Congo has an international exchange of information agreement in effect that allows for the automatic exchange of tax information. This recommendation remains unchanged since the 2018/2019 peer review.

5. It is recommended that Congo take steps to implement processes or written procedures to ensure that the exchange of information is conducted in a manner consistent with the terms of reference (OECD, 2017[3]) relating to the exchange of information framework ahead of the first exchanges of information. This recommendation remains unchanged since the 2018/2019 peer review.

6. It is recommended that Congo take steps to ensure that the appropriate use condition is met ahead of the first exchanges of information. This recommendation remains unchanged since the 2018/2019 peer review.

Part A: The domestic legal and administrative framework

7. Congo does not yet have legislation in place for implementing the BEPS Action 13 minimum standard.

(a) Parent entity filing obligation

(b) Scope and timing of parent entity filing

(c) Limitation on local filing obligation

(d) Limitation on local filing in case of surrogate filing

(e) Effective implementation

Conclusion

8. It is recommended that Congo take steps to implement a domestic legal and administrative framework to impose and enforce CbC reporting requirements as soon as possible.

Part B: The exchange of information framework

(a) Exchange of information framework

9. As of 31 March 2020, Congo has no bilateral relationships in place for the exchange of CbC reports. It is recommended that Congo take steps to have qualifying competent authority agreements in effect with jurisdictions of the Inclusive Framework that meet the confidentiality, consistency and appropriate use conditions and with which Congo has an international exchange of information agreement in effect that allows for the automatic exchange of tax information.

(b) Content of information exchanged

10. No changes were identified.

(c) Completeness of exchanges

11. No changes were identified.

(d) Timeliness of exchanges

12. No changes were identified.

(e) Temporary suspension of exchange or termination of QCAA

13. No changes were identified.

(f) Consultation with other Competent Authority before determining systemic failure or significant non-compliance

14. No changes were identified.

(g) Format for information exchange

15. No changes were identified.

(h) Method for transmission

16. No changes were identified.

Conclusion

17. It is recommended that Congo take steps to have qualifying competent authority agreements in effect with jurisdictions of the Inclusive Framework that meet the confidentiality, consistency and appropriate use conditions and with which Congo has an international exchange of information agreement in effect that allows for the automatic exchange of tax information. This recommendation remains unchanged since the 2018/2019 peer review.

18. It is recommended that Congo take steps to implement processes or written procedures to ensure that the exchange of information is conducted in a manner consistent with the terms of reference relating to the exchange of information framework ahead of its first exchanges of information. This recommendation remains unchanged since the 2018/2019 peer review.

Part C: Appropriate use

Appropriate use

19. No changes were identified.

Conclusion

20. It is recommended that Congo take steps to ensure that the appropriate use condition is met ahead of its first exchanges of information. This recommendation remains unchanged since the 2018/2019 peer review.

Summary of recommendations on the implementation of Country-by-Country Reporting

Aspect of the implementation that should be improved		**Recommendation for improvement**
Part A	Domestic legal and administrative framework	It is recommended that Congo take steps to implement a domestic legal and administrative framework to impose and enforce CbC requirements as soon as possible.
Part B	Exchange of information framework	It is recommended that Congo take steps to have qualifying competent authority agreements in effect with jurisdictions of the Inclusive Framework that meet the confidentiality, consistency and appropriate use conditions and with which Congo has an international exchange of information agreement in effect that allows for the automatic exchange of tax information.
Part B	Exchange of information framework	It is recommended that Congo take steps to implement the necessary processes or written procedures to ensure that the exchange of information is conducted in a manner consistent with the terms of reference relating to the exchange of information framework.
Part C	Appropriate use	It is recommended that Congo take steps to ensure that the appropriate use condition is met ahead of the first exchanges of information.

References

OECD (2018), *Country-by-Country Reporting – Compilation of Peer Review Reports (Phase 1): Inclusive Framework on BEPS: Action 13*, OECD/G20 Base Erosion and Profit Shifting Project, OECD Publishing, Paris, https://dx.doi.org/10.1787/9789264300057-en. [2]

OECD (2017), *Terms of reference for the conduct of peer review of the Action 13 minimum standard on country-by-country reporting*, OECD Publishing, https://www.oecd.org/tax/beps/beps-action-13-on-country-by-country-reporting-peer-review-documents.pdf. [3]

Costa Rica

1. Costa Rica was reviewed as part of the 2017/2018 and the 2018/2019 peer reviews. This report is supplementary to those previous reports (OECD, 2019[1]) (OECD, 2018[2]) .

2. The first filing obligation for a CbC report in Costa Rica commences in respect of reporting fiscal years on or after 1 January 2017.

Summary of key findings

3. Costa Rica's domestic legal and administrative framework meets all applicable terms of reference (OECD, 2017[3]), except for the following:

- It is recommended that Costa Rica complete its definition of "Ultimate Parent Entity" to be in line with the terms of reference.
- It is recommended that Costa Rica amend its rules or otherwise ensures that a CbC report is not filed later than 12 months after the end of the accounting period and not subsequently exchanged more than 15 months after the end of the accounting period with partner jurisdictions.
- These recommendations remain unchanged since the 2017/2018 peer review.

4. It is recommended that Costa Rica take steps to implement the necessary processes and written procedures to ensure that the exchange of information is conducted in a manner consistent with the terms of reference relating to the exchange of information framework. This recommendation remains unchanged since the 2018/2019 peer review.

Part A: The domestic legal and administrative framework

5. Costa Rica has rules in place to implement the BEPS Action 13 minimum standard.

(a) Parent entity filing obligation

6. It is recommended that Costa Rica amend or otherwise clarify that the definition of "Ultimate Parent Entity" applies only to those entities in which no other entities hold an interest[1]. This recommendation remains in place since the 2017/2018 peer review.

(b) Scope and timing of parent entity filing

7. The 2017/2018 peer review included a recommendation to Costa Rica amend its rules on the filing deadline or otherwise ensure that a CbC report is not filed later than 12 months after the end of the accounting period and that is not subsequently exchanged later than 15 months after the end of the accounting period with partner jurisdictions. This recommendation remains in place.[2]

(c) Limitation on local filing obligation

8. No changes were identified.

(d) Limitation on local filing in case of surrogate filing

9. No changes were identified.

(e) Effective implementation

10. No changes were identified.[3]

Conclusion

11. It is recommended that Costa Rica complete its definition of "Ultimate Parent Entity" to be in line with the terms of reference. This recommendation remains since the 2017/2018 peer review.

12. It is recommended that Costa Rica amend its rules or otherwise ensures that a CbC report is not filed later than 12 months after the end of the accounting period and not subsequently exchanged more than 15 months after the end of the accounting period with partner jurisdictions. This recommendation remains since the 2017/2018 peer review.

Part B: The exchange of information framework

(a) Exchange of information framework

13. Costa Rica's 2017/2018 peer review included a recommendation to continue to take steps to have Qualifying Competent Authority agreements in effect with jurisdictions of the Inclusive Framework that meet the confidentiality, consistency and appropriate use conditions and with which Costa Rica has an international exchange of information agreement in effect that allows for the automatic exchange of tax information. Bilateral relationships are now in place so this recommendation is removed.

14. As of 31 March 2020, Costa Rica has 54 bilateral relationships activated under the CbC MCAA. Within the context of its international exchange of information agreements that allow automatic exchange of information, Costa Rica has taken steps to have qualifying competent authority agreements in effect with jurisdictions of the Inclusive Framework that meet the confidentiality, consistency and appropriate use conditions and with which Costa Rica has an international exchange of information agreement in effect that allows for the automatic exchange of tax information.[4] Regarding Costa Rica's exchange of information framework, no inconsistencies with the terms of reference were identified.

(b) Content of information exchanged

15. Costa Rica does not have procedures in place that are intended to ensure that each of the mandatory fields of information as required in the CbC template are present in the information exchanged.

(c) Completeness of exchanges

16. Costa Rica does not have processes in place that are intended to ensure that CbC reports are exchanged with all tax jurisdictions listed in Table 1 of a CbC reporting template with which it should exchange information as per the relevant QCAAs.

(d) Timeliness of exchanges

17. Costa Rica does not have yet processes in place that are intended to ensure that the information to be exchanged is transmitted to the relevant jurisdictions in accordance with the timelines provided for in the relevant QCAAs and terms of reference.

(e) Temporary suspension of exchange or termination of QCAA

18. Costa Rica does not have yet processes in place that are intended to ensure that a temporary suspension of the exchange of information or termination of a relevant QCAA be carried out only as per the conditions set out in the QCAA.

(f) Consultation with other Competent Authority before determining systemic failure or significant non-compliance

19. Costa Rica does not have yet processes in place that are intended to ensure that the Competent Authority consults with the other Competent Authority prior to making a determination that there is or has been significant non-compliance with the terms of the relevant QCAA or that the other Competent Authority has caused a systemic failure.

(g) Format for information exchange

20. Costa Rica confirms that it uses the OECD XML Schema and User Guide (OECD, 2017[4]) for the international exchange of CbC reports.

(h) Method for transmission

21. Costa Rica indicates that it intends to use the Common Transmission System to exchange CbC reports.

Conclusion

22. It is recommended that Costa Rica take steps to implement the necessary processes and written procedures to ensure that the exchange of information is conducted in a manner consistent with the terms of reference relating to the exchange of information framework. This recommendation remain from the2018/2019 peer review.

Part C: Appropriate use

Appropriate use

23. No changes were identified.

Conclusion

24. Costa Rica is a non-reciprocal jurisdiction and, as such, will not receive CbC reports submitted to tax authorities in other jurisdictions, and will not apply local filing. It is not necessary for this peer review evaluation to reach any conclusion with respect to Costa Rica's compliance with the terms of reference on appropriate use.

Summary of recommendations on the implementation of country-by-country reporting

Aspect of the implementation that should be improved		Recommendation for improvement
Part A	Domestic legal and administrative framework – parent filing obligation	It is recommended that Costa Rica complete its definition of "Ultimate Parent Entity" to be in line with the terms of reference.
Part A	Domestic legal and administrative framework - Scope and timing of parent entity filing – filing date	It is recommended that Costa Rica amend its rules or otherwise ensures that a CbC report is not filed later than 12 months after the end of the accounting period and not subsequently exchanged more than 15 months after the end of the accounting period with partner jurisdictions.
Part B	Exchange of information framework	It is recommended that Costa Rica take steps to have the necessary processes in place ahead of the first exchanges of CbC reports.
Part C	Appropriate use	-

References

OECD (2019), *Country-by-Country Reporting – Compilation of Peer Review Reports (Phase 2): Inclusive Framework on BEPS: Action 13*, OECD/G20 Base Erosion and Profit Shifting Project, OECD Publishing, Paris, https://dx.doi.org/10.1787/f9bf1157-en. [1]

OECD (2018), *Country-by-Country Reporting – Compilation of Peer Review Reports (Phase 1): Inclusive Framework on BEPS: Action 13*, OECD/G20 Base Erosion and Profit Shifting Project, OECD Publishing, Paris, https://dx.doi.org/10.1787/9789264300057-en. [2]

OECD (2017), *Terms of reference for the conduct of peer review of the Action 13 minimum standard on country-by-country reporting*, OECD Publishing, https://www.oecd.org/tax/beps/beps-action-13-on-country-by-country-reporting-peer-review-documents.pdf. [3]

Notes

[1] Article 1, item 6 of Costa Rica's rules does not make it clear that an entity cannot be an Ultimate Parent Entity if another Constituent Entity holds an interest in that entity (i.e. the ultimate holding company must be the top level holding company in the MNE group).

[2] The 2017/2018 peer review also included a monitoring point for the first year exchanges, to ensure that the filing deadline will not impact the ability of the Costa Rica to meet its obligations relating to the exchange of information under the terms of reference. This monitoring point remains in place.

[3] Costa Rica's 2017/2018 peer review included a monitoring point relating to the absence of specific processes in place that would allow Costa Rica to take appropriate measures in case it is notified by another jurisdiction that such other jurisdiction has reason to believe that an error may have led to incorrect or incomplete information reporting by a Reporting Entity or that there is non-compliance of a Reporting Entity with respect to its obligation to file a CbC report. This aspect will be further monitored once the actual exchanges of CbC reports will commence. This monitoring point remains in place.

[4] No inconsistency with the terms of reference will be identified where a QCAA is not in effect with one or more jurisdictions of the Inclusive Framework that meet the confidentiality, consistency and appropriate use conditions, but this is due to circumstances that are not under the control of the reviewed jurisdiction. This may include, for example, where the other jurisdiction intends to exchange CbC reports using the MCAA but it does not have the Convention in effect for the relevant fiscal period, or where the other jurisdiction has declined to have a QCAA in effect with the reviewed jurisdiction.

Côte d'Ivoire

1. Côte d'Ivoire was reviewed as part of the 2017/2018 and the 2018/2019 peer reviews. This report is supplementary to those previous reports (OECD, 2019[1]) (OECD, 2018[2]).

2. The first filing obligation for a CbC report in Côte d'Ivoire commences in respect of reporting fiscal years commencing on or after 1 January 2018.

Summary of key findings

3. Côte d'Ivoire's implementation of the Action 13 minimum standard meets all applicable terms of reference (OECD, 2017[3]).

4. Côte d'Ivoire's 2018/2019 peer review recommended that Côte d'Ivoire amend the rule relating to the filing threshold, which should be determined in relation to the fiscal year preceding the reporting fiscal year. The rule has been amended so the recommendation is removed.

5. Côte d'Ivoire's 2018/2019 peer review recommended that Côte d'Ivoire have enforcement measures in case of an incomplete or erroneous filing of a CbC report. These measures are now in place so the recommendation is removed.

6. It is recommended that Côte d'Ivoire take steps to have QCAAs in effect with jurisdictions of the Inclusive Framework which meet the confidentiality, consistency and appropriate use prerequisites and with which Côte d'Ivoire has an international exchange of information agreement in effect that allows for the automatic exchange of tax information. This recommendation remains in place since Côte d'Ivoire's 2017/2018 peer review.

7. It is recommended that Côte d'Ivoire have in place the necessary processes or written procedures to ensure that the exchange of information is conducted in a manner consistent with the terms of reference relating to the exchange of information framework. This recommendation remains unchanged since the 2018/2019 peer review.

8. It is recommended that Côte d'Ivoire take steps to ensure that the appropriate use condition is met ahead of the first exchanges of information. This recommendation remains in place since Côte d'Ivoire's 2017/2018 peer review.

Part A: The domestic legal and administrative framework

9. Côte d'Ivoire has legislation in place to implement the BEPS Action 13 minimum standard.

(a) Parent entity filing obligation

10. Côte d'Ivoire's 2018/2019 peer review recommended that Côte d'Ivoire amend the rule relating to the filing threshold, which should be determined in relation to the fiscal year preceding the reporting fiscal year. The rule has been amended so the recommendation is removed.[1]

(b) Scope and timing of parent entity filing

11. No changes were identified.

(c) Limitation on local filing obligation

12. No changes were identified.

(d) Limitation on local filing in case of surrogate filing

13. No changes were identified.

(e) Effective implementation

14. Côte d'Ivoire's 2018/2019 peer review recommended that Côte d'Ivoire have enforcement measures in case of an incomplete or erroneous filing of a CbC report. These measures are now in place so the recommendation is removed [2] [3].

Conclusion

15. Côte d'Ivoire meets the terms of reference relating to the domestic legal and administrative framework.

Part B: The exchange of information framework

(a) Exchange of information framework

16. As of 31 March 2020, Côte d'Ivoire has no bilateral relationships in place for the exchange of CbC reports. It is recommended that Côte d'Ivoire take steps to have qualifying competent authority agreements in effect with jurisdictions of the Inclusive Framework that meet the confidentiality, consistency and appropriate use conditions and with which Côte d'Ivoire has an international exchange of information agreement in effect that allows for the automatic exchange of tax information. This recommendation is unchanged since the 2017/2018 peer review.

(b) Content of information exchanged

17. No changes were identified.

(c) Completeness of exchange

18. No changes were identified.

(d) Timeliness of exchanges

19. No changes were identified.

(e) Temporary suspension of exchange or termination of QCAA

20. No changes were identified.

(f) Consultation with other Competent Authority before determining systemic failure or significant non-compliance

21. No changes were identified.

(g) Format for information exchange

22. No changes were identified.

(h) Method for transmission

23. No changes were identified.

Conclusion

24. It is recommended that Côte d'Ivoire take steps to have qualifying competent authority agreements in effect with jurisdictions of the Inclusive Framework that meet the confidentiality, consistency and appropriate use conditions and with which Côte d'Ivoire has an international exchange of information agreement in effect that allows for the automatic exchange of tax information. This recommendation remains unchanged since the 2017/2018 review.

25. It is recommended that Côte d'Ivoire take steps to implement processes or written procedures to ensure that the exchange of information is conducted in a manner consistent with the terms of reference relating to the exchange of information framework ahead of its first exchanges of information. This recommendation remains unchanged since the 2018/2019 peer review.

Part C: Appropriate use

Appropriate use

26. No changes were identified.

Conclusion

27. It is recommended that Côte d'Ivoire take steps to ensure that the appropriate use condition is met ahead of its first exchanges of information remain in place. This recommendation remains unchanged since the 2018/2019 peer review.

Summary of recommendations on the implementation of country-by-country reporting

Aspect of the implementation that should be improved		Recommendation for improvement
Part A	Domestic legal and administrative framework	-
Part B	Exchange of information framework	It is recommended that Côte d'Ivoire take steps to have QCAAs in effect with jurisdictions of the Inclusive Framework which meet the confidentiality, consistency and appropriate use pre-requisites and with which Côte d'Ivoire has an international exchange of information agreement in effect that allows for the automatic exchange of tax information.
Part B	Exchange of information framework	It is also recommended that Côte d'Ivoire have in place the necessary processes or written procedures to ensure that the exchange of information is conducted in a manner consistent with the terms of reference relating to the exchange of information framework.
Part C	Appropriate use	It is recommended that Côte d'Ivoire take steps to ensure that the appropriate use condition is met ahead of the first exchanges of information

References

OECD (2019), *Country-by-Country Reporting – Compilation of Peer Review Reports (Phase 2): Inclusive Framework on BEPS: Action 13*, OECD/G20 Base Erosion and Profit Shifting Project, OECD Publishing, Paris, https://dx.doi.org/10.1787/f9bf1157-en. [1]

OECD (2018), *Country-by-Country Reporting – Compilation of Peer Review Reports (Phase 1): Inclusive Framework on BEPS: Action 13*, OECD/G20 Base Erosion and Profit Shifting Project, OECD Publishing, Paris, https://dx.doi.org/10.1787/9789264300057-en. [2]

OECD (2017), *Terms of reference for the conduct of peer review of the Action 13 minimum standard on country-by-country reporting*, OECD Publishing, https://www.oecd.org/tax/beps/beps-action-13-on-country-by-country-reporting-peer-review-documents.pdf. [3]

Notes

[1] http://www.dgi.gouv.ci/images/PDF/ANNEXE_FISCALE_2020.pdf. (accessed on 24 August 2020).

[2] http://www.dgi.gouv.ci/images/PDF/ANNEXE_FISCALE_2020.pdf. (accessed on 24 August 2020).

[3] Cote d'Ivoire's 2017/2018 peer review included a general monitoring point relating to a specific process to that would allow to take appropriate measures in case Cote d'Ivoire is notified by another jurisdiction that such other jurisdiction has reason to believe that an error may have led to incorrect or incomplete information reporting by a Reporting Entity or that there is non-compliance of a Reporting Entity with respect to its obligation to file a CbC report. This monitoring point remains in place.

Croatia

1. Croatia was reviewed as part of the 2017/2018 and the 2018/2019 peer reviews. This report is supplementary to those previous reports (OECD, 2019[1]) (OECD, 2018[2]).

2. The first filing obligation for a CbC report in Croatia applies to reporting fiscal years commencing on or after 1 January 2016.

Summary of key findings

3. Croatia's implementation of the Action 13 minimum standard meets all applicable terms of reference (OECD, 2017[3]).

Part A: The domestic legal and administrative framework

4. Croatia has legislation in place to implement the BEPS Action 13 minimum standard.

(a) Parent entity filing obligation

5. No changes were identified.

(b) Scope and timing of parent entity filing

6. No changes were identified.[1]

(c) Limitation on local filing obligation

7. No changes were identified.

(d) Limitation on local filing in case of surrogate filing

8. No changes were identified.

(e) Effective implementation

9. No changes were identified.

Conclusion

10. Croatia meets all the terms of reference relating to the domestic legal and administrative framework.

Part B: The exchange of information framework

(a) Exchange of information framework

11. As of 31 March 2020, Croatia has 67 bilateral relationships in place, including those activated under the CbC MCAA, bilateral QCAAs and under the EU Council Directive (2016/881/EU). Within the context of its international exchange of information agreements that allow automatic exchange of information, Croatia has taken steps to have qualifying competent authority agreements in effect with jurisdictions of the Inclusive Framework that meet the confidentiality, consistency and appropriate use

conditions.[2] Regarding Croatia's exchange of information framework, no inconsistencies with the terms of reference were identified.

(b) Content of information exchanged

12. No changes were identified.

(c) Completeness of exchanges

13. No changes were identified.

(d) Timeliness of exchanges

14. No changes were identified.

(e) Temporary suspension of exchange or termination of QCAA

15. No changes were identified.

(f) Consultation with other Competent Authority before determining systemic failure or significant non-compliance

16. No changes were identified.

(g) Format for information exchange

17. No changes were identified.

(h) Method for transmission

18. No changes were identified.

Conclusion

19. Croatia meets all the terms of reference regarding the exchange of information.

Part C: Appropriate use

Appropriate use

20. No changes were identified.

Conclusion

21. Croatia meets all the terms of reference relating to appropriate use of CbC reports.

Summary of recommendations on the implementation of Country-by-Country Reporting

Aspect of the implementation that should be improved		Recommendation for improvement
Part A	Domestic legal and administrative framework	-
Part B	Exchange of information framework	-
Part C	Appropriate use	-

References

OECD (2019), *Country-by-Country Reporting – Compilation of Peer Review Reports (Phase 2): Inclusive Framework on BEPS: Action 13*, OECD/G20 Base Erosion and Profit Shifting Project, OECD Publishing, Paris, https://dx.doi.org/10.1787/f9bf1157-en. [1]

OECD (2018), *Country-by-Country Reporting – Compilation of Peer Review Reports (Phase 1): Inclusive Framework on BEPS: Action 13*, OECD/G20 Base Erosion and Profit Shifting Project, OECD Publishing, Paris, https://dx.doi.org/10.1787/9789264300057-en. [2]

OECD (2017), *Terms of reference for the conduct of peer review of the Action 13 minimum standard on country-by-country reporting*, OECD Publishing, https://www.oecd.org/tax/beps/beps-action-13-on-country-by-country-reporting-peer-review-documents.pdf. [3]

Notes

[1] Croatia's 2017/2018 peer review included a monitoring point relating to the definition of "related enterprises". This monitoring point remains in place.

[2] No inconsistency with the terms of reference will be identified where a QCAA is not in effect with one or more jurisdictions of the Inclusive Framework that meet the confidentiality, consistency and appropriate use conditions, but this is due to circumstances that are not under the control of the reviewed jurisdiction. This may include, for example, where the other jurisdiction intends to exchange CbC reports using the MCAA but it does not have the Convention in effect for the relevant fiscal period, or where the other jurisdiction has declined to have a QCAA in effect with the reviewed jurisdiction.

Curaçao

1. Curaçao was reviewed as part of the 2017/2018 and the 2018/2019 peer reviews. This report is supplementary to those previous reports (OECD, 2019[1]) (OECD, 2018[2]).

2. The first filing obligation for a CbC report in Curaçao applies to reporting fiscal years commencing on or after 1 January 2018 or end/ing after 1 January 2018. Curaçao also allows its MNE groups to file a CbC report on a voluntary basis, for reporting fiscal years ending prior to 1 January 2018.

Summary of key findings

3. Curaçao's implementation of the Action 13 minimum standard meets all the terms of reference (OECD, 2017[3]).

Part A: The domestic legal and administrative framework

4. Curaçao has legislation in place to implement the BEPS Action 13 minimum standard.

(a) Parent entity filing obligation

5. No changes were identified.

(b) Scope and timing of parent entity filing

6. No changes were identified.

(c) Limitation on local filing obligation

7. No changes were identified.

(d) Limitation on local filing in case of surrogate filing

8. No changes were identified.

(e) Effective implementation

9. No changes were identified.

Conclusion

10. Curaçao meets all the terms of reference relating to the domestic legal and administrative framework.

Part B: The exchange of information framework

(a) Exchange of information framework

11. As of 31 March 2020, Curaçao has 49 bilateral relationships in place for the exchange of CbC reports, activated under the CbC MCAA. Within the context of its international exchange of information agreements that allow automatic exchange of tax information, Curaçao has taken steps to have

qualifying competent authority agreements in effect with jurisdictions of the Inclusive Framework that currently meet the confidentiality, consistency and appropriate use conditions. Regarding Curaçao's exchange of information framework, no inconsistencies with the terms of reference were identified.[1]

(b) Content of information exchanged

12. No changes were identified.

(c) Completeness of exchanges

13. No changes were identified.

(d) Timeliness of exchanges

14. No changes were identified.

(e) Temporary suspension of exchange or termination of QCAA

15. No changes were identified.

(f) Consultation with other Competent Authority before determining systemic failure or significant non-compliance

16. No changes were identified.

(g) Format for information exchange

17. No changes were identified.

(h) Method for transmission

18. No changes were identified.

Conclusion

19. Curaçao meets all the terms of reference regarding the exchange of information.

Part C: Appropriate use

Appropriate use

20. No changes were identified.

Conclusion

21. Curaçao is a non-reciprocal jurisdiction and, as such, will not receive CbC reports submitted to tax authorities in other jurisdictions, and will not apply local filing. It is therefore not necessary for this peer review evaluation to reach any conclusions with respect to Curaçao's compliance with the terms of reference on appropriate use.

Summary of recommendations on the implementation of Country-by-Country Reporting

Aspect of the implementation that should be improved		Recommendation for improvement
Part A	Domestic legal and administrative framework	-
Part B	Exchange of information framework	-
Part C	Appropriate use	-

References

OECD (2019), *Country-by-Country Reporting – Compilation of Peer Review Reports (Phase 2): Inclusive Framework on BEPS: Action 13*, OECD/G20 Base Erosion and Profit Shifting Project, OECD Publishing, Paris, https://dx.doi.org/10.1787/f9bf1157-en. [1]

OECD (2018), *Country-by-Country Reporting – Compilation of Peer Review Reports (Phase 1): Inclusive Framework on BEPS: Action 13*, OECD/G20 Base Erosion and Profit Shifting Project, OECD Publishing, Paris, https://dx.doi.org/10.1787/9789264300057-en. [2]

OECD (2017), *Terms of reference for the conduct of peer review of the Action 13 minimum standard on country-by-country reporting*, OECD Publishing, https://www.oecd.org/tax/beps/beps-action-13-on-country-by-country-reporting-peer-review-documents.pdf. [3]

Note

[1] No inconsistency with the terms of reference will be identified where a QCAA is not in effect with one or more jurisdictions of the Inclusive Framework that meet the confidentiality, consistency and appropriate use conditions, but this is due to circumstances that are not under the control of the reviewed jurisdiction. This may include, for example, where the other jurisdiction intends to exchange CbC reports using the MCAA but it does not have the Convention in effect for the relevant fiscal period, or where the other jurisdiction has declined to have a QCAA in effect with the reviewed jurisdiction.

Czech Republic

1. The Czech Republic was reviewed as part of the 2017/2018 and the 2018/2019 peer reviews. This report is supplementary to those previous reports (OECD, 2019[1]) (OECD, 2018[2]).

2. The first filing obligation for a CbC report in the Czech Republic applies to reporting fiscal years commencing on or after 1 January 2016.

Summary of key findings

3. The Czech Republic's implementation of the Action 13 minimum standard meets all applicable terms of reference (OECD, 2017[3]).

Part A: The domestic legal and administrative framework

4. The Czech Republic has legislation in place to implement the BEPS Action 13 minimum standard.

(a) Parent entity filing obligation

5. No changes were identified.

(b) Scope and timing of parent entity filing

6. No changes were identified.

(c) Limitation on local filing obligation

7. No changes were identified.

(d) Limitation on local filing in case of surrogate filing

8. No changes were identified.

(e) Effective implementation

9. No changes were identified.

Conclusion

10. The Czech Republic meets all the terms of reference relating to the domestic legal and administrative framework.

Part B: The exchange of information framework

(a) Exchange of information framework

11. As of 31 March 2020, the Czech Republic has 68 bilateral relationships in place for the exchange of CbC reports, including those activated under the CbC MCAA, under bilateral CAAs and under the EU Council Directive (2016/881/EU). Within the context of its international exchange of information agreements that allow automatic exchange of tax information, the Czech Republic has taken steps to have

qualifying competent authority agreements in effect with jurisdictions of the Inclusive Framework that currently meet the confidentiality, consistency and appropriate use conditions. Regarding the Czech Republic's exchange of information framework, no inconsistencies with the terms of reference were identified.[1]

(b) Content of information exchanged

12. No changes were identified.

(c) Completeness of exchanges

13. No changes were identified.

(d) Timeliness of exchanges

14. No changes were identified.

(e) Temporary suspension of exchange or termination of QCAA

15. No changes were identified.

(f) Consultation with other Competent Authority before determining systemic failure or significant non-compliance

16. No changes were identified.

(g) Format for information exchange

17. No changes were identified.

(h) Method for transmission

18. No changes were identified.

Conclusion

19. The Czech Republic meets all the terms of reference regarding the exchange of information.

Part C: Appropriate use

Appropriate use

20. No changes were identified.

Conclusion

21. The Czech Republic meets all the terms of reference relating to appropriate use of CbC reports.

Summary of recommendations on the implementation of country-by-country reporting

	Aspect of the implementation that should be improved	Recommendation for improvement
Part A	Domestic legal and administrative framework - Parent entity filing obligation annual consolidated group revenue threshold	
Part B	Exchange of information framework	
Part C	Appropriate use	

References

OECD (2019), *Country-by-Country Reporting – Compilation of Peer Review Reports (Phase 2): Inclusive Framework on BEPS: Action 13*, OECD/G20 Base Erosion and Profit Shifting Project, OECD Publishing, Paris, https://dx.doi.org/10.1787/f9bf1157-en. [1]

OECD (2018), *Country-by-Country Reporting – Compilation of Peer Review Reports (Phase 1): Inclusive Framework on BEPS: Action 13*, OECD/G20 Base Erosion and Profit Shifting Project, OECD Publishing, Paris, https://dx.doi.org/10.1787/9789264300057-en. [2]

OECD (2017), *Terms of reference for the conduct of peer review of the Action 13 minimum standard on country-by-country reporting*, OECD Publishing, https://www.oecd.org/tax/beps/beps-action-13-on-country-by-country-reporting-peer-review-documents.pdf. [3]

Note

[1] No inconsistency with the terms of reference will be identified where a QCAA is not in effect with one or more jurisdictions of the Inclusive Framework that meet the confidentiality, consistency and appropriate use conditions, but this is due to circumstances that are not under the control of the reviewed jurisdiction. This may include, for example, where the other jurisdiction intends to exchange CbC reports using the MCAA but it does not have the Convention in effect for the relevant fiscal period, or where the other jurisdiction has declined to have a QCAA in effect with the reviewed jurisdiction.

Democratic Republic of the Congo

1. The Democratic Republic of the Congo was reviewed as part of the 2017/2018 and the 2018/2019 peer reviews. This report is supplementary to those previous reports (OECD, 2019[1]) (OECD, 2018[2]).

2. There is no filing obligation for a CbC report in the Democratic Republic of the Congo yet.

Summary of key findings

3. It is recommended that the Democratic Republic of the Congo take steps to implement a domestic legal and administrative framework to impose and enforce CbC reporting requirements as soon as possible. This recommendation remains unchanged since the 2017/2018 peer review.

4. It is recommended that the Democratic Republic of the Congo take steps to have QCAAs in effect with jurisdictions of the Inclusive Framework which meet the confidentiality, consistency and appropriate use prerequisites and with which they have an international exchange of information agreement in effect that allows for the automatic exchange of tax information. This recommendation remains unchanged since the 2017/2018 peer review.

5. It is recommended that the Democratic Republic of the Congo take steps to implement processes or written procedures to ensure that the exchange of information is conducted in a manner consistent with the terms of reference (OECD, 2017[3]) relating to the exchange of information framework ahead of the first exchanges of information. This recommendation remains unchanged since the 2018/2019 peer review.

6. It is recommended that the Democratic Republic of the Congo take steps to ensure that the appropriate use condition is met ahead of the first exchanges of information. This recommendation remains unchanged since the 2017/2018 peer review.

Part A: The domestic legal and administrative framework

7. The Democratic Republic of the Congo does not yet have legislation in place for implementing the BEPS Action 13 minimum standard.

(a) Parent entity filing obligation

8. No changes were identified.

(b) Scope and timing of parent entity filing

9. No changes were identified.

(c) Limitation on local filing obligation

10. No changes were identified.

(d) Limitation on local filing in case of surrogate filing

11. No changes were identified.

(e) Effective implementation

12. No changes were identified.

Conclusion

13. It is recommended that the Democratic Republic of the Congo take steps to implement a domestic legal and administrative framework to impose and enforce CbC reporting requirements as soon as possible. This recommendation remains unchanged since the 2017/2018 peer review.

Part B: The exchange of information framework

(a) Exchange of information framework

14. As of 31 March 2020, the Democratic Republic of the Congo has no bilateral relationships in place for the exchange of CbC reports. It is recommended that the Democratic Republic of the Congo take steps to have qualifying competent authority agreements in effect with jurisdictions of the Inclusive Framework that meet the confidentiality, consistency and appropriate use conditions and with which the Democratic Republic of the Congo has an international exchange of information agreement in effect that allows for the automatic exchange of tax information. This recommendation remains unchanged from the 2017/2018 review.

(b) Content of information exchanged

15. No changes were identified.

(c) Completeness of exchanges

16. No changes were identified.

(d) Timeliness of exchanges

17. No changes were identified.

(e) Temporary suspension of exchange or termination of QCAA

18. No changes were identified.

(f) Consultation with other Competent Authority before determining systemic failure or significant non-compliance

19. No changes were identified.

(g) Format for information exchange

20. No changes were identified.

(h) Method for transmission

21. No changes were identified.

Conclusion

22. It is recommended that the Democratic Republic of the Congo to take steps to have QCAAs in effect with jurisdictions of the Inclusive Framework which meet the confidentiality, consistency and appropriate use prerequisites and with which they have an international exchange of information agreement in effect that allows for the automatic exchange of tax information. This recommendation remains unchanged since the 2017/2018 peer review.

23. It is recommended that the Democratic Republic of the Congo take steps to implement processes or written procedures to ensure that the exchange of information is conducted in a manner consistent with

the terms of reference relating to the exchange of information framework ahead of its first exchanges of information. This recommendation remains unchanged since the 2018/2019 peer review.

Part C: Appropriate use

Appropriate use

24. No changes were identified.

Conclusion

25. It is recommended that the Democratic Republic of the Congo to take steps to ensure that the appropriate use condition is met ahead of its first exchanges of information remains in place. This recommendation remains unchanged since the 2017/2018 peer review.

Summary of recommendations on the implementation of Country-by-Country Reporting

Aspect of the implementation that should be improved		Recommendation for improvement
Part A	Domestic legal and administrative framework	It is recommended that the Democratic Republic of the Congo take steps to implement a domestic legal and administrative framework to impose and enforce CbC requirements as soon as possible.
Part B	Exchange of information framework	It is recommended that the Democratic Republic of the Congo take steps to have QCAAs in effect with jurisdictions of the Inclusive Framework which meet the confidentiality, consistency and appropriate use prerequisites and with which they have an international exchange of information agreement in effect that allows for the automatic exchange of tax information.
Part B	Exchange of information framework	It is recommended that the Democratic Republic of the Congo take steps to implement the necessary processes or written procedures to ensure that the exchange of information is conducted in a manner consistent with the terms of reference relating to the exchange of information framework.
Part C	Appropriate use	It is recommended that the Democratic Republic of the Congo take steps to ensure that the appropriate use condition is met ahead of the first exchanges of information.

References

OECD (2019), *Country-by-Country Reporting – Compilation of Peer Review Reports (Phase 2): Inclusive Framework on BEPS: Action 13*, OECD/G20 Base Erosion and Profit Shifting Project, OECD Publishing, Paris, https://dx.doi.org/10.1787/f9bf1157-en. [1]

OECD (2018), *Country-by-Country Reporting – Compilation of Peer Review Reports (Phase 1): Inclusive Framework on BEPS: Action 13*, OECD/G20 Base Erosion and Profit Shifting Project, OECD Publishing, Paris, https://dx.doi.org/10.1787/9789264300057-en. [2]

OECD (2017), *Terms of reference for the conduct of peer review of the Action 13 minimum standard on country-by-country reporting*, OECD Publishing, https://www.oecd.org/tax/beps/beps-action-13-on-country-by-country-reporting-peer-review-documents.pdf. [3]

Denmark

1. Denmark was reviewed as part of the 2017/2018 and the 2018/2019 peer reviews. This report is supplementary to those previous reports (OECD, 2019[1]) (OECD, 2018[2]).

2. The first filing obligation for a CbC report in Denmark applies to reporting fiscal years commencing on or after 1 January 2016.

Summary of key findings

3. Denmark's implementation of the Action 13 minimum standard meets all applicable terms of reference (OECD, 2017[3]).

Part A: The domestic legal and administrative framework

4. Denmark has legislation in place for implementing the BEPS Action 13 minimum standard.

(a) Parent entity filing obligation

5. No changes were identified.

(b) Scope and timing of parent entity filing

6. No changes were identified.

(c) Limitation on local filing obligation

7. No changes were identified.

(d) Limitation on local filing in case of surrogate filing

8. No changes were identified.

(e) Effective implementation

9. No changes were identified.

Conclusion

10. Denmark meets all the terms of reference relating to the domestic legal and administrative framework.

Part B: The exchange of information framework

(a) Exchange of information framework

11. As of 31 March 2020, Denmark has 63 bilateral relationships in place, including those activated under the CbC MCAA, under bilateral CAAs and under the EU Council Directive (2016/881/EU). Within the context of its international exchange of information agreements that allow automatic exchange of information, Denmark has taken steps to have qualifying competent authority agreements in effect with

jurisdictions of the Inclusive Framework that meet the confidentiality, consistency and appropriate use conditions. Regarding Denmark's exchange of information framework, no inconsistencies with the terms of reference were identified.

(b) Content of information exchanged

12. No changes were identified.

(c) Completeness of exchanges

13. No changes were identified.

(d) Timeliness of exchanges

14. No changes were identified.

(e) Temporary suspension of exchange or termination of QCAA

15. No changes were identified.

(f) Consultation with other Competent Authority before determining systemic failure or significant non-compliance

16. No changes were identified.

(g) Format for information exchange

17. No changes were identified.

(h) Method for transmission

18. No changes were identified.

Conclusion

19. Denmark meets all the terms of reference regarding the exchange of information.

Part C: Appropriate use

Appropriate use

20. No changes were identified.

Conclusion

21. Denmark meets all the terms of reference relating to appropriate use of CbC reports.

Summary of recommendations on the implementation of country-by-country reporting

Aspect of the implementation that should be improved		Recommendation for improvement
Part A	Domestic legal and administrative framework	-
Part B	Exchange of information framework	-
Part C	Appropriate use	-

References

OECD (2019), *Country-by-Country Reporting – Compilation of Peer Review Reports (Phase 2): Inclusive Framework on BEPS: Action 13*, OECD/G20 Base Erosion and Profit Shifting Project, OECD Publishing, Paris, https://dx.doi.org/10.1787/f9bf1157-en. [1]

OECD (2018), *Country-by-Country Reporting – Compilation of Peer Review Reports (Phase 1): Inclusive Framework on BEPS: Action 13*, OECD/G20 Base Erosion and Profit Shifting Project, OECD Publishing, Paris, https://dx.doi.org/10.1787/9789264300057-en. [2]

OECD (2017), *Terms of reference for the conduct of peer review of the Action 13 minimum standard on country-by-country reporting*, OECD Publishing, https://www.oecd.org/tax/beps/beps-action-13-on-country-by-country-reporting-peer-review-documents.pdf. [3]

Djibouti

1. Djibouti was first reviewed during the 2018/2019 peer review. This report is supplementary to that previous report (OECD, 2018[2]).

2. There is no filing obligation for a CbC report in Djibouti yet.

Summary of key findings

3. Djibouti does not yet have legislation in place for implementing the BEPS Action 13 minimum standard. It is recommended that Djibouti take steps to implement a domestic legal and administrative framework to impose and enforce CbC reporting requirements as soon as possible. This recommendation remains unchanged since the 2018/2019 peer review.

4. It is recommended that Djibouti take steps to have qualifying competent authority agreements in effect with jurisdictions of the Inclusive Framework that meet the confidentiality, consistency and appropriate use conditions and with which Djibouti has an international exchange of information agreement in effect that allows for the automatic exchange of tax information. This recommendation remains unchanged since the 2018/2019 peer review.

5. It is recommended that Djibouti take steps to implement processes or written procedures to ensure that the exchange of information is conducted in a manner consistent with the terms of reference (OECD, 2017[3]) relating to the exchange of information framework ahead of the first exchanges of information. This recommendation remains unchanged since the 2018/2019 peer review.

6. It is recommended that Djibouti take steps to ensure that the appropriate use condition is met ahead of the first exchanges of information. This recommendation remains unchanged since the 2018/2019 peer review.

Part A: The domestic legal and administrative framework

7. Djibouti does not yet have legislation in place for implementing the BEPS Action 13 minimum standard.

(a) Parent entity filing obligation

(b) Scope and timing of parent entity filing

(c) Limitation on local filing obligation

(d) Limitation on local filing in case of surrogate filing

(e) Effective implementation

Conclusion

8. It is recommended that Djibouti take steps to implement a domestic legal and administrative framework to impose and enforce CbC reporting requirements as soon as possible. This recommendation remains unchanged since the 2018/2019 peer review.

Part B: The exchange of information framework

(a) Exchange of information framework

9. As of 31 March 2020, Djibouti has no bilateral relationships in place for the exchange of CbC reports. It is recommended that Djibouti take steps to put in place an exchange of information framework that allows Automatic Exchange of Information and have QCAAs in effect with jurisdictions of the Inclusive Framework which meet the confidentiality, consistency and appropriate use prerequisites and with which Djibouti has an international exchange of information agreement in effect that allows for the automatic exchange of tax information.

(b) Content of information exchanged

10. No changes were identified.

(c) Completeness of exchanges

11. No changes were identified.

(d) Timeliness of exchanges

12. No changes were identified.

(e) Temporary suspension of exchange or termination of QCAA

13. No changes were identified.

(f) Consultation with other Competent Authority before determining systemic failure or significant non-compliance

14. No changes were identified.

(g) Format for information exchange

15. No changes were identified.

(h) Method for transmission

16. No changes were identified.

Conclusion

17. It is recommended that Djibouti take steps to put in place an exchange of information framework that allows Automatic Exchange of Information and have QCAAs in effect with jurisdictions of the Inclusive Framework which meet the confidentiality, consistency and appropriate use prerequisites and with which Djibouti has an international exchange of information agreement in effect that allows for the automatic exchange of tax information. This recommendation remains unchanged since the 2018/2019 peer review.

18. It is recommended that Djibouti take steps to implement processes or written procedures to ensure that the exchange of information is conducted in a manner consistent with the terms of reference relating to the exchange of information framework ahead of its first exchanges of information. This recommendation remains unchanged since the 2018/2019 peer review.

Part C: Appropriate use

Appropriate use

19. No changes were identified.

Conclusion

20. It is recommended that Djibouti take steps to ensure that the appropriate use condition is met ahead of its first exchanges of information. This recommendation remains unchanged since the 2018/2019 peer review.

Summary of recommendations on the implementation of Country-by-Country Reporting

Aspect of the implementation that should be improved		Recommendation for improvement
Part A	Domestic legal and administrative framework	It is recommended that Djibouti take steps to implement a domestic legal and administrative framework to impose and enforce CbC requirements as soon as possible.
Part B	Exchange of information framework	It is recommended that Djibouti take steps to put in place an exchange of information framework that allows Automatic Exchange of Information and have QCAAs in effect with jurisdictions of the Inclusive Framework which meet the confidentiality, consistency and appropriate use prerequisites and with which Djibouti has an international exchange of information agreement in effect that allows for the automatic exchange of tax information
Part B	Exchange of information framework	It is recommended that Djibouti take steps to implement the necessary processes or written procedures to ensure that the exchange of information is conducted in a manner consistent with the terms of reference relating to the exchange of information framework.
Part C	Appropriate use	It is recommended that Djibouti take steps to ensure that the appropriate use condition is met ahead of the first exchanges of information.

References

OECD (2018), *Country-by-Country Reporting – Compilation of Peer Review Reports (Phase 1): Inclusive Framework on BEPS: Action 13*, OECD/G20 Base Erosion and Profit Shifting Project, OECD Publishing, Paris, https://dx.doi.org/10.1787/9789264300057-en. [2]

OECD (2017), *Terms of reference for the conduct of peer review of the Action 13 minimum standard on country-by-country reporting*, OECD Publishing, https://www.oecd.org/tax/beps/beps-action-13-on-country-by-country-reporting-peer-review-documents.pdf. [3]

Dominica

1. This report is Dominica's first annual peer review report. Consistent with the agreed methodology this report covers: (i) the domestic legal and administrative framework, (ii) the exchange of information framework as well as (iii) the appropriate use of CbC reports.

2. There is no filing obligation for a CbC report in Dominica yet.

Summary of key findings

3. Dominica does not yet have legislation in place for implementing the BEPS Action 13 minimum standard.

4. It is recommended that Dominica take steps to implement a domestic legal and administrative framework to impose and enforce CbC reporting requirements as soon as possible.

5. It is recommended that Dominica take steps to put in place an exchange of information framework that allows automatic exchange of information and have QCAAs in effect with jurisdictions of the Inclusive Framework which meet the confidentiality, consistency and appropriate use prerequisites and with which Dominica has an international exchange of information agreement in effect that allows for the automatic exchange of tax information.

6. It is recommended that Dominica take steps to implement processes or written procedures to ensure that the exchange of information is conducted in a manner consistent with the terms of reference (OECD, 2017[3]) relating to the exchange of information framework ahead of the first exchanges of information.

7. It is recommended that Dominica take steps to ensure that the appropriate use condition is met ahead of the first exchanges of information.

Part A: The domestic legal and administrative framework

8. Dominica does not yet have legislation in place for implementing the BEPS Action 13 minimum standard.

(a) Parent entity filing obligation

(b) Scope and timing of parent entity filing

(c) Limitation on local filing obligation

(d) Limitation on local filing in case of surrogate filing

(e) Effective implementation

Conclusion

9. It is recommended that Dominica take steps to implement a domestic legal and administrative framework to impose and enforce CbC reporting requirements as soon as possible.

Part B: The exchange of information framework

(a) Exchange of information framework

10. As of 31 March 2020, Dominica has no bilateral relationships in place for the exchange of CbC reports. It is recommended that Dominica take steps to have qualifying competent authority agreements in effect with jurisdictions of the Inclusive Framework that meet the confidentiality, consistency and appropriate use conditions and with which Dominica has an international exchange of information agreement in effect that allows for the automatic exchange of tax information.

(b) Content of information exchanged

11. Dominica does not have processes or written procedures in place that are intended to ensure that each of the mandatory fields of information required in the CbC reporting template are present in the information exchanged.

(c) Completeness of exchanges

12. Dominica does not have processes or written procedures in place that are intended to ensure that CbC reports are exchanged with all tax jurisdictions listed in Table 1 of a CbC report with which it should exchange information as per the relevant QCAA.

(d) Timeliness of exchanges

13. Dominica does not have processes or written procedures in place that are intended to ensure that the information to be exchanged is transmitted to the relevant jurisdictions in accordance with the timelines provided for in the relevant QCAAs.

(e) Temporary suspension of exchange or termination of QCAA

14. Dominica does not have processes or written procedures in place that are intended to ensure that a temporary suspension of the exchange of information or termination of a relevant QCAA would be carried out only as per the conditions set out in the relevant QCAA.

(f) Consultation with other Competent Authority before determining systemic failure or significant non-compliance

15. Dominica does not have processes or written procedures in place that are intended to ensure that its Competent Authority consults with the other Competent Authority before making a determination of systemic failure or significant non-compliance with the terms of the relevant QCAA by that other Competent Authority.

(g) Format for information exchange

16. Dominica has not confirmed the format that will be used for the international exchange of CbC reports.

(h) Method for transmission

17. Dominica has not confirmed the mechanism that it will use to exchange CbC reports.

Conclusion

18. It is recommended that Dominica take steps to have qualifying competent authority agreements in effect with jurisdictions of the Inclusive Framework that meet the confidentiality, consistency and

appropriate use conditions and with which Dominica has an international exchange of information agreement in effect that allows for the automatic exchange of tax information.

19. It is recommended that Dominica take steps to implement processes or written procedures to ensure that the exchange of information is conducted in a manner consistent with the terms of reference (OECD, 2017[3]) relating to the exchange of information framework ahead of its first exchanges of information.

Part C: Appropriate use

Appropriate use

20. Dominica does not yet have measures in place relating to appropriate use.

21. It is recommended that Dominica take steps to have measures in place relating to appropriate use ahead of the first exchanges of information.

Conclusion

22. It is recommended that Dominica take steps to ensure that the appropriate use condition is met ahead of its first exchanges of information.

Summary of recommendations on the implementation of Country-by-Country Reporting

Aspect of the implementation that should be improved		Recommendation for improvement
Part A	Domestic legal and administrative framework	It is recommended that Dominica take steps to implement a domestic legal and administrative framework to impose and enforce CbC requirements as soon as possible.
Part B	Exchange of information framework	It is recommended that Dominica take steps to put in place an exchange of information framework that allows Automatic Exchange of Information and have QCAAs in effect with jurisdictions of the Inclusive Framework which meet the confidentiality, consistency and appropriate use prerequisites and with which Dominica has an international exchange of information agreement in effect that allows for the automatic exchange of tax information.
Part B	Exchange of information framework	It is recommended that Dominica take steps to implement the necessary processes or written procedures to ensure that the exchange of information is conducted in a manner consistent with the terms of reference relating to the exchange of information framework.
Part C	Appropriate use	It is recommended that Dominica take steps to ensure that the appropriate use condition is met ahead of the first exchanges of information.

References

OECD (2017), *Terms of reference for the conduct of peer review of the Action 13 minimum standard on country-by-country reporting*, OECD Publishing, https://www.oecd.org/tax/beps/beps-action-13-on-country-by-country-reporting-peer-review-documents.pdf. [3]

Dominican Republic

1. This report is Dominican Republic's first annual peer review report. Consistent with the agreed methodology this report covers: (i) the domestic legal and administrative framework, (ii) the exchange of information framework as well as (iii) the appropriate use of CbC reports.

2. There is no filing obligation for a CbC report in Dominican Republic yet.

Summary of key findings

3. Dominican Republic does not yet have legislation in place for implementing the BEPS Action 13 minimum standard.

4. It is recommended that Dominican Republic take steps to implement a domestic legal and administrative framework to impose and enforce CbC reporting requirements as soon as possible.

5. It is recommended that Dominican Republic take steps to put in place an exchange of information framework that allows automatic exchange of information and have QCAAs in effect with jurisdictions of the Inclusive Framework which meet the confidentiality, consistency and appropriate use prerequisites and with which Dominican Republic has an international exchange of information agreement in effect that allows for the automatic exchange of tax information.

6. It is recommended that Dominican Republic take steps to implement processes or written procedures to ensure that the exchange of information is conducted in a manner consistent with the terms of reference (OECD, 2017[3]) relating to the exchange of information framework ahead of the first exchanges of information.

7. It is recommended that Dominican Republic take steps to ensure that the appropriate use condition is met ahead of the first exchanges of information.

Part A: The domestic legal and administrative framework

8. Dominican Republic does not yet have legislation in place for implementing the BEPS Action 13 minimum standard.

(a) Parent entity filing obligation

(b) Scope and timing of parent entity filing

(c) Limitation on local filing obligation

(d) Limitation on local filing in case of surrogate filing

(e) Effective implementation

Conclusion

9. It is recommended that Dominican Republic take steps to implement a domestic legal and administrative framework to impose and enforce CbC reporting requirements as soon as possible.

Part B: The exchange of information framework

(a) Exchange of information framework

10. As of 31 March 2020, Dominican Republic has no bilateral relationships in place for the exchange of CbC reports. It is recommended that Dominican Republic take steps to have qualifying competent authority agreements in effect with jurisdictions of the Inclusive Framework that meet the confidentiality, consistency and appropriate use conditions and with which Dominican Republic has an international exchange of information agreement in effect that allows for the automatic exchange of tax information.

(b) Content of information exchanged

11. Dominican Republic does not have processes or written procedures in place that are intended to ensure that each of the mandatory fields of information required in the CbC reporting template are present in the information exchanged.

(c) Completeness of exchanges

12. Dominican Republic does not have processes or written procedures in place that are intended to ensure that CbC reports are exchanged with all tax jurisdictions listed in Table 1 of a CbC report with which it should exchange information as per the relevant QCAA.

(d) Timeliness of exchanges

13. Dominican Republic does not have processes or written procedures in place that are intended to ensure that the information to be exchanged is transmitted to the relevant jurisdictions in accordance with the timelines provided for in the relevant QCAAs.

(e) Temporary suspension of exchange or termination of QCAA

14. Dominican Republic does not have processes or written procedures in place that are intended to ensure that a temporary suspension of the exchange of information or termination of a relevant QCAA would be carried out only as per the conditions set out in the relevant QCAA.

(f) Consultation with other Competent Authority before determining systemic failure or significant non compliance

15. Dominican Republic does not have processes or written procedures in place that are intended to ensure that its Competent Authority consults with the other Competent Authority before making a determination of systemic failure or significant non-compliance with the terms of the relevant QCAA by that other Competent Authority.

(g) Format for information exchange

16. Dominican Republic has not confirmed the format that will be used for the international exchange of CbC reports.

(h) Method for transmission

17. Dominican Republic has not confirmed the mechanism that it will use to exchange CbC reports.

Conclusion

18. It is recommended that Dominican Republic take steps to have qualifying competent authority agreements in effect with jurisdictions of the Inclusive Framework that meet the confidentiality, consistency

and appropriate use conditions and with which Dominican Republic has an international exchange of information agreement in effect that allows for the automatic exchange of tax information.

19. It is recommended that Dominican Republic take steps to implement processes or written procedures to ensure that the exchange of information is conducted in a manner consistent with the terms of reference (OECD, 2017[3]) relating to the exchange of information framework ahead of its first exchanges of information.

Part C: Appropriate use

Appropriate use

20. Dominican Republic does not yet have measures in place relating to appropriate use.

21. It is recommended that Dominican Republic take steps to have measures in place relating to appropriate use ahead of the first exchanges of information.

Conclusion

22. It is recommended that Dominican Republic take steps to ensure that the appropriate use condition is met ahead of its first exchanges of information.

Summary of recommendations on the implementation of Country-by-Country Reporting

Aspect of the implementation that should be improved		Recommendation for improvement
Part A	Domestic legal and administrative framework	It is recommended that Dominican Republic take steps to implement a domestic legal and administrative framework to impose and enforce CbC requirements as soon as possible.
Part B	Exchange of information framework	It is recommended that Dominican Republic take steps to put in place an exchange of information framework that allows Automatic Exchange of Information and have QCAAs in effect with jurisdictions of the Inclusive Framework which meet the confidentiality, consistency and appropriate use prerequisites and with which Dominican Republic has an international exchange of information agreement in effect that allows for the automatic exchange of tax information.
Part B	Exchange of information framework	It is recommended that Dominican Republic take steps to implement the necessary processes or written procedures to ensure that the exchange of information is conducted in a manner consistent with the terms of reference relating to the exchange of information framework.
Part C	Appropriate use	It is recommended that Dominican Republic take steps to ensure that the appropriate use condition is met ahead of the first exchanges of information.

References

OECD (2017), *Terms of reference for the conduct of peer review of the Action 13 minimum standard on country-by-country reporting*, OECD Publishing, https://www.oecd.org/tax/beps/beps-action-13-on-country-by-country-reporting-peer-review-documents.pdf. [3]

Egypt

1. Egypt was reviewed as part of the 2017/2018 and the 2018/2019 peer reviews. This report is supplementary to those previous reports (OECD, 2019[1]) (OECD, 2018[2]).

2. The first filing obligation for a CbC report in Egypt applies to reporting fiscal years ending on or after the 31 December 2018.

Summary of key findings

3. Egypt's legal and administrative framework to implement Action 13 meets all applicable terms of reference (OECD, 2017[3]), except for the following:

- It is recommended that Egypt take steps to ensure that its definition of Group of Associated Enterprises is in line with the required definition of Group. This recommendation remains unchanged since the 2018/2019 peer review.
- It is recommended that Egypt take steps to ensure that its definition of Egyptian Parented GAE is in line with the required definition of Ultimate Parent Entity and Multinational Enterprise Group. This recommendation remains unchanged since the 2018/2019 peer review.
- It is recommended that Egypt take steps to ensure that its definition of multinational group is in line with the required definition of Multinational Enterprise Group. This recommendation remains unchanged since the 2018/2019 peer review.
- It is recommended that Egypt take steps to ensure that enforcement provisions and monitoring relating to the enforcement of CbCR filing obligations are implemented. This recommendation remains unchanged since the 2018/2019 peer review.

4. It is recommended that Egypt take steps to have qualifying competent authority agreements in effect with jurisdictions of the Inclusive Framework that meet the confidentiality, consistency and appropriate use conditions and with which Egypt has an international exchange of information agreement in effect that allows for the automatic exchange of tax information. This recommendation remains unchanged since the 2017/2018 peer review.

5. It is recommended that Egypt take steps to implement processes or written procedures to ensure that the exchange of information is conducted in a manner consistent with the terms of reference relating to the exchange of information framework ahead of the first exchanges of information. This recommendation remains unchanged since the 2018/2019 peer review.

6. It is recommended that Egypt take steps to ensure that the appropriate use condition is met ahead of the first exchanges of information. This recommendation remains unchanged since the 2017/2018 peer review.

Part A: The domestic legal and administrative framework

7. Egypt has Transfer Pricing Guidelines issued by Ministerial Decree in place to implement the BEPS Action 13 minimum standard.

(a) Parent entity filing obligation

8. No changes were identified.

b) Scope and timing of parent entity filing

9. No changes were identified.

(c) Limitation on local filing obligation

10. No changes were identified.

(d) Limitation on local filing in case of surrogate filing

11. No changes were identified.

(e) Effective implementation

12. No changes were identified.

Conclusion

13. The recommendation in the 2017/18 peer review, that Egypt finalise its domestic legal and administrative framework in relation to CbC requirements as soon as possible, is removed.

14. Egypt's domestic legal framework meets all applicable terms of reference, except for the following:

- It is recommended that Egypt take steps to ensure that its definition of group is in line with the required definition of Group.
- It is recommended that Egypt take steps to ensure that its definition of parent entity is in line with the required definition of Ultimate Parent Entity.
- It is recommended that Egypt take steps to ensure that its definition of multinational group is in line with the required definition of Multinational Enterprise Group.
- It is recommended that Egypt take steps to ensure that enforcement provisions and monitoring relating to the enforcement of CbCR filing obligations are implemented.

Part B: The exchange of information framework

(a) Exchange of information framework

15. As of 31 March 2020, Egypt has no bilateral relationships in place for the exchange of CbC reports. It is recommended that Egypt take steps to have qualifying competent authority agreements in effect with jurisdictions of the Inclusive Framework that meet the confidentiality, consistency and appropriate use conditions and with which Egypt has an international exchange of information agreement in effect that allows for the automatic exchange of tax information.

(b) Content of information exchanged

16. No changes were identified.

(c) Completeness of exchanges

17. No changes were identified.

(d) Timeliness of exchanges

18. No changes were identified.

(e) Temporary suspension of exchange or termination of QCAA

19. No changes were identified.

(f) Consultation with other Competent Authority before determining systemic failure or significant non-compliance

20. No changes were identified.

(g) Format for information exchange

21. No changes were identified.

(h) Method for transmission

22. No changes were identified.

Conclusion

23. It is recommended that Egypt take steps to have QCAAs in effect with jurisdictions of the Inclusive Framework which meet the confidentiality, consistency and appropriate use prerequisites and with which Egypt has an international exchange of information agreement in effect that allows for the automatic exchange of tax information remains in place. This recommendation remains unchanged since the 2017/2018 peer review.

24. It is recommended that Egypt take steps to implement processes or written procedures to ensure that the exchange of information is conducted in a manner consistent with the terms of reference relating to the exchange of information framework ahead of its first exchanges of information. This recommendation remains unchanged since the 2018/2019 peer review.

Part C: Appropriate use

Appropriate use

25. No changes were identified.

Conclusion

26. The recommendation for Egypt to take steps to ensure that the appropriate use condition is met ahead of its first exchanges of information remain in place.

27. This recommendation remains unchanged since the 2017/2018 peer review.

Summary of recommendations on the implementation of Country-by-Country Reporting

Aspect of the implementation that should be improved		Recommendation for improvement
Part A	Domestic legal and administrative framework	It is recommended that Egypt finalise its domestic legal and administrative framework in relation to CbC requirements as soon as possible. Specifically it is recommended that: Egypt take steps to ensure that its definition of Group of Associated Enterprises is in line with the required definition of Group. Egypt take steps to ensure that its definition of Egyptian Parented GAE is in line with the required definition of Ultimate Parent Entity and Multinational Enterprise Group. Egypt take steps to ensure that its definition of multinational group is in line with the required definition of Multinational Enterprise Group. Egypt take steps to ensure that enforcement provisions and monitoring relating to the enforcement of CbCR filing obligations are implemented.
Part B	Exchange of information framework	It is recommended that Egypt take steps to have qualifying competent authority agreements in effect with jurisdictions of the Inclusive Framework that meet the confidentiality, consistency and appropriate use conditions and with which Egypt has an international exchange of information agreement in effect that allows for the automatic exchange of tax information
Part B	Exchange of information framework	It is recommended that Egypt take steps to implement the necessary processes or written procedures to ensure that the exchange of information is conducted in a manner consistent with the terms of reference relating to the exchange of information framework.
Part C	Appropriate use	It is recommended that Egypt take steps to ensure that the appropriate use condition is met ahead of the first exchanges of information.

References

OECD (2019), *Country-by-Country Reporting – Compilation of Peer Review Reports (Phase 2): Inclusive Framework on BEPS: Action 13*, OECD/G20 Base Erosion and Profit Shifting Project, OECD Publishing, Paris, https://dx.doi.org/10.1787/f9bf1157-en. [1]

OECD (2018), *Country-by-Country Reporting – Compilation of Peer Review Reports (Phase 1): Inclusive Framework on BEPS: Action 13*, OECD/G20 Base Erosion and Profit Shifting Project, OECD Publishing, Paris, https://dx.doi.org/10.1787/9789264300057-en. [2]

OECD (2017), *Terms of reference for the conduct of peer review of the Action 13 minimum standard on country-by-country reporting*, OECD Publishing, https://www.oecd.org/tax/beps/beps-action-13-on-country-by-country-reporting-peer-review-documents.pdf. [3]

Estonia

1. Estonia was reviewed as part of the 2017/2018 and the 2018/2019 peer reviews. This report is supplementary to those previous reports (OECD, 2019[1]) (OECD, 2018[2]).

2. The first filing obligation for a CbC report in Estonia applies to reporting fiscal years commencing on or after 1 January 2016.

Summary of key findings

3. Estonia's implementation of the Action 13 minimum standard meets all applicable terms of reference (OECD, 2017[3]).

Part A: The domestic legal and administrative framework

4. Estonia has legislation in place for implementing the BEPS Action 13 minimum standard.

(a) Parent entity filing obligation

5. No changes were identified.[1]

(b) Scope and timing of parent entity filing

6. No changes were identified.

(c) Limitation on local filing obligation

7. No changes were identified.

(d) Limitation on local filing in case of surrogate filing

8. No changes were identified.

(e) Effective implementation

9. No changes were identified.[2]

Conclusion

10. Estonia meets all the terms of reference relating to the domestic legal and administrative framework.

Part B: The exchange of information framework

(a) Exchange of information framework

11. As of 31 March 2020, Estonia has 67 bilateral relationships in place, including those activated under the CbC MCAA, under bilateral CAAs and under the EU Council Directive (2016/881/EU). Within the context of its international exchange of information agreements that allow automatic exchange of information, Estonia has taken steps to have qualifying competent authority agreements in effect with

jurisdictions of the Inclusive Framework that meet the confidentiality, consistency and appropriate use conditions. Regarding Estonia's exchange of information framework, no inconsistencies with the terms of reference were identified.

(b) Content of information exchanged

12. No changes were identified.

(c) Completeness of exchanges

13. No changes were identified.

(d) Timeliness of exchanges

14. No changes were identified.

(e) Temporary suspension of exchange or termination of QCAA

15. No changes were identified.

(f) Consultation with other Competent Authority before determining systemic failure or significant non-compliance

16. No changes were identified.

(g) Format for information exchange

17. No changes were identified.

(h) Method for transmission

18. No changes were identified.[3]

Conclusion

19. Estonia meets all the terms of reference regarding the exchange of information.

Part C: Appropriate use

Appropriate use

20. No changes were identified.

Conclusion

21. Estonia meets all the terms of reference relating to appropriate use of CbC reports.

Summary of recommendations on the implementation of country-by-country reporting

Aspect of the implementation that should be improved		Recommendation for improvement
Part A	Domestic legal and administrative framework	-
Part B	Exchange of information framework	-
Part C	Appropriate use	-

References

OECD (2019), *Country-by-Country Reporting – Compilation of Peer Review Reports (Phase 2): Inclusive Framework on BEPS: Action 13*, OECD/G20 Base Erosion and Profit Shifting Project, OECD Publishing, Paris, https://dx.doi.org/10.1787/f9bf1157-en. [1]

OECD (2018), *Country-by-Country Reporting – Compilation of Peer Review Reports (Phase 1): Inclusive Framework on BEPS: Action 13*, OECD/G20 Base Erosion and Profit Shifting Project, OECD Publishing, Paris, https://dx.doi.org/10.1787/9789264300057-en. [2]

OECD (2017), *Terms of reference for the conduct of peer review of the Action 13 minimum standard on country-by-country reporting*, OECD Publishing, https://www.oecd.org/tax/beps/beps-action-13-on-country-by-country-reporting-peer-review-documents.pdf. [3]

Notes

[1] Estonia's 2017/2018 peer review included a monitoring point relating to the threshold calculation rule which would be applied in a manner consistent with the OECD guidance on currency fluctuations (paragraph 8 (a) ii. of the terms of reference) This monitoring point remains in place.

[2] Estonia's 2017/2018 peer review included a general monitoring point relating to a specific process to that would allow to take appropriate measures in case Estonia is notified by another jurisdiction that such other jurisdiction has reason to believe that an error may have led to incorrect or incomplete information reporting by a Reporting Entity or that there is non-compliance of a Reporting Entity with respect to its obligation to file a CbC report. This monitoring point remains in place.

[3] Countries exchanging under the EU Council Directive (2016/881/EU) use the Common Communication Network (CCN).

Eswatini (Kingdom of)

1. This report is the Kingdom of Eswatini's (Eswatini) first annual peer review report. Consistent with the agreed methodology this report covers: (i) the domestic legal and administrative framework, (ii) the exchange of information framework as well as (iii) the appropriate use of CbC reports.

2. There is no filing obligation for a CbC report in Eswatini yet.

Summary of key findings

3. Eswatini does not yet have legislation in place for implementing the BEPS Action 13 minimum standard.

4. It is recommended that Eswatini take steps to implement a domestic legal and administrative framework to impose and enforce CbC reporting requirements as soon as possible.

5. It is recommended that Eswatini take steps to put in place an exchange of information framework that allows automatic exchange of information and have QCAAs in effect with jurisdictions of the Inclusive Framework which meet the confidentiality, consistency and appropriate use prerequisites and with which Eswatini has an international exchange of information agreement in effect that allows for the automatic exchange of tax information.

6. It is recommended that Eswatini take steps to implement processes or written procedures to ensure that the exchange of information is conducted in a manner consistent with the terms of reference (OECD, 2017[3]) relating to the exchange of information framework ahead of the first exchanges of information.

7. It is recommended that Eswatini take steps to ensure that the appropriate use condition is met ahead of the first exchanges of information.

Part A: The domestic legal and administrative framework

8. Eswatini does not yet have legislation in place for implementing the BEPS Action 13 minimum standard.

(a) Parent entity filing obligation

(b) Scope and timing of parent entity filing

(c) Limitation on local filing obligation

(d) Limitation on local filing in case of surrogate filing

(e) Effective implementation

Conclusion

9. It is recommended that Eswatini take steps to implement a domestic legal and administrative framework to impose and enforce CbC reporting requirements as soon as possible.

Part B: The exchange of information framework

(a) Exchange of information framework

10. As of 31 March 2020, Eswatini has no bilateral relationships in place for the exchange of CbC reports. It is recommended that Eswatini take steps to have qualifying competent authority agreements in effect with jurisdictions of the Inclusive Framework that meet the confidentiality, consistency and appropriate use conditions and with which Eswatini has an international exchange of information agreement in effect that allows for the automatic exchange of tax information.

(b) Content of information exchanged

11. Eswatini does not have processes or written procedures in place that are intended to ensure that each of the mandatory fields of information required in the CbC reporting template are present in the information exchanged.

(c) Completeness of exchanges

12. Eswatini does not have processes or written procedures in place that are intended to ensure that CbC reports are exchanged with all tax jurisdictions listed in Table 1 of a CbC report with which it should exchange information as per the relevant QCAA.

(d) Timeliness of exchanges

13. Eswatini does not have processes or written procedures in place that are intended to ensure that the information to be exchanged is transmitted to the relevant jurisdictions in accordance with the timelines provided for in the relevant QCAAs.

(e) Temporary suspension of exchange or termination of QCAA

14. Eswatini does not have processes or written procedures in place that are intended to ensure that a temporary suspension of the exchange of information or termination of a relevant QCAA would be carried out only as per the conditions set out in the relevant QCAA.

(f) Consultation with other Competent Authority before determining systemic failure or significant non compliance

15. Eswatini does not have processes or written procedures in place that are intended to ensure that its Competent Authority consults with the other Competent Authority before making a determination of systemic failure or significant non-compliance with the terms of the relevant QCAA by that other Competent Authority.

(g) Format for information exchange

16. Eswatini has not confirmed the format that will be used for the international exchange of CbC reports.

(h) Method for transmission

17. Eswatini has not confirmed the mechanism that it will use to exchange CbC reports.

Conclusion

18. It is recommended that Eswatini take steps to have qualifying competent authority agreements in effect with jurisdictions of the Inclusive Framework that meet the confidentiality, consistency and

appropriate use conditions and with which Eswatini has an international exchange of information agreement in effect that allows for the automatic exchange of tax information.

19. It is recommended that Eswatini take steps to implement processes or written procedures to ensure that the exchange of information is conducted in a manner consistent with the terms of reference (OECD, 2017[3]) relating to the exchange of information framework ahead of its first exchanges of information.

Part C: Appropriate use

Appropriate use

20. Eswatini does not yet have measures in place relating to appropriate use.

21. It is recommended that Eswatini take steps to have measures in place relating to appropriate use ahead of the first exchanges of information remains in place.

Conclusion

22. It is recommended that Eswatini take steps to ensure that the appropriate use conditions is met ahead of its first exchanges of information.

Summary of recommendations on the implementation of Country-by-Country Reporting

Aspect of the implementation that should be improved		Recommendation for improvement
Part A	Domestic legal and administrative framework	It is recommended that Eswatini take steps to implement a domestic legal and administrative framework to impose and enforce CbC requirements as soon as possible.
Part B	Exchange of information framework	It is recommended that Eswatini take steps to put in place an exchange of information framework that allows Automatic Exchange of Information and have QCAAs in effect with jurisdictions of the Inclusive Framework which meet the confidentiality, consistency and appropriate use prerequisites and with which Eswatini has an international exchange of information agreement in effect that allows for the automatic exchange of tax information.
Part B	Exchange of information framework	It is recommended that Eswatini take steps to implement the necessary processes or written procedures to ensure that the exchange of information is conducted in a manner consistent with the terms of reference relating to the exchange of information framework.
Part C	Appropriate use	It is recommended that Eswatini take steps to ensure that the appropriate use condition is met ahead of the first exchanges of information.

References

OECD (2017), *Terms of reference for the conduct of peer review of the Action 13 minimum standard on country-by-country reporting*, OECD Publishing, https://www.oecd.org/tax/beps/beps-action-13-on-country-by-country-reporting-peer-review-documents.pdf. [3]

Faroe Islands

1. This report is the Faroe Islands' first annual peer review report. Consistent with the agreed methodology this report covers: (i) the domestic legal and administrative framework, (ii) the exchange of information framework as well as (iii) the appropriate use of CbC reports.

2. The first filing obligation for a CbC report in the Faroe Islands applies to reporting fiscal years commencing on or after 20 December 2019.

Summary of key findings

3. The Faroe Islands implementation of the Action 13 minimum standard meets all the applicable terms of reference (OECD, 2017[3]) relating to the domestic legal and administrative framework, with the exceptions that:

- It is recommended that the Faroe Islands take steps to amend legislation or otherwise clarify that an MNE Group should consider its requirement to file using the turnover for the year before any reporting year for comparison with the threshold.
- It is recommended that the Faroe Islands take steps to amend legislation or otherwise clarify that there are no exemptions form the filing requirement for groups who meet the threshold requirement in the Faroe Islands.
- It is recommended that the Faroe Islands take steps to amend legislation or otherwise clarify that a CbC report should be filed within 12 months of the end of the reporting period the report applies to.
- It is recommended that the Faroe Islands take steps to implement procedures to ensure effective implementation of the filing requirement.
- It is recommended that the Faroe Islands clarify that the annual consolidated group revenue threshold calculation rule applies in line with the OECD guidance on currency fluctuations in respect of an MNE Group whose Ultimate Parent Entity is located in a jurisdiction other than the Faroe Islands.

4. It is recommended that the Faroe Islands take steps to put in place an exchange of information framework that allows automatic exchange of information and have QCAAs in effect with jurisdictions of the Inclusive Framework which meet the confidentiality, consistency and appropriate use prerequisites and with which the Faroe Islands has an international exchange of information agreement in effect that allows for the automatic exchange of tax information.

5. It is recommended that the Faroe Islands take steps to implement processes or written procedures to ensure that the exchange of information is conducted in a manner consistent with the terms of reference (OECD, 2017[3]) relating to the exchange of information framework ahead of the first exchanges of information.

6. It is recommended that the Faroe Islands take steps to ensure that the appropriate use condition is met ahead of the first exchanges of information.

Part A: The domestic legal and administrative framework

7. The Faroe Islands has published legislation and guidance that imposes and enforces a CbC filing requirement for fiscal years commencing on or after 20 December 2019.

(a) Parent entity filing obligation

8. The Faroe Islands has introduced a filing requirement which applies to Ultimate Parent Entities of MNE Groups above a certain threshold and which requires inclusion of all constituent entities.

9. The Faroe Islands legislation specifies that the threshold requirement applies to the turnover of an MNE group in the reporting year, rather than turnover over of the year before the reporting year as required by the standard.

10. It is recommended that the Faroe Islands take steps to amend legislation or otherwise clarify that an MNE Group should consider its requirement to file using the turnover for the year before any reporting year for comparison with the threshold.

11. The filing requirement applies to all MNE Groups that are fully taxable in the Faroe Islands. This may not apply for some non-resident entities and may therefore lead to some exemptions from the filing requirement, which are not in line with the standard.

12. It is recommended that the Faroe Islands take steps to amend legislation or otherwise clarify that there are no exemptions from the filing requirement for groups who meet the threshold requirement in the Faroe Islands.

13. It is recommended that the Faroe Islands clarify that the annual consolidated group revenue threshold calculation rule applies in line with the OECD guidance on currency fluctuations in respect of an MNE Group whose Ultimate Parent Entity is located in a jurisdiction other than the Faroe Islands.

(b) Scope and timing of parent entity filing

14. Primary legislation in the Faroe Islands sets a filing deadline within 12 months after the end of the reporting year but secondary legislation appears to set a deadline of the end of the reporting year itself.

15. It is recommended that the Faroe Islands take steps to amend legislation or otherwise clarify that a CbC report should be filed within 12 months of the end of the reporting period.

(c) Limitation on local filing obligation

16. The Faroe Islands has introduced local filing requirements, which apply to reporting fiscal years commencing on or after 20 December 2019.

17. No inconsistencies were identified with respect to the limitation on local filing obligations.

(d) Limitation on local filing in case of surrogate filing

18. The Faroe Islands' local filing requirements will not apply if there is surrogate filing in another jurisdiction.

19. No inconsistencies were identified with respect to the limitation on local filing obligations in the case of surrogate filing.

(e) Effective implementation

20. The Faroe Islands has provisions to apply a penalty to ensure compliance with the filing requirement but does not have a mechanism to check that all Ultimate Parent Entities and Surrogate Parent Entities that are required to file do so.

21. It is recommended that the Faroe Islands take steps to implement procedures to ensure effective implementation of the filing requirement.

Conclusion

22. The Faroe Islands implementation of the Action 13 minimum standard meets all the applicable terms of reference (OECD, 2017[3]) relating to the domestic legal and administrative framework, with the exceptions that:

- It is recommended that the Faroe Islands take steps to amend legislation or otherwise clarify that an MNE Group should consider its requirement to file using the turnover for the year before any reporting year for comparison with the threshold.
- It is recommended that the Faroe Islands take steps to amend legislation or otherwise clarify that there are no exemptions from the filing requirement for groups who meet the threshold requirement in the Faroe Islands.
- It is recommended that the Faroe Islands take steps to amend legislation or otherwise clarify that a CbC report should be filed within 12 months of the end of the reporting period the report applies to.
- It is recommended that the Faroe Islands take steps to implement procedures to ensure effective implementation of the filing requirement.
- It is recommended that the Faroe Islands clarify that the annual consolidated group revenue threshold calculation rule applies in line with the OECD guidance on currency fluctuations in respect of an MNE Group whose Ultimate Parent Entity is located in a jurisdiction other than the Faroe Islands.

Part B: The exchange of information framework

(a) Exchange of information framework

23. As of 31 March 2020, Faroe Islands has no bilateral relationships in place for the exchange of CbC reports. It is recommended that Faroe Islands take steps to have qualifying competent authority agreements in effect with jurisdictions of the Inclusive Framework that meet the confidentiality, consistency and appropriate use conditions and with which Faroe Islands has an international exchange of information agreement in effect that allows for the automatic exchange of tax information.

(b) Content of information exchanged

24. Faroe Islands does not have processes or written procedures in place that are intended to ensure that each of the mandatory fields of information required in the CbC reporting template are present in the information exchanged.

(c) Completeness of exchanges

25. Faroe Islands does not have processes or written procedures in place that are intended to ensure that CbC reports are exchanged with all tax jurisdictions listed in Table 1 of a CbC report with which it should exchange information as per the relevant QCAA.

(d) Timeliness of exchanges

26. Faroe Islands does not have processes or written procedures in place that are intended to ensure that the information to be exchanged is transmitted to the relevant jurisdictions in accordance with the timelines provided for in the relevant QCAAs.

(e) Temporary suspension of exchange or termination of QCAA

27. Faroe Islands does not have processes or written procedures in place that are intended to ensure that a temporary suspension of the exchange of information or termination of a relevant QCAA would be carried out only as per the conditions set out in the relevant QCAA.

(f) Consultation with other Competent Authority before determining systemic failure or significant non-compliance

28. Faroe Islands does not have processes or written procedures in place that are intended to ensure that its Competent Authority consults with the other Competent Authority before making a determination of systemic failure or significant non-compliance with the terms of the relevant QCAA by that other Competent Authority.

(g) Format for information exchange

29. Faroe Islands has not confirmed the format that will be used for the international exchange of CbC reports.

(h) Method for transmission

30. Faroe Islands has not confirmed the mechanism that it will use to exchange CbC reports.

Conclusion

31. It is recommended that Faroe Islands take steps to have qualifying competent authority agreements in effect with jurisdictions of the Inclusive Framework that meet the confidentiality, consistency and appropriate use conditions and with which Faroe Islands has an international exchange of information agreement in effect that allows for the automatic exchange of tax information.

32. It is recommended that Faroe Islands take steps to implement processes or written procedures to ensure that the exchange of information is conducted in a manner consistent with the terms of reference (OECD, 2017[3]) relating to the exchange of information framework ahead of its first exchanges of information.

Part C: Appropriate use

Appropriate use

33. Faroe Islands does not yet have measures in place relating to appropriate use.

34. It is recommended that Faroe Islands take steps to have measures in place relating to appropriate use ahead of the first exchanges of information remains in place.

Conclusion

35. It is recommended that Faroe Islands take steps to ensure that the appropriate use condition is met ahead of its first exchanges of information.

Summary of recommendations on the implementation of Country-by-Country Reporting

Aspect of the implementation that should be improved		Recommendation for improvement
Part A	Domestic legal and administrative framework	It is recommended that the Faroe Islands take steps to amend legislation or otherwise clarify that an MNE Group should consider its requirement to file using the turnover for the year before any reporting year for comparison with the threshold. It is recommended that the Faroe Islands take steps to amend legislation or otherwise clarify that there are no exemptions from the filing requirement for groups who meet the threshold requirement in the Faroe Islands. It is recommended that the Faroe Islands take steps to amend legislation or otherwise clarify that a CbC report should be filed within 12 months of the end of the reporting period the report applies to. It is recommended that the Faroe Islands take steps to implement procedures to ensure effective implementation of the filing requirement. It is recommended that the Faroe Islands clarify that the annual consolidated group revenue threshold calculation rule applies in line with the OECD guidance on currency fluctuations in respect of an MNE Group whose Ultimate Parent Entity is located in a jurisdiction other than the Faroe Islands.
Part B	Exchange of information framework	It is recommended that Faroe Islands take steps to put in place an exchange of information framework that allows Automatic Exchange of Information and have QCAAs in effect with jurisdictions of the Inclusive Framework which meet the confidentiality, consistency and appropriate use prerequisites and with which Faroe Islands has an international exchange of information agreement in effect that allows for the automatic exchange of tax information.
Part B	Exchange of information framework	It is recommended that Faroe Islands take steps to implement the necessary processes or written procedures to ensure that the exchange of information is conducted in a manner consistent with the terms of reference relating to the exchange of information framework.
Part C	Appropriate use	It is recommended that Faroe Islands take steps to ensure that the appropriate use condition is met ahead of the first exchanges of information.

References

OECD (2017), *Terms of reference for the conduct of peer review of the Action 13 minimum standard on country-by-country reporting*, OECD Publishing, https://www.oecd.org/tax/beps/beps-action-13-on-country-by-country-reporting-peer-review-documents.pdf. [3]

Finland

1. Finland was reviewed as part of the 2017/2018 and the 2018/2019 peer reviews. This report is supplementary to those previous reports (OECD, 2019[1]) (OECD, 2018[2]).

2. The first filing obligation for a CbC report in Finland applies to reporting fiscal years commencing on or after 1 January 2016.

Summary of key findings

3. Finland's implementation of the Action 13 minimum standard meets all applicable terms of reference (OECD, 2017[3]).

Part A: The domestic legal and administrative framework

4. Finland has legislation in place for implementing the BEPS Action 13 minimum standard establishing the necessary requirements.

(a) Parent entity filing obligation

5. No changes were identified.

(b) Scope and timing of parent entity filing

6. No changes were identified.

(c) Limitation on local filing obligation

7. No changes were identified.

(d) Limitation on local filing in case of surrogate filing

8. No changes were identified.

(e) Effective implementation

9. No changes were identified.

Conclusion

10. Finland meets all the terms of reference (OECD, 2017[3]) relating to the domestic legal and administrative framework.

Part B: The exchange of information framework

(a) Exchange of information framework

11. As of 31 March 2020, Finland has 62 bilateral relationships in place for the exchange of CbC reports, including those activated under the CbC MCAA, under bilateral CAAs and under the EU Council Directive (2016/881/EU). Within the context of its international exchange of information agreements that

allow automatic exchange of information, Finland has taken steps to have qualifying competent authority agreements in effect with jurisdictions of the Inclusive Framework that meet the confidentiality, consistency and appropriate use conditions.[1] Regarding Finland's exchange of information framework, no inconsistencies with the terms of reference were identified.

(b) Content of information exchanged

12. No changes were identified.

(c) Completeness of exchanges

13. No changes were identified.

(d) Timeliness of exchanges

14. No changes were identified.

(e) Temporary suspension of exchange or termination of QCAA

15. No changes were identified.

(f) Consultation with other Competent Authority before determining systemic failure or significant non-compliance

16. No changes were identified.

(g) Format for information exchange

17. No changes were identified.

(h) Method for transmission

18. No changes were identified.

Conclusion

19. Finland meets all the terms of reference regarding the exchange of information.

Part C: Appropriate use

Appropriate use

20. No changes were identified.

Conclusion

21. Finland meets all the terms of reference relating to appropriate use of CbC reports.

Summary of recommendations on the implementation of Country-by-Country Reporting

Aspect of the implementation that should be improved		Recommendation for improvement
Part A	Domestic legal and administrative framework	-
Part B	Exchange of information framework	-
Part C	Appropriate use	-

References

OECD (2019), *Country-by-Country Reporting – Compilation of Peer Review Reports (Phase 2): Inclusive Framework on BEPS: Action 13*, OECD/G20 Base Erosion and Profit Shifting Project, OECD Publishing, Paris, https://dx.doi.org/10.1787/f9bf1157-en. [1]

OECD (2018), *Country-by-Country Reporting – Compilation of Peer Review Reports (Phase 1): Inclusive Framework on BEPS: Action 13*, OECD/G20 Base Erosion and Profit Shifting Project, OECD Publishing, Paris, https://dx.doi.org/10.1787/9789264300057-en. [2]

OECD (2017), *Terms of reference for the conduct of peer review of the Action 13 minimum standard on country-by-country reporting*, OECD Publishing, https://www.oecd.org/tax/beps/beps-action-13-on-country-by-country-reporting-peer-review-documents.pdf. [3]

Note

[1] No inconsistency with the terms of reference will be identified where a QCAA is not in effect with one or more jurisdictions of the Inclusive Framework that meet the confidentiality, consistency and appropriate use conditions, but this is due to circumstances that are not under the control of the reviewed jurisdiction. This may include, for example, where the other jurisdiction intends to exchange CbC reports using the MCAA but it does not have the Convention in effect for the relevant fiscal period, or where the other jurisdiction has declined to have a QCAA in effect with the reviewed jurisdiction.

France

1. France was reviewed as part of the 2017/2018 and the 2018/2019 peer reviews. This report is supplementary to those previous reports (OECD, 2019[1]) (OECD, 2018[2]).

2. The first filing obligation for a CbC report in France commences in respect of fiscal years commencing on or after 1 January 2016.

Summary of key findings

3. France's implementation of the Action 13 minimum standard meets all applicable terms of reference, except for the following:

- It is recommended that France introduce a provision which would have an equivalent effect as the "deemed listing provision", i.e. ensuring that all entities that are not legally required to prepare Consolidated Financial Statements (whether under commercial / company law, or under regulations governing the relevant stock exchange / market, or other) be included in the scope of the parent entity filing obligation.
- It is recommended that France ensure that local filing only occurs in the circumstances contained in the terms of reference (OECD, 2017[3]).

Part A: The domestic legal and administrative framework

4. France has legislation in place for implementing the BEPS Action 13 minimum standard.

(a) Parent entity filing obligation

5. It is recommended that France to complete the definition of an "Ultimate Parent Entity" in a manner consistent with the terms of reference, by introducing a provision which would have an equivalent effect as the "deemed listing provision" remains in place. This recommendation remains unchanged since the 2017/2018 peer review. France's 2017/2018 peer review also included three monitoring point on the parent entity filing obligation.

(b) Scope and timing of parent entity filing

6. No changes were identified.

(c) Limitation on local filing obligation

7. It is recommended that France to ensure that local filing only occurs in the circumstances permitted under the minimum standard and to prevent local filing in the absence on an international agreement remains in place. This recommendation remains unchanged since the 2017/2018 peer review. France's 2017/2018 peer review also included a monitoring point on the limitation on local filing obligation that remains in place.[1]

(d) Limitation on local filing in case of surrogate filing

8. No changes were identified.

(e) Effective implementation

9. No changes were identified.

Conclusion

10. France's implementation of the Action 13 minimum standard meets all applicable terms of reference, except for the following:

- It is recommended that France introduce a provision which would have an equivalent effect as the "deemed listing provision", i.e. ensuring that all entities that are not legally required to prepare Consolidated Financial Statements (whether under commercial / company law, or under regulations governing the relevant stock exchange / market, or other) be included in the scope of the parent entity filing obligation. This recommendation remains unchanged since the 2017/2018 peer review.
- It is recommended that France ensure that local filing only occurs in the circumstances contained in the terms of reference. This recommendation remains unchanged since the 2017/2018 peer review.

Part B: The exchange of information framework

(a) Exchange of information framework

11. As of 31 March 2020, France has 67 bilateral relationships, including those activated under the CbC MCAA and under the EU Council Directive (2016/881/EU). Within the context of its international exchange of information agreements that allow automatic exchange of information, France has taken steps to have Qualifying Competent Authority agreements in effect with jurisdictions of the Inclusive Framework that meet the confidentiality, consistency and appropriate use conditions. Regarding France's exchange of information framework, no inconsistencies with the terms of reference were identified.

(b) Content of information exchanged

12. No changes were identified.

(c) Completeness of exchanges

13. No changes were identified.

(d) Timeliness of exchanges

14. No changes were identified.

(e) Temporary suspension of exchange or termination of QCAA

15. No changes were identified.

(f) Consultation with other Competent Authority before determining systemic failure or significant non-compliance

16. No changes were identified.

(g) Format for information exchange

17. No changes were identified.

(h) Method for transmission

18. No changes were identified.

Conclusion

19. France meets all the terms of reference regarding the exchange of information.

Part C: Appropriate use

Appropriate use

20. No changes were identified.

Conclusion

21. France meets all the terms of reference relating to appropriate use of CbC reports.

Summary of recommendations on the implementation of Country-by-Country Reporting

Aspect of the implementation that should be improved		Recommendation for improvement
Part A	Domestic legal and administrative framework – definition of an Ultimate Parent Entity	It is recommended that France introduce a provision which would have an equivalent effect as the "deemed listing provision", i.e. ensuring that all entities that are not legally required to prepare Consolidated Financial Statements (whether under commercial / company law, or under regulations governing the relevant stock exchange / market, or other) be included in the scope of the parent entity filing obligation.
Part A	Domestic legal and administrative framework – limitation on local filing obligation	It is recommended that France ensure that local filing only occurs in the circumstances contained in the terms of reference.
Part B	Exchange of information framework	-
Part C	Appropriate use	-

References

OECD (2019), *Country-by-Country Reporting – Compilation of Peer Review Reports (Phase 2): Inclusive Framework on BEPS: Action 13*, OECD/G20 Base Erosion and Profit Shifting Project, OECD Publishing, Paris, https://dx.doi.org/10.1787/f9bf1157-en. [1]

OECD (2018), *Country-by-Country Reporting – Compilation of Peer Review Reports (Phase 1): Inclusive Framework on BEPS: Action 13*, OECD/G20 Base Erosion and Profit Shifting Project, OECD Publishing, Paris, https://dx.doi.org/10.1787/9789264300057-en. [2]

OECD (2017), *Terms of reference for the conduct of peer review of the Action 13 minimum standard on country-by-country reporting*, OECD Publishing, https://www.oecd.org/tax/beps/beps-action-13-on-country-by-country-reporting-peer-review-documents.pdf. [3]

Note

[1] France's 2017/2018 peer review included a monitoring point with respect to the limitation of local filing to the instances of "Systemic Failure" as defined in paragraph 21 of the terms of reference. France confirms that its legislation implies that the obligations under the CbC MCAA are complied with (in particular the obligation for a prior consultation between Competent Authorities under Section 6 of the CbC MCAA) and will only apply local filing if there is a "Systemic Failure". This monitoring point remains in place.

Gabon

1. Gabon was reviewed as part of the 2017/2018 and the 2018/2019 peer reviews. This report is supplementary to those previous reports (OECD, 2019[1]) (OECD, 2018[2]).

2. The first filing obligation for CbC reporting in Gabon commences in respect of periods commencing on or after 1 January 2017.

Summary of key findings

3. It is recommended that Gabon finalise its requirements particularly to:

- complete or introduce the definitions of "Constituent Entity", "Group" and "MNE Group" which appear to be incomplete or missing, and
- define the requirements on the content of a CbC report.

4. This recommendation remains unchanged since the 2017/2018 peer review.

5. It is recommended that Gabon take steps to have qualifying competent authority agreements in effect with jurisdictions of the Inclusive Framework that meet the confidentiality, consistency and appropriate use conditions and with which Gabon has an international exchange of information agreement in effect that allows for the automatic exchange of tax information. This recommendation remains unchanged since the 2017/2018 peer review.

6. It is recommended that Gabon take steps to implement the necessary processes or written procedures to ensure that the exchange of information is conducted in a manner consistent with the terms of reference relating to the exchange of information framework. This recommendation remains unchanged since the 2018/2019 peer review.

7. It is recommended that Gabon take steps to ensure that the appropriate use condition is met ahead of the first exchanges of CbC reports. This recommendation remain unchanged since the 2017/2018 peer review.

Part A: The domestic legal and administrative framework

8. Gabon has legislation in place to implement the BEPS Action 13 minimum standard.

(a) Parent entity filing obligation

9. No changes were identified.

(b) Scope and timing of parent entity filing

10. No changes were identified.

(c) Limitation on local filing obligation

11. No changes were identified.

(d) Limitation on local filing in case of surrogate filing

12. No changes were identified.

(e) Effective implementation

13. No changes were identified.

Conclusion

14. It is recommended that Gabon finalise its legislation around (i) the definitions of "Constituent Entities", "Group" and "MNE Group" and (ii) the information to be reported in the CbC report). This recommendation remains unchanged since the 2017/2018 peer review.

Part B: The exchange of information framework

(a) Exchange of information framework

15. As of 31 March 2020, Gabon has no bilateral relationships in place for the exchange of CbC reports. It is recommended that Gabon take steps to have qualifying competent authority agreements in effect with jurisdictions of the Inclusive Framework that meet the confidentiality, consistency and appropriate use conditions and with which Gabon has an international exchange of information agreement in effect that allows for the automatic exchange of tax information.

(b) Content of information exchanged

16. No changes were identified.

(c) Completeness of exchanges

17. No changes were identified.

(d) Timeliness of exchanges

18. No changes were identified.

(e) Temporary suspension of exchange or termination of QCAA

19. No changes were identified.

(f) Consultation with other Competent Authority before determining systemic failure or significant non-compliance

20. No changes were identified.

(g) Format for information exchange

21. No changes were identified.

(h) Method for transmission

22. No changes were identified.

Conclusion

23. It is recommended that Gabon take steps to have QCAAs in effect with jurisdictions of the Inclusive Framework which meet the confidentiality, consistency and appropriate use prerequisites and with which Gabon has an international exchange of information agreement in effect that allows for the automatic exchange of tax information. This recommendation remains unchanged since the 2017/2018 peer review.

24. It is recommended that Gabon take steps to implement processes or written procedures to ensure that the exchange of information is conducted in a manner consistent with the terms of reference relating to the exchange of information framework ahead of its first exchanges of information. This recommendation remains unchanged since the 2018/2019 peer review.

Part C: Appropriate use

Appropriate use

25. No changes were identified.

Conclusion

26. The recommendation for Gabon to take steps to ensure that the appropriate use condition is met ahead of its first exchanges of information remains in place.

Summary of recommendations on the implementation of country-by-country reporting

Aspect of the implementation that should be improved		Recommendation for improvement
Part A	Domestic legal and administrative framework	It is recommended that Gabon finalise its domestic legal and administrative framework as soon as possible. Specifically, it is recommended that Gabon: - introduce or complete the definitions of an "MNE Group", "Group" and "Constituent Entity" in a manner consistent with the terms of reference; - publish the administrative circular as soon as possible, prescribing all of, and only, the information as contained in the template in the Action 13 Report.
Part B	Exchange of information framework	It is recommended that Gabon take steps to have qualifying competent authority agreements in effect with jurisdictions of the Inclusive Framework that meet the confidentiality, consistency and appropriate use conditions and with which Gabon has an international exchange of information agreement in effect that allows for the automatic exchange of tax information.
Part B	Exchange of information framework	It is recommended that Gabon take steps to implement the necessary processes or written procedures to ensure that the exchange of information is conducted in a manner consistent with the terms of reference relating to the exchange of information framework.
Part C	Appropriate use	It is recommended that Gabon take steps to ensure that the appropriate use condition is met ahead of the first exchanges of information.

References

OECD (2019), *Country-by-Country Reporting – Compilation of Peer Review Reports (Phase 2): Inclusive Framework on BEPS: Action 13*, OECD/G20 Base Erosion and Profit Shifting Project, OECD Publishing, Paris, https://dx.doi.org/10.1787/f9bf1157-en. [1]

OECD (2018), *Country-by-Country Reporting – Compilation of Peer Review Reports (Phase 1): Inclusive Framework on BEPS: Action 13*, OECD/G20 Base Erosion and Profit Shifting Project, OECD Publishing, Paris, https://dx.doi.org/10.1787/9789264300057-en. [2]

Georgia

1. Georgia was reviewed as part of the 2017/2018 and the 2018/2019 peer reviews. This report is supplementary to those previous reports (OECD, 2019[1]) (OECD, 2018[2]).

2. There is no filing obligation for a CbC report in Georgia yet.

Summary of key findings

3. Georgia does not yet have legislation in place for implementing the BEPS Action 13 minimum standard. It is recommended that Georgia take steps to implement a domestic legal and administrative framework to impose and enforce CbC reporting requirements as soon as possible. This recommendation remains unchanged since the 2017/2018 peer review.

4. It is recommended that Georgia take steps to have QCAAs in effect with jurisdictions of the Inclusive Framework which meet the confidentiality, consistency and appropriate use prerequisites and with which they have an international exchange of information agreement in effect that allows for the automatic exchange of tax information. This recommendation remains unchanged since the 2017/2018 peer review.

5. It is recommended that Georgia take steps to implement processes or written procedures to ensure that the exchange of information is conducted in a manner consistent with the terms of reference (OECD, 2017[3]) relating to the exchange of information framework ahead of the first exchanges of information. This recommendation remains unchanged since the 2018/2019 peer review.

6. It is recommended that Georgia take steps to ensure that the appropriate use condition is met ahead of the first exchanges of information. This recommendation remains unchanged since the 2017/2018 peer review.

Part A: The domestic legal and administrative framework

7. Georgia does not yet have legislation in place for implementing the BEPS Action 13 minimum standard. Georgia indicates that it is in the final stages of amending its Tax Code to provide the legal basis for CbC reporting and estimates that the amendments will come into effect during the year 2019.

(a) Parent entity filing obligation

8. No changes were identified.

(b) Scope and timing of parent entity filing

9. No changes were identified.

(c) Limitation on local filing obligation

10. No changes were identified.

(d) Limitation on local filing in case of surrogate filing

11. No changes were identified.

(e) Effective implementation

12. No changes were identified.

Conclusion

13. It is recommended that Georgia take steps to implement a domestic legal and administrative framework to impose and enforce CbC reporting requirements as soon as possible. This recommendation remains unchanged since the 2017/2018 peer review.

Part B: The exchange of information framework

(a) Exchange of information framework

14. As of 31 March 2020, Georgia has no bilateral relationships in place for the exchange of CbC reports. It is recommended that Georgia take steps to have qualifying competent authority agreements in effect with jurisdictions of the Inclusive Framework that meet the confidentiality, consistency and appropriate use conditions and with which Georgia has an international exchange of information agreement in effect that allows for the automatic exchange of tax information.

(b) Content of information exchanged

15. No changes were identified.

(c) Completeness of exchanges

16. No changes were identified.

(d) Timeliness of exchanges

17. No changes were identified.

(e) Temporary suspension of exchange or termination of QCAA

18. No changes were identified.

(f) Consultation with other Competent Authority before determining systemic failure or significant non-compliance

19. No changes were identified.

(g) Format for information exchange

20. No changes were identified.

(h) Method for transmission

21. No changes were identified.

Conclusion

22. It is recommended that Georgia take steps to have qualifying competent authority agreements in effect with jurisdictions of the Inclusive Framework that meet the confidentiality, consistency and appropriate use conditions and with which Georgia has an international exchange of information agreement in effect that allows for the automatic exchange of tax information. This recommendation remains unchanged since the 2017/2018 peer review.

23. It is recommended that Georgia take steps to implement the necessary processes or written procedures to ensure that the exchange of information is conducted in a manner consistent with the terms of reference relating to the exchange of information framework. This recommendation remains unchanged since the 2018/2019 peer review.

Part C: Appropriate use

Appropriate use

24. No changes were identified.

Conclusion

25. It is recommended that Georgia take steps to ensure that the appropriate use condition is met ahead of its first exchanges of information remains in place. This recommendation remains unchanged since the 2017/2018 peer review.

Summary of recommendations on the implementation of Country-by-Country

Aspect of the implementation that should be improved		Recommendation for improvement
Part A	Domestic legal and administrative framework	It is recommended that Georgia take steps to implement a domestic legal and administrative framework to impose and enforce CbC requirements as soon as possible.
Part B	Exchange of information framework	It is recommended that Georgia take steps to have QCAAs in effect with jurisdictions of the Inclusive Framework which meet the confidentiality, consistency and appropriate use prerequisites and with which they have an international exchange of information agreement in effect that allows for the automatic exchange of tax information.
Part B	Exchange of information framework	It is recommended that Georgia take steps to implement the necessary processes or written procedures to ensure that the exchange of information is conducted in a manner consistent with the terms of reference relating to the exchange of information framework.
Part C	Appropriate use	It is recommended that Georgia take steps to ensure that the appropriate use condition is met ahead of the first exchanges of information.

References

OECD (2019), *Country-by-Country Reporting – Compilation of Peer Review Reports (Phase 2): Inclusive Framework on BEPS: Action 13*, OECD/G20 Base Erosion and Profit Shifting Project, OECD Publishing, Paris, https://dx.doi.org/10.1787/f9bf1157-en. [1]

OECD (2018), *Country-by-Country Reporting – Compilation of Peer Review Reports (Phase 1): Inclusive Framework on BEPS: Action 13*, OECD/G20 Base Erosion and Profit Shifting Project, OECD Publishing, Paris, https://dx.doi.org/10.1787/9789264300057-en. [2]

OECD (2017), *Terms of reference for the conduct of peer review of the Action 13 minimum standard on country-by-country reporting*, OECD Publishing, https://www.oecd.org/tax/beps/beps-action-13-on-country-by-country-reporting-peer-review-documents.pdf. [3]

Germany

1. Germany was reviewed as part of the 2017/2018 and the 2018/2019 peer reviews. This report is supplementary to those previous reports (OECD, 2019[1]) (OECD, 2018[2]).

2. The first filing obligation for a CbC report in Germany applies in respect of reporting fiscal years commencing on or after 1 January 2016.

Summary of key findings

3. Germany's implementation of the Action 13 minimum standard meets all applicable terms of reference (OECD, 2017[3]).

Part A: The domestic legal and administrative framework

4. Germany has legislation in place to implement the BEPS Action 13 minimum standard.

(a) Parent entity filing obligation

5. No changes were identified.

(b) Scope and timing of parent entity filing

6. No changes were identified.

(c) Limitation on local filing obligation

7. Germany's 2018/2019 peer review included a monitoring point on Germany's intention to publish guidance externally to clarify its local filing requirements. This has now been published and the monitoring point is removed.

(d) Limitation on local filing in case of surrogate filing

8. No changes were identified.

(e) Effective implementation

9. No changes were identified.

Conclusion

10. Germany meets all the terms of reference relating to the domestic legal and administrative framework.

Part B: The exchange of information framework

(a) Exchange of information framework

11. As of 31 March 2020, Germany has 67 bilateral relationships in place for the exchange of CbC reports, including those activated under the CbC MCAA, under bilateral CAAs and under the EU Council Directive (2016/881/EU). Within the context of its international exchange of information agreements that

allow automatic exchange of tax information, Germany has taken steps to have qualifying competent authority agreements in effect with jurisdictions of the Inclusive Framework that currently meet the confidentiality, consistency and appropriate use conditions. Regarding Germany's exchange of information framework, no inconsistencies with the terms of reference were identified.[1]

(b) Content of information exchanged

12. No changes were identified.

(c) Completeness of exchanges

13. No changes were identified.

(d) Timeliness of exchanges

14. No changes were identified.

(e) Temporary suspension of exchange or termination of QCAA

15. No changes were identified.

(f) Consultation with other Competent Authority before determining systemic failure or significant non-compliance

16. No changes were identified.

(g) Format for information exchange

17. No changes were identified.

(h) Method for transmission

18. No changes were identified.

Conclusion

19. Germany meets all the terms of reference regarding the exchange of information.

Part C: Appropriate use

Appropriate use

20. No changes were identified.

Conclusion

21. Germany meets all the terms of reference relating to appropriate use of CbC reports.

Summary of recommendations on the implementation of country-by-country reporting

Aspect of the implementation that should be improved		Recommendation for improvement
Part A	Domestic legal and administrative framework – limitation on local filing obligation	-
Part B	Exchange of information framework	-
Part C	Appropriate use	-

References

OECD (2019), *Country-by-Country Reporting – Compilation of Peer Review Reports (Phase 2): Inclusive Framework on BEPS: Action 13*, OECD/G20 Base Erosion and Profit Shifting Project, OECD Publishing, Paris, https://dx.doi.org/10.1787/f9bf1157-en. [1]

OECD (2018), *Country-by-Country Reporting – Compilation of Peer Review Reports (Phase 1): Inclusive Framework on BEPS: Action 13*, OECD/G20 Base Erosion and Profit Shifting Project, OECD Publishing, Paris, https://dx.doi.org/10.1787/9789264300057-en. [2]

OECD (2017), *Terms of reference for the conduct of peer review of the Action 13 minimum standard on country-by-country reporting*, OECD Publishing, https://www.oecd.org/tax/beps/beps-action-13-on-country-by-country-reporting-peer-review-documents.pdf. [3]

Note

[1] No inconsistency with the terms of reference will be identified where a QCAA is not in effect with one or more jurisdictions of the Inclusive Framework that meet the confidentiality, consistency and appropriate use conditions, but this is due to circumstances that are not under the control of the reviewed jurisdiction. This may include, for example, where the other jurisdiction intends to exchange CbC reports using the MCAA but it does not have the Convention in effect for the relevant fiscal period, or where the other jurisdiction has declined to have a QCAA in effect with the reviewed jurisdiction.

Gibraltar

1. This report is Gibraltar's first annual peer review report. Consistent with the methodology this report covers: (i) the domestic legal and administrative framework, (ii) the exchange of information framework as well as (iii) the appropriate use of CbC reports.

2. The first filing obligation for a CbC report in Gibraltar applies to reporting fiscal years beginning on or after 1 January 2016.

Summary of key findings

3. Gibraltar's implementation of the Action 13 minimum standard meets all the applicable terms of reference (OECD, 2017[3]).

Part A: The domestic legal and administrative framework

4. Gibraltar has published legislation that imposes and enforces a CbC filing requirement for fiscal years commencing on or after 1 January 2016.[1]

(a) Parent entity filing obligation

5. Gibraltar has introduced a filing requirement which applies to all Ultimate Parent Entities of MNE Groups above a certain threshold and which requires inclusion of all constituent entities.

6. No inconsistencies were identified.

(b) Scope and timing of parent entity filing

7. The first filing requirements for MNE Groups in Gibraltar enforce a CbC filing requirement for fiscal years commencing on or after 1 January 2016 and filing is required 12 months after the reporting year end.

8. No inconsistencies were identified.

(c) Limitation on local filing obligation

9. Gibraltar has introduced a local filing requirement which applied to reporting fiscal years commencing on or after 1 January 2017.

10. No inconsistencies were identified.

(d) Limitation on local filing in case of surrogate filing

11. Gibraltar's local filing requirements will not apply if there is surrogate filing in another jurisdiction.

12. No inconsistencies were identified.

(e) Effective implementation

13. Gibraltar has notification and penalty requirements to ensure compliance with CbC reporting through its primary legislation.

14. No inconsistencies were identified.

Conclusion

15. Gibraltar's legal framework meets all the terms of reference. .

Part B: The exchange of information framework

(a) Exchange of information framework

16. As of 31 March 2020, Gibraltar has 52 bilateral relationships in place, including those activated under the CbC MCAA, a bilateral CAA, and the EU Council Directive (2016/881/EU). Within the context of its international exchange of information agreements that allow automatic exchange of information, Gibraltar has taken steps to have qualifying competent authority agreements in effect with jurisdictions of the Inclusive Framework that meet the confidentiality, consistency and appropriate use conditions.[2] Regarding Gibraltar's exchange of information framework, no inconsistencies with the terms of reference were identified.

(b) Content of information exchanged

17. Gibraltar has processes in place that are intended to ensure that each of the mandatory fields of information as required in the CbC template are present in the information exchanged.

18. No inconsistencies were identified.

(c) Completeness of exchanges

19. Gibraltar has processes or written procedures in place that are intended to ensure that CbC reports are exchanged with all tax jurisdictions listed in Table 1 of a CbC report with which it should exchange information as per the relevant QCAA.

20. No inconsistencies were identified.

(d) Timeliness of exchanges

21. Gibraltar has processes or written procedures in place that are intended to ensure that the information to be exchanged is transmitted to the relevant jurisdictions in accordance with the timelines provided for in the relevant QCAA.

22. No inconsistencies were identified.

(e) Temporary suspension of exchange or termination of QCAA

23. Gibraltar has processes or written procedures in place that are intended to ensure that a temporary suspension of the exchange of information or termination of a relevant QCAA would be carried out only as per the conditions set out in the relevant QCAA.

24. No inconsistencies were identified.

(f) Consultation with other Competent Authority before determining systemic failure or significant non-compliance

25. Gibraltar has processes or written procedures in place that are intended to ensure that its Competent Authority consults with the other Competent Authority before making a determination of systemic failure or significant non-compliance with the terms of the relevant QCAA by that other Competent Authority.

26. No inconsistencies were identified.

(g) Format for information exchange

27. Gibraltar confirms that it uses the OECD XML Schema and User Guide (OECD, 2017[4]) for the international exchange of CbC reports.

(h) Method for transmission

28. Gibraltar uses the Common Transmission System to exchange CbC reports.[3]

Conclusion

29. Gibraltar meets all the terms of reference regarding the exchange of information.

Part C: Appropriate use

Appropriate use

30. Gibraltar has provided information to confirm that it has the processes required to meet the appropriate use condition

Conclusion

31. Gibraltar meets all of the terms of reference with regard to appropriate use of CbC reports.

Summary of recommendations on the implementation of Country-by-Country Reporting

Aspect of the implementation that should be improved		Recommendation for improvement
Part A	Domestic legal and administrative framework	-
Part B	Exchange of information framework	-
Part C	Appropriate use	-

References

OECD (2017), *Terms of reference for the conduct of peer review of the Action 13 minimum standard on country-by-country reporting*, OECD Publishing, https://www.oecd.org/tax/beps/beps-action-13-on-country-by-country-reporting-peer-review-documents.pdf. [3]

Notes

[1] https://www.gibraltarlaws.gov.gi/articles/2010-21o.pdf (accessed on 24 August 2020).

[2] No inconsistency with the terms of reference will be identified where a QCAA is not in effect with one or more jurisdictions of the Inclusive Framework that meet the confidentiality, consistency and appropriate use conditions, but this is due to circumstances that are not under the control of the reviewed jurisdiction. This may include, for example, where the other jurisdiction intends to exchange CbC reports using the MCAA but it does not have the Convention in effect for the relevant fiscal period, or where the other jurisdiction has declined to have a QCAA in effect with the reviewed jurisdiction.

[3] Countries exchanging under the EU Council Directive (2016/881/EU) use the Common Communication Network (CCN).

Greece

1. Greece was reviewed as part of the 2017/2018 and the 2018/2019 peer reviews. This report is supplementary to those previous reports (OECD, 2019[1]) (OECD, 2018[2]).

2. The first filing obligation for a CbC report in Greece applies to reporting fiscal years commencing on or after 1 January 2016.

Summary of key findings

3. Greece's implementation of the Action 13 minimum standard meets all applicable terms of reference (OECD, 2017[3]).

Part A: The domestic legal and administrative framework

4. Greece has legislation in place for implementing the BEPS Action 13 minimum standard.

(a) Parent entity filing obligation

5. No changes were identified.

(b) Scope and timing of parent entity filing

6. No changes were identified.

(c) Limitation on local filing obligation

7. No changes were identified.

(d) Limitation on local filing in case of surrogate filing

8. No changes were identified.

(e) Effective implementation

9. No changes were identified.[1]

Conclusion

10. Greece meets all the terms of reference relating to the domestic legal and administrative framework.

Part B: The exchange of information framework

(a) Exchange of information framework

11. As of 31 March 2020, Greece has 75 bilateral relationships in place, including those activated under the CbC MCAA, under bilateral CAAs and under the EU Council Directive (2016/881/EU). Within the context of its international exchange of information agreements that allow automatic exchange of information, Greece has taken steps to have qualifying competent authority agreements in effect with jurisdictions of the Inclusive Framework that meet the confidentiality, consistency and appropriate use

conditions.[2] Regarding Greece's exchange of information framework, no inconsistencies with the terms of reference were identified.

(b) Content of information exchanged

12. No changes were identified.

(c) Completeness of exchanges

13. No changes were identified.

(d) Timeliness of exchanges

14. No changes were identified.

(e) Temporary suspension of exchange or termination of QCAA

15. No changes were identified.

(f) Consultation with other Competent Authority before determining systemic failure or significant non-compliance

16. No changes were identified.

(g) Format for information exchange

17. No changes were identified.

(h) Method for transmission

18. No changes were identified.

Conclusion

19. Greece meets all the terms of reference regarding the exchange of information.

Part C: Appropriate use

Appropriate use

20. No changes were identified.

Conclusion

21. Greece meets all the terms of reference relating to appropriate use of CbC reports.

Summary of recommendations on the implementation of country-by-country reporting

Aspect of the implementation that should be improved		Recommendation for improvement
Part A	Domestic legal and administrative framework	-
Part B	Exchange of information framework	-
Part C	Appropriate use	-

References

OECD (2019), *Country-by-Country Reporting – Compilation of Peer Review Reports (Phase 2): Inclusive Framework on BEPS: Action 13*, OECD/G20 Base Erosion and Profit Shifting Project, OECD Publishing, Paris, https://dx.doi.org/10.1787/f9bf1157-en. [1]

OECD (2018), *Country-by-Country Reporting – Compilation of Peer Review Reports (Phase 1): Inclusive Framework on BEPS: Action 13*, OECD/G20 Base Erosion and Profit Shifting Project, OECD Publishing, Paris, https://dx.doi.org/10.1787/9789264300057-en. [2]

OECD (2017), *Terms of reference for the conduct of peer review of the Action 13 minimum standard on country-by-country reporting*, OECD Publishing, https://www.oecd.org/tax/beps/beps-action-13-on-country-by-country-reporting-peer-review-documents.pdf. [3]

Notes

[1] Greece's 2017/2018 peer review included a general monitoring point relating to a specific process to that would allow to take appropriate measures in case Greece is notified by another jurisdiction that such other jurisdiction has reason to believe that an error may have led to incorrect or incomplete information reporting by a Reporting Entity or that there is non-compliance of a Reporting Entity with respect to its obligation to file a CbC report. This monitoring point remains in place.

[2] No inconsistency with the terms of reference will be identified where a QCAA is not in effect with one or more jurisdictions of the Inclusive Framework that meet the confidentiality, consistency and appropriate use conditions, but this is due to circumstances that are not under the control of the reviewed jurisdiction. This may include, for example, where the other jurisdiction intends to exchange CbC reports using the MCAA but it does not have the Convention in effect for the relevant fiscal period, or where the other jurisdiction has declined to have a QCAA in effect with the reviewed jurisdiction.

Note by Turkey

The information in this document with reference to "Cyprus" relates to the southern part of the Island. There is no single authority representing both Turkish and Greek Cypriot people on the Island. Turkey recognises the Turkish Republic of Northern Cyprus. Until a lasting and equitable solution is found within the context of the United Nations, Turkey shall preserve its position concerning the "Cyprus issue".

Note by all the European Union Member States of the OECD and the European Union

The Republic of Cyprus is recognised by all members of the United Nations with the exception of Turkey. The information in this document relates to the area under the effective control of the Government of the Republic of Cyprus.

Greenland

1. This report is Greenland's first annual peer review report. Consistent with the agreed methodology this report covers: (i) the domestic legal and administrative framework, (ii) the exchange of information framework as well as (iii) the appropriate use of CbC reports.

2. The first filing obligation for a CbC report in Greenland commences in respect of fiscal periods commencing on or after 1 January 2019.

Summary of key findings

3. Greenland has legislation to impose and enforce a CbC filing requirement that meets all of the terms of reference, with the exception that:

- It is recommended that Greenland clarify that the annual consolidated group revenue threshold calculation rule applies in line with the OECD guidance on currency fluctuations in respect of an MNE Group whose Ultimate Parent Entity is located in a jurisdiction other than Greenland.

4. It is recommended that Greenland take steps to put in place an exchange of information framework that allows Automatic Exchange of Information and have QCAAs in effect with jurisdictions of the Inclusive Framework which meet the confidentiality, consistency and appropriate use prerequisites and with which Greenland has an international exchange of information agreement in effect that allows for the automatic exchange of tax information.

5. It is recommended that Greenland take steps to implement processes or written procedures to ensure that the exchange of information is conducted in a manner consistent with the terms of reference (OECD, 2017[3]) relating to the exchange of information framework ahead of the first exchanges of information.

6. It is recommended that Greenland take steps to ensure that the appropriate use condition is met ahead of the first exchanges of information.

Part A: The domestic legal and administrative framework

7. Greenland has legislation in place for implementing the BEPS Action 13 minimum standard.[1]

(a) Parent entity filing obligation

8. Greenland has introduced a filing requirement which applies to all Ultimate Parent Entities of MNE Groups above a certain threshold and which requires inclusion of all constituent entities.

With respect to the annual consolidated group revenue threshold where the MNE Group draws up, or would draw up, its Consolidated Financial Statements in a currency other than that specified by Greenland, the reference to Greenland's threshold has the effect as if it were a reference to the equivalent in that currency at the average exchange rate for the accounting period. While this provision would not create an issue for MNE Groups whose Ultimate Parent Entity is a tax resident in Greenland, it may be incompatible with the guidance on currency fluctuations for MNE Groups whose Ultimate Parent Entity is located in another jurisdiction, if local filing requirements were applied in respect of a Constituent Entity (which is a Greenland tax resident) of an MNE Group which does not reach the threshold as determined in the jurisdiction of the Ultimate Parent Entity of such a Group

9. This is an unintended consequence of having a local filing requirement and it its therefore recommended that Greenland clarify that the annual consolidated group revenue threshold calculation rule applies in line with the OECD guidance on currency fluctuations in respect of an MNE Group whose Ultimate Parent Entity is located in a jurisdiction other than Greenland.

10. No other inconsistencies were identified

(b) Scope and timing of parent entity filing

11. The first filing requirements for MNE Groups in Greenland enforce a CbC filing requirement for fiscal years commencing on or after 1 January 2019 and filing is required 12 months after the reporting year end.

12. No inconsistencies were identified.

(c) Limitation on local filing obligations

13. Greenland has introduced a local filing requirement which is in line with the terms of reference with regard to the circumstances in which a local filing requirement can be imposed.

14. No inconsistencies were identified.

(d) Limitation on local filing in case of surrogate filing

15. Greenland's local filing requirements will not apply if there is surrogate filing in another jurisdiction.

16. No inconsistencies were identified.

(e) Effective implementation

17. Greenland has systems to ensure effective implementation of the CbC filing requirement which include a notification requirement and a penalty regime in the case of late, inaccurate or non-filing of CbC reports.

Conclusion

18. Greenland has legislation to impose and enforce a CbC filing requirement that meets all of the terms of reference, with the exception that:

- It is recommended that Greenland clarify that the annual consolidated group revenue threshold calculation rule applies in line with the OECD guidance on currency fluctuations in respect of an MNE Group whose Ultimate Parent Entity is located in a jurisdiction other than Greenland.

Part B: The exchange of information framework

(a) Exchange of information framework

19. As of 31 March 2020, Greenland has no bilateral relationships in place for the exchange of CbC reports. It is recommended that Greenland take steps to have qualifying competent authority agreements in effect with jurisdictions of the Inclusive Framework that meet the confidentiality, consistency and appropriate use conditions and with which Greenland has an international exchange of information agreement in effect that allows for the automatic exchange of tax information.[2]

(b) Content of information exchanged

20. Greenland does not have processes or written procedures in place that are intended to ensure that each of the mandatory fields of information required in the CbC reporting template are present in the information exchanged.

(c) Completeness of exchanges

21. Greenland does not have processes or written procedures in place that are intended to ensure that CbC reports are exchanged with all tax jurisdictions listed in Table 1 of a CbC report with which it should exchange information as per the relevant QCAA.

(d) Timeliness of exchanges

22. Greenland does not have processes or written procedures in place that are intended to ensure that the information to be exchanged is transmitted to the relevant jurisdictions in accordance with the timelines provided for in the relevant QCAAs.

(e) Temporary suspension of exchange or termination of QCAA

23. Greenland does not have processes or written procedures in place that are intended to ensure that a temporary suspension of the exchange of information or termination of a relevant QCAA would be carried out only as per the conditions set out in the relevant QCAA.

(f) Consultation with other Competent Authority before determining systemic failure or significant non-compliance

24. Greenland does not have processes or written procedures in place that are intended to ensure that its Competent Authority consults with the other Competent Authority before making a determination of systemic failure or significant non-compliance with the terms of the relevant QCAA by that other Competent Authority.

(g) Format for information exchange

25. Greenland has not confirmed the format that will be used for the international exchange of CbC reports.

(h) Method for transmission

26. Greenland has not confirmed the mechanism that it will use to exchange CbC reports.

Conclusion

27. It is recommended that Greenland take steps to put in place an exchange of information framework that allows Automatic Exchange of Information and have QCAAs in effect with jurisdictions of the Inclusive Framework which meet the confidentiality, consistency and appropriate use prerequisites and with which Greenland has an international exchange of information agreement in effect that allows for the automatic exchange of tax information.

28. It is recommended that Greenland take steps to implement processes or written procedures to ensure that the exchange of information is conducted in a manner consistent with the terms of reference (OECD, 2017[3]) relating to the exchange of information framework ahead of the first exchanges of information.

Part C: Appropriate use

Appropriate use

29. Greenland does not yet have measures in place relating to appropriate use.

30. It is recommended that Greenland take steps to have measures in place relating to appropriate use ahead of the first exchanges of information.

Conclusion

31. It is recommended that Greenland take steps to ensure that the appropriate use condition is met ahead of its first exchanges of information.

Summary of recommendations on the implementation of Country-by-Country Reporting

Aspect of the implementation that should be improved		Recommendation for improvement
Part A	Domestic legal and administrative framework	It is recommended that Greenland clarify that the annual consolidated group revenue threshold calculation rule applies in line with the OECD guidance on currency fluctuations in respect of an MNE Group whose Ultimate Parent Entity is located in a jurisdiction other than Greenland
Part B	Exchange of information framework	It is recommended that Greenland take steps to put in place an exchange of information framework that allows Automatic Exchange of Information and have QCAAs in effect with jurisdictions of the Inclusive Framework which meet the confidentiality, consistency and appropriate use prerequisites and with which Greenland has an international exchange of information agreement in effect that allows for the automatic exchange of tax information
Part B	Exchange of information framework	It is recommended that Greenland take steps to implement the necessary processes or written procedures to ensure that the exchange of information is conducted in a manner consistent with the terms of reference relating to the exchange of information framework.
Part C	Appropriate use	It is recommended that Greenland take steps to ensure that the appropriate use condition is met ahead of the first exchanges of information.

Refrences

OECD (2017), *Terms of reference for the conduct of peer review of the Action 13 minimum standard on country-by-country reporting*, OECD Publishing, https://www.oecd.org/tax/beps/beps-action-13-on-country-by-country-reporting-peer-review-documents.pdf. [3]

Notes

[1] The Danish version can be found here: http://lovgivning.gl/lov?rid={7F2072AE-B840-4DC7-9726-17D79B879831} (accessed on 24 August 2020).

The Greenlandic version can be found here: http://inatsisit.gl/Lov?rid=%7b7F2072AE-B840-4DC7-9726-17D79B879831%7d&sc_lang=kl-GL (accessed on 24 August 2020).

[2] No inconsistency with the terms of reference will be identified where a QCAA is not in effect with one or more jurisdictions of the Inclusive Framework that meet the confidentiality, consistency and appropriate use conditions, but this is due to circumstances that are not under the control of the reviewed jurisdiction. This may include, for example, where the other jurisdiction intends to exchange CbC reports using the MCAA but it does not have the Convention in effect for the relevant fiscal period, or where the other jurisdiction has declined to have a QCAA in effect with the reviewed jurisdiction.

Grenada

1. This report is Grenada's first annual peer review report. Consistent with the agreed methodology this report covers: (i) the domestic legal and administrative framework, (ii) the exchange of information framework as well as (iii) the appropriate use of CbC reports.

2. There is no filing obligation for a CbC report in Grenada yet.

Summary of key findings

3. Grenada does not yet have legislation in place for implementing the BEPS Action 13 minimum standard.

4. It is recommended that Grenada take steps to implement a domestic legal and administrative framework to impose and enforce CbC reporting requirements as soon as possible.

5. It is recommended that Grenada take steps to put in place an exchange of information framework that allows automatic exchange of information and have QCAAs in effect with jurisdictions of the Inclusive Framework which meet the confidentiality, consistency and appropriate use prerequisites and with which Grenada has an international exchange of information agreement in effect that allows for the automatic exchange of tax information.

6. It is recommended that Grenada take steps to implement processes or written procedures to ensure that the exchange of information is conducted in a manner consistent with the terms of reference (OECD, 2017[3]) relating to the exchange of information framework ahead of the first exchanges of information.

7. It is recommended that Grenada take steps to ensure that the appropriate use condition is met ahead of the first exchanges of information.

Part A: The domestic legal and administrative framework

8. Grenada does not yet have legislation in place for implementing the BEPS Action 13 minimum standard.

(a) Parent entity filing obligation

(b) Scope and timing of parent entity filing

(c) Limitation on local filing obligation

(d) Limitation on local filing in case of surrogate filing

(e) Effective implementation

Conclusion

9. It is recommended that Grenada take steps to implement a domestic legal and administrative framework to impose and enforce CbC reporting requirements as soon as possible.

Part B: The exchange of information framework

(a) Exchange of information framework

10. As of 31 March 2020, Grenada has no bilateral relationships in place for the exchange of CbC reports. It is recommended that Grenada take steps to have qualifying competent authority agreements in effect with jurisdictions of the Inclusive Framework that meet the confidentiality, consistency and appropriate use conditions and with which Grenada has an international exchange of information agreement in effect that allows for the automatic exchange of tax information.

(b) Content of information exchanged

11. Grenada does not have processes or written procedures in place that are intended to ensure that each of the mandatory fields of information required in the CbC reporting template are present in the information exchanged.

(c) Completeness of exchanges

12. Grenada does not have processes or written procedures in place that are intended to ensure that CbC reports are exchanged with all tax jurisdictions listed in Table 1 of a CbC report with which it should exchange information as per the relevant QCAA.

(d) Timeliness of exchanges

13. Grenada does not have processes or written procedures in place that are intended to ensure that the information to be exchanged is transmitted to the relevant jurisdictions in accordance with the timelines provided for in the relevant QCAAs.

(e) Temporary suspension of exchange or termination of QCAA

14. Grenada does not have processes or written procedures in place that are intended to ensure that a temporary suspension of the exchange of information or termination of a relevant QCAA would be carried out only as per the conditions set out in the relevant QCAA.

(f) Consultation with other Competent Authority before determining systemic failure or significant non-compliance

15. Grenada does not have processes or written procedures in place that are intended to ensure that its Competent Authority consults with the other Competent Authority before making a determination of systemic failure or significant non-compliance with the terms of the relevant QCAA by that other Competent Authority.

(g) Format for information exchange

16. Grenada has not confirmed the format that will be used for the international exchange of CbC reports.

(h) Method for transmission

17. Grenada has not confirmed the mechanism that it will use to exchange CbC reports.

Conclusion

18. It is recommended that Grenada take steps to have qualifying competent authority agreements in effect with jurisdictions of the Inclusive Framework that meet the confidentiality, consistency and

appropriate use conditions and with which Grenada has an international exchange of information agreement in effect that allows for the automatic exchange of tax information.

19. It is recommended that Grenada take steps to implement processes or written procedures to ensure that the exchange of information is conducted in a manner consistent with the terms of reference (OECD, 2017[3]) relating to the exchange of information framework ahead of its first exchanges of information.

Part C: Appropriate use

Appropriate use

20. Grenada does not yet have measures in place relating to appropriate use.

21. It is recommended that Grenada take steps to have measures in place relating to appropriate use ahead of the first exchanges of information remains in place.

Conclusion

22. It is recommended that Grenada take steps to ensure that the appropriate use condition is met ahead of its first exchanges of information.

Summary of recommendations on the implementation of Country-by-Country Reporting

Aspect of the implementation that should be improved		Recommendation for improvement
Part A	Domestic legal and administrative framework	It is recommended that Grenada take steps to implement a domestic legal and administrative framework to impose and enforce CbC requirements as soon as possible.
Part B	Exchange of information framework	It is recommended that Grenada take steps to put in place an exchange of information framework that allows Automatic Exchange of Information and have QCAAs in effect with jurisdictions of the Inclusive Framework which meet the confidentiality, consistency and appropriate use prerequisites and with which Grenada has an international exchange of information agreement in effect that allows for the automatic exchange of tax information.
Part B	Exchange of information framework	It is recommended that Grenada take steps to implement the necessary processes or written procedures to ensure that the exchange of information is conducted in a manner consistent with the terms of reference relating to the exchange of information framework.
Part C	Appropriate use	It is recommended that Grenada take steps to ensure that the appropriate use condition is met ahead of the first exchanges of information.

References

OECD (2017), *Terms of reference for the conduct of peer review of the Action 13 minimum standard on country-by-country reporting*, OECD Publishing, https://www.oecd.org/tax/beps/beps-action-13-on-country-by-country-reporting-peer-review-documents.pdf. [3]

Guernsey

1. Guernsey was reviewed as part of the 2017/2018 and the 2018/2019 peer reviews. This report is supplementary to those previous reports (OECD, 2019[1]) (OECD, 2018[2]).

2. The first filing obligation for a CbC report in Guernsey applies to reporting fiscal years commencing on or after 1 January 2016.

Summary of key findings

3. Guernsey's implementation of the Action 13 minimum standard meets all applicable terms of reference (OECD, 2017[3]).

Part A: The domestic legal and administrative framework

4. Guernsey has legislation in place for implementing the BEPS Action 13 minimum standard.

(a) Parent entity filing obligation

5. No changes were identified.

(b) Scope and timing of parent entity filing

6. No changes were identified.

(c) Limitation on local filing obligation

7. No changes were identified.

(d) Limitation on local filing in case of surrogate filing

8. No changes were identified.

(e) Effective implementation

9. No changes were identified.[1]

Conclusion

10. There is no change to the conclusion in relation to the domestic legal and administration framework for Guernsey since the previous peer review. Guernsey meets all the terms of reference relating to the domestic legal and administrative framework.

Part B: The exchange of information framework

(a) Exchange of information framework

11. As of 31 March 2020, Guernsey has 62 bilateral relationships in place, including those activated under the CbC MCAA and under bilateral CAAs. Within the context of its international exchange of information agreements that allow automatic exchange of information, Guernsey has taken steps to have qualifying competent authority agreements in effect with jurisdictions of the Inclusive Framework that meet

the confidentiality, consistency and appropriate use conditions.[2] Regarding Guernsey's exchange of information framework, no inconsistencies with the terms of reference were identified.

(b) Content of information exchanged

12. No changes were identified.

(c) Completeness of exchanges

13. No changes were identified.

(d) Timeliness of exchanges

14. No changes were identified.

(e) Temporary suspension of exchange or termination of QCAA

15. No changes were identified.

(f) Consultation with other Competent Authority before determining systemic failure or significant non-compliance

16. No changes were identified.

(g) Format for information exchange

17. No changes were identified.

(h) Method for transmission

18. No changes were identified.

Conclusion

19. Guernsey meets all the terms of reference regarding the exchange of information.

Part C: Appropriate use

Appropriate use

20. No changes were identified.

Conclusion

21. Guernsey meets all the terms of reference relating to appropriate use of CbC reports.

Summary of recommendations on the implementation of country-by-country reporting

Aspect of the implementation that should be improved		Recommendation for improvement
Part A	Domestic legal and administrative framework	-
Part B	Exchange of information framework	-
Part C	Appropriate use	-

References

OECD (2019), *Country-by-Country Reporting – Compilation of Peer Review Reports (Phase 2): Inclusive Framework on BEPS: Action 13*, OECD/G20 Base Erosion and Profit Shifting Project, OECD Publishing, Paris, https://dx.doi.org/10.1787/f9bf1157-en. [1]

OECD (2018), *Country-by-Country Reporting – Compilation of Peer Review Reports (Phase 1): Inclusive Framework on BEPS: Action 13*, OECD/G20 Base Erosion and Profit Shifting Project, OECD Publishing, Paris, https://dx.doi.org/10.1787/9789264300057-en. [2]

OECD (2017), *Terms of reference for the conduct of peer review of the Action 13 minimum standard on country-by-country reporting*, OECD Publishing, https://www.oecd.org/tax/beps/beps-action-13-on-country-by-country-reporting-peer-review-documents.pdf. [3]

Notes

[1] Guernsey's 2017/2018 peer review included a general monitoring point relating to a specific process to that would allow to take appropriate measures in case Guernsey is notified by another jurisdiction that such other jurisdiction has reason to believe that an error may have led to incorrect or incomplete information reporting by a Reporting Entity or that there is non-compliance of a Reporting Entity with respect to its obligation to file a CbC report. This monitoring point remains in place.

[2] No inconsistency with the terms of reference will be identified where a QCAA is not in effect with one or more jurisdictions of the Inclusive Framework that meet the confidentiality, consistency and appropriate use conditions, but this is due to circumstances that are not under the control of the reviewed jurisdiction. This may include, for example, where the other jurisdiction intends to exchange CbC reports using the MCAA but it does not have the Convention in effect for the relevant fiscal period, or where the other jurisdiction has declined to have a QCAA in effect with the reviewed jurisdiction.

Haiti

1. Haiti was reviewed as part of the 2017/2018 and the 2018/2019 peer reviews. This report is supplementary to those previous reports (OECD, 2019[1]) (OECD, 2018[2]).

2. There is no filing obligation for a CbC report in Haiti yet.

Summary of key findings

3. Haiti does not yet have legislation in place for implementing the BEPS Action 13 minimum standard. It is recommended that Haiti take steps to implement a domestic legal and administrative framework to impose and enforce CbC reporting requirements as soon as possible. This recommendation remains unchanged since the 2017/2018 peer review.

4. It is recommended that Haiti take steps to have QCAAs in effect with jurisdictions of the Inclusive Framework which meet the confidentiality, consistency and appropriate use prerequisites and with which they have an international exchange of information agreement in effect that allows for the automatic exchange of tax information. This recommendation remains unchanged since the 2017/2018 peer review.

5. It is recommended that Haiti take steps to implement processes or written procedures to ensure that the exchange of information is conducted in a manner consistent with the terms of reference (OECD, 2017[3]) relating to the exchange of information framework ahead of the first exchanges of information. This recommendation remains unchanged since the 2018/2019 peer review.

6. It is recommended that Haiti take steps to ensure that the appropriate use condition is met ahead of the first exchanges of information. This recommendation remains unchanged since the 2017/2018 peer review.

Part A: The domestic legal and administrative framework

7. Haiti does not yet have legislation in place for implementing the BEPS Action 13 minimum standard.[1]

(a) Parent entity filing obligation

(b) Scope and timing of parent entity filing

(c) Limitation on local filing obligation

(d) Limitation on local filing in case of surrogate filing

(e) Effective implementation

Conclusion

8. It is recommended that Haiti take steps to implement a domestic legal and administrative framework to impose and enforce CbC reporting requirements as soon as possible. This recommendation remains unchanged since the 2017/2018 peer review.

Part B: The exchange of information framework

(a) Exchange of information framework

9. As of 31 March 2020, Haiti has no bilateral relationships in place for the exchange of CbC reports. However, it is noted that Haiti does not currently have any international exchange of information agreements in effect that allow for the automatic exchange of tax information. Within the context of Haiti's exchange of information framework, no inconsistencies with the terms of reference were identified. As such, no recommendation is made, but Haiti is encouraged to expand the coverage of its international agreements for the exchange of tax information.

(b) Content of information exchanged

10. No changes were identified.

(c) Completeness of exchanges

11. No changes were identified.

(d) Timeliness of exchanges

12. No changes were identified.

(e) Temporary suspension of exchange or termination of QCAA

13. No changes were identified.

(f) Consultation with other Competent Authority before determining systemic failure or significant non-compliance

14. No changes were identified.

(g) Format for information exchange

15. No changes were identified.

(h) Method for transmission

16. No changes were identified.

Conclusion

17. It is recommended that Haiti to take steps to have QCAAs in effect with jurisdictions of the Inclusive Framework which meet the confidentiality, consistency and appropriate use prerequisites and with which they have an international exchange of information agreement in effect that allows for the automatic exchange of tax information remains in place. This recommendation remains unchanged since the 2017/2018 peer review.

18. It is recommended that Haiti take steps to implement processes or written procedures to ensure that the exchange of information is conducted in a manner consistent with the terms of reference relating to the exchange of information framework ahead of its first exchanges of information. This recommendation remains unchanged since the 2018/2019 peer review.

Part C: Appropriate use

Appropriate use

19. No changes were identified.

Conclusion

20. It is recommended that Haiti to take steps to ensure that the appropriate use condition is met ahead of its first exchanges of information. This recommendation remains unchanged since the 2017/2018 peer review.

Summary of recommendations on the implementation of Country-by-Country Reporting

Aspect of the implementation that should be improved		Recommendation for improvement
Part A	Domestic legal and administrative framework	It is recommended that Haiti take steps to implement a domestic legal and administrative framework to impose and enforce CbC requirements as soon as possible.
Part B	Exchange of information framework	It is recommended that Haiti take steps to have QCAAs in effect with jurisdictions of the Inclusive Framework which meet the confidentiality, consistency and appropriate use prerequisites and with which they have an international exchange of information agreement in effect that allows for the automatic exchange of tax information.
Part B	Exchange of information framework	It is recommended that Haiti take steps to implement the necessary processes or written procedures to ensure that the exchange of information is conducted in a manner consistent with the terms of reference relating to the exchange of information framework.
Part C	Appropriate use	It is recommended that Haiti take steps to ensure that the appropriate use condition is met ahead of the first exchanges of information.

References

OECD (2019), *Country-by-Country Reporting – Compilation of Peer Review Reports (Phase 2): Inclusive Framework on BEPS: Action 13*, OECD/G20 Base Erosion and Profit Shifting Project, OECD Publishing, Paris, https://dx.doi.org/10.1787/f9bf1157-en. [1]

OECD (2018), *Country-by-Country Reporting – Compilation of Peer Review Reports (Phase 1): Inclusive Framework on BEPS: Action 13*, OECD/G20 Base Erosion and Profit Shifting Project, OECD Publishing, Paris, https://dx.doi.org/10.1787/9789264300057-en. [2]

OECD (2017), *Terms of reference for the conduct of peer review of the Action 13 minimum standard on country-by-country reporting*, OECD Publishing, https://www.oecd.org/tax/beps/beps-action-13-on-country-by-country-reporting-peer-review-documents.pdf. [3]

Note

[1] According to the latest information provided, the draft legislation was submitted to the parliamentary budgetary session, but it has not been approved yet.

Hong Kong (China)

1. Hong Kong was reviewed as part of the 2017/2018 and the 2018/2019 peer reviews. This report is supplementary to those previous (OECD, 2019[1]) (OECD, 2018[2]).

2. The filing obligation for a CbC report in Hong Kong applies to reporting fiscal years commencing on or after 1 January 2018. Hong Kong also allows Hong Kong's MNE groups to file a CbC report on a voluntary basis, for reporting fiscal years beginning between 1 January 2016 and 31 December 2017.

Summary of key findings

3. Hong Kong's implementation of the Action 13 minimum standard meets all applicable terms of reference (OECD, 2017[3]).

4. Hong Kong's 2017/2018 peer review included a recommendation that Hong Kong continues to take steps to enable exchanges of CbC reports under existing international agreements for reporting fiscal years commencing in 2017 and 2018. With respect to reporting fiscal years commencing on or after 1 January 2019, Hong Kong has taken steps to ensure bilateral relationships for the exchange of CbC reports under the CbC MCAA are in place and so the recommendation no longer applies and is now removed.

Part A: The domestic legal and administrative framework

5. Hong Kong has legislation to implement the BEPS Action 13 minimum standard.

(a) Parent entity filing obligation

6. No changes were identified.

(b) Scope and timing of parent entity filing

7. No changes were identified.

(c) Limitation on local filing obligation

8. No changes were identified.

(d) Limitation on local filing in case of surrogate filing

9. No changes were identified.

(e) Effective implementation

10. No changes were identified.

Conclusion

11. Hong Kong meets all the terms of reference relating to the domestic legal and administrative framework.

Part B: The exchange of information framework

(a) Exchange of information framework

12. Hong Kong's 2017/2018 peer review included a recommendation that Hong Kong continues to take steps to enable exchanges of CbC reports under existing international agreements for reporting periods commencing in 2017 and 2018. With respect to reporting periods commencing on or after 1 January 2019, Hong Kong has taken steps to ensure bilateral relationships for the exchange of CbC reports under the CbC MCAA are in place and so the recommendation no longer applies and is now removed.

13. As of 31 March 2020, Hong Kong has 66 bilateral relationships in place for the exchange of CbC reports, including those activated under the CbC MCAA and bilateral CAAs. Within the context of its international exchange of information agreements that allow automatic exchange of tax information, Hong Kong has taken steps to have qualifying competent authority agreements in effect with jurisdictions of the Inclusive Framework that currently meet the confidentiality, consistency and appropriate use conditions. Regarding Hong Kong's exchange of information framework, no inconsistencies with the terms of reference were identified.[1]

(b) Content of information exchanged

14. No changes were identified.

(c) Completeness of exchanges

15. No changes were identified.

(d) Timeliness of exchanges

16. No changes were identified.

(e) Temporary suspension of exchange or termination of QCAA

17. No changes were identified.

(f) Consultation with other Competent Authority before determining systemic failure or significant non-compliance

18. No changes were identified.

(g) Format for information exchange

19. No changes were identified.

(h) Method for transmission

20. No changes were identified.

Conclusion

21. Hong Kong's 2017/2018 peer review included a recommendation that Hong Kong continues to take steps to enable exchanges of CbC reports under existing international agreements for reporting fiscal years commencing in 2017 and 2018. With respect to reporting fiscal years commencing on or after 1 January 2019, Hong Kong has taken steps to ensure bilateral relationships for the exchange of CbC reports under the CbC MCAA are in place and so the recommendation no longer applies and is now removed.

22. Hong Kong meets all the terms of reference with regard to the exchange of information.

Part C: Appropriate use

Appropriate use

23. No changes were identified.

Conclusion

24. Hong Kong meets all the terms of reference relating to appropriate use of CbC reports.

Summary of recommendations on the implementation of Country-by-Country Reporting

Aspect of the implementation that should be improved		Recommendation for improvement
Part A	Domestic legal and administrative framework	-
Part B	Exchange of information framework	-
Part C	Appropriate use	-

References

OECD (2019), *Country-by-Country Reporting – Compilation of Peer Review Reports (Phase 2): Inclusive Framework on BEPS: Action 13*, OECD/G20 Base Erosion and Profit Shifting Project, OECD Publishing, Paris, https://dx.doi.org/10.1787/f9bf1157-en. [1]

OECD (2018), *Country-by-Country Reporting – Compilation of Peer Review Reports (Phase 1): Inclusive Framework on BEPS: Action 13*, OECD/G20 Base Erosion and Profit Shifting Project, OECD Publishing, Paris, https://dx.doi.org/10.1787/9789264300057-en. [2]

OECD (2017), *Terms of reference for the conduct of peer review of the Action 13 minimum standard on country-by-country reporting*, OECD Publishing, https://www.oecd.org/tax/beps/beps-action-13-on-country-by-country-reporting-peer-review-documents.pdf. [3]

Note

[1] No inconsistency with the terms of reference will be identified where a QCAA is not in effect with one or more jurisdictions of the Inclusive Framework that meet the confidentiality, consistency and appropriate use conditions, but this is due to circumstances that are not under the control of the reviewed jurisdiction. This may include, for example, where the other jurisdiction intends to exchange CbC reports using the MCAA but it does not have the Convention in effect for the relevant fiscal period, or where the other jurisdiction has declined to have a QCAA in effect with the reviewed jurisdiction.

Hungary

1. Hungary was reviewed as part of the 2017/2018 and the 2018/2019 peer reviews. This report is supplementary to those previous reports (OECD, 2019[1]) (OECD, 2018[2]).

2. The first filing obligation for a CbC report in Hungary applies to reporting fiscal years commencing on or after 1 January 2016.

Summary of key findings

3. Hungary's implementation of the Action 13 minimum standard meets all applicable terms of reference (OECD, 2017[3]).

Part A: The domestic legal and administrative framework

4. Hungary has legislation in place for implementing the BEPS Action 13 minimum standard.

(a) Parent entity filing obligation

5. No changes were identified.

(b) Scope and timing of parent entity filing

6. No changes were identified.

(c) Limitation on local filing obligation

7. No changes were identified.

(d) Limitation on local filing in case of surrogate filing

8. No changes were identified.

(e) Effective implementation

9. No changes were identified.

Conclusion

10. Hungary meets all the terms of reference relating to the domestic legal and administrative framework.

Part B: The exchange of information framework

(a) Exchange of information framework

11. As of 31 March 2020, Hungary has 64 bilateral relationships in place, including those activated under the CbC MCAA, under bilateral CAAs and under the EU Council Directive (2016/881/EU). Within the context of its international exchange of information agreements that allow automatic exchange of information, Hungary has taken steps to have qualifying competent authority agreements in effect with jurisdictions of the Inclusive Framework that meet the confidentiality, consistency and appropriate use

conditions. Regarding Hungary's exchange of information framework, no inconsistencies with the terms of reference were identified.[1]

(b) Content of information exchanged

12. No changes were identified.

(c) Completeness of exchanges

13. No changes were identified.

(d) Timeliness of exchanges

14. No changes were identified.

(e) Temporary suspension of exchange or termination of QCAA

15. No changes were identified.

(f) Consultation with other Competent Authority before determining systemic failure or significant non-compliance

16. No changes were identified.

(g) Format for information exchange

17. No changes were identified.

(h) Method for transmission

18. No changes were identified.

Conclusion

19. Hungary meets all the terms of reference regarding the exchange of information.

Part C: Appropriate use

Appropriate use

20. No changes were identified.

Conclusion

21. Hungary meets all the terms of reference relating to appropriate use of CbC reports.

Summary of recommendations on the implementation of country-by-country reporting

Aspect of the implementation that should be improved		Recommendation for improvement
Part A	Domestic legal and administrative framework	-
Part B	Exchange of information framework	-
Part C	Appropriate use	-

References

OECD (2019), *Country-by-Country Reporting – Compilation of Peer Review Reports (Phase 2): Inclusive Framework on BEPS: Action 13*, OECD/G20 Base Erosion and Profit Shifting Project, OECD Publishing, Paris, https://dx.doi.org/10.1787/f9bf1157-en. [1]

OECD (2018), *Country-by-Country Reporting – Compilation of Peer Review Reports (Phase 1): Inclusive Framework on BEPS: Action 13*, OECD/G20 Base Erosion and Profit Shifting Project, OECD Publishing, Paris, https://dx.doi.org/10.1787/9789264300057-en. [2]

OECD (2017), *Terms of reference for the conduct of peer review of the Action 13 minimum standard on country-by-country reporting*, OECD Publishing, https://www.oecd.org/tax/beps/beps-action-13-on-country-by-country-reporting-peer-review-documents.pdf. [3]

Note

[1] No inconsistency with the terms of reference will be identified where a QCAA is not in effect with one or more jurisdictions of the Inclusive Framework that meet the confidentiality, consistency and appropriate use conditions, but this is due to circumstances that are not under the control of the reviewed jurisdiction. This may include, for example, where the other jurisdiction intends to exchange CbC reports using the MCAA but it does not have the Convention in effect for the relevant fiscal period, or where the other jurisdiction has declined to have a QCAA in effect with the reviewed jurisdiction

Iceland

1. Iceland was reviewed as part of the 2017/2018 and the 2018/2019 peer reviews. This report is supplementary to those previous reports (OECD, 2019[1]) (OECD, 2018[2]).

2. The first filing obligation for a CbC report in Iceland applies to reporting fiscal years commencing on or after 1 January 2017.

Summary of key findings

3. Iceland's implementation of the Action 13 minimum standard meets all applicable terms of reference (OECD, 2017[3]), except for the following:

- It is recommended that Iceland amend or otherwise clarify the definition of 'Ultimate Parent Entity" in a manner consistent with the definition contained in the terms of reference. This recommendation remains unchanged since the 2017/2018 peer review.

4. Iceland's 2017/2018 peer reviews recommended that Iceland clarify that the annual consolidated group revenue threshold calculation rule applies in line with the OECD guidance on currency fluctuations in respect of an MNE Group whose Ultimate Parent Entity is located in a jurisdiction other than Iceland. Guidance has been issued and the recommendation is removed.

5. Iceland's previous peer reviews included a recommendation that Iceland amend or otherwise clarify the definitions of "Constituent Entity" and "MNE Group" in a manner consistent with the definition contained in the terms of reference. These definitions have now been amended and the recommendation is removed.

6. Iceland's previous peer reviews recommended that Iceland clarify the scope of two conditions for local filing to ensure that local filing can only be required in the circumstances contained in the terms of reference. This has now been clarified and the recommendation is removed.

7. Iceland's previous peer reviews included a recommendation that Iceland introduce rules providing that local filing will not apply in case of Surrogate Parent Entity. This rule has now been introduced and the recommendation is removed.

Part A: The domestic legal and administrative framework

8. Iceland has legislation in place to implement the BEPS Action 13 minimum standard.

(a) Parent entity filing obligation

9. It was previously recommended that Iceland amend or otherwise clarify its rule for the calculation of the annual consolidated group revenue threshold calculation so that it applies in a manner consistent with the OECD guidance on currency fluctuations in respect of an MNE Group whose Ultimate Parent Entity is located in a jurisdiction other than Iceland, when local filing requirements are applicable.[1] Iceland has issued clarifying guidance on this point and the recommendation is removed.

(b) Scope and timing of parent entity filing

10. No changes were identified.[2]

(c) Limitation on local filing obligation

11. Iceland's 2017/2018 peer review included a recommendation that Iceland amend its legislation or otherwise take steps to ensure that local filing is only required in the circumstances contained in the terms of reference. This amendment has been made and the recommendation is removed.

(d) Limitation on local filing in case of surrogate filing

12. Iceland's 2017/2018 peer review included a recommendation that Iceland introduce rules providing that local filing will not apply for a Constituent Entity resident in Iceland when the CbC report of the CbC Group to which it belongs has been filed by a Surrogate Parent Entity in its jurisdiction of tax residence. This amendment has been made and the recommendation is removed

(e) Effective implementation

13. No changes were identified.[3]

Conclusion

14. Iceland meets all the terms of reference relating to the domestic legal and administrative framework, with the exception that:

- It is recommended that Iceland amend or otherwise clarify the definition of 'Ultimate Parent Entity" in a manner consistent with the definition contained in the terms of reference. This recommendation remains unchanged since the 2017/2018 peer review.

Part B: The exchange of information framework

(a) Exchange of information framework

15. As of 31 March 2020 Iceland has 72 bilateral relationships, including those activated under the CbC MCAA, under bilateral CAAs and under the Nordic Convention. Within the context of its international exchange of information agreements that allow automatic exchange of information, Iceland has taken steps to have qualifying competent authority agreements in effect with jurisdictions of the Inclusive Framework that meet the confidentiality, consistency and appropriate use conditions.[4] Regarding Iceland's exchange of information framework, no inconsistencies with the terms of reference were identified.

(b) Content of information exchanged

16. No changes were identified.

(c) Completeness of exchanges

17. No changes were identified.

(d) Timeliness of exchanges

18. No changes were identified.

(e) Temporary suspension of exchange or termination of QCAA

19. No changes were identified.

(f) Consultation with other Competent Authority before determining systemic failure or significant non-compliance

20. No changes were identified.

(g) Format for information exchange

21. No changes were identified.

(h) Method for transmission

22. No changes were identified.

Conclusion

23. Iceland meets all the terms of reference regarding the exchange of information.

Part C: Appropriate use

Appropriate use

24. No changes were identified.

Conclusion

25. Iceland meets all the terms of reference relating to appropriate use of CbC reports.

Summary of recommendations on the implementation of country-by-country reporting

Aspect of the implementation that should be improved		Recommendation for improvement
Part A	Domestic legal and administrative framework - Parent entity filing obligation definitions	It is recommended that Iceland amend or otherwise clarify the definition of an "Ultimate Parent Entity".
Part B	Exchange of information	-
Part C	Appropriate use	-

References

OECD (2019), *Country-by-Country Reporting – Compilation of Peer Review Reports (Phase 2): Inclusive Framework on BEPS: Action 13*, OECD/G20 Base Erosion and Profit Shifting Project, OECD Publishing, Paris, https://dx.doi.org/10.1787/f9bf1157-en. [1]

OECD (2018), *Country-by-Country Reporting – Compilation of Peer Review Reports (Phase 1): Inclusive Framework on BEPS: Action 13*, OECD/G20 Base Erosion and Profit Shifting Project, OECD Publishing, Paris, https://dx.doi.org/10.1787/9789264300057-en. [2]

OECD (2017), *Terms of reference for the conduct of peer review of the Action 13 minimum standard on country-by-country reporting*, OECD Publishing, https://www.oecd.org/tax/beps/beps-action-13-on-country-by-country-reporting-peer-review-documents.pdf. [3]

Notes

[1] https://www.rsk.is/fagadilar/cbc/leidbeiningar/riki-fyrir-riki-skyrsla-rsk-430 (accessed on 24 August 2020).

[2] Iceland's 2017/2018 peer review included a monitoring point in relation to the issuance of updated interpretation or clarification of "Revenues – Related Party" within a reasonable timeframe to ensure consistency with OECD guidance. Iceland indicates it is in the process of updating existing guidance. This monitoring point remains in place.

[3] Iceland's 2017/2018 peer review included a general monitoring point relating to a specific process to that would allow to take appropriate measures in case Iceland is notified by another jurisdiction that such other jurisdiction has reason to believe that an error may have led to incorrect or incomplete information reporting by a Reporting Entity or that there is non-compliance of a Reporting Entity with respect to its obligation to file a CbC report. This monitoring point remains in place.

[4] No inconsistency with the terms of reference will be identified where a QCAA is not in effect with one or more jurisdictions of the Inclusive Framework that meet the confidentiality, consistency and appropriate use conditions, but this is due to circumstances that are not under the control of the reviewed jurisdiction. This may include, for example, where the other jurisdiction intends to exchange CbC reports using the MCAA but it does not have the Convention in effect for the relevant fiscal period, or where the other jurisdiction has declined to have a QCAA in effect with the reviewed jurisdiction.

India

1. India was reviewed as part of the 2017/2018 and the 2018/2019 peer reviews. This report is supplementary to those previous reports (OECD, 2019[1]) (OECD, 2018[2]).

2. The first filing obligation for a CbC report in India commences in respect of financial years beginning on or after 1 April 2016.

Summary of key findings

3. India's implementation of Action 13 minimum standard meets all applicable terms of reference (OECD, 2017[3]) relating to the domestic legal and administrative framework, with the following exception:

- It is recommended that India amend or otherwise clarify that the annual consolidated group revenue threshold calculation rule applies in a manner consistent with the OECD guidance on currency fluctuations in respect of an MNE Group whose Ultimate Parent Entity is located in a jurisdiction other than India. This recommendation remains unchanged since the 2017/2018 peer review.
- It is recommended that India amend its legislation or otherwise takes steps to ensure that local filing is only required in the circumstances contained in the terms of reference. This recommendation remains unchanged since the 2017/2018 peer review.

4. India does not yet have in place all the necessary processes and written procedures to ensure that the exchange of information is conducted in a manner consistent with the terms of reference relating to the exchange of information framework. It is recommended that India take steps to implement such processes and written procedures as soon as possible. This recommendation remains unchanged since the 2018/2019 peer review.

Part A: The domestic legal and administrative framework

5. India has legislation in place to implement the BEPS Action 13 minimum standard.

(a) Parent entity filing obligation

6. It is recommended that India amend or otherwise clarify that the annual consolidated group revenue threshold calculation rule applies in a manner consistent with the OECD guidance on currency fluctuations in respect of an MNE Group whose Ultimate Parent Entity is located in a jurisdiction other than India. This recommendation remains in place since the 2017/2018 peer review.

(b) Scope and timing of parent entity filing

7. No changes were identified.

(c) Limitation on local filing obligation

8. It is recommended that India amend its legislation or otherwise takes steps to ensure that local filing is only required in the circumstances contained in the terms of reference. This recommendation remains unchanged since the 2017/2018 peer review.

(d) Limitation on local filing in case of surrogate filing

9. No changes were identified.

(e) Effective implementation

10. No changes were identified.

Conclusion

11. It is recommended that India amend or otherwise clarify that the annual consolidated group revenue threshold calculation rule applies in a manner consistent with the OECD guidance on currency fluctuations in respect of an MNE Group whose Ultimate Parent Entity is located in a jurisdiction other than India. This recommendation remains unchanged since the 2017/2018 peer review.

12. It is recommended that India amend its legislation or otherwise takes steps to ensure that local filing is only required in the circumstances contained in the terms of reference. This recommendation remains unchanged since the 2017/2018 peer review.

Part B: The exchange of information framework

(a) Exchange of information framework

13. As at 31 March 2020, India has 71 bilateral relationships activated under the CbC MCAA. Within the context of its international exchange of information agreements that allow automatic exchange of information, India has taken steps to have qualifying competent authority agreements in effect with jurisdictions of the Inclusive Framework that meet the confidentiality, consistency and appropriate use conditions.[1] Regarding India's exchange of information framework, no inconsistencies with the terms of reference were identified.

(b) Content of information exchanged

14. No changes were identified.

(c) Completeness of exchanges

15. No changes were identified.

(d) Timeliness of exchange

16. No changes were identified.

(e) Temporary suspension of exchange or termination of QCAA

17. No changes were identified.

(f) Consultation with other Competent Authority before determining systemic failure or significant non-compliance

18. No changes were identified.

(g) Format for information exchange

19. No changes were identified.

(h) Method for transmission

20. No changes were identified.

Conclusion

21. It is recommended that India take steps to implement such processes and written procedures as soon as possible.

Part C: Appropriate use

Appropriate use

22. No changes were identified.

Conclusion

23. India meets all the terms of reference relating to appropriate use of CbC reports.

Summary of recommendations on the implementation of Country-by-Country Reporting

Aspect of the implementation that should be improved		Recommendation for improvement
Part A	Domestic legal and administrative framework	It is recommended that India amend or otherwise clarify that the annual consolidated group revenue threshold calculation rule applies in a manner consistent with the OECD guidance on currency fluctuations in respect of an MNE Group whose Ultimate Parent Entity is located in a jurisdiction other than India. This recommendation remains unchanged since the 2017/2018 peer review.
Part A	Domestic legal and administrative framework	It is recommended that India amend its legislation or otherwise take steps to ensure that local filing is only required in the circumstances contained in the terms of reference.
Part B	Exchange of information framework	It is recommended that India take steps to implement the necessary processes or written procedures to ensure that the exchange of information is conducted in a manner consistent with the terms of reference relating to the exchange of information framework.
Part C	Appropriate Use	-

References

OECD (2019), *Country-by-Country Reporting – Compilation of Peer Review Reports (Phase 2): Inclusive Framework on BEPS: Action 13*, OECD/G20 Base Erosion and Profit Shifting Project, OECD Publishing, Paris, https://dx.doi.org/10.1787/f9bf1157-en. [1]

OECD (2018), *Country-by-Country Reporting – Compilation of Peer Review Reports (Phase 1): Inclusive Framework on BEPS: Action 13*, OECD/G20 Base Erosion and Profit Shifting Project, OECD Publishing, Paris, https://dx.doi.org/10.1787/9789264300057-en. [2]

OECD (2017), *Terms of reference for the conduct of peer review of the Action 13 minimum standard on country-by-country reporting*, OECD Publishing, https://www.oecd.org/tax/beps/beps-action-13-on-country-by-country-reporting-peer-review-documents.pdf. [3]

Note

[1] No inconsistency with the terms of reference will be identified where a QCAA is not in effect with one or more jurisdictions of the Inclusive Framework that meet the confidentiality, consistency and appropriate use conditions, but this is due to circumstances that are not under the control of the reviewed jurisdiction. This may include, for example, where the other jurisdiction intends to exchange CbC reports using the MCAA but it does not have the Convention in effect for the relevant fiscal period, or where the other jurisdiction has declined to have a QCAA in effect with the reviewed jurisdiction.

Indonesia

1. Indonesia was reviewed as part of the 2017/2018 and the 2018/2019 peer reviews. This report is supplementary to those previous reports (OECD, 2019[1]) (OECD, 2018[2]).

2. The first filing obligation for a CbC report in Indonesia commences in respect of periods commencing on or after 1 January 2016.

Summary of key findings

3. Indonesia's implementation of the Action 13 minimum standard meets all applicable terms of reference (OECD, 2017[3]).

Part A: The domestic legal and administrative framework

4. Indonesia has legislation in place for implementing the BEPS Action 13 minimum standard.

(a) Parent entity filing obligation

5. No changes were identified.

(b) Scope and timing of parent entity filing

6. No changes were identified.

(c) Limitation on local filing obligation

7. No changes were identified.[1]

(d) Limitation on local filing in case of surrogate filing

8. No changes were identified.[2]

(e) Effective implementation

9. Indonesia's 2017/2018 peer review included a general monitoring point relating to a specific process to that would allow to take appropriate measures in case Indonesia is notified by another jurisdiction that such other jurisdiction has reason to believe that an error may have led to incorrect or incomplete information reporting by a Reporting Entity or that there is non-compliance of a Reporting Entity with respect to its obligation to file a CbC report. A Ministry of Finance internal regulation has been issued by Indonesia which clarifies these measures and the monitoring point is removed.

Conclusion

10. Indonesia meets all the terms of reference relating to the domestic legal and administrative framework.

Part B: The exchange of information framework

(a) Exchange of information framework

11. As of 31 March 2020, Indonesia has 73 bilateral relationships, including those activated under the CbC MCAA and under bilateral CAAs. Within the context of its international exchange of information agreements that allow automatic exchange of information, Indonesia has taken steps to have qualifying competent authority agreements in effect with jurisdictions of the Inclusive Framework that meet the confidentiality, consistency and appropriate use conditions.[3] Regarding Indonesia's exchange of information framework, no inconsistencies with the terms of reference were identified.

(b) Content of information exchanged

12. No changes were identified.

(c) Completeness of exchanges

13. No changes were identified.

(d) Timeliness of exchanges

14. No changes were identified.

(e) Temporary suspension of exchange or termination of QCAA

15. No changes were identified.

(f) Consultation with other Competent Authority before determining systemic failure or significant non-compliance

16. No changes were identified.

(g) Format for information exchange

17. No changes were identified.

(h) Method for transmission

18. No changes were identified.

Conclusion

19. Indonesia meets all the terms of reference regarding the exchange of information.

Part C: Appropriate use

Appropriate use

20. No changes were identified.

Conclusion

21. Indonesia meets all the terms of reference relating to appropriate use of CbC reports.

Summary of recommendations on the implementation of country-by-country reporting

Aspect of the implementation that should be improved		Recommendation for improvement
Part A	Domestic legal and administrative framework	-
Part B	Exchange of information framework	-
Part C	Appropriate use	-

References

OECD (2019), *Country-by-Country Reporting – Compilation of Peer Review Reports (Phase 2): Inclusive Framework on BEPS: Action 13*, OECD/G20 Base Erosion and Profit Shifting Project, OECD Publishing, Paris, https://dx.doi.org/10.1787/f9bf1157-en. [1]

OECD (2018), *Country-by-Country Reporting – Compilation of Peer Review Reports (Phase 1): Inclusive Framework on BEPS: Action 13*, OECD/G20 Base Erosion and Profit Shifting Project, OECD Publishing, Paris, https://dx.doi.org/10.1787/9789264300057-en. [2]

OECD (2017), *Terms of reference for the conduct of peer review of the Action 13 minimum standard on country-by-country reporting*, OECD Publishing, https://www.oecd.org/tax/beps/beps-action-13-on-country-by-country-reporting-peer-review-documents.pdf. [3]

Notes

[1] Indonesia's 2017/2018 peer review included a monitoring point in relation to the local filing in case of "systemic failure". This monitoring point remains in place.

[2] Indonesia's 2017/2018 peer review included a monitoring point in relation to one of the conditions to deactivate the local filing obligation in case of surrogate filing. This monitoring point remains in place.

[3] No inconsistency with the terms of reference will be identified where a QCAA is not in effect with one or more jurisdictions of the Inclusive Framework that meet the confidentiality, consistency and appropriate use conditions, but this is due to circumstances that are not under the control of the reviewed jurisdiction. This may include, for example, where the other jurisdiction intends to exchange CbC reports using the MCAA but it does not have the Convention in effect for the relevant fiscal period, or where the other jurisdiction has declined to have a QCAA in effect with the reviewed jurisdiction.

Ireland

1. Ireland was reviewed as part of the 2017/2018 and the 2018/2019 peer reviews. This report is supplementary to those previous reports (OECD, 2019[1]) (OECD, 2018[2]).

2. The first filing obligation for a CbC report in Ireland applies to reporting fiscal years commencing on or after 1 January 2016.

Summary of key findings

3. Ireland's implementation of the Action 13 minimum standard meets all applicable terms of reference (OECD, 2017[3]).

Part A: The domestic legal and administrative framework

4. Ireland has legislation in place to implement the BEPS Action 13 minimum standard.

(a) Parent entity filing obligation

5. No changes were identified.

(b) Scope and timing of parent entity filing

6. No changes were identified.

(c) Limitation on local filing obligation

7. No changes were identified.[1]

(d) Limitation on local filing in case of surrogate filing

8. No changes were identified.

(e) Effective implementation

9. No changes were identified.

Conclusion

10. Ireland meets all the terms of reference relating to the domestic legal and administrative framework.

Part B: The exchange of information framework

(a) Exchange of information framework

11. As of 31 March 2020, Ireland has 67 bilateral relationships in place, including those activated under the CbC MCAA, under bilateral CAAs and under the EU Council Directive (2016/881/EU). Within the context of its international exchange of information agreements that allow automatic exchange of information, Ireland has taken steps to have qualifying competent authority agreements in effect with jurisdictions of the Inclusive Framework that meet the confidentiality, consistency and appropriate use

conditions.[23] Regarding Ireland's exchange of information framework, no inconsistencies with the terms of reference were identified.

(b) Content of information exchanged

12. No changes were identified.

(c) Completeness of exchanges

13. No changes were identified.

(d) Timeliness of exchanges

14. Ireland reports that some late exchanges have occurred. These were due a technical issue with their exchange mechanism that was not picked up until after status messages were received. This issue is expected to be solved by an upgrade in the system used to connect EU jurisdictions to the CTS but in any case Ireland has brought forward its post exchange review process to ensure that any future issues are picked up and corrected before the exchange deadline. As the issue has been addressed no recommendation is required.

(e) Temporary suspension of exchange or termination of QCAA

15. No changes were identified.

(f) Consultation with other Competent Authority before determining systemic failure or significant non-compliance

16. No changes were identified.

(g) Format for information exchange

17. No changes were identified.

(h) Method for transmission

18. No changes were identified.

Conclusion

19. Ireland meets all the terms of reference regarding the exchange of information.

Part C: Appropriate use

Appropriate use

20. No changes were identified.

Conclusion

21. Ireland meets all the terms of reference relating to appropriate use of CbC reports.

Summary of recommendations on the implementation of country-by-country reporting

Aspect of the implementation that should be improved		Recommendation for improvement
Part A	Domestic legal and administrative framework	-
Part B	Exchange of information framework	-
Part C	Appropriate use	-

References

OECD (2019), *Country-by-Country Reporting – Compilation of Peer Review Reports (Phase 2): Inclusive Framework on BEPS: Action 13*, OECD/G20 Base Erosion and Profit Shifting Project, OECD Publishing, Paris, https://dx.doi.org/10.1787/f9bf1157-en. [1]

OECD (2018), *Country-by-Country Reporting – Compilation of Peer Review Reports (Phase 1): Inclusive Framework on BEPS: Action 13*, OECD/G20 Base Erosion and Profit Shifting Project, OECD Publishing, Paris, https://dx.doi.org/10.1787/9789264300057-en. [2]

OECD (2017), *Terms of reference for the conduct of peer review of the Action 13 minimum standard on country-by-country reporting*, OECD Publishing, https://www.oecd.org/tax/beps/beps-action-13-on-country-by-country-reporting-peer-review-documents.pdf. [3]

Notes

[1] Ireland's 2017/2018 peer review included a monitoring point relating to the conditions under which local filing may be required (paragraph 8 (c) iv. b) of the terms of reference). This monitoring point remains in place.

[2] No inconsistency with the terms of reference will be identified where a QCAA is not in effect with one or more jurisdictions of the Inclusive Framework that meet the confidentiality, consistency and appropriate use conditions, but this is due to circumstances that are not under the control of the reviewed jurisdiction. This may include, for example, where the other jurisdiction intends to exchange CbC reports using the MCAA but it does not have the Convention in effect for the relevant fiscal period, or where the other jurisdiction has declined to have a QCAA in effect with the reviewed jurisdiction.

[3] It is also noted that Ireland deposited a Unilateral Declaration on "the effective date for exchanges of information under the Multilateral Competent Authority Agreement on the exchange of Country-by-Country Reports" with the Depository of the Convention on Mutual Administrative Assistance in Tax Matters to allow for an earlier date of entry into effect of the Convention for jurisdictions that will sign the Convention at a later date.

Isle of Man

1. The Isle of Man was reviewed as part of the 2017/2018 and the 2018/2019 peer reviews. This report is supplementary to those previous reports (OECD, 2019[1]) (OECD, 2018[2]).

2. The first filing obligation for a CbC report in the Isle of Man applies to reporting fiscal years commencing on or after 1 January 2017. The Isle of Man also allowed its MNE groups to file a CbC report on a voluntary basis, for reporting fiscal years beginning between 1 January 2016 and 31 December 2016.

Summary of key findings

3. The Isle of Man's implementation of the Action 13 minimum standard meets all applicable terms of reference (OECD, 2017[3]).

Part A: The domestic legal and administrative framework

4. The Isle of Man has legislation in place for implementing the BEPS Action 13 minimum standard.

(a) Parent entity filing obligation

5. No changes were identified.

(b) Scope and timing of parent entity filing

6. No changes were identified.

(c) Limitation on local filing obligation

7. No changes were identified.

(d) Limitation on local filing in case of surrogate filing

8. No changes were identified.

(e) Effective implementation

9. No changes were identified.

Conclusion

10. The Isle of Man meets all the terms of reference relating to the domestic legal and administrative framework.

Part B: The exchange of information framework

(a) Exchange of information framework

11. As of 31 March 2020, the Isle of Man has 58 bilateral relationships in place, including those activated under the CbC MCAA and under bilateral CAAs. Within the context of its international exchange of information agreements that allow automatic exchange of information, the Isle of Man has taken steps to have qualifying competent authority agreements in effect with jurisdictions of the Inclusive Framework

that meet the confidentiality, consistency and appropriate use conditions.[1] Regarding the Isle of Man's exchange of information framework, no inconsistencies with the terms of reference were identified.

(b) Content of information exchanged

12. No changes were identified.

(c) Completeness of exchanges

13. No changes were identified.

(d) Timeliness of exchanges

14. No changes were identified.

(e) Temporary suspension of exchange or termination of QCAA

15. No changes were identified.

(f) Consultation with other Competent Authority before determining systemic failure or significant non-compliance

16. No changes were identified.

(g) Format for information exchange

17. No changes were identified.

(h) Method for transmission

18. No changes were identified.

Conclusion

19. The Isle of Man meets all the terms of reference regarding the exchange of information.

Part C: Appropriate use

Appropriate use

20. No changes were identified.

Conclusion

21. The Isle of Man meets all the terms of reference relating to appropriate use of CbC reports.

Summary of recommendations on the implementation of country-by-country reporting

Aspect of the implementation that should be improved		Recommendation for improvement
Part A	Domestic legal and administrative framework	-
Part B	Exchange of information framework	-
Part C	Appropriate use	-

References

OECD (2019), *Country-by-Country Reporting – Compilation of Peer Review Reports (Phase 2): Inclusive Framework on BEPS: Action 13*, OECD/G20 Base Erosion and Profit Shifting Project, OECD Publishing, Paris, https://dx.doi.org/10.1787/f9bf1157-en. [1]

OECD (2018), *Country-by-Country Reporting – Compilation of Peer Review Reports (Phase 1): Inclusive Framework on BEPS: Action 13*, OECD/G20 Base Erosion and Profit Shifting Project, OECD Publishing, Paris, https://dx.doi.org/10.1787/9789264300057-en. [2]

OECD (2017), *Terms of reference for the conduct of peer review of the Action 13 minimum standard on country-by-country reporting*, OECD Publishing, https://www.oecd.org/tax/beps/beps-action-13-on-country-by-country-reporting-peer-review-documents.pdf. [3]

Note

[1] It is noted that a few Qualifying Competent Authority agreements are not in effect with jurisdictions of the Inclusive Framework that meet the confidentiality condition and have legislation in place: this may be because the partner jurisdictions considered do not have the Convention in effect for the first reporting period, or may not have listed the reviewed jurisdiction in their notifications under Section 8 of the CbC MCAA.

Israel

1. Israel was reviewed as part of the 2017/2018 and the 2018/2019 peer reviews. This report is supplementary to those previous reports (OECD, 2019[1]) (OECD, 2018[2]).

2. There is no filing obligation for a CbC report in Israel yet.

Summary of key findings

3. Israel does not yet have legislation in place for implementing the BEPS Action 13 minimum standard. It is recommended that Israel take steps to implement a domestic legal and administrative framework to impose and enforce CbC reporting requirements as soon as possible. This recommendation remains unchanged since the 2017/2018 peer review.

4. It is recommended that Israel take steps to have qualifying competent authority agreements in effect with jurisdictions of the Inclusive Framework that meet the confidentiality, consistency and appropriate use conditions and with which Israel has an international exchange of information agreement in effect that allows for the automatic exchange of tax information. This recommendation remains unchanged since the 2017/2018 peer review.

5. It is recommended that Israel take steps to implement processes or written procedures to ensure that the exchange of information is conducted in a manner consistent with the terms of reference (OECD, 2017[3]) relating to the exchange of information framework ahead of the first exchanges of information. This recommendation remains unchanged since the 2018/2019 peer review.

6. It is recommended that Israel take steps to ensure that the appropriate use condition is met ahead of the first exchanges of information. This recommendation remains unchanged since the 2017/2018 peer review.

Part A: The domestic legal and administrative framework

7. Israel does not yet have legislation in place for implementing the BEPS Action 13 minimum standard. Israel indicates that primary legislation has been submitted to the Israeli Knesset for approval and that secondary legislation is in draft.

(a) Parent entity filing obligation

(b) Scope and timing of parent entity filing

(c) Limitation on local filing obligation

(d) Limitation on local filing in case of surrogate filing

(e) Effective implementation

Conclusion

8. It is recommended that Israel take steps to implement a domestic legal and administrative framework to impose and enforce CbC reporting requirements as soon as possible, remains in place. This recommendation remains unchanged since the 2017/2018 peer review.

Part B: The exchange of information framework

(a) Exchange of information framework

9. As of 31 March 2020, Israel has no bilateral relationships in place for the exchange of CbC reports. It is recommended that Israel take steps to have qualifying competent authority agreements in effect with jurisdictions of the Inclusive Framework that meet the confidentiality, consistency and appropriate use conditions and with which Israel has an international exchange of information agreement in effect that allows for the automatic exchange of tax information.

(b) Content of information exchanged

10. No changes were identified.

(c) Completeness of exchanges

11. No changes were identified.

(d) Timeliness of exchanges

12. No changes were identified.

(e) Temporary suspension of exchange or termination of QCAA

13. No changes were identified

(f) Consultation with other Competent Authority before determining systemic failure or significant non-compliance

14. No changes were identified.

(g) Format for information exchange

15. No changes were identified.

(h) Method for transmission

16. No changes were identified.

Conclusion

17. It is recommended that Israel take steps to have the QCAAs in effect with jurisdictions of the Inclusive Framework which meet the confidentiality, consistency and appropriate use prerequisites and with which Israel has an international exchange of information agreement in effect that allows for the automatic exchange of tax information. This recommendation remains unchanged since the 2017/2018 peer review.

18. It is recommended that Israel take steps to implement processes or written procedures to ensure that the exchange of information is conducted in a manner consistent with the terms of reference relating to the exchange of information framework ahead of its first exchanges of information. This recommendation remains unchanged since the 2018/2019 peer review.

Part C: Appropriate use

Appropriate use

19. No changes were identified.

Conclusion

20. It is recommended that Israel take steps to ensure that the appropriate use condition is met ahead of its first exchanges of information. This recommendation remains unchanged since the 2017/2018 peer review.

Summary of recommendations on the implementation of Country-by-Country Reporting

Aspect of the implementation that should be improved		Recommendation for improvement
Part A	Domestic legal and administrative framework	It is recommended that Israel take steps to implement a domestic legal and administrative framework to impose and enforce CbC requirements as soon as possible.
Part B	Exchange of information framework	It is recommended that Israel take steps to have QCAAs in effect with jurisdictions of the Inclusive Framework which meet the confidentiality, consistency and appropriate use prerequisites and with which Israel has an international exchange of information agreement in effect that allows for the automatic exchange of tax information
Part B	Exchange of information framework	It is recommended that Israel take steps to implement the necessary processes or written procedures to ensure that the exchange of information is conducted in a manner consistent with the terms of reference relating to the exchange of information framework.
Part C	Appropriate use	It is recommended that Israel take steps to ensure that the appropriate use condition is met ahead of the first exchanges of information.

References

OECD (2019), *Country-by-Country Reporting – Compilation of Peer Review Reports (Phase 2): Inclusive Framework on BEPS: Action 13*, OECD/G20 Base Erosion and Profit Shifting Project, OECD Publishing, Paris, https://dx.doi.org/10.1787/f9bf1157-en. [1]

OECD (2018), *Country-by-Country Reporting – Compilation of Peer Review Reports (Phase 1): Inclusive Framework on BEPS: Action 13*, OECD/G20 Base Erosion and Profit Shifting Project, OECD Publishing, Paris, https://dx.doi.org/10.1787/9789264300057-en. [2]

OECD (2017), *Terms of reference for the conduct of peer review of the Action 13 minimum standard on country-by-country reporting*, OECD Publishing, https://www.oecd.org/tax/beps/beps-action-13-on-country-by-country-reporting-peer-review-documents.pdf. [3]

Italy

1. Italy was reviewed as part of the 2017/2018 and the 2018/2019 peer reviews. This report is supplementary to those previous reports (OECD, 2019[1]) (OECD, 2018[2]).

2. The first filing obligation for a CbC report in Italy applies to reporting fiscal years commencing on or after 1 January 2016.

Summary of key findings

3. Italy's implementation of the Action 13 minimum standard meets all applicable terms of reference (OECD, 2017[3]).

Part A: The domestic legal and administrative framework

4. Italy has legislation in place which implements the BEPS Action 13 minimum standard.

(a) Parent entity filing obligation

5. No changes were identified.

(b) Scope and timing of parent entity filing

6. No changes were identified.

(c) Limitation on local filing obligation

7. No changes were identified.

(d) Limitation on local filing in case of surrogate filing

8. No changes were identified.

(e) Effective implementation

9. No changes were identified.

Conclusion

10. Italy meets all the terms of reference relating to the domestic legal and administrative framework.

Part B: The exchange of information framework

(a) Exchange of information framework

11. As of 31 March 2020, Italy has 75 bilateral relationships in place, including those activated under the CbC MCAA, a bilateral CAA, and the EU Council Directive (2016/881/EU). Within the context of its international exchange of information agreements that allow automatic exchange of information, Italy has taken steps to have qualifying competent authority agreements in effect with jurisdictions of the Inclusive

Framework that meet the confidentiality, consistency and appropriate use conditions.[1] Regarding Italy's exchange of information framework, no inconsistencies with the terms of reference were identified.

(b) Content of information exchanged

12. No changes were identified.

(c) Completeness of exchanges

13. No changes were identified.

(d) Timeliness of exchanges

14. No changes were identified.

(e) Temporary suspension of exchange or termination of QCAA

15. No changes were identified.

(f) Consultation with other Competent Authority before determining systemic failure or significant non-compliance

16. No changes were identified.

(g) Format for information exchange

17. No changes were identified.

(h) Method for transmission

18. No changes were identified.

Conclusion

19. Italy meets all the terms of reference regarding the exchange of information.

Part C: Appropriate use

Appropriate use

20. No changes were identified.

Conclusion

21. Italy meets all the terms of reference relating to appropriate use of CbC reports.

Summary of recommendations on the implementation of country-by-country reporting

Aspect of the implementation that should be improved		Recommendation for improvement
Part A	Domestic legal and administrative framework	-
Part B	Exchange of information framework	-
Part C	Appropriate use	-

References

OECD (2019), *Country-by-Country Reporting – Compilation of Peer Review Reports (Phase 2): Inclusive Framework on BEPS: Action 13*, OECD/G20 Base Erosion and Profit Shifting Project, OECD Publishing, Paris, https://dx.doi.org/10.1787/f9bf1157-en. [1]

OECD (2018), *Country-by-Country Reporting – Compilation of Peer Review Reports (Phase 1): Inclusive Framework on BEPS: Action 13*, OECD/G20 Base Erosion and Profit Shifting Project, OECD Publishing, Paris, https://dx.doi.org/10.1787/9789264300057-en. [2]

OECD (2017), *Terms of reference for the conduct of peer review of the Action 13 minimum standard on country-by-country reporting*, OECD Publishing, https://www.oecd.org/tax/beps/beps-action-13-on-country-by-country-reporting-peer-review-documents.pdf. [3]

Note

[1]: No inconsistency with the terms of reference will be identified where a QCAA is not in effect with one or more jurisdictions of the Inclusive Framework that meet the confidentiality, consistency and appropriate use conditions, but this is due to circumstances that are not under the control of the reviewed jurisdiction. This may include, for example, where the other jurisdiction intends to exchange CbC reports using the MCAA but it does not have the Convention in effect for the relevant fiscal period, or where the other jurisdiction has declined to have a QCAA in effect with the reviewed jurisdiction.

Jamaica

1. Jamaica was first reviewed during the 2018/2019 peer review. This report is supplementary to that previous report (OECD, 2018[2]).

2. There is no filing obligation for a CbC report in Jamaica yet.

Summary of key findings

3. Jamaica does not yet have legislation in place for implementing the BEPS Action 13 minimum standard. It is recommended that Jamaica take steps to implement a domestic legal and administrative framework to impose and enforce CbC reporting requirements as soon as possible. This recommendation remains unchanged since the 2018/2019 peer review.

4. It is recommended that Jamaica take steps to have QCAAs in effect with jurisdictions of the Inclusive Framework which meet the confidentiality, consistency and appropriate use prerequisites and with which Jamaica has an international exchange of information agreement in effect that allows for the automatic exchange of tax information. This recommendation remains unchanged since the 2018/2019 peer review.

5. It is recommended that Jamaica take steps to implement processes or written procedures to ensure that the exchange of information is conducted in a manner consistent with the terms of reference (OECD, 2017[3]) relating to the exchange of information framework ahead of the first exchanges of information. This recommendation remains unchanged since the 2018/2019 peer review.

6. It is recommended that Jamaica take steps to ensure that the appropriate use condition is met ahead of the first exchanges of information. This recommendation remains unchanged since the 2018/2019 peer review.

Part A: The domestic legal and administrative framework

7. Jamaica does not have legislation in place for implementing the BEPS Action 13 minimum standard.

(a) Parent entity filing obligation

(b) Scope and timing of parent entity filing

(c) Limitation on local filing obligation

(d) Limitation on local filing in case of surrogate filing

(e) Effective implementation

8. It is recommended that Jamaica take steps to implement a domestic legal and administrative framework to impose and enforce CbC reporting requirements as soon as possible.

Conclusion

9. It is recommended that Jamaica take steps to implement a domestic legal and administrative framework to impose and enforce CbC reporting requirements as soon as possible.

Part B: The exchange of information framework

(a) Exchange of information framework

10. As of 31 March 2020, Jamaica has no bilateral relationships in place for the exchange of CbC reports. It is recommended that Jamaica take steps to have qualifying competent authority agreements in effect with jurisdictions of the Inclusive Framework that meet the confidentiality, consistency and appropriate use conditions and with which Jamaica has an international exchange of information agreement in effect that allows for the automatic exchange of tax information.

(b) Content of information exchanged

11. No changes were identified.

(c) Completeness of exchanges

12. No changes were identified.

(d) Timeliness of exchanges

13. No changes were identified.

(e) Temporary suspension of exchange or termination of QCAA

14. No changes were identified.

(f) Consultation with other Competent Authority before determining systemic failure or significant non-compliance

15. No changes were identified.

(g) Format for information exchange

16. No changes were identified.

(h) Method for transmission

17. No changes were identified.

Conclusion

18. It is recommended that Jamaica take steps to put QCAAs in effect with jurisdictions of the Inclusive Framework which meet the confidentiality, consistency and appropriate use prerequisites and with which it has an international exchange of information agreement in effect that allows for the automatic exchange of tax information. This recommendation remains unchanged since the 2018/2019 peer review.

19. It is recommended that Jamaica take steps to implement processes or written procedures to ensure that the exchange of information is conducted in a manner consistent with the terms of reference relating to the exchange of information framework ahead of its first exchanges of information. This recommendation remains unchanged since the 2018/2019 peer review.

Part C: Appropriate use

Appropriate use

20. No changes were identified.

Conclusion

21. It is recommended that Jamaica take steps to ensure that the appropriate use condition is met ahead of its first exchanges of information. This recommendation remains unchanged since the 2018/2019 peer review.

Summary of recommendations on the implementation of Country-by-Country Reporting

Aspect of the implementation that should be improved		Recommendation for improvement
Part A	Domestic legal and administrative framework	It is recommended that Jamaica take steps to implement a domestic legal and administrative framework to impose and enforce CbC requirements as soon as possible.
Part B	Exchange of information framework	It is recommended that Jamaica take steps to put QCAAs in effect with jurisdictions of the Inclusive Framework which meet the confidentiality, consistency and appropriate use prerequisites and with which Jamaica has an international exchange of information agreement in effect that allows for the automatic exchange of tax information.
Part B	Exchange of information framework	It is recommended that Jamaica take steps to implement the necessary processes or written procedures to ensure that the exchange of information is conducted in a manner consistent with the terms of reference relating to the exchange of information framework.
Part C	Appropriate use	It is recommended that Jamaica take steps to ensure that the appropriate use condition is met ahead of its first exchanges of information.

References

OECD (2018), *Country-by-Country Reporting – Compilation of Peer Review Reports (Phase 1): Inclusive Framework on BEPS: Action 13*, OECD/G20 Base Erosion and Profit Shifting Project, OECD Publishing, Paris, https://dx.doi.org/10.1787/9789264300057-en. [2]

OECD (2017), *Terms of reference for the conduct of peer review of the Action 13 minimum standard on country-by-country reporting*, OECD Publishing, https://www.oecd.org/tax/beps/beps-action-13-on-country-by-country-reporting-peer-review-documents.pdf. [3]

Japan

1. Japan was reviewed as part of the 2017/2018 and the 2018/2019 peer reviews. This report is supplementary to those previous reports (OECD, 2019[1]) (OECD, 2018[2]).

2. The first filing obligation for a CbC report in Japan commences in respect of fiscal years commencing on or after 1 April 2016. Japan also allows its MNE groups to file a CbC report on a voluntary basis, for reporting fiscal years beginning between 1 January 2016 and 31 March 2016.

Summary of key findings

3. Japan's implementation of the Action 13 minimum standard meets all applicable terms of reference (OECD, 2017[3]).

Part A: The domestic legal and administrative framework

4. Japan has legislation in place which implements the BEPS Action 13 minimum standard.

(a) Parent entity filing obligation

5. No changes were identified.

(b) Scope and timing of parent entity filing

6. No changes were identified.

(c) Limitation on local filing obligation

7. No changes were identified.

(d) Limitation on local filing in case of surrogate filing

8. No changes were identified.

(e) Effective implementation

9. No changes were identified.

Conclusion

10. Japan meets all the terms of reference relating to the domestic legal and administrative framework.

Part B: The exchange of information framework

(a) Exchange of information framework

11. As of 31 March 2020, Japan has 65 bilateral relationships in place, including those activated under the CbC MCAA and a bilateral QCAA. Within the context of its international exchange of information agreements that allow automatic exchange of information, Japan has taken steps to have qualifying competent authority agreements in effect with jurisdictions of the Inclusive Framework that meet the

confidentiality, consistency and appropriate use conditions. Regarding Japan's exchange of information framework, no inconsistencies with the terms of reference were identified. [1]

(b) Content of information exchanged

12. No changes were identified.

(c) Completeness of exchanges

13. No changes were identified.

(d) Timeliness of exchanges

14. No changes were identified.

(e) Temporary suspension of exchange or termination of QCAA

15. No changes were identified.

(f) Consultation with other Competent Authority before determining systemic failure or significant non-compliance

16. No changes were identified.

(g) Format for information exchange

17. No changes were identified.

(h) Method for transmission

18. No changes were identified.

Conclusion

19. Japan meets all the terms of reference regarding the exchange of information.

Part C: Appropriate use

Appropriate use

20. No changes were identified.

Conclusion

21. Japan meets all the terms of reference relating to appropriate use of CbC reports.

Summary of recommendations on the implementation of country-by-country reporting

Aspect of the implementation that should be improved		Recommendation for improvement
Part A	Domestic legal and administrative framework	-
Part B	Exchange of information framework	-
Part C	Appropriate use	-

References

OECD (2019), *Country-by-Country Reporting – Compilation of Peer Review Reports (Phase 2): Inclusive Framework on BEPS: Action 13*, OECD/G20 Base Erosion and Profit Shifting Project, OECD Publishing, Paris, https://dx.doi.org/10.1787/f9bf1157-en. [1]

OECD (2018), *Country-by-Country Reporting – Compilation of Peer Review Reports (Phase 1): Inclusive Framework on BEPS: Action 13*, OECD/G20 Base Erosion and Profit Shifting Project, OECD Publishing, Paris, https://dx.doi.org/10.1787/9789264300057-en. [2]

OECD (2017), *Terms of reference for the conduct of peer review of the Action 13 minimum standard on country-by-country reporting*, OECD Publishing, https://www.oecd.org/tax/beps/beps-action-13-on-country-by-country-reporting-peer-review-documents.pdf. [3]

Note

[1] No inconsistency with the terms of reference will be identified where a QCAA is not in effect with one or more jurisdictions of the Inclusive Framework that meet the confidentiality, consistency and appropriate use conditions, but this is due to circumstances that are not under the control of the reviewed jurisdiction. This may include, for example, where the other jurisdiction intends to exchange CbC reports using the MCAA but it does not have the Convention in effect for the relevant fiscal period, or where the other jurisdiction has declined to have a QCAA in effect with the reviewed jurisdiction.

Jersey

1. Jersey was reviewed as part of the 2017/2018 and the 2018/2019 peer reviews. This report is supplementary to those previous reports (OECD, 2019[1]) (OECD, 2018[2]).

2. The first filing obligation for a CbC report in Jersey commences in respect of fiscal years commencing on or after 1 January 2016.

Summary of key findings

3. Jersey's implementation of the Action 13 minimum standard meets all applicable terms of reference (OECD, 2017[3]).

Part A: The domestic legal and administrative framework

4. Jersey has legislation in place which implements the BEPS Action 13 minimum standard.

(a) Parent entity filing obligation

5. No changes were identified.

(b) Scope and timing of parent entity filing

6. No changes were identified.

(c) Limitation on local filing obligation

7. No changes were identified.

(d) Limitation on local filing in case of surrogate filing

8. No changes were identified.

(e) Effective implementation

9. No changes were identified.

Conclusion

10. Jersey meets all the terms of reference relating to the domestic legal and administrative framework.

Part B: The exchange of information framework

(a) Exchange of information framework

11. As of 31 March 2020, Jersey has 65 bilateral relationships in place, including those activated under the CbC MCAA and bilateral QCAAs. Within the context of its international exchange of information agreements that allow automatic exchange of information, Jersey has taken steps to have qualifying competent authority agreements in effect with jurisdictions of the Inclusive Framework that meet the

confidentiality, consistency and appropriate use conditions.[1] Regarding Jersey's exchange of information framework, no inconsistencies with the terms of reference were identified.

(b) Content of information exchanged

12. No changes were identified.

(c) Completeness of exchanges

13. No changes were identified.

(d) Timeliness of exchanges

14. No changes were identified.

(e) Temporary suspension of exchange or termination of QCAA

15. No changes were identified.

(f) Consultation with other Competent Authority before determining systemic failure or significant non-compliance

16. No changes were identified.

(g) Format for information exchange

17. No changes were identified.

(h) Method for transmission

18. No changes were identified.

Conclusion

19. Jersey meets all the terms of reference regarding the exchange of information.

Part C: Appropriate use

Appropriate use

20. No changes were identified.

Conclusion

21. Jersey meets all the terms of reference relating to appropriate use of CbC reports.

Summary of recommendations on the implementation of country-by-country reporting

Aspect of the implementation that should be improved		Recommendation for improvement
Part A	Domestic legal and administrative framework	-
Part B	Exchange of information framework	-
Part C	Appropriate use	-

References

OECD (2019), *Country-by-Country Reporting – Compilation of Peer Review Reports (Phase 2): Inclusive Framework on BEPS: Action 13*, OECD/G20 Base Erosion and Profit Shifting Project, OECD Publishing, Paris, https://dx.doi.org/10.1787/f9bf1157-en. [1]

OECD (2018), *Country-by-Country Reporting – Compilation of Peer Review Reports (Phase 1): Inclusive Framework on BEPS: Action 13*, OECD/G20 Base Erosion and Profit Shifting Project, OECD Publishing, Paris, https://dx.doi.org/10.1787/9789264300057-en. [2]

OECD (2017), *Terms of reference for the conduct of peer review of the Action 13 minimum standard on country-by-country reporting*, OECD Publishing, https://www.oecd.org/tax/beps/beps-action-13-on-country-by-country-reporting-peer-review-documents.pdf. [3]

Note

[1] No inconsistency with the terms of reference will be identified where a QCAA is not in effect with one or more jurisdictions of the Inclusive Framework that meet the confidentiality, consistency and appropriate use conditions, but this is due to circumstances that are not under the control of the reviewed jurisdiction. This may include, for example, where the other jurisdiction intends to exchange CbC reports using the MCAA but it does not have the Convention in effect for the relevant fiscal period, or where the other jurisdiction has declined to have a QCAA in effect with the reviewed jurisdiction.

Jordan

1. This report is Jordan's first annual peer review report. Consistent with the agreed methodology this report covers: (i) the domestic legal and administrative framework, (ii) the exchange of information framework as well as (iii) the appropriate use of CbC reports.

2. There is no filing obligation for a CbC report in Jordan yet.

Summary of key findings

3. Jordan does not yet have legislation in place for implementing the BEPS Action 13 minimum standard.

4. It is recommended that Jordan take steps to implement a domestic legal and administrative framework to impose and enforce CbC reporting requirements as soon as possible.

5. It is recommended that Jordan take steps to put in place an exchange of information framework that allows automatic exchange of information and have QCAAs in effect with jurisdictions of the Inclusive Framework which meet the confidentiality, consistency and appropriate use prerequisites and with which Jordan has an international exchange of information agreement in effect that allows for the automatic exchange of tax information.

6. It is recommended that Jordan take steps to implement processes or written procedures to ensure that the exchange of information is conducted in a manner consistent with the terms of reference (OECD, 2017[3]) relating to the exchange of information framework ahead of the first exchanges of information.

7. It is recommended that Jordan take steps to ensure that the appropriate use condition is met ahead of the first exchanges of information.

Part A: The domestic legal and administrative framework

8. Jordan does not yet have legislation in place for implementing the BEPS Action 13 minimum standard.

(a) Parent entity filing obligation

(b) Scope and timing of parent entity filing

(c) Limitation on local filing obligation

(d) Limitation on local filing in case of surrogate filing

(e) Effective implementation

Conclusion

9. It is recommended that Jordan take steps to implement a domestic legal and administrative framework to impose and enforce CbC reporting requirements as soon as possible.

Part B: The exchange of information framework

(a) Exchange of information framework

10. As of 31 March 2020, Jordan has no bilateral relationships in place for the exchange of CbC reports. It is recommended that Jordan take steps to have qualifying competent authority agreements in effect with jurisdictions of the Inclusive Framework that meet the confidentiality, consistency and appropriate use conditions and with which Jordan has an international exchange of information agreement in effect that allows for the automatic exchange of tax information.

(b) Content of information exchanged

11. Jordan does not have processes or written procedures in place that are intended to ensure that each of the mandatory fields of information required in the CbC reporting template are present in the information exchanged.

(c) Completeness of exchanges

12. Jordan does not have processes or written procedures in place that are intended to ensure that CbC reports are exchanged with all tax jurisdictions listed in Table 1 of a CbC report with which it should exchange information as per the relevant QCAA.

(d) Timeliness of exchanges

13. Jordan does not have processes or written procedures in place that are intended to ensure that the information to be exchanged is transmitted to the relevant jurisdictions in accordance with the timelines provided for in the relevant QCAAs.

(e) Temporary suspension of exchange or termination of QCAA

14. Jordan does not have processes or written procedures in place that are intended to ensure that a temporary suspension of the exchange of information or termination of a relevant QCAA would be carried out only as per the conditions set out in the relevant QCAA.

(f) Consultation with other Competent Authority before determining systemic failure or significant non-compliance

15. Jordan does not have processes or written procedures in place that are intended to ensure that its Competent Authority consults with the other Competent Authority before making a determination of systemic failure or significant non-compliance with the terms of the relevant QCAA by that other Competent Authority.

(g) Format for information exchange

16. Jordan has not confirmed the format that will be used for the international exchange of CbC reports.

(h) Method for transmission

17. Jordan has not confirmed the mechanism that it will use to exchange CbC reports.

Conclusion

18. It is recommended that Jordan take steps to have qualifying competent authority agreements in effect with jurisdictions of the Inclusive Framework that meet the confidentiality, consistency and

appropriate use conditions and with which Jordan has an international exchange of information agreement in effect that allows for the automatic exchange of tax information.

19. It is recommended that Jordan take steps to implement processes or written procedures to ensure that the exchange of information is conducted in a manner consistent with the terms of reference (OECD, 2017[3]) relating to the exchange of information framework ahead of its first exchanges of information.

Part C: Appropriate use

Appropriate use

20. Jordan does not yet have measures in place relating to appropriate use.

21. It is recommended that Jordan take steps to ensure that the appropriate use condition is met ahead of its first exchanges of information

Conclusion

22. It is recommended that Jordan take steps to ensure that the appropriate use condition is met ahead of its first exchanges of information.

Summary of recommendations on the implementation of Country-by-Country Reporting

Aspect of the implementation that should be improved		Recommendation for improvement
Part A	Domestic legal and administrative framework	It is recommended that Jordan take steps to implement a domestic legal and administrative framework to impose and enforce CbC requirements as soon as possible.
Part B	Exchange of information framework	It is recommended that Jordan take steps to put in place an exchange of information framework that allows Automatic Exchange of Information and have QCAAs in effect with jurisdictions of the Inclusive Framework which meet the confidentiality, consistency and appropriate use prerequisites and with which Jordan has an international exchange of information agreement in effect that allows for the automatic exchange of tax information.
Part B	Exchange of information framework	It is recommended that Jordan take steps to implement the necessary processes or written procedures to ensure that the exchange of information is conducted in a manner consistent with the terms of reference relating to the exchange of information framework.
Part C	Appropriate use	It is recommended that Jordan take steps to ensure that the appropriate use condition is met ahead of the first exchanges of information.

References

OECD (2017), *Terms of reference for the conduct of peer review of the Action 13 minimum standard on country-by-country reporting*, OECD Publishing, https://www.oecd.org/tax/beps/beps-action-13-on-country-by-country-reporting-peer-review-documents.pdf. [3]

Kazakhstan

1. Kazakhstan was reviewed as part of the 2017/2018 and the 2018/2019 peer reviews. This report is supplementary to those previous reports (OECD, 2019[1]) (OECD, 2018[2]).

2. The first filing obligation for a CbC report in Kazakhstan commences in respect of reporting fiscal years starting on or after 1 January 2016.

Summary of key findings

3. Kazakhstan's implementation of legislation for the Action 13 minimum standard meets all applicable terms of reference (OECD, 2017[3]), except for the following:

- It is recommended that Kazakhstan clarify the exact scope, conditions and legal basis under the minimum standard and/ or the exchange of information framework for the exemption in case of state secrets.

4. It is recommended that Kazakhstan take steps to have QCAAs in effect with jurisdictions of the Inclusive Framework which will meet the confidentiality, consistency and appropriate use prerequisites and with which Kazakhstan has an international exchange of information agreement in effect that allows for the automatic exchange of tax information. This recommendation remains unchanged since the 2017/2018 peer review.

5. It is recommended that Kazakhstan take steps to implement processes or written procedures to ensure that the exchange of information is conducted in a manner consistent with the terms of reference relating to the exchange of information framework ahead of its first exchanges of information. This recommendation remains unchanged since the 2018/2019 peer review.

6. It is recommended that Kazakhstan take steps to ensure that the appropriate use condition is met ahead of the first exchanges of information. This recommendation remains unchanged since the 2017/2018 peer review.

Part A: The domestic legal and administrative framework

7. Kazakhstan has legislation in place to implement the BEPS Action 13 minimum standard.

(a) Parent entity filing obligation

8. It is recommended that Kazakhstan clarify the exact scope, conditions and legal basis under the minimum standard and/ or the exchange of information framework for the exemption given in their legislation in the case of inclusion of state secrets.

(b) Scope and timing of parent entity filing

9. No changes were identified.

(c) Limitation on local filing obligation

10. No changes were identified.[1]

(d) Limitation on local filing in case of surrogate filing

11. No changes were identified. [2]

(e) Effective implementation

12. No changes were identified.[3]

Conclusion

13. It is recommended that Kazakhstan clarify the exact scope, conditions and legal basis under the minimum standard and/or the exchange of information framework for the exemption in case of state secrets

Part B: The exchange of information framework

(a) Exchange of information framework

14. As of 31 March 2020, Kazakhstan has no bilateral relationships in place for the exchange of CbC reports. It is recommended that Kazakhstan take steps to have qualifying competent authority agreements in effect with jurisdictions of the Inclusive Framework that meet the confidentiality, consistency and appropriate use conditions and with which Kazakhstan has an international exchange of information agreement in effect that allows for the automatic exchange of tax information

(b) Content of information exchanged

15. No changes were identified.

(c) Completeness of exchanges

16. No changes were identified.

(d) Timeliness of exchanges

17. No changes were identified.

(e) Temporary suspension of exchange or termination of QCAA

18. No changes were identified.

(f) Consultation with other Competent Authority before determining systemic failure or significant non-compliance

19. No changes were identified.

(g) Format for information exchange

20. No changes were identified.

(h) Method for transmission

21. No changes were identified.

Conclusion

22. It is recommended that Kazakhstan take steps to have QCAAs in effect with jurisdictions of the Inclusive Framework which meet the confidentiality, consistency and appropriate use prerequisites and with which Kazakhstan has an international exchange of information agreement in effect that allows for the

automatic exchange of tax information. This recommendation remains unchanged since the 2017/2018 peer review.

23. It is recommended that Kazakhstan take steps to implement processes or written procedures to ensure that the exchange of information is conducted in a manner consistent with the terms of reference relating to the exchange of information framework ahead of its first exchanges of information. This recommendation remains unchanged since the 2018/2019 peer review.

Part C: Appropriate use

Appropriate use

24. No changes were identified.

Conclusion

25. It is recommended that Kazakhstan take steps to ensure that the appropriate use condition is met ahead of the first exchanges of information.

Summary of recommendations on the implementation of country-by-country reporting

Aspect of the implementation that should be improved		Recommendation for improvement
Part A	Domestic legal and administrative framework	It is recommended that Kazakhstan clarify the exact scope, conditions and legal basis under the minimum standard and/ or the exchange of information framework for the exemption in case of state secrets.
Part B	Exchange of information framework	It is recommended that Kazakhstan take steps to have qualifying competent authority agreements in effect with jurisdictions of the Inclusive Framework that meet the confidentiality, consistency and appropriate use conditions and with which Kazakhstan has an international exchange of information agreement in effect that allows for the automatic exchange of tax information.
Part B	Exchange of information framework	It is recommended that Kazakhstan take steps to implement processes or written procedures to ensure that the exchange of information is conducted in a manner consistent with the terms of reference relating to the exchange of information framework ahead of its first exchanges of information.
Part C	Appropriate use	It is recommended that Kazakhstan take steps to ensure that the appropriate use condition is met ahead of the first exchanges of information.

References

OECD (2019), *Country-by-Country Reporting – Compilation of Peer Review Reports (Phase 2): Inclusive Framework on BEPS: Action 13*, OECD/G20 Base Erosion and Profit Shifting Project, OECD Publishing, Paris, https://dx.doi.org/10.1787/f9bf1157-en. [1]

OECD (2018), *Country-by-Country Reporting – Compilation of Peer Review Reports (Phase 1): Inclusive Framework on BEPS: Action 13*, OECD/G20 Base Erosion and Profit Shifting Project, OECD Publishing, Paris, https://dx.doi.org/10.1787/9789264300057-en. [2]

OECD (2017), *Terms of reference for the conduct of peer review of the Action 13 minimum standard on country-by-country reporting*, OECD Publishing, https://www.oecd.org/tax/beps/beps-action-13-on-country-by-country-reporting-peer-review-documents.pdf. [3]

Notes

[1] It was recommended in Kazakhstan's 2017/2018 report that Kazakhstan implement a provision whereby a single Constituent Entity of the same MNE Group may be designated to file the CbC report which would satisfy the local filing requirement of all the Constituent Entities in Kazakhstan. As Kazakhstan's local filing requirement is currently suspended until further notice, this recommendation was removed but the situation will be monitored.

[2] It is unclear whether Kazakhstan's legislation provides for the deactivation of local filing in case of surrogate filing. Kazakhstan state that this is the case, this point will be monitored

[3] There are no specific processes to take appropriate measures in case Kazakhstan is notified by another jurisdiction that it has reason to believe with respect to a Reporting Entity that an error may have led to incorrect or incomplete information reporting or that there is non-compliance of a Reporting Entity with respect to its obligation to file a CbC report. As no exchange of CbC reports has yet occurred, no recommendation is made but this aspect will be monitored.

Kenya

1. Kenya was reviewed as part of the 2017/2018 and the 2018/2019 peer reviews. This report is supplementary to those previous reports (OECD, 2019[1]) (OECD, 2018[2]).

2. There is no filing obligation for a CbC report in Kenya yet.

Summary of key findings

3. It is recommended that Kenya take steps to implement a domestic legal and administrative framework to impose and enforce CbC reporting requirements as soon as possible. This recommendation remains unchanged since the 2017/2018 peer review.

4. It is recommended that Kenya take steps to have qualifying competent authority agreements in effect with jurisdictions of the Inclusive Framework that meet the confidentiality, consistency and appropriate use conditions and with which Kenya has an international exchange of information agreement in effect that allows for the automatic exchange of tax information. This recommendation remains unchanged since the 2017/2018 peer review.

5. It is recommended that Kenya take steps to implement processes or written procedures to ensure that the exchange of information is conducted in a manner consistent with the terms of reference (OECD, 2017[3]) relating to the exchange of information framework ahead of the first exchanges of information. This recommendation remains unchanged since the 2018/2019 peer review.

6. It is recommended that Kenya take steps to ensure that the appropriate use condition is met ahead of the first exchanges of information. This recommendation remains unchanged since the 2017/2018 peer review.

Part A: The domestic legal and administrative framework

7. Kenya does not yet have legislation in place for implementing the BEPS Action 13 minimum standard.

(a) Parent entity filing obligation

(b) Scope and timing of parent entity filing

(c) Limitation on local filing obligation

(d) Limitation on local filing in case of surrogate filing

(e) Effective implementation

Conclusion

8. It is recommended that Kenya take steps to implement a domestic legal and administrative framework to impose and enforce CbC reporting requirements as soon as possible.

Part B: The exchange of information framework

(a) Exchange of information framework

9. As of 31 March 2020, Kenya has no bilateral relationships in place for the exchange of CbC reports. It is recommended that Kenya take steps to have qualifying competent authority agreements in effect with jurisdictions of the Inclusive Framework that meet the confidentiality, consistency and appropriate use conditions and with which they have an international exchange of information agreement in effect that allows for the automatic exchange of tax information. This recommendation remains unchanged since the 2017/2018 peer review.

(b) Content of information exchanged

10. No changes were identified.

(c) Completeness of exchanges

11. No changes were identified.

(d) Timeliness of exchanges

12. No changes were identified.

(e) Temporary suspension of exchange or termination of QCAA

13. No changes were identified.

(f) Consultation with other Competent Authority before determining systemic failure or significant non-compliance

14. No changes were identified.

(g) Format for information exchange

15. No changes were identified.

(h) Method for transmission

16. No changes were identified.

Conclusion

17. It is recommended that Kenya take steps to put in place an exchange of information framework that allows Automatic Exchange of Information and have QCAAs in effect with jurisdictions of the Inclusive Framework which meet the confidentiality, consistency and appropriate use prerequisites and with which Kenya has an international exchange of information agreement in effect that allows for the automatic exchange of tax information. This recommendation remains unchanged since the 2017/2018 peer review.

18. It is recommended that Kenya take steps to implement processes or written procedures to ensure that the exchange of information is conducted in a manner consistent with the terms of reference relating to the exchange of information framework ahead of its first exchanges of information. This recommendation remains unchanged since the 2018/2019 peer review.

Part C: Appropriate use

Appropriate use

19. No changes were identified.

Conclusion

20. It is recommended that Kenya take steps to ensure that the appropriate use condition is met ahead of its first exchanges of information. This recommendation remains unchanged since the 2017/2018 peer review.

Summary of recommendations on the implementation of Country-by-Country Reporting

Aspect of the implementation that should be improved		Recommendation for improvement
Part A	Domestic legal and administrative framework	It is recommended that Kenya take steps to implement a domestic legal and administrative framework to impose and enforce CbC requirements as soon as possible.
Part B	Exchange of information framework	It is recommended that Kenya take steps to have QCAAs in effect with jurisdictions of the Inclusive Framework which meet the confidentiality, consistency and appropriate use prerequisite and with which it has international agreement that allow the automatic exchange of information.
Part B	Exchange of information framework	It is recommended that Kenya take steps to implement the necessary processes or written procedures to ensure that the exchange of information is conducted in a manner consistent with the terms of reference relating to the exchange of information framework.
Part C	Appropriate use	It is recommended that Kenya take steps to ensure that the appropriate use condition is met ahead of the first exchanges of information.

References

OECD (2019), *Country-by-Country Reporting – Compilation of Peer Review Reports (Phase 2): Inclusive Framework on BEPS: Action 13*, OECD/G20 Base Erosion and Profit Shifting Project, OECD Publishing, Paris, https://dx.doi.org/10.1787/f9bf1157-en. [1]

OECD (2018), *Country-by-Country Reporting – Compilation of Peer Review Reports (Phase 1): Inclusive Framework on BEPS: Action 13*, OECD/G20 Base Erosion and Profit Shifting Project, OECD Publishing, Paris, https://dx.doi.org/10.1787/9789264300057-en. [2]

OECD (2017), *Terms of reference for the conduct of peer review of the Action 13 minimum standard on country-by-country reporting*, OECD Publishing, https://www.oecd.org/tax/beps/beps-action-13-on-country-by-country-reporting-peer-review-documents.pdf. [3]

Korea

1. Korea was reviewed as part of the 2017/2018 and the 2018/2019 peer reviews. This report is supplementary to those previous reports (OECD, 2019[1]) (OECD, 2018[2]).

2. The first filing obligation for a CbC report in Korea commences in respect of fiscal years commencing on or after 1 April 2016.

Summary of key findings

3. Korea's implementation of the Action 13 minimum standard meets all applicable terms of reference (OECD, 2017[3]).

Part A: The domestic legal and administrative framework

4. Korea has legislation in place which implements the BEPS Action 13 minimum standard.

(a) Parent entity filing obligation

5. No changes were identified.

(b) Scope and timing of parent entity filing

6. No changes were identified.

(c) Limitation on local filing obligation

7. No changes were identified.

(d) Limitation on local filing in case of surrogate filing

8. No changes were identified.

(e) Effective implementation

9. No changes were identified.

Conclusion

10. Korea meets all the terms of reference relating to the domestic legal and administrative framework.

Part B: The exchange of information framework

(a) Exchange of information framework

11. As of 31 March 2020, Korea has 65 bilateral relationships in place, including those activated under the CbC MCAA and bilateral QCAAs. Within the context of its international exchange of information agreements that allow automatic exchange of information, Korea has taken steps to have qualifying competent authority agreements in effect with jurisdictions of the Inclusive Framework that meet the

confidentiality, consistency and appropriate use conditions. Regarding Korea's exchange of information framework, no inconsistencies with the terms of reference were identified.

(b) Content of information exchanged

12. No changes were identified.

(c) Completeness of exchanges

13. No changes were identified.

(d) Timeliness of exchanges

14. No changes were identified.

(e) Temporary suspension of exchange or termination of QCAA

15. No changes were identified.

(f) Consultation with other Competent Authority before determining systemic failure or significant non-compliance

16. No changes were identified.

(g) Format for information exchange

17. No changes were identified.

(h) Method for transmission

18. No changes were identified.

Conclusion

19. Korea meets all the terms of reference regarding the exchange of information.

Part C: Appropriate use

Appropriate use

20. No changes were identified.

Conclusion

21. Korea meets all the terms of reference relating to appropriate use of CbC reports.

Summary of recommendations on the implementation of country-by-country reporting

Aspect of the implementation that should be improved		Recommendation for improvement
Part A	Domestic legal and administrative framework – limitation on local filing obligation	-
Part B	Exchange of information framework	-
Part C	Appropriate use	-

References

OECD (2019), *Country-by-Country Reporting – Compilation of Peer Review Reports (Phase 2): Inclusive Framework on BEPS: Action 13*, OECD/G20 Base Erosion and Profit Shifting Project, OECD Publishing, Paris, https://dx.doi.org/10.1787/f9bf1157-en. [1]

OECD (2018), *Country-by-Country Reporting – Compilation of Peer Review Reports (Phase 1): Inclusive Framework on BEPS: Action 13*, OECD/G20 Base Erosion and Profit Shifting Project, OECD Publishing, Paris, https://dx.doi.org/10.1787/9789264300057-en. [2]

OECD (2017), *Terms of reference for the conduct of peer review of the Action 13 minimum standard on country-by-country reporting*, OECD Publishing, https://www.oecd.org/tax/beps/beps-action-13-on-country-by-country-reporting-peer-review-documents.pdf. [3]

Latvia

1. Latvia was reviewed as part of the 2017/2018 and the 2018/2019 peer reviews. This report is supplementary to those previous reports (OECD, 2019[1]) (OECD, 2018[2]).

2. The first filing obligation for a CbC report in Latvia commences in respect of reporting fiscal years starting on or after 1 January 2016.

Summary of key findings

3. Latvia's implementation of the Action 13 minimum standard meets all applicable terms of reference (OECD, 2017[3]), except for the following:

- It is recommended that Latvia amend or otherwise clarify that the annual consolidated group revenue threshold calculation rule applies in a manner consistent with the OECD guidance on currency fluctuations in respect of an MNE Group whose Ultimate Parent Entity is located in a jurisdiction other than Latvia. This recommendation remains unchanged since the 2017/2018 peer review.

4. Latvia's 2017/2018 review recommended that Latvia take steps to change its legislation or otherwise implement a provision whereby a single Constituent Entity of the same MNE Group may be designated to file the CbC report which would satisfy the local filing requirement of all the Constituent Entities. This amendment has been made and the recommendation is removed.

Part A: The domestic legal and administrative framework

5. Latvia has legislation in place to implement the BEPS Action 13 minimum standard, establishing the necessary requirements including the filing and reporting obligations.

(a) Parent entity filing obligation

6. It is recommended that Latvia amend or otherwise clarify its rule for the calculation of the annual consolidated group revenue threshold calculation so that it applies in a manner consistent with the OECD guidance on currency fluctuations in respect of an MNE Group whose Ultimate Parent Entity is located in a jurisdiction other than Latvia, when local filing requirements are applicable. This recommendation remains in place since the 2017/2018 peer review.

(b) Scope and timing of parent entity filing

7. No changes were identified.[1]

(c) Limitation on local filing obligation

8. Latvia's 2017/2018 review recommended that Latvia take steps to change its legislation or otherwise implement a provision whereby a single Constituent Entity of the same MNE Group may be designated to file the CbC report which would satisfy the local filing requirement of all the Constituent Entities. This amendment has been made and the recommendation is removed.[2]

(d) Limitation on local filing in case of surrogate filing

9. No changes were identified.

(e) Effective implementation

10. No changes were identified.

Conclusion

11. Latvia meets the terms of reference relating to the domestic legal and administrative framework, with the exceptions that:

- It is recommended that Latvia amend or otherwise clarify that the annual consolidated group revenue threshold calculation rule applies in a manner consistent with the OECD guidance on currency fluctuations in respect of an MNE Group whose Ultimate Parent Entity is located in a jurisdiction other than Latvia. This recommendation remains unchanged since the 2017/2018 peer review.

Part B: The exchange of information framework

(a) Exchange of information framework

12. As of 31 March 2020, Latvia has 75 bilateral relationships in place, including those activated under the CbC MCAA, under bilateral CAAs and under the EU Council Directive (2016/881/EU). Within the context of its international exchange of information agreements that allow automatic exchange of information, Latvia has taken steps to have qualifying competent authority agreements in effect with jurisdictions of the Inclusive Framework that meet the confidentiality, consistency and appropriate use conditions.[3] Regarding Latvia's exchange of information framework, no inconsistencies with the terms of reference were identified.

(b) Content of information exchanged

13. No changes were identified.

(c) Completeness of exchanges

14. No changes were identified.

(d) Timeliness of exchanges

15. No changes were identified.

(e) Temporary suspension of exchange or termination of QCAA

16. No changes were identified.

(f) Consultation with other Competent Authority before determining systemic failure or significant non-compliance

17. No changes were identified.

(g) Format for information exchange

18. No changes were identified.

(h) Method for transmission

19. No changes were identified.

Conclusion

20. Latvia meets all the terms of reference regarding the exchange of information.

Part C: Appropriate use

Appropriate use

21. No changes were identified.

Conclusion

22. Latvia meets all the terms of reference relating to appropriate use of CbC reports.

Summary of recommendations on the implementation of country-by-country reporting

Aspect of the implementation that should be improved		Recommendation for improvement
Part A	Domestic legal and administrative	It is recommended that Latvia amend or otherwise clarify that the annual consolidated group revenue threshold calculation rule applies in line with the OECD guidance on currency fluctuations in respect of an MNE Group whose Ultimate Parent Entity is located in a jurisdiction other than Latvia.
Part B	Exchange of information framework	-
Part C	Appropriate use	-

References

OECD (2019), *Country-by-Country Reporting – Compilation of Peer Review Reports (Phase 2): Inclusive Framework on BEPS: Action 13*, OECD/G20 Base Erosion and Profit Shifting Project, OECD Publishing, Paris, https://dx.doi.org/10.1787/f9bf1157-en. [1]

OECD (2018), *Country-by-Country Reporting – Compilation of Peer Review Reports (Phase 1): Inclusive Framework on BEPS: Action 13*, OECD/G20 Base Erosion and Profit Shifting Project, OECD Publishing, Paris, https://dx.doi.org/10.1787/9789264300057-en. [2]

OECD (2017), *Terms of reference for the conduct of peer review of the Action 13 minimum standard on country-by-country reporting*, OECD Publishing, https://www.oecd.org/tax/beps/beps-action-13-on-country-by-country-reporting-peer-review-documents.pdf. [3]

Note

[1] Latvia's 2017/2018 peer review included a monitoring point relating to the interpretation of the definitions of "Revenues – Related Party". This monitoring point remains in place.

[2] https://likumi.lv/ta/id/292196 (accessed on 24 August 2020).

[3] No inconsistency with the terms of reference will be identified where a QCAA is not in effect with one or more jurisdictions of the Inclusive Framework that meet the confidentiality, consistency and appropriate use conditions, but this is due to circumstances that are not under the control of the reviewed jurisdiction. This may include, for example, where the other jurisdiction intends to exchange CbC reports using the MCAA but it does not have the Convention in effect for the relevant fiscal period, or where the other jurisdiction has declined to have a QCAA in effect with the reviewed jurisdiction.

Liberia

1. Liberia was first reviewed during the 2018/2019 peer review. This report is supplementary to that previous report (OECD, 2018[2]).

2. There is no filing obligation for a CbC report in Liberia yet.

Summary of key findings

3. Liberia does not yet have legislation in place for implementing the BEPS Action 13 minimum standard. It is recommended that Liberia take steps to implement a domestic legal and administrative framework to impose and enforce CbC reporting requirements as soon as possible. This recommendation remains unchanged since the 2018/2019 peer review.

4. It is recommended that Liberia take steps to have QCAAs in effect with jurisdictions of the Inclusive Framework which meet the confidentiality, consistency and appropriate use prerequisites and with which it has an international agreement which allows for the automatic exchange of information. This recommendation remains unchanged since the 2018/2019 peer review.

5. It is recommended that Liberia take steps to implement processes or written procedures to ensure that the exchange of information is conducted in a manner consistent with the terms of reference (OECD, 2017[3]) relating to the exchange of information framework ahead of the first exchanges of information. This recommendation remains unchanged since the 2018/2019 peer review.

6. It is recommended that Liberia take steps to ensure that the appropriate use condition is met ahead of the first exchanges of information. This recommendation remains unchanged since the 2018/2019 peer review.

Part A: The domestic legal and administrative framework

7. Liberia does not yet have legislation in place for implementing the BEPS Action 13 minimum standard.

(a) Parent entity filing obligation

(b) Scope and timing of parent entity filing

(c) Limitation on local filing obligation

(d) Limitation on local filing in case of surrogate filing

(e) Effective implementation

8. It is recommended that Liberia take steps to implement a domestic legal and administrative framework to impose and enforce CbC reporting requirements as soon as possible.

Conclusion

9. It is recommended that Liberia take steps to implement a domestic legal and administrative framework to impose and enforce CbC reporting requirements as soon as possible.

Part B: The exchange of information framework

(a) Exchange of information framework

10. As of 31 March 2020, Liberia has no bilateral relationships in place for the exchange of CbC reports. It is recommended that Liberia take steps to have qualifying competent authority agreements in effect with jurisdictions of the Inclusive Framework that meet the confidentiality, consistency and appropriate use conditions and with which it has an international exchange of information agreement in effect that allows for the automatic exchange of tax information.

(b) Content of information exchanged

11. No changes were identified.

(c) Completeness of exchanges

12. No changes were identified.

(d) Timeliness of exchanges

13. No changes were identified.

(e) Temporary suspension of exchange or termination of QCAA

14. No changes were identified.

(f) Consultation with other Competent Authority before determining systemic failure or significant non-compliance

15. No changes were identified.

(g) Format for information exchange

16. No changes were identified.

(h) Method for transmission

17. No changes were identified.

Conclusion

18. It is recommended that Liberia take steps to put in place an exchange of information framework that allows Automatic Exchange of Information and have QCAAs in effect with jurisdictions of the Inclusive Framework which meet the confidentiality, consistency and appropriate use prerequisites and with which Liberia has an international exchange of information agreement in effect that allows for the automatic exchange of tax information. This recommendation remains unchanged since the 2018/2019 peer review.

19. It is recommended that Liberia take steps to implement processes or written procedures to ensure that the exchange of information is conducted in a manner consistent with the terms of reference relating to the exchange of information framework ahead of its first exchanges of information. This recommendation remains unchanged since the 2018/2019 peer review.

Part C: Appropriate use

Appropriate use

20. No changes were identified.

Conclusion

21. It is recommended that Liberia take steps to ensure that the appropriate use condition is met ahead of its first exchanges of information. This recommendation remains unchanged since the 2018/2019 peer review.

Summary of recommendations on the implementation of Country-by-Country Reporting

Aspect of the implementation that should be improved		Recommendation for improvement
Part A	Domestic legal and administrative framework	It is recommended that Liberia take steps to implement a domestic legal and administrative framework to impose and enforce CbC requirements as soon as possible.
Part B	Exchange of information framework	It is recommended that Liberia take steps to put in place an exchange of information framework that allows Automatic Exchange of Information and have QCAAs in effect with jurisdictions of the Inclusive Framework which meet the confidentiality, consistency and appropriate use prerequisites and with which Liberia have an international agreement which allows for automatic exchange of tax information.
Part B	Exchange of information framework	It is recommended that Liberia take steps to implement the necessary processes or written procedures to ensure that the exchange of information is conducted in a manner consistent with the terms of reference relating to the exchange of information framework.
Part C	Appropriate use	It is recommended that Liberia take steps to ensure that the appropriate use condition is met ahead of the first exchanges of information.

References

OECD (2018), *Country-by-Country Reporting – Compilation of Peer Review Reports (Phase 1): Inclusive Framework on BEPS: Action 13*, OECD/G20 Base Erosion and Profit Shifting Project, OECD Publishing, Paris, https://dx.doi.org/10.1787/9789264300057-en. [2]

OECD (2017), *Terms of reference for the conduct of peer review of the Action 13 minimum standard on country-by-country reporting*, OECD Publishing, https://www.oecd.org/tax/beps/beps-action-13-on-country-by-country-reporting-peer-review-documents.pdf. [3]

Liechtenstein

1. Liechtenstein was reviewed as part of the 2017/2018 and the 2018/2019 peer reviews. This report is supplementary to those previous reports (OECD, 2019[1]) (OECD, 2018[2]).

2. The first filing obligation for a CbC report in Liechtenstein applies to reporting fiscal years commencing on or after 1 January 2017. Liechtenstein also allows its MNE groups to file a CbC report on a voluntary basis, for reporting fiscal years beginning between 1 January 2016 and 31 December 2016.

Summary of key findings

3. Liechtenstein's implementation of the Action 13 minimum standard meets all applicable terms of reference (OECD, 2017[3]).

Part A: The domestic legal and administrative framework

4. Liechtenstein has legislation in place which implements the BEPS Action 13 minimum standard.

(a) Parent entity filing obligation

5. No changes were identified.

(b) Scope and timing of parent entity filing

6. No changes were identified.

(c) Limitation on local filing obligation

7. No changes were identified.

(d) Limitation on local filing in case of surrogate filing

8. No changes were identified.[1]

(e) Effective implementation

9. No changes were identified.

Conclusion

10. Liechtenstein meets all the terms of reference relating to the domestic legal and administrative framework.

Part B: The exchange of information framework

(a) Exchange of information framework

11. As of 31 March 2020, Liechtenstein has 66 bilateral relationships in place, including those activated under the CbC MCAA and bilateral QCAAs. Within the context of its international exchange of information agreements that allow automatic exchange of information, Liechtenstein has taken steps to have qualifying competent authority agreements in effect with jurisdictions of the Inclusive Framework that meet the

confidentiality, consistency and appropriate use conditions.[2] Regarding Liechtenstein's exchange of information framework, no inconsistencies with the terms of reference were identified.

(b) Content of information exchanged

12. No changes were identified.

(c) Completeness of exchanges

13. No changes were identified.

(d) Timeliness of exchanges

14. No changes were identified.

(e) Temporary suspension of exchange or termination of QCAA

15. No changes were identified.

(f) Consultation with other Competent Authority before determining systemic failure or significant non-compliance

16. No changes were identified.

(g) Format for information exchange

17. No changes were identified.

(h) Method for transmission

18. No changes were identified.

Conclusion

19. Liechtenstein meets all the terms of reference regarding the exchange of information.

Part C: Appropriate use

Appropriate use

20. No changes were identified.

Conclusion

21. Liechtenstein meets all the terms of reference relating to appropriate use of CbC reports.

Summary of recommendations on the implementation of country-by-country reporting

Aspect of the implementation that should be improved		Recommendation for improvement
Part A	Domestic legal and administrative framework	-
Part B	Exchange of information framework	-
Part C	Appropriate use	-

References

OECD (2019), *Country-by-Country Reporting – Compilation of Peer Review Reports (Phase 2): Inclusive Framework on BEPS: Action 13*, OECD/G20 Base Erosion and Profit Shifting Project, OECD Publishing, Paris, https://dx.doi.org/10.1787/f9bf1157-en. [1]

OECD (2018), *Country-by-Country Reporting – Compilation of Peer Review Reports (Phase 1): Inclusive Framework on BEPS: Action 13*, OECD/G20 Base Erosion and Profit Shifting Project, OECD Publishing, Paris, https://dx.doi.org/10.1787/9789264300057-en. [2]

OECD (2017), *Terms of reference for the conduct of peer review of the Action 13 minimum standard on country-by-country reporting*, OECD Publishing, https://www.oecd.org/tax/beps/beps-action-13-on-country-by-country-reporting-peer-review-documents.pdf. [3]

Notes

[1] Liechtenstein's 2017/2018 peer review included a general monitoring point to ensure that legislation setting out local filing requirements is not interpreted as applying to situations where there is no current international agreement between Liechtenstein and the residence jurisdiction of the Ultimate Parent Entity (which is not permitted under the terms of reference).This monitoring point remains in place.

[2] No inconsistency with the terms of reference will be identified where a QCAA is not in effect with one or more jurisdictions of the Inclusive Framework that meet the confidentiality, consistency and appropriate use conditions, but this is due to circumstances that are not under the control of the reviewed jurisdiction. This may include, for example, where the other jurisdiction intends to exchange CbC reports using the MCAA but it does not have the Convention in effect for the relevant fiscal period, or where the other jurisdiction has declined to have a QCAA in effect with the reviewed jurisdiction.

Lithuania

1. Lithuania was reviewed as part of the 2017/2018 and the 2018/2019 peer reviews. This report is supplementary to those previous reports (OECD, 2019[1]) (OECD, 2018[2]).

2. The first filing obligation for a CbC report in Lithuania applies to reporting fiscal years commencing on or after 1 January 2016.

Summary of key findings

3. Lithuania's implementation of the Action 13 minimum standard meets all applicable terms of reference (OECD, 2017[3]).

Part A: The domestic legal and administrative framework

4. Lithuania has legislation in place which implements the BEPS Action 13 minimum standard.

(a) Parent entity filing obligation

5. No changes were identified.[1]

(b) Scope and timing of parent entity filing

6. No changes were identified.[2]

(c) Limitation on local filing obligation

7. No changes were identified.

(d) Limitation on local filing in case of surrogate filing

8. No changes were identified.

(e) Effective implementation

9. No changes were identified.

Conclusion

10. Lithuania meets all the terms of reference relating to the domestic legal and administrative framework.

Part B: The exchange of information framework

(a) Exchange of information framework

11. As of 31 March 2020, Lithuania has 75 bilateral relationships in place, including those activated under the CbC MCAA, bilateral QCAAs and under the EU Council Directive (2016/881/EU). Within the context of its international exchange of information agreements that allow automatic exchange of information, Lithuania has taken steps to have qualifying competent authority agreements in effect with jurisdictions of the Inclusive Framework that meet the confidentiality, consistency and appropriate use

conditions.[3] Regarding Lithuania's exchange of information framework, no inconsistencies with the terms of reference were identified.

(b) Content of information exchanged

12. No changes were identified.

(c) Completeness of exchanges

13. No changes were identified.

(d) Timeliness of exchanges

14. No changes were identified.

(e) Temporary suspension of exchange or termination of QCAA

15. No changes were identified.

(f) Consultation with other Competent Authority before determining systemic failure or significant non-compliance

16. No changes were identified.

(g) Format for information exchange

17. No changes were identified.

(h) Method for transmission

18. No changes were identified.

Conclusion

19. Lithuania meets all the terms of reference regarding the exchange of information.

Part C: Appropriate use

Appropriate use

20. No changes were identified.

Conclusion

21. Lithuania meets all the terms of reference relating to appropriate use of CbC reports.

Summary of recommendations on the implementation of country-by-country reporting

Aspect of the implementation that should be improved		Recommendation for improvement
Part A	Domestic legal and administrative framework	-
Part B	Exchange of information framework	-
Part C	Appropriate use	-

References

OECD (2019), *Country-by-Country Reporting – Compilation of Peer Review Reports (Phase 2): Inclusive Framework on BEPS: Action 13*, OECD/G20 Base Erosion and Profit Shifting Project, OECD Publishing, Paris, https://dx.doi.org/10.1787/f9bf1157-en. [1]

OECD (2018), *Country-by-Country Reporting – Compilation of Peer Review Reports (Phase 1): Inclusive Framework on BEPS: Action 13*, OECD/G20 Base Erosion and Profit Shifting Project, OECD Publishing, Paris, https://dx.doi.org/10.1787/9789264300057-en. [2]

OECD (2017), *Terms of reference for the conduct of peer review of the Action 13 minimum standard on country-by-country reporting*, OECD Publishing, https://www.oecd.org/tax/beps/beps-action-13-on-country-by-country-reporting-peer-review-documents.pdf. [3]

Notes

[1] Lithuania's 2017/2018 peer review included a monitoring point relating to the definition of "International Corporation Group". This monitoring point remains in place.

[2] Lithuania's 2017/2018 peer review included a monitoring point relating to the interpretation of the definitions of "Revenues – Related Party". This monitoring point remains in place.

[3] No inconsistency with the terms of reference will be identified where a QCAA is not in effect with one or more jurisdictions of the Inclusive Framework that meet the confidentiality, consistency and appropriate use conditions, but this is due to circumstances that are not under the control of the reviewed jurisdiction. This may include, for example, where the other jurisdiction intends to exchange CbC reports using the MCAA but it does not have the Convention in effect for the relevant fiscal period, or where the other jurisdiction has declined to have a QCAA in effect with the reviewed jurisdiction.

Luxembourg

1. Luxembourg was reviewed as part of the 2017/2018 and the 2018/2019 peer reviews. This report is supplementary to those previous reports (OECD, 2019[1]) (OECD, 2018[2]).

2. The first filing obligation for a CbC report in Luxembourg applies to reporting fiscal years commencing on or after 1 January 2016.

Summary of key findings

3. Luxembourg's implementation of the Action 13 minimum standard meets all applicable terms of reference (OECD, 2017[3]).

Part A: The domestic legal and administrative framework

4. Luxembourg has legislation in place which implements the BEPS Action 13 minimum standard.

(a) Parent entity filing obligation

5. No changes were identified.

(b) Scope and timing of parent entity filing

6. No changes were identified.

(c) Limitation on local filing obligation

7. No changes were identified.

(d) Limitation on local filing in case of surrogate filing

8. No changes were identified.

(e) Effective implementation

9. No changes were identified.

Conclusion

10. Luxembourg meets all the terms of reference relating to the domestic legal and administrative framework.

Part B: The exchange of information framework

(a) Exchange of information framework

11. As of 31 March 2020, Luxembourg has 68 bilateral relationships in place, including those activated under the CbC MCAA, bilateral QCAAs and under the EU Council Directive (2016/881/EU). Within the context of its international exchange of information agreements that allow automatic exchange of information, Luxembourg has taken steps to have qualifying competent authority agreements in effect with jurisdictions of the Inclusive Framework that meet the confidentiality, consistency and appropriate use

conditions.[1] Regarding Luxembourg's exchange of information framework, no inconsistencies with the terms of reference were identified.

(b) Content of information exchanged

12. No changes were identified.

(c) Completeness of exchanges

13. No changes were identified.

(d) Timeliness of exchanges

14. No changes were identified.

(e) Temporary suspension of exchange or termination of QCAA

15. No changes were identified.

(f) Consultation with other Competent Authority before determining systemic failure or significant non-compliance

16. No changes were identified.

(g) Format for information exchange

17. No changes were identified.

(h) Method for transmission

18. No changes were identified.

Conclusion

19. Luxembourg meets all the terms of reference regarding the exchange of information.

Part C: Appropriate use

Appropriate use

20. No changes were identified.

Conclusion

21. Luxembourg meets all the terms of reference relating to appropriate use of CbC reports.

Summary of recommendations on the implementation of country-by-country reporting

Aspect of the implementation that should be improved		Recommendation for improvement
Part A	Domestic legal and administrative framework	-
Part B	Exchange of information framework	-
Part C	Appropriate use	-

References

OECD (2019), *Country-by-Country Reporting – Compilation of Peer Review Reports (Phase 2): Inclusive Framework on BEPS: Action 13*, OECD/G20 Base Erosion and Profit Shifting Project, OECD Publishing, Paris, https://dx.doi.org/10.1787/f9bf1157-en. [1]

OECD (2018), *Country-by-Country Reporting – Compilation of Peer Review Reports (Phase 1): Inclusive Framework on BEPS: Action 13*, OECD/G20 Base Erosion and Profit Shifting Project, OECD Publishing, Paris, https://dx.doi.org/10.1787/9789264300057-en. [2]

OECD (2017), *Terms of reference for the conduct of peer review of the Action 13 minimum standard on country-by-country reporting*, OECD Publishing, https://www.oecd.org/tax/beps/beps-action-13-on-country-by-country-reporting-peer-review-documents.pdf. [3]

Note

[1] No inconsistency with the terms of reference will be identified where a QCAA is not in effect with one or more jurisdictions of the Inclusive Framework that meet the confidentiality, consistency and appropriate use conditions, but this is due to circumstances that are not under the control of the reviewed jurisdiction. This may include, for example, where the other jurisdiction intends to exchange CbC reports using the MCAA but it does not have the Convention in effect for the relevant fiscal period, or where the other jurisdiction has declined to have a QCAA in effect with the reviewed jurisdiction.

Macau (China)

1. Macau was reviewed as part of the 2017/2018 and the 2018/2019 peer reviews. This report is supplementary to those previous reports (OECD, 2019[1]) (OECD, 2018[2]).

2. The first filing obligation for a CbC report in Macau commences in respect of fiscal periods commencing on or after 1 January 2019.

Summary of key findings

3. The 2017/2018 peer review recommended that Macau take steps to implement a domestic legal and administrative framework to impose and enforce CbC reporting requirements. Legislation is now in effect and this recommendation is removed

4. It is recommended that Macau take steps to have qualifying competent authority agreements in effect with jurisdictions of the Inclusive Framework that meet the confidentiality, consistency and appropriate use conditions and with which it has an international exchange of information agreement in effect that allows for the automatic exchange of tax information. This recommendation remains unchanged since the 2017/2018 peer review.

5. The 2017/2018 peer review recommended that Macau take steps to implement processes or written procedures to ensure that the exchange of information is conducted in a manner consistent with the terms of reference relating to the exchange of information framework ahead of its first exchanges of information. Process are now in place and this recommendation is removed.

6. The 2017/2018 recommended that Macau take steps to ensure that the appropriate use condition is met ahead of the first exchanges of information. This condition is now met and the recommendation is removed.

Part A: The domestic legal and administrative framework

7. Macau has legislation in place for implementing the BEPS Action 13 minimum standard, requiring filing of CbC reports for fiscal years commencing on or after 1 January 2019.[1]

(a) Parent entity filing obligation

8. Macau has introduced a filing requirement which applies to all Ultimate Parent Entities of MNE Groups above a certain threshold and which requires inclusion of all constituent entities.

9. No inconsistencies were identified

(b) Scope and timing of parent entity filing

10. The first filing requirements for MNE Groups in Macau enforce a CbC filing requirement for fiscal years commencing on or after 1 January 2019 and filing is required 12 months after the reporting year end.

11. No inconsistencies were identified

(c) Limitation on local filing obligation

12. Macau does not have a local filing requirement.

(d) Limitation on local filing in case of surrogate filing

13. Macau does not have a local filing requirement.

(e) Effective implementation

14. Macau has systems to ensure effective implementation of the CbC filing requirement which include a notification requirement and a penalty regime in the case of late, inaccurate or non-filing of CbC reports.

Conclusion

15. Macau's legal framework meets all of the terms of reference.

Part B: The exchange of information framework

(a) Exchange of information framework

16. As of 31 March 2020, Macau has no bilateral relationships in place for the exchange of CbC reports. It is recommended that Macau take steps to have qualifying competent authority agreements in effect with jurisdictions of the Inclusive Framework that meet the confidentiality, consistency and appropriate use conditions and with which Macau has an international exchange of information agreement in effect that allows for the automatic exchange of tax information

(b) Content of information exchanged

17. Macau has processes in place that are intended to ensure that each of the mandatory fields of information as required in the CbC template are present in the information exchanged. It has provided details in relation to these processes and written procedures.

(c) Completeness of exchanges

18. Macau has processes and written procedures in place that are intended to ensure that CbC reports are exchanged with all tax jurisdictions listed in Table 1 of a CbC reporting template with which it should exchange information as per the relevant QCAAs. It has provided details in relation to these processes and written procedures.

(d) Timeliness of exchanges

19. Macau has processes and written procedures in place that are intended to ensure that the information to be exchanged is transmitted to the relevant jurisdictions in accordance with the timelines provided for in the relevant QCAAs and terms of reference. It has provided details in relation to these processes and written procedures.

(e) Temporary suspension of exchange or termination of QCAA

20. Macau has processes in place that are intended to ensure that a temporary suspension of the exchange of information or termination of a relevant QCAA be carried out only as per the conditions set out in the QCAA. It has provided details in relation to those processes.

(f) Consultation with other Competent Authority before determining systemic failure or significant non-compliance

21. Macau has processes in place that are intended to ensure that the Competent Authority consults with the other Competent Authority prior to making a determination that there is or has been significant

non-compliance with the terms of the relevant QCAA or that the other Competent Authority has caused a systemic failure. It has provided details in relation to those processes.

(g) Format for information exchange

22. Macau confirms that it will use the OECD XML Schema and User Guide for the international exchange of CbC reports.

(h) Method for transmission

23. Macau confirms that it will use the Common Transmission System for the exchange of CbC reports.

Conclusion

24. The 2018/2019 peer review recommended that Macau take steps to implement processes or written procedures to ensure that the exchange of information is conducted in a manner consistent with the terms of reference relating to the exchange of information framework ahead of its first exchanges of information. The processes are in place and the recommendation is removed.

25. It is recommended that Macau take steps to have QCAAs in effect with jurisdictions of the Inclusive Framework which meet the confidentiality, consistency and appropriate use prerequisites and with which Macau has an international exchange of information agreement in effect that allows for the automatic exchange of tax information. This recommendation remains unchanged since the 2017/2018 peer review.

Part C: Appropriate use

Appropriate use

26. The 2017/2018 recommended that Macau take steps to ensure that the appropriate use condition is met ahead of the first exchanges of information. This condition is now met and the recommendation is removed.

Conclusion

27. The 2017/2018 recommended that Macau take steps to ensure that the appropriate use condition is met ahead of the first exchanges of information. This condition is now met and the recommendation is removed.

Summary of recommendations on the implementation of Country-by-Country Reporting

<table>
<tr><th colspan="2">Aspect of the implementation that should be improved</th><th>Recommendation for improvement</th></tr>
<tr><td>Part A</td><td>Domestic legal and administrative framework</td><td>-</td></tr>
<tr><td>Part B</td><td>Exchange of information framework</td><td>It is recommended that Macau take steps to have QCAAs in effect with jurisdictions of the Inclusive Framework which meet the confidentiality, consistency and appropriate use prerequisites and with which Macau has an international exchange of information agreement in effect that allows for the automatic exchange of tax information</td></tr>
<tr><td>Part C</td><td>Appropriate use</td><td>-</td></tr>
</table>

References

OECD (2019), *Country-by-Country Reporting – Compilation of Peer Review Reports (Phase 2): Inclusive Framework on BEPS: Action 13*, OECD/G20 Base Erosion and Profit Shifting Project, OECD Publishing, Paris, https://dx.doi.org/10.1787/f9bf1157-en. [1]

OECD (2018), *Country-by-Country Reporting – Compilation of Peer Review Reports (Phase 1): Inclusive Framework on BEPS: Action 13*, OECD/G20 Base Erosion and Profit Shifting Project, OECD Publishing, Paris, https://dx.doi.org/10.1787/9789264300057-en. [2]

Note

[1] Law 21/2019 https://bo.io.gov.mo/bo/i/2019/51/lei21.asp; (accessed on 24 August 2020). Administrative Regulation 1/2020 https://bo.io.gov.mo/bo/i/2020/03/regadm01.asp (accessed on 24 August 2020).

Malaysia

1. Malaysia was reviewed as part of the 2017/2018 and the 2018/2019 peer reviews. This report is supplementary to those previous reports (OECD, 2019[1]) (OECD, 2018[2]).

2. The first filing obligation for a CbC report in Malaysia applies in respect of reporting fiscal years commencing on 1 January 2017. Malaysia also allows its MNE groups to file a CbC report on a voluntary basis, for reporting fiscal years beginning between 1 January 2016 and 31 December 2016.

Summary of key findings

3. Malaysia's implementation of the Action 13 minimum standard meets all applicable terms of reference (OECD, 2017[3]).

Part A: The domestic legal and administrative framework

4. Malaysia has legislation in place which implements the BEPS Action 13 minimum standard.

(a) Parent entity filing obligation

5. No changes were identified.

(b) Scope and timing of parent entity filing

6. No changes were identified.

(c) Limitation on local filing obligation

7. No changes were identified.

(d) Limitation on local filing in case of surrogate filing

8. No changes were identified.

(e) Effective implementation

9. No changes were identified.

Conclusion

10. Malaysia meets all the terms of reference relating to the domestic legal and administrative framework.

Part B: The exchange of information framework

(a) Exchange of information framework

11. As of 31 March 2020, Malaysia has 63 bilateral relationships in place, including those activated under the CbC MCAA and bilateral QCAAs. Within the context of its international exchange of information agreements that allow automatic exchange of information, Malaysia has taken steps to have qualifying competent authority agreements in effect with jurisdictions of the Inclusive Framework that meet the

confidentiality, consistency and appropriate use conditions. Regarding Malaysia's exchange of information framework, no inconsistencies with the terms of reference were identified.

(b) Content of information exchanged

12. No changes were identified.

(c) Completeness of exchanges

13. No changes were identified.

(d) Timeliness of exchanges

14. No changes were identified.

(e) Temporary suspension of exchange or termination of QCAA

15. No changes were identified.

(f) Consultation with other Competent Authority before determining systemic failure or significant non-compliance

16. No changes were identified.

(g) Format for information exchange

17. No changes were identified.

(h) Method for transmission

18. No changes were identified.

Conclusion

19. Malaysia meets all the terms of reference regarding the exchange of information.

Part C: Appropriate use

Appropriate use

20. No changes were identified.

Conclusion

21. Malaysia meets all the terms of reference relating to appropriate use of CbC reports.

Summary of recommendations on the implementation of country-by-country reporting

Aspect of the implementation that should be improved		Recommendation for improvement
Part A	Domestic legal and administrative framework	-
Part B	Exchange of information framework	-
Part C	Appropriate use	-

References

OECD (2019), *Country-by-Country Reporting – Compilation of Peer Review Reports (Phase 2): Inclusive Framework on BEPS: Action 13*, OECD/G20 Base Erosion and Profit Shifting Project, OECD Publishing, Paris, https://dx.doi.org/10.1787/f9bf1157-en. [1]

OECD (2018), *Country-by-Country Reporting – Compilation of Peer Review Reports (Phase 1): Inclusive Framework on BEPS: Action 13*, OECD/G20 Base Erosion and Profit Shifting Project, OECD Publishing, Paris, https://dx.doi.org/10.1787/9789264300057-en. [2]

OECD (2017), *Terms of reference for the conduct of peer review of the Action 13 minimum standard on country-by-country reporting*, OECD Publishing, https://www.oecd.org/tax/beps/beps-action-13-on-country-by-country-reporting-peer-review-documents.pdf. [3]

Maldives

1. Maldives was reviewed as part of the 2017/2018 and the 2018/2019 peer reviews. This report is supplementary to those previous reports (OECD, 2019[1]) (OECD, 2018[2]).

2. There is no filing obligation for a CbC report in Maldives yet.

Summary of key findings

3. It is recommended that Maldives take steps to finalise its domestic legal and administrative framework in relation to CbC requirements as soon as possible. This recommendation remains unchanged since the 2017/2018 peer review.

4. It is recommended that Maldives take steps to have QCAAs in effect with jurisdictions of the Inclusive Framework which meet the confidentiality, consistency and appropriate use prerequisites and with which it has international agreements for the automatic exchange of information. This recommendation remains unchanged since the 2017/2018 peer review.

5. It is recommended that Maldives have in place the necessary processes or written procedures to ensure that the exchange of information is conducted in a manner consistent with the terms of reference (OECD, 2017[3]) relating to the exchange of information framework. This recommendation remains unchanged since the 2018/2019 peer review.

6. It is recommended that Maldives take steps to ensure that the appropriate use condition is met ahead of the first exchanges of CbC reports. This recommendation remains unchanged since the 2017/2018 peer review.

Part A: The domestic legal and administrative framework

7. Maldives does not yet have legislation in place for implementing the BEPS Action 13 minimum standard. Maldives indicates that Tax Administration Act is being amended to provide the legal basis for the CbC Reporting implementation.

(a) Parent entity filing obligation

(b) Scope and timing of parent entity filing

(c) Limitation on local filing obligation

(d) Limitation on local filing in case of surrogate filing

(e) Effective implementation

Conclusion

8. It is recommended that the Maldives take steps to implement a domestic legal and administrative framework to impose and enforce CbC reporting requirements as soon as possible. This recommendation remains unchanged since the 2017/2018 peer review.

Part B: The exchange of information framework

(a) Exchange of information framework

9. As of 31 March 2020, Maldives has no bilateral relationships in place for the exchange of CbC reports. It is recommended that Maldives take steps to have qualifying competent authority agreements in effect with jurisdictions of the Inclusive Framework that meet the confidentiality, consistency and appropriate use conditions and with which Maldives has an international exchange of information agreement in effect that allows for the automatic exchange of tax information.

(b) Content of information exchanged

10. No changes were identified.

(c) Completeness of exchanges

11. No changes were identified.

(d) Timeliness of exchanges

12. No changes were identified.

(e) Temporary suspension of exchange or termination of QCAA

13. No changes were identified.

(f) Consultation with other Competent Authority before determining systemic failure or significant non-compliance

14. No changes were identified.

(g) Format for information exchange

15. No changes were identified.

(h) Method for transmission

16. No changes were identified.

Conclusion

17. It is recommended that Maldives take steps to have QCAAs in effect with jurisdictions of the Inclusive Framework which meet the confidentiality, consistency and appropriate use prerequisites and with which it has international agreements for the automatic exchange of information. This recommendation remains unchanged since the 2017/2018 peer review.

18. It is recommended that Maldives take steps to implement processes or written procedures to ensure that the exchange of information is conducted in a manner consistent with the terms of reference relating to the exchange of information framework ahead of its first exchanges of information. This recommendation remains unchanged since the 2018/2019 peer review.

Part C: Appropriate use

Appropriate use

19. No changes were identified

Conclusion

20. It is recommended that Maldives take steps to ensure that the appropriate use condition is met ahead of its first exchanges of information remain in place. This recommendation remains unchanged since the 2017/2018 peer review.

Summary of recommendations on the implementation of country-by-country reporting

Aspect of the implementation that should be improved		Recommendation for improvement
Part A	Domestic legal and administrative framework	It is recommended that Maldives finalize its domestic legal and administrative framework in relation to CbC requirements as soon as possible.
Part B	Exchange of information framework	It is recommended that Maldives take steps to have QCAAs in effect with jurisdictions of the Inclusive Framework which meet the confidentiality, consistency and appropriate use prerequisites and with which it has international agreements for the automatic exchange of information.
Part B	Exchange of information framework	It is recommended that Maldives have in place the necessary processes or written procedures to ensure that the exchange of information is conducted in a manner consistent with the terms of reference relating to the exchange of information framework.
Part C	Appropriate use	It is recommended that Maldives take steps to ensure that the appropriate use condition is met ahead of the first exchanges of information.

References

OECD (2019), *Country-by-Country Reporting – Compilation of Peer Review Reports (Phase 2): Inclusive Framework on BEPS: Action 13*, OECD/G20 Base Erosion and Profit Shifting Project, OECD Publishing, Paris, https://dx.doi.org/10.1787/f9bf1157-en. [1]

OECD (2018), *Country-by-Country Reporting – Compilation of Peer Review Reports (Phase 1): Inclusive Framework on BEPS: Action 13*, OECD/G20 Base Erosion and Profit Shifting Project, OECD Publishing, Paris, https://dx.doi.org/10.1787/9789264300057-en. [2]

OECD (2017), *Terms of reference for the conduct of peer review of the Action 13 minimum standard on country-by-country reporting*, OECD Publishing, https://www.oecd.org/tax/beps/beps-action-13-on-country-by-country-reporting-peer-review-documents.pdf. [3]

Malta

1. Malta was reviewed as part of the 2017/2018 and the 2018/2019 peer reviews. This report is supplementary to those previous reports (OECD, 2019[1]) (OECD, 2018[2]).

2. The first filing obligation for a CbC report in Malta applies in respect of reporting fiscal years commencing on 1 January 2016.

Summary of key findings

3. Malta's implementation of the Action 13 minimum standard meets all applicable terms of reference (OECD, 2017[3]).

Part A: The domestic legal and administrative framework

4. Malta has legislation in place which implements the BEPS Action 13 minimum standard.

(a) Parent entity filing obligation

5. No changes were identified.

(b) Scope and timing of parent entity filing

6. No changes were identified.

(c) Limitation on local filing obligation

7. No changes were identified.

(d) Limitation on local filing in case of surrogate filing

8. No changes were identified.

(e) Effective implementation

9. No changes were identified.

Conclusion

10. Malta meets all the terms of reference relating to the domestic legal and administrative framework.

Part B: The exchange of information framework

(a) Exchange of information framework

11. As of 31 March 2020, Malta has 66 bilateral relationships in place, including those activated under the CbC MCAA, bilateral QCAAs and under the EU Council Directive (2016/881/EU). Within the context of its international exchange of information agreements that allow automatic exchange of information, Malta has taken steps to have qualifying competent authority agreements in effect with jurisdictions of the

Inclusive Framework that meet the confidentiality, consistency and appropriate use conditions.[1] Regarding Malta's exchange of information framework, no inconsistencies with the terms of reference were identified.

(b) Content of information exchanged

12. No changes were identified.

(c) Completeness of exchanges

13. No changes were identified.

(d) Timeliness of exchanges

14. No changes were identified.

(e) Temporary suspension of exchange or termination of QCAA

15. No changes were identified.

(f) Consultation with other Competent Authority before determining systemic failure or significant non-compliance

16. No changes were identified.

(g) Format for information exchange

17. No changes were identified.

(h) Method for transmission

18. No changes were identified.

Conclusion

19. Malta meets all the terms of reference regarding the exchange of information.

Part C: Appropriate use

Appropriate use

20. No changes were identified.

Conclusion

21. Malta meets all the terms of reference relating to appropriate use of CbC reports.

Summary of recommendations on the implementation of country-by-country reporting

Aspect of the implementation that should be improved		Recommendation for improvement
Part A	Domestic legal and administrative framework	-
Part B	Exchange of information framework	-
Part C	Appropriate use	-

References

OECD (2019), *Country-by-Country Reporting – Compilation of Peer Review Reports (Phase 2): Inclusive Framework on BEPS: Action 13*, OECD/G20 Base Erosion and Profit Shifting Project, OECD Publishing, Paris, https://dx.doi.org/10.1787/f9bf1157-en. [1]

OECD (2018), *Country-by-Country Reporting – Compilation of Peer Review Reports (Phase 1): Inclusive Framework on BEPS: Action 13*, OECD/G20 Base Erosion and Profit Shifting Project, OECD Publishing, Paris, https://dx.doi.org/10.1787/9789264300057-en. [2]

OECD (2017), *Terms of reference for the conduct of peer review of the Action 13 minimum standard on country-by-country reporting*, OECD Publishing, https://www.oecd.org/tax/beps/beps-action-13-on-country-by-country-reporting-peer-review-documents.pdf. [3]

Note

[1] No inconsistency with the terms of reference will be identified where a QCAA is not in effect with one or more jurisdictions of the Inclusive Framework that meet the confidentiality, consistency and appropriate use conditions, but this is due to circumstances that are not under the control of the reviewed jurisdiction. This may include, for example, where the other jurisdiction intends to exchange CbC reports using the MCAA but it does not have the Convention in effect for the relevant fiscal period, or where the other jurisdiction has declined to have a QCAA in effect with the reviewed jurisdiction.

Mauritius

1. Mauritius was reviewed as part of the 2017/2018 and the 2018/2019 peer reviews. This report is supplementary to those previous reports (OECD, 2019[1]) (OECD, 2018[2]).

2. The first filing obligation for a CbC report in Mauritius applies to reporting fiscal years commencing on or after 1 July 2018.

Summary of key findings

3. Mauritius's implementation of the Action 13 minimum standard meets all applicable terms of reference (OECD, 2017[3]).

Part A: The domestic legal and administrative framework

4. Mauritius has legislation in place to implement the BEPS Action 13 minimum standard.

(a) Parent entity filing obligation

5. No changes were identified.

(b) Scope and timing of parent entity filing

6. No changes were identified.

(c) Limitation on local filing obligation

7. No changes were identified.

(d) Limitation on local filing in case of surrogate filing

8. No changes were identified.

(e) Effective implementation

9. No changes were identified.[12]

Conclusion

10. Mauritius meets all the terms of reference relating to the domestic legal and administrative framework.

Part B: The exchange of information framework

(a) Exchange of information framework

11. As of 31 March 2020, Mauritius has 72 bilateral relationships in place for the exchange of CbC reports, including those activated under the CbC MCAA and under bilateral CAAs. Within the context of its international exchange of information agreements that allow automatic exchange of tax information, Mauritius has taken steps to have qualifying competent authority agreements in effect with jurisdictions of the Inclusive Framework that meet the confidentiality, consistency and appropriate use conditions.

Regarding Mauritius's exchange of information framework, no inconsistencies with the terms of reference were identified.[3]

(b) Content of information exchanged

12. No changes were identified.

(c) Completeness of exchanges

13. No changes were identified.

(d) Timeliness of exchanges

14. No changes were identified.

(e) Temporary suspension of exchange or termination of QCAA

15. No changes were identified.

(f) Consultation with other Competent Authority before determining systemic failure or significant non-compliance

16. No changes were identified.

(g) Format for information exchange

17. No changes were identified.

(h) Method for transmission

18. No changes were identified.

Conclusion

19. Mauritius meets all the terms of reference regarding the exchange of information.

Part C: Appropriate use

Appropriate use

20. No changes were identified.

Conclusion

21. Mauritius meets all the terms of reference relating to appropriate use of CbC reports.

Summary of recommendations on the implementation of Country-by-Country Reporting

Aspect of the implementation that should be improved		Recommendation for improvement
Part A	Domestic legal and administrative framework	-
Part B	Exchange of information framework	-
Part C	Appropriate use	-

References

OECD (2019), *Country-by-Country Reporting – Compilation of Peer Review Reports (Phase 2): Inclusive Framework on BEPS: Action 13*, OECD/G20 Base Erosion and Profit Shifting Project, OECD Publishing, Paris, https://dx.doi.org/10.1787/f9bf1157-en. [1]

OECD (2018), *Country-by-Country Reporting – Compilation of Peer Review Reports (Phase 1): Inclusive Framework on BEPS: Action 13*, OECD/G20 Base Erosion and Profit Shifting Project, OECD Publishing, Paris, https://dx.doi.org/10.1787/9789264300057-en. [2]

OECD (2017), *Terms of reference for the conduct of peer review of the Action 13 minimum standard on country-by-country reporting*, OECD Publishing, https://www.oecd.org/tax/beps/beps-action-13-on-country-by-country-reporting-peer-review-documents.pdf. [3]

Notes

[1] Mauritius intends to implement penalties through amended CbCR Regulations, which are expected to be in force before the end of June 2019. Based on Article 7A of the draft amended CbCR Regulations: 1) Any person who fails to comply with the provisions of the CbCR Regulations is liable to a penalty of 5,000 rupees. 2) Where the failure to comply continues, the person will be liable to a further penalty of 10,000 rupees per month or part of the month during which the failure continues, for an aggregate not exceeding 120,000 rupees. 3) A person will be liable to a penalty not exceeding 50,000 rupees where the person provides inaccurate information. This aspect will be monitored. This monitoring point remains in place form the 2017/2018 peer review.

[2] There are no specific processes in place that would allow appropriate measures in case Mauritius is notified by another jurisdiction that such other jurisdiction has reason to believe that an error may have led to incorrect or incomplete information reported by a Reporting Entity or that a Reporting Entity is failing to comply with respect to CbC reporting obligations. As no exchange of CbC reports has yet occurred, no recommendation is made but this aspect will be further monitored

[3] No inconsistency with the terms of reference will be identified where a QCAA is not in effect with one or more jurisdictions of the Inclusive Framework that meet the confidentiality, consistency and appropriate use conditions, but this is due to circumstances that are not under the control of the reviewed jurisdiction. This may include, for example, where the other jurisdiction intends to exchange CbC reports using the MCAA but it does not have the Convention in effect for the relevant fiscal period, or where the other jurisdiction has declined to have a QCAA in effect with the reviewed jurisdiction.

Mexico

1. Mexico was reviewed as part of the 2017/2018 and the 2018/2019 peer reviews. This report is supplementary to those previous reports (OECD, 2019[1]) (OECD, 2018[2]).

2. The first filing obligation for a CbC report in Mexico commences in respect of periods commencing on or after 1 January 2016.

Summary of key findings

3. Mexico's implementation of the Action 13 minimum standard meets all applicable terms of reference (OECD, 2017[3]).

Part A: The domestic legal and administrative framework

4. Mexico has legislation in place to implement the BEPS Action 13 minimum standard.

(a) Parent entity filing obligation

5. No changes were identified.[1]

(b) Scope and timing of parent entity filing

6. No changes were identified.[2]

(c) Limitation on local filing obligation

7. Mexico's 2017/2018 peer review included a general monitoring point with respect to the local filing conditions. The beginning of the timeframe for the tax authority to require CbC Report under local filing requirements is not express in the legislation. Mexico confirms that CbC reports will not be requested under local filing requirements before a reasonable timeframe. Mexico confirms that local filing will be applied in line with paragraph 60 of the Action 13 Report and that this is clarified in an internal manual for tax inspectors in order to ensure that local filing can only be required in the circumstances defined by the minimum standard and terms of reference. This monitoring point is removed.

(d) Limitation on local filing in case of surrogate filing

8. Mexico's 2017/2018 peer review included a general monitoring point with respect to the limitation on local filing in case of surrogate filing. Mexico indicates that even though there is no express limitation, if the conditions in the terms of reference are met, the deactivation of local filing will apply. Mexico confirms that the limitation on local filing in case of surrogate filing is clarified in an internal manual for tax inspectors in order to ensure that local filing will be deactivated in the circumstances defined in terms of reference. This monitoring point is removed.

(e) Effective implementation

9. No changes were identified.[3]

Conclusion

10. Mexico meets all the terms of reference relating to the domestic legal and administrative framework.

Part B: The exchange of information framework

(a) Exchange of information framework

11. As of 31 March 2020, Mexico has 73 bilateral relationships, including those activated under the CbC MCAA and under bilateral CAAs. Within the context of its international exchange of information agreements that allow automatic exchange of information, Mexico has taken steps to have qualifying competent authority agreements in effect with jurisdictions of the Inclusive Framework that meet the confidentiality, consistency and appropriate use conditions.[4] Regarding Mexico's exchange of information framework, no inconsistencies with the terms of reference were identified.

(b) Content of information exchanged

12. No changes were identified.

(c) Completeness of exchanges

13. No changes were identified.

(d) Timeliness of exchanges

14. No changes were identified.

(e) Temporary suspension of exchange or termination of QCAA

15. No changes were identified.

(f) Consultation with other Competent Authority before determining systemic failure or significant non-compliance

16. No changes were identified.

(g) Format for information exchange

17. No changes were identified.

(h) Method for transmission

18. No changes were identified.

Conclusion

19. Mexico meets all the terms of reference regarding the exchange of information.

Part C: Appropriate use

Appropriate use

20. No changes were identified.

Conclusion

21. Mexico meets all the terms of reference relating to appropriate use of CbC reports.

Summary of recommendations on the implementation of country-by-country reporting

Aspect of the implementation that should be improved		Recommendation for improvement
Part A	Domestic legal and administrative framework	-
Part B	Exchange of information framework	-
Part C	Appropriate use	-

References

OECD (2019), *Country-by-Country Reporting – Compilation of Peer Review Reports (Phase 2): Inclusive Framework on BEPS: Action 13*, OECD/G20 Base Erosion and Profit Shifting Project, OECD Publishing, Paris, https://dx.doi.org/10.1787/f9bf1157-en. [1]

OECD (2018), *Country-by-Country Reporting – Compilation of Peer Review Reports (Phase 1): Inclusive Framework on BEPS: Action 13*, OECD/G20 Base Erosion and Profit Shifting Project, OECD Publishing, Paris, https://dx.doi.org/10.1787/9789264300057-en. [2]

OECD (2017), *Terms of reference for the conduct of peer review of the Action 13 minimum standard on country-by-country reporting*, OECD Publishing, https://www.oecd.org/tax/beps/beps-action-13-on-country-by-country-reporting-peer-review-documents.pdf. [3]

Notes

[1] Mexico's 2017/2018 peer review included a general monitoring point with respect to the annual consolidated group revenue threshold under article 76-A, paragraph III.c.6. of the Mexican Income Tax Law, which may be inconsistent with paragraph 8 a) ii. of the terms of reference, as it may generate fluctuations from year to year on the threshold to require the filing of CbC reports. Mexico indicates that the sole purpose of this provision is to have a legal vehicle in order change the threshold if such change arises from the 2020 revision. Mexico confirms that there were no yearly fluctuations to the annual consolidated group revenue threshold under article 76-A during the year in review. This monitoring point remains in place.

[2] Mexico's 2017/2018 peer review included a monitoring point relating to the definition of "number of employees" in its legislation. The definition in Mexico's legislation does not mirror the Action 13 Report's specific instructions by not providing flexibility to taxpayers to report independent contractors as employees. However, this does not seem to raise any significant concern, taking into account the particular domestic context as described by Mexico. Mexico confirms that the definition of "number of employees" remains as established since it is intended to address specific issues related to certain tax planning set-ups relevant in the Mexican context. This monitoring point remains in place.

[3] Mexico's 2017/2018 peer review included a general monitoring point relating to processes that would allow Mexico to take appropriate measures in case it is notified by another jurisdiction that such other jurisdiction has reason to believe that an error may have led to incorrect or incomplete information reporting by a Reporting Entity or that there is non-compliance of a Reporting Entity with respect to its obligation to file a CbC report. This monitoring point remains in place.

[4] No inconsistency with the terms of reference will be identified where a QCAA is not in effect with one or more jurisdictions of the Inclusive Framework that meet the confidentiality, consistency and appropriate use conditions, but this is due to circumstances that are not under the control of the reviewed jurisdiction. This may include, for example, where the other jurisdiction intends to exchange CbC reports using the MCAA but it does not have the Convention in effect for the relevant fiscal period, or where the other jurisdiction has declined to have a QCAA in effect with the reviewed jurisdiction.

Monaco

1. Monaco was reviewed as part of the 2017/2018 and the 2018/2019 peer reviews. This report is supplementary to those previous reports (OECD, 2019[1]) (OECD, 2018[2]).

2. The first filing obligation for a CbC report in Monaco commences in respect of periods commending on or after 1 January 2018.

Summary of key findings

3. Monaco's legal and domestic framework for implementation of the Action 13 minimum standard meets all applicable terms of reference (OECD, 2017[3]).

4. It is recommended to have the necessary processes and written procedures to ensure that the exchange of information is conducted in a manner consistent with the terms of reference relating to the exchange of information framework. This recommendation remains unchanged since the 2018/2019 peer review.

5. Monaco's previous peer reviews included a recommendation that Monaco should continue to work actively towards putting in place qualifying competent authority agreements with jurisdictions of the Inclusive Framework that meet the confidentiality, consistency and appropriate use conditions and with which Monaco has an international exchange of information agreement in effect that allows for the automatic exchange of tax information. Bilateral relationships are now in place and this recommendation is removed.

Part A: The domestic legal and administrative framework

6. Monaco has legislation in place to implement the BEPS Action 13 minimum standard.

(a) Parent entity filing obligation

7. No changes were identified.

(b) Scope and timing of parent entity filing

8. No changes were identified.

(c) Limitation on local filing obligation

9. No changes were identified.

(d) Limitation on local filing in case of surrogate filing

10. No changes were identified.

(e) Effective implementation

11. No changes were identified.

Conclusion

12. Monaco meets all the terms of reference relating to the domestic legal and administrative framework.

Part B: The exchange of information framework

(a) Exchange of information framework

13. Monaco's previous peer reviews included a recommendation that Monaco should continue to work actively towards putting in place qualifying competent authority agreements with jurisdictions of the Inclusive Framework that meet the confidentiality, consistency and appropriate use conditions and with which Monaco has an international exchange of information agreement in effect that allows for the automatic exchange of tax information. Bilateral relationships are now in place and this recommendation is removed.

14. As of 31 March 2020, Monaco has 58 bilateral relationships in place for the exchange of CbC reports activated under the CbC MCAA. Within the context of its international exchange of information agreements that allow automatic exchange of information, Monaco has taken steps to have qualifying competent authority agreements in effect with jurisdictions of the Inclusive Framework that meet the confidentiality, consistency and appropriate use conditions. Regarding Monaco's exchange of information framework, no inconsistencies with the terms of reference were identified.

(b) Content of information exchanged

15. No changes were identified.

(c) Completeness of exchanges

16. No changes were identified.

(d) Timeliness of exchanges

17. No changes were identified.

(e) Temporary suspension of exchange or termination of QCAA

18. No changes were identified.

(f) Consultation with other Competent Authority before determining systemic failure or significant non-compliance

19. No changes were identified.

(g) Format for information exchange

20. No changes were identified.

(h) Method for transmission

21. No changes were identified.

Conclusion

22. Monaco's previous peer reviews included a recommendation that it take steps to have QCAAs in effect with jurisdictions of the Inclusive Framework which will meet the confidentiality, consistency and appropriate use prerequisites and with which Monaco has international agreements which allow for the

automatic exchange of tax information. Bilateral relationships are now in place so the recommendation is removed.

23. It is recommended that Monaco take steps to implement processes and written procedures to ensure that the exchange of information is conducted in a manner consistent with the terms of reference relating to the exchange of information framework. This recommendation remains unchanged since the 2018/2019 peer review.

Part C: Appropriate use

Appropriate use

24. No changes were identified.

Conclusion

25. Monaco meets all the terms of reference relating to appropriate use of CbC reports.

Summary of recommendations on the implementation of country-by-country reporting

Aspect of the implementation that should be improved		Recommendation for improvement
Part A	Domestic legal and administrative framework	-
Part B	Exchange of information framework	It is recommended that Monaco take steps to have all the necessary processes and written procedures in place to ensure that the exchange of information is conducted in a manner consistent with the terms of reference relating to the exchange of information framework.
Part C	Appropriate use	-

References

OECD (2019), *Country-by-Country Reporting – Compilation of Peer Review Reports (Phase 2): Inclusive Framework on BEPS: Action 13*, OECD/G20 Base Erosion and Profit Shifting Project, OECD Publishing, Paris, https://dx.doi.org/10.1787/f9bf1157-en. [1]

OECD (2018), *Country-by-Country Reporting – Compilation of Peer Review Reports (Phase 1): Inclusive Framework on BEPS: Action 13*, OECD/G20 Base Erosion and Profit Shifting Project, OECD Publishing, Paris, https://dx.doi.org/10.1787/9789264300057-en. [2]

OECD (2017), *Terms of reference for the conduct of peer review of the Action 13 minimum standard on country-by-country reporting*, OECD Publishing, https://www.oecd.org/tax/beps/beps-action-13-on-country-by-country-reporting-peer-review-documents.pdf. [3]

Mongolia

1. Mongolia was first reviewed during the 2018/2019 peer review. This report is supplementary to that previous report (OECD, 2018[2]).

2. There is no filing obligation for a CbC report in Mongolia yet.

Summary of key findings

3. Mongolia does not have legislation in place for implementing the BEPS Action 13 minimum standard. It is recommended that Mongolia take steps to implement a domestic legal and administrative framework to impose and enforce CbC reporting requirements as soon as possible. This recommendation remains in place since the 2018/2019 peer review.

4. It is recommended that Mongolia take steps to put QCAAs in effect with jurisdictions of the Inclusive Framework which meet the confidentiality, consistency and appropriate use prerequisites and with which they have an international exchange of information agreement in effect that allows for the automatic exchange of tax information. This recommendation remains in place since the 2018/2019 peer review.

5. It is recommended that Mongolia take steps to implement processes or written procedures to ensure that the exchange of information is conducted in a manner consistent with the terms of reference (OECD, 2017[3]) relating to the exchange of information framework ahead of the first exchanges of information. This recommendation remains in place since the 2018/2019 peer review.

6. It is recommended that Mongolia take steps to ensure that the appropriate use condition is met ahead of the first exchanges of information. This recommendation remains in place since the 2018/2019 peer review.

Part A: The domestic legal and administrative framework

7. Mongolia does not yet have legislation in place for implementing the BEPS Action 13 minimum standard. Mongolia indicates that it intends to have legislation implementing the CbC reporting requirements in force in 2020.

(a) Parent entity filing obligation

(b) Scope and timing of parent entity filing

(c) Limitation on local filing obligation

(d) Limitation on local filing in case of surrogate filing

(e) Effective implementation

8. Mongolia does not yet have its legal and administrative framework in place to implement CbC Reporting.

9. It is recommended that Mongolia take steps to implement a domestic legal and administrative framework to impose and enforce CbC reporting requirements as soon as possible.

Conclusion

10. It is recommended that Mongolia take steps to implement a domestic legal and administrative framework to impose and enforce CbC reporting requirements as soon as possible.

Part B: The exchange of information framework

(a) Exchange of information framework

11. As of 31 March 2020, Mongolia has no bilateral relationships in place for the exchange of CbC reports. It is recommended that Mongolia take steps to have qualifying competent authority agreements in effect with jurisdictions of the Inclusive Framework that meet the confidentiality, consistency and appropriate use conditions and with which Mongolia has an international exchange of information agreement in effect that allows for the automatic exchange of tax information.

(b) Content of information exchanged

12. No changes were identified.

(c) Completeness of exchanges

13. No changes were identified.

(d) Timeliness of exchanges

14. No changes were identified.

(e) Temporary suspension of exchange or termination of QCAA

15. No changes were identified.

(f) Consultation with other Competent Authority before determining systemic failure or significant non-compliance

16. No changes were identified.

(g) Format for information exchange

17. No changes were identified.

(h) Method for transmission

18. No changes were identified.

Conclusion

19. It is recommended that Mongolia take steps to have QCAAs in effect with jurisdictions of the Inclusive Framework which meet the confidentiality, consistency and appropriate use prerequisites and with which they have an international exchange of information agreement in effect that allows for the automatic exchange of tax information. This recommendation remains unchanged since the 2018/2019 peer review.

20. It is recommended that Mongolia take steps to implement processes or written procedures to ensure that the exchange of information is conducted in a manner consistent with the terms of reference relating to the exchange of information framework ahead of its first exchanges of information. This recommendation remains unchanged since the 2018/2019 peer review.

Part C: Appropriate use

Appropriate use

21. No changes were identified.

Conclusion

22. It is recommended that Mongolia take steps to ensure that the appropriate use condition is met ahead of its first exchanges of information. This recommendation remains unchanged since the 2018/2019 peer review.

Summary of recommendations on the implementation of Country-by-Country Reporting

Aspect of the implementation that should be improved		Recommendation for improvement
Part A	Domestic legal and administrative framework	It is recommended that Mongolia take steps to implement a domestic legal and administrative framework to impose and enforce CbC requirements as soon as possible.
Part B	Exchange of information framework	It is recommended that Mongolia take steps to put in place an exchange of information framework that allows Automatic Exchange of Information and have QCAAs in effect with jurisdictions of the Inclusive Framework which meet the confidentiality, consistency and appropriate use prerequisites and with which they have an international exchange of information agreement in effect that allows for the automatic exchange of tax information
Part B	Exchange of information framework	It is recommended that Mongolia take steps to implement the necessary processes or written procedures to ensure that the exchange of information is conducted in a manner consistent with the terms of reference relating to the exchange of information framework.
Part C	Appropriate use	It is recommended that Mongolia take steps to ensure that the appropriate use condition is met ahead of the first exchanges of information.

References

OECD (2018), *Country-by-Country Reporting – Compilation of Peer Review Reports (Phase 1): Inclusive Framework on BEPS: Action 13*, OECD/G20 Base Erosion and Profit Shifting Project, OECD Publishing, Paris, https://dx.doi.org/10.1787/9789264300057-en. [2]

OECD (2017), *Terms of reference for the conduct of peer review of the Action 13 minimum standard on country-by-country reporting*, OECD Publishing, https://www.oecd.org/tax/beps/beps-action-13-on-country-by-country-reporting-peer-review-documents.pdf. [3]

Montserrat

1. Montserrat was first reviewed during the 2018/2019 peer review. This report is supplementary to that previous report (OECD, 2018[2]).

2. There is no filing obligation for a CbC report in Montserrat yet.

Summary of key findings

3. Montserrat does not have legislation in place for implementing the BEPS Action 13 minimum standard. It is recommended that Montserrat take steps to implement a domestic legal and administrative framework to impose and enforce CbC reporting requirements as soon as possible. This recommendation remains unchanged since the 2018/2019 peer review.

4. It is recommended that Montserrat take steps to have QCAAs in effect with jurisdictions of the Inclusive Framework which meet the confidentiality, consistency and appropriate use prerequisites and with which Montserrat has an international exchange of information agreement in effect that allows for the automatic exchange of tax information. This recommendation remains unchanged since the 2018/2019 peer review.

5. It is recommended that Montserrat take steps to implement processes or written procedures to ensure that the exchange of information is conducted in a manner consistent with the terms of reference (OECD, 2017[3]) relating to the exchange of information framework ahead of the first exchanges of information. This recommendation remains unchanged since the 2018/2019 peer review.

6. It is recommended that Montserrat take steps to ensure that the appropriate use condition is met ahead of the first exchanges of information. This recommendation remains unchanged since the 2018/2019 peer review.

Part A: The domestic legal and administrative framework

7. Montserrat does not yet have legislation in place for implementing the BEPS Action 13 minimum standard.

(a) Parent entity filing obligation

(b) Scope and timing of parent entity filing

(c) Limitation on local filing obligation

(d) Limitation on local filing in case of surrogate filing

(e) Effective implementation

Conclusion

8. It is recommended that Montserrat take steps to implement a domestic legal and administrative framework to impose and enforce CbC reporting requirements as soon as possible. This recommendation remains unchanged since the 2018/2019 peer review.

Part B: The exchange of information framework

(a) Exchange of information framework

9. As of 31 March 2020, Montserrat has no bilateral relationships in place for the exchange of CbC reports. It is recommended that Montserrat take steps to have qualifying competent authority agreements in effect with jurisdictions of the Inclusive Framework that meet the confidentiality, consistency and appropriate use conditions and with which Montserrat has an international exchange of information agreement in effect that allows for the automatic exchange of tax information. This recommendation remains unchanged since the 2018/2019 peer review.

(b) Content of information exchanged

10. No changes were identified.

(c) Completeness of exchanges

11. No changes were identified.

(d) Timeliness of exchanges

12. No changes were identified.

(e) Temporary suspension of exchange or termination of QCAA

13. No changes were identified.

(f) Consultation with other Competent Authority before determining systemic failure or significant non-compliance

14. No changes were identified.

(g) Format for information exchange

15. No changes were identified.

(h) Method for transmission

16. No changes were identified.

Conclusion

17. It is recommended that Montserrat take steps to have qualifying competent authority agreements in effect with jurisdictions of the Inclusive Framework that meet the confidentiality, consistency and appropriate use conditions and with which Montserrat has an international exchange of information agreement in effect that allows for the automatic exchange of tax information. This recommendation remains unchanged since the 2018/2019 peer review.

18. It is recommended that Montserrat take steps to implement processes or written procedures to ensure that the exchange of information is conducted in a manner consistent with the terms of reference relating to the exchange of information framework ahead of its first exchanges of information. This recommendation remains unchanged since the 2018/2019 peer review.

Part C: Appropriate use

Appropriate use

19. No changes were identified.

Conclusion

20. It is recommended that Montserrat take steps to ensure that the appropriate use condition is met ahead of its first exchanges of information. This recommendation remains unchanged since the 2018/2019 peer review.

Summary of recommendations on the implementation of Country-by-Country Reporting

Aspect of the implementation that should be improved		Recommendation for improvement
Part A	Domestic legal and administrative framework	It is recommended that Montserrat take steps to implement a domestic legal and administrative framework to impose and enforce CbC requirements as soon as possible.
Part B	Exchange of information framework	It is recommended that Montserrat take steps to have QCAAs in effect with jurisdictions of the Inclusive Framework which meet the confidentiality, consistency and appropriate use prerequisites and with which Montserrat has an international exchange of information agreement in effect that allows for the automatic exchange of tax information.
Part B	Exchange of information framework	It is recommended that Montserrat take steps to implement the necessary processes or written procedures to ensure that the exchange of information is conducted in a manner consistent with the terms of reference relating to the exchange of information framework.
Part C	Appropriate use	It is recommended that Montserrat take steps to ensure that the appropriate use condition is met ahead of the first exchanges of information.

References

OECD (2018), *Country-by-Country Reporting – Compilation of Peer Review Reports (Phase 1): Inclusive Framework on BEPS: Action 13*, OECD/G20 Base Erosion and Profit Shifting Project, OECD Publishing, Paris, https://dx.doi.org/10.1787/9789264300057-en. [2]

OECD (2017), *Terms of reference for the conduct of peer review of the Action 13 minimum standard on country-by-country reporting*, OECD Publishing, https://www.oecd.org/tax/beps/beps-action-13-on-country-by-country-reporting-peer-review-documents.pdf. [3]

Morocco

1. This report is Morocco's first annual peer review report. Consistent with the agreed methodology this report covers: (i) the domestic legal and administrative framework, (ii) the exchange of information framework as well as (iii) the appropriate use of CbC reports.

2. The first filing obligation for a CbC report in Morocco commences in respect of fiscal periods commencing on or after 1 January 2021.

Summary of key findings

3. Morocco has implemented CbC legislation in budget law 2020. This legislation is in effect and will be reviewed in the next review.

4. It is recommended that Morocco take steps to put in place an exchange of information framework that allows automatic exchange of information and have QCAAs in effect with jurisdictions of the Inclusive Framework which meet the confidentiality, consistency and appropriate use prerequisites and with which Morocco has an international exchange of information agreement in effect that allows for the automatic exchange of tax information.

5. It is recommended that Morocco take steps to implement processes or written procedures to ensure that the exchange of information is conducted in a manner consistent with the terms of reference (OECD, 2017[3]) relating to the exchange of information framework ahead of the first exchanges of information.

6. It is recommended that Morocco take steps to ensure that the appropriate use condition is met ahead of the first exchanges of information.

Part A: The domestic legal and administrative framework

7. Morocco has implemented legislation in its budget law 2020 to meet the BEPS Action 13 minimum standard. This legislation will be reviewed in the next peer review.

(a) Parent entity filing obligation

(b) Scope and timing of parent entity filing

(c) Limitation on local filing obligation

(d) Limitation on local filing in case of surrogate filing

(e) Effective implementation

Conclusion

8. Morocco has legislation in place for implementing the BEPS Action 13 minimum standard. Review of this legislation will take place next year.

Part B: The exchange of information framework

(a) Exchange of information framework

9. As of 31 March 2020, Morocco has no bilateral relationships in place for the exchange of CbC reports. It is recommended that Morocco take steps to have qualifying competent authority agreements in effect with jurisdictions of the Inclusive Framework that meet the confidentiality, consistency and appropriate use conditions and with which Morocco has an international exchange of information agreement in effect that allows for the automatic exchange of tax information.

(b) Content of information exchanged

10. Morocco does not have processes or written procedures in place that are intended to ensure that each of the mandatory fields of information required in the CbC reporting template are present in the information exchanged.

(c) Completeness of exchanges

11. Morocco does not have processes or written procedures in place that are intended to ensure that CbC reports are exchanged with all tax jurisdictions listed in Table 1 of a CbC report with which it should exchange information as per the relevant QCAA.

(d) Timeliness of exchanges

12. Morocco does not have processes or written procedures in place that are intended to ensure that the information to be exchanged is transmitted to the relevant jurisdictions in accordance with the timelines provided for in the relevant QCAAs.

(e) Temporary suspension of exchange or termination of QCAA

13. Morocco does not have processes or written procedures in place that are intended to ensure that a temporary suspension of the exchange of information or termination of a relevant QCAA would be carried out only as per the conditions set out in the relevant QCAA.

(f) Consultation with other Competent Authority before determining systemic failure or significant non-compliance

14. Morocco does not have processes or written procedures in place that are intended to ensure that its Competent Authority consults with the other Competent Authority before making a determination of systemic failure or significant non-compliance with the terms of the relevant QCAA by that other Competent Authority.

(g) Format for information exchange

15. Morocco has not confirmed the format that will be used for the international exchange of CbC reports.

(h) Method for transmission

16. Morocco has not confirmed the mechanism that it will use to exchange CbC reports.

Conclusion

17. It is recommended that Morocco take steps to have qualifying competent authority agreements in effect with jurisdictions of the Inclusive Framework that meet the confidentiality, consistency and

appropriate use conditions and with which Morocco has an international exchange of information agreement in effect that allows for the automatic exchange of tax information.

18. It is recommended that Morocco take steps to implement processes or written procedures to ensure that the exchange of information is conducted in a manner consistent with the terms of reference (OECD, 2017[3]) relating to the exchange of information framework ahead of its first exchanges of information.

Part C: Appropriate use

Appropriate use

19. Morocco does not yet have measures in place relating to appropriate use.

20. It is recommended that Morocco take steps to have measures in place relating to appropriate use ahead of the first exchanges of information.

Conclusion

21. It is recommended that Morocco take steps to ensure that the appropriate use condition is met ahead of its first exchanges of information.

Summary of recommendations on the implementation of Country-by-Country Reporting

Aspect of the implementation that should be improved		Recommendation for improvement
Part A	Domestic legal and administrative framework	A review of Morocco's domestic legal and administrative framework will be undertaken as part of the next BEPS Action 13 peer review..
Part B	Exchange of information framework	It is recommended that Morocco take steps to put in place an exchange of information framework that allows Automatic Exchange of Information and have QCAAs in effect with jurisdictions of the Inclusive Framework which meet the confidentiality, consistency and appropriate use prerequisites and with which Morocco has an international exchange of information agreement in effect that allows for the automatic exchange of tax information.
Part B	Exchange of information framework	It is recommended that Morocco take steps to implement the necessary processes or written procedures to ensure that the exchange of information is conducted in a manner consistent with the terms of reference relating to the exchange of information framework.
Part C	Appropriate use	It is recommended that Morocco take steps to ensure that the appropriate use condition is met ahead of the first exchanges of information.

References

OECD (2017), *Terms of reference for the conduct of peer review of the Action 13 minimum standard on country-by-country reporting*, OECD Publishing, https://www.oecd.org/tax/beps/beps-action-13-on-country-by-country-reporting-peer-review-documents.pdf. [3]

Namibia

1. This report is Namibia's first annual peer review report. Consistent with the agreed methodology this report covers: (i) the domestic legal and administrative framework, (ii) the exchange of information framework as well as (iii) the appropriate use of CbC reports.

2. There is no filing obligation for a CbC report in Namibia yet.

Summary of key findings

3. Namibia does not yet have legislation in place for implementing the BEPS Action 13 minimum standard.

4. It is recommended that Namibia take steps to implement a domestic legal and administrative framework to impose and enforce CbC reporting requirements as soon as possible.

5. It is recommended that Namibia take steps to put in place an exchange of information framework that allows automatic exchange of information and have QCAAs in effect with jurisdictions of the Inclusive Framework which meet the confidentiality, consistency and appropriate use prerequisites and with which Namibia has an international exchange of information agreement in effect that allows for the automatic exchange of tax information.

6. It is recommended that Namibia take steps to implement processes or written procedures to ensure that the exchange of information is conducted in a manner consistent with the terms of reference (OECD, 2017[3]) relating to the exchange of information framework ahead of the first exchanges of information.

7. It is recommended that Namibia take steps to ensure that the appropriate use condition is met ahead of the first exchanges of information.

Part A: The domestic legal and administrative framework

8. Namibia does not yet have legislation in place for implementing the BEPS Action 13 minimum standard.

(a) Parent entity filing obligation

(b) Scope and timing of parent entity filing

(c) Limitation on local filing obligation

(d) Limitation on local filing in case of surrogate filing

(e) Effective implementation

Conclusion

9. It is recommended that Namibia take steps to implement a domestic legal and administrative framework to impose and enforce CbC reporting requirements as soon as possible.

Part B: The exchange of information framework

(a) Exchange of information framework

10. As of 31 May 2020, Namibia has no bilateral relationships in place for the exchange of CbC reports. It is recommended that Namibia take steps to have qualifying competent authority agreements in effect with jurisdictions of the Inclusive Framework that meet the confidentiality, consistency and appropriate use conditions and with which Namibia has an international exchange of information agreement in effect that allows for the automatic exchange of tax information.

(b) Content of information exchanged

11. Namibia does not have processes or written procedures in place that are intended to ensure that each of the mandatory fields of information required in the CbC reporting template are present in the information exchanged.

(c) Completeness of exchanges

12. Namibia does not have processes or written procedures in place that are intended to ensure that CbC reports are exchanged with all tax jurisdictions listed in Table 1 of a CbC report with which it should exchange information as per the relevant QCAA.

(d) Timeliness of exchanges

13. Namibia does not have processes or written procedures in place that are intended to ensure that the information to be exchanged is transmitted to the relevant jurisdictions in accordance with the timelines provided for in the relevant QCAAs.

(e) Temporary suspension of exchange or termination of QCAA

14. Namibia does not have processes or written procedures in place that are intended to ensure that a temporary suspension of the exchange of information or termination of a relevant QCAA would be carried out only as per the conditions set out in the relevant QCAA.

(f) Consultation with other Competent Authority before determining systemic failure or significant non-compliance

15. Namibia does not have processes or written procedures in place that are intended to ensure that its Competent Authority consults with the other Competent Authority before making a determination of systemic failure or significant non-compliance with the terms of the relevant QCAA by that other Competent Authority.

(g) Format for information exchange

16. Namibia has not confirmed the format that will be used for the international exchange of CbC reports.

(h) Method for transmission

17. Namibia has not confirmed the mechanism that it will use to exchange CbC reports.

Conclusion

18. It is recommended that Namibia take steps to have qualifying competent authority agreements in effect with jurisdictions of the Inclusive Framework that meet the confidentiality, consistency and

appropriate use conditions and with which Namibia has an international exchange of information agreement in effect that allows for the automatic exchange of tax information.

19. It is recommended that Namibia take steps to implement processes or written procedures to ensure that the exchange of information is conducted in a manner consistent with the terms of reference (OECD, 2017[3]) relating to the exchange of information framework ahead of its first exchanges of information.

Part C: Appropriate use

Appropriate use

20. Namibia does not yet have measures in place relating to appropriate use.

21. It is recommended that Namibia take steps to have measures in place relating to appropriate use ahead of the first exchanges of information remains in place.

Conclusion

22. It is recommended that Namibia take steps to ensure that the appropriate use condition is met ahead of its first exchanges of information.

Summary of recommendations on the implementation of Country-by-Country Reporting

Aspect of the implementation that should be improved		Recommendation for improvement
Part A	Domestic legal and administrative framework	It is recommended that Namibia take steps to implement a domestic legal and administrative framework to impose and enforce CbC requirements as soon as possible.
Part B	Exchange of information framework	It is recommended that Namibia take steps to put in place an exchange of information framework that allows Automatic Exchange of Information and have QCAAs in effect with jurisdictions of the Inclusive Framework which meet the confidentiality, consistency and appropriate use prerequisites and with which Namibia has an international exchange of information agreement in effect that allows for the automatic exchange of tax information.
Part B	Exchange of information framework	It is recommended that Namibia take steps to implement the necessary processes or written procedures to ensure that the exchange of information is conducted in a manner consistent with the terms of reference relating to the exchange of information framework.
Part C	Appropriate use	It is recommended that Namibia take steps to ensure that the appropriate use condition is met ahead of the first exchanges of information.

References

OECD (2017), *Terms of reference for the conduct of peer review of the Action 13 minimum standard on country-by-country reporting*, OECD Publishing, https://www.oecd.org/tax/beps/beps-action-13-on-country-by-country-reporting-peer-review-documents.pdf. [3]

Netherlands

1. The Netherlands was reviewed as part of the 2017/2018 and the 2018/2019 peer reviews. This report is supplementary to those previous reports (OECD, 2019[1]) (OECD, 2018[2]).

2. The first filing obligation for a CbC report in the Netherlands applies to reporting fiscal years commencing on or after 1 January 2016.

Summary of key findings

3. The Netherlands' implementation of the Action 13 minimum standard meets all applicable terms of reference (OECD, 2017[3]).

Part A: The domestic legal and administrative framework

4. The Netherlands has primary and secondary laws in place for implementing the BEPS Action 13 minimum standard[1] establishing the necessary requirements, including the filing and reporting obligations. Guidance has also been published.[2] Since the 2017/2018 peer review, guidance has been updated. The Netherlands has provided an update with respect to the procedures it has in place to ensure effective implementation.

(a) Parent entity filing obligation

5. The Netherlands' 2017/2018 peer review included a monitoring point concerning the threshold used to determine an Excluded MNE Group. Since the 2017/2018 peer review, the Netherlands has updated national guidance[3] in a manner consistent with the terms of reference relating to the threshold used to determine an Excluded MNE Group. In view of this update, the monitoring point is removed.

6. No other changes were identified with respect to the parent entity filing obligation.

(b) Scope and timing of parent entity filing

7. No changes were identified with respect to the scope and timing of parent entity filing.

(c) Limitation on local filing obligation

8. No changes were identified with respect to the limitation on local filing obligation.

(d) Limitation on local filing in case of surrogate filing

9. The Netherlands indicates that a legislative basis for voluntary parent surrogate filing has been provided[4] by the Corporate Income Act 1969 as per 1 January 2018. No other changes were identified with respect to the limitation on local filing in case of surrogate filing.

(e) Effective implementation

10. The Netherlands' 2017/2018 peer review included a general monitoring point concerning the fact that was no specific process that would allow it to take appropriate measures in case the Netherlands is notified by another jurisdiction that such other jurisdiction has reason to believe that an error may have led to incorrect or incomplete information reporting by a Reporting Entity or that there is non-compliance of a Reporting Entity with respect to its obligation to file a CbC report. Since the 2017/2018 peer review, the

Netherlands has issued a written procedure, explaining that, in such a situation, the Central Liaison Office (CLO) will forward the message to the coordinator of the CbC team within one week. The coordinator will assess the message and, if necessary, notify the Reporting Entity within one month. Subsequently, the CbC team will monitor the appropriate action taken by the Reporting Entity. In addition, the coordinator will determine which follow-up action is to be used (penalty or other means) in case of late filing. In view of this update and specific procedure, the monitoring point is removed.

11. No changes were identified with respect to the effective implementation.

Conclusion

12. There is no change to the conclusion in relation to the domestic legal and administration framework for The Netherlands since the previous peer review. The Netherlands meets all the terms of reference relating to the domestic legal and administrative framework.

Part B: The exchange of information framework

(a) Exchange of information framework

13. As of 31 March 2020, The Netherlands has 66 bilateral relationships in place, including those activated under the CbC MCAA, under bilateral CAAs and under the EU Council Directive (2016/881/EU). Within the context of its international exchange of information agreements that allow automatic exchange of information, The Netherlands has taken steps to have qualifying competent authority agreements in effect with jurisdictions of the Inclusive Framework that meet the confidentiality, consistency and appropriate use conditions.[5] Regarding The Netherlands's exchange of information framework, no inconsistencies with the terms of reference were identified.

(b) Content of information exchanged

14. The Netherlands has processes in place that are intended to ensure that each of the mandatory fields of information as required in the CbC template are present in the information exchanged. It has provided details in relation to these processes.

15. Peer input was received from one jurisdiction in relation to the content of information exchanged. There are no concerns to be reported in respect of the content of information exchanged.

(c) Completeness of exchanges

16. The Netherlands has processes in place that are intended to ensure that CbC reports are exchanged with all tax jurisdictions listed in Table 1 of a CbC reporting template with which it should exchange information as per the relevant QCAAs. It has provided details in relation to these processes.

17. Peer input was received from one jurisdiction in relation to the completeness of exchanges. There are no concerns to be reported in respect of the completeness of exchanges.

(d) Timeliness of exchanges

18. The Netherlands has processes in place that are intended to ensure that the information to be exchanged is transmitted to the relevant jurisdictions in accordance with the timelines provided for in the relevant QCAAs and terms of reference. It has provided details in relation to these processes.

19. Despite these procedures, The Netherlands indicates that a few CbC reports were exchanged late.. These late exchanges were due to errors contained in the CbC reports submitted by Reporting Entities and the first exchanges where transmitted close to the deadline. The Netherlands indicates that

any future errors will be discovered and corrected before the deadline. As such, no recommendation is required.

(e) Temporary suspension of exchange or termination of QCAA

20. The Netherlands has processes in place that are intended to ensure that a temporary suspension of the exchange of information or termination of a relevant QCAA be carried out only as per the conditions set out in the QCAA. It has provided details in relation to those processes.

21. Peer input was received from one jurisdiction in relation to a temporary suspension of exchange or termination of a QCAA. There are no concerns to be reported in respect of the temporary suspension of exchange or termination of QCAA.

(f) Consultation with other Competent Authority before determining systemic failure or significant non-compliance

22. The Netherlands has processes in place that are intended to ensure that the Competent Authority consults with the other Competent Authority prior to making a determination that there is or has been significant non-compliance with the terms of the relevant QCAA or that the other Competent Authority has caused a systemic failure. It has provided details in relation to those processes.

23. Peer input was received from one jurisdiction in relation to the requirement for a consultation before determining systemic failure or significant non-compliance. There are no concerns to be reported in respect of consultation with the other Competent Authority before determining systemic failure or significant non-compliance.

(g) Format for information exchange

24. The Netherlands confirms that it uses the OECD XML Schema and User Guide (OECD, 2017[4]) for the international exchange of CbC reports.

25. Peer input was received from one jurisdiction in relation to the format for information exchange. There are no concerns to be reported in respect of the format of information exchange.

(h) Method for transmission

26. The Netherlands indicates that it uses the Common Transmission System to exchange CbC reports.[6]

27. Peer input was received from one jurisdiction in relation to the method for transmission. There are no concerns to be reported in respect of the method used for transmission.

Conclusion

28. The Netherlands has in place the necessary processes to ensure that the exchange of information is conducted in a manner consistent with the terms of reference relating to the exchange of information framework. The Netherlands meets all the terms of reference regarding the exchange of information.

Part C: Appropriate use

Appropriate use

29. There are no concerns to be reported in respect of appropriate use.

Conclusion

30. The Netherlands meets all the terms of reference relating to appropriate use of CbC reports.

Summary of recommendations on the implementation of Country-by-Country Reporting

Aspect of the implementation that should be improved		Recommendation for improvement
Part A	Domestic legal and administrative framework	-
Part B	Exchange of information framework	-
Part C	Appropriate use	-

References

OECD (2019), *Country-by-Country Reporting – Compilation of Peer Review Reports (Phase 2): Inclusive Framework on BEPS: Action 13*, OECD/G20 Base Erosion and Profit Shifting Project, OECD Publishing, Paris, https://dx.doi.org/10.1787/f9bf1157-en. [1]

OECD (2018), *Country-by-Country Reporting – Compilation of Peer Review Reports (Phase 1): Inclusive Framework on BEPS: Action 13*, OECD/G20 Base Erosion and Profit Shifting Project, OECD Publishing, Paris, https://dx.doi.org/10.1787/9789264300057-en. [2]

OECD (2017), *Terms of reference for the conduct of peer review of the Action 13 minimum standard on country-by-country reporting*, OECD Publishing, https://www.oecd.org/tax/beps/beps-action-13-on-country-by-country-reporting-peer-review-documents.pdf. [3]

Notes

[1] Primary law consists of Chapter VIIA of the Corporate Income Tax Act 1969 (CITA): http://wetten.overheid.nl/BWBR0002672/2017-01-01#HoofdstukVIIa. Secondary law consists of Government Gazette No. 47457/2015, providing for regulations on additional transfer pricing documentation requirements: http://wetten.overheid.nl/BWBR0037475/2016-01-01 (accessed on 24 August 2020).

[2] Guidance consists on the 2016 Manual for Filing CbC Reports which was replaced by the 2018 Manual for Filing CbC Reports, from the Tax and Customs Administration. The Netherlands indicates that this explains more details about CbC and contains instructions for filling out the fields in the notification portal and important remarks and is available at: https://gegevensportaal.belastingdienst.nl/portal/document/74/ (accessed on 24 August 2020). In addition, the Netherlands published a Policy decision on notification aspects dated November 15, 2016, nr. DGBel 2016-0000184128M, Staatscourant (Official Gazette), November 21, 2016, nr. 63121, https://zoek.officielebekendmakingen.nl/stcrt-2016-63121.html (accessed on 24 August 2020).

[3] The Netherlands indicates that national guidance has been updated as follows: As set out in the Action 13 Report, the agreed threshold is EUR 750 million or a near equivalent amount in domestic currency as of January 2015. Provided that the jurisdiction of the Ultimate Parent Entity has implemented a reporting

threshold that is a near equivalent of EUR 750 million in domestic currency as it was at January 2015, a MNE Group that complies with this local threshold will not be exposed to local filing in the Netherlands.

[4] See articles 34f and 34g of the Corporate Income Act 1969.

[5] No inconsistency with the terms of reference will be identified where a QCAA is not in effect with one or more jurisdictions of the Inclusive Framework that meet the confidentiality, consistency and appropriate use conditions, but this is due to circumstances that are not under the control of the reviewed jurisdiction. This may include, for example, where the other jurisdiction intends to exchange CbC reports using the MCAA but it does not have the Convention in effect for the relevant fiscal period, or where the other jurisdiction has declined to have a QCAA in effect with the reviewed jurisdiction.

[6] Countries exchanging under the EU Council Directive (2016/881/EU) use the Common Communication Network (CCN).

New Zealand

1. New Zealand was reviewed as part of the 2017/2018 and the 2018/2019 peer reviews. This report is supplementary to those previous reports (OECD, 2019[1]) (OECD, 2018[2]).

2. The first filing obligation for a CbC report in New Zealand applies to reporting fiscal years commencing on or after 1 January 2016.

Summary of key findings

3. New Zealand's implementation of the Action 13 minimum standard meets all applicable terms of reference (OECD, 2017[3]).

Part A: The domestic legal and administrative framework

4. New Zealand has legislation in place which implements the BEPS Action 13 minimum standard, establishing the necessary requirements

(a) Parent entity filing obligation

5. No changes were identified. New Zealand's 2017/18 peer review included monitoring points which remain in place.[1] [2]

(b) Scope and timing of parent entity filing

6. No changes were identified.

(c) Limitation on local filing obligation

7. No changes were identified.

(d) Limitation on local filing in case of surrogate filing

8. No changes were identified.

(e) Effective implementation

9. No changes were identified.[3]

Conclusion

10. New Zealand meets all the terms of reference in relating to the domestic legal and administrative framework.

Part B: The exchange of information framework

(a) Exchange of information framework

11. As of 31 March 2020, New Zealand has 65 bilateral relationships in place, including those activated under the CbC MCAA and under bilateral CAAs. Within the context of its international exchange of information agreements that allow automatic exchange of information, New Zealand has taken steps to have qualifying competent authority agreements in effect with jurisdictions of the Inclusive Framework that meet the confidentiality, consistency and appropriate use conditions.[4] Regarding New Zealand's exchange of information framework, no inconsistencies with the terms of reference were identified.

(b) Content of information exchanged

12. No changes were identified.

(c) Completeness of exchanges

13. No changes were identified.

(d) Timeliness of exchanges

14. No changes were identified.

(e) Temporary suspension of exchange or termination of QCAA

15. No changes were identified.

(f) Consultation with other Competent Authority before determining systemic failure or significant non-compliance

16. No changes were identified.

(g) Format for information exchange

17. No changes were identified.

(h) Method for transmission

18. No changes were identified.

Conclusion

19. New Zealand meets all the terms of reference regarding the exchange of information.

Part C: Appropriate use

Appropriate use

20. No changes were identified.

Conclusion

21. New Zealand meets all the terms of reference relating to appropriate use of CbC reports.

Summary of recommendations on the implementation of country-by-country reporting

Aspect of the implementation that should be improved		Recommendation for improvement
Part A	Domestic legal and administrative framework	-
Part B	Exchange of information framework	-
Part C	Appropriate use	-

References

OECD (2019), *Country-by-Country Reporting – Compilation of Peer Review Reports (Phase 2): Inclusive Framework on BEPS: Action 13*, OECD/G20 Base Erosion and Profit Shifting Project, OECD Publishing, Paris, https://dx.doi.org/10.1787/f9bf1157-en. [1]

OECD (2018), *Country-by-Country Reporting – Compilation of Peer Review Reports (Phase 1): Inclusive Framework on BEPS: Action 13*, OECD/G20 Base Erosion and Profit Shifting Project, OECD Publishing, Paris, https://dx.doi.org/10.1787/9789264300057-en. [2]

OECD (2017), *Terms of reference for the conduct of peer review of the Action 13 minimum standard on country-by-country reporting*, OECD Publishing, https://www.oecd.org/tax/beps/beps-action-13-on-country-by-country-reporting-peer-review-documents.pdf. [3]

Notes

[1] The definition of a "large multinational group" in the legislation does not include the "deemed listing provision" as required under the terms of reference.[1] However, New Zealand notes that the financial reporting requirements in New Zealand apply to large entities (including companies, partnerships and limited partnerships) regardless of whether they are listed on a stock exchange. A "large entity" is defined in the Financial Reporting Act 2013 as an entity that earns over NZD 30m of consolidated revenues (which is much lower than EUR 750m) or that have over NZD 60m of consolidated assets in the previous two years. New Zealand also confirms that in the very unlikely event that an entity did not prepare consolidated financial statements and would be considered as an "Ultimate Parent Entity" further to the "deemed listing provision" (as per paragraph 18.i. of the terms of reference), the existing powers of Section 17 of the Tax Administration Act 1994 will be relied on to request the information. This will be monitored.

[2] As New Zealand continues to rely on existing powers in the Tax Administration Act 1994 until legislation is finalised, and because the effectiveness of this system still relies on the fact that the Inland Revenue correctly identifies all New Zealand resident entities that are the Ultimate Parent Entity of an MNE group within the scope of CbC Reporting and issues a notification, the monitoring point in the 2017/2018 peer review relating to New Zealand's framework remains.

[3] New Zealand's 2017/2018 peer review included a general monitoring point relating to a specific process to that would allow to take appropriate measures in case New Zealand is notified by another jurisdiction that such other jurisdiction has reason to believe that an error may have led to incorrect or incomplete

information reporting by a Reporting Entity or that there is non-compliance of a Reporting Entity with respect to its obligation to file a CbC report. This monitoring point remains in place.

[4] No inconsistency with the terms of reference will be identified where a QCAA is not in effect with one or more jurisdictions of the Inclusive Framework that meet the confidentiality, consistency and appropriate use conditions, but this is due to circumstances that are not under the control of the reviewed jurisdiction. This may include, for example, where the other jurisdiction intends to exchange CbC reports using the MCAA but it does not have the Convention in effect for the relevant fiscal period, or where the other jurisdiction has declined to have a QCAA in effect with the reviewed jurisdiction.

Nigeria

1. Nigeria was reviewed as part of the 2017/2018 and the 2018/2019 peer reviews. This report is supplementary to those previous reports (OECD, 2019[1]) (OECD, 2018[2]).

2. The first filing obligation for a CbC report in Nigeria applies to reporting fiscal years commencing on or after 1 January 2018.

Summary of key findings

3. Nigeria's implementation of the Action 13 minimum standard meets all applicable terms of reference (OECD, 2017[3]), except for the following:

- It is recommended that Nigeria take steps to amend its legislation or otherwise ensure that local filing requirements only apply in accordance with the terms of reference. This recommendation remains unchanged since the 2018/2019 peer review.

4. It is recommended that Nigeria have in place the necessary processes or written procedures to ensure that the exchange of information is conducted in a manner consistent with the terms of reference relating to the exchange of information framework. This recommendation remains unchanged since the 2018/2019 peer review.

Part A: The domestic legal and administrative framework

5. Nigeria has legislation in place for implementing the BEPS Action 13 minimum standard.

(a) Parent entity filing obligation

6. No changes were identified.[1]

(b) Scope and timing of parent entity filing

7. No changes were identified.

(c) Limitation on local filing obligation

8. No changes were identified.

(d) Limitation on local filing in case of surrogate filing

9. No changes were identified.

(e) Effective implementation

10. No changes were identified.

Conclusion

11. It is recommended that Nigeria take steps to amend its legislation or otherwise ensure that local filing requirements only apply in accordance with the terms of reference.

Part B: The exchange of information framework

(a) Exchange of information framework

12. As at 31 March 2020, Nigeria has 51 bilateral relationships activated under the CbC MCAA. Within the context of its international exchange of information agreements that allow automatic exchange of information, Nigeria has taken steps to have qualifying competent authority agreements in effect with jurisdictions of the Inclusive Framework that meet the confidentiality, consistency and appropriate use conditions.[2] Regarding Nigeria's exchange of information framework, no inconsistencies with the terms of reference were identified.

(b) Content of information exchanged

13. No changes were identified.

(c) Completeness of exchanges

14. No changes were identified.

(d) Timeliness of exchanges

15. No changes were identified.

(e) Temporary suspension of exchange or termination of QCAA

16. No changes were identified.

(f) Consultation with other Competent Authority before determining systemic failure or significant non-compliance

17. No changes were identified.

(g) Format for information exchange

18. No changes were identified.

(h) Method for transmission

19. No changes were identified.

Conclusion

20. It is recommended that Nigeria take steps to implement processes or written procedures to ensure that the exchange of information is conducted in a manner consistent with the terms of reference relating to the exchange of information framework ahead of its first exchanges of information. This recommendation remains unchanged since the 2018/2019 peer review.

Part C: Appropriate use

Appropriate use

21. No changes were identified.

Conclusion

22. Nigeria is a non-reciprocal jurisdiction and, as such, will not receive CbC reports submitted to tax authorities in other jurisdictions, and will not apply local filing. The recommendation is removed and it is not necessary for this peer review evaluation to reach any conclusion with respect to Nigeria's compliance with the terms of reference on appropriate use.

Summary of recommendations on the implementation of Country-by-Country Reporting

Aspect of the implementation that should be improved		Recommendation for improvement
Part A	Domestic legal and administrative framework	It is recommended that Nigeria take steps to amend its legislation or otherwise ensure that local filing requirements only apply in accordance with the terms of reference.
Part B	Exchange of information framework	It is recommended that Nigeria have in place the necessary processes or written procedures to ensure that the exchange of information is conducted in a manner consistent with the terms of reference relating to the exchange of information framework.
Part C	Appropriate use	-

References

OECD (2019), *Country-by-Country Reporting – Compilation of Peer Review Reports (Phase 2): Inclusive Framework on BEPS: Action 13*, OECD/G20 Base Erosion and Profit Shifting Project, OECD Publishing, Paris, https://dx.doi.org/10.1787/f9bf1157-en. [1]

OECD (2018), *Country-by-Country Reporting – Compilation of Peer Review Reports (Phase 1): Inclusive Framework on BEPS: Action 13*, OECD/G20 Base Erosion and Profit Shifting Project, OECD Publishing, Paris, https://dx.doi.org/10.1787/9789264300057-en. [2]

OECD (2017), *Terms of reference for the conduct of peer review of the Action 13 minimum standard on country-by-country reporting*, OECD Publishing, https://www.oecd.org/tax/beps/beps-action-13-on-country-by-country-reporting-peer-review-documents.pdf. [3]

Notes

1 Nigeria's 2017/2018 peer review included a monitoring point relating to the definition of "Excluded MNE group". This monitoring point remains in place.

2 No inconsistency with the terms of reference will be identified where a QCAA is not in effect with one or more jurisdictions of the Inclusive Framework that meet the confidentiality, consistency and appropriate use conditions, but this is due to circumstances that are not under the control of the reviewed jurisdiction. This may include, for example, where the other jurisdiction intends to exchange CbC reports using the MCAA but it does not have the Convention in effect for the relevant fiscal period, or where the other jurisdiction has declined to have a QCAA in effect with the reviewed jurisdiction.

North Macedonia (Republic of)

1. The Republic of North Macedonia (North Macedonia) was first reviewed during the 2018/2019 peer review. This report is supplementary to that previous report (OECD, 2018[2]).

2. There is no filing obligation for a CbC report in North Macedonia yet.

Summary of key findings

3. North Macedonia does not yet have legislation in place for implementing the BEPS Action 13 minimum standard. It is recommended that North Macedonia take steps to implement a domestic legal and administrative framework to impose and enforce CbC reporting requirements as soon as possible.

4. It is recommended that North Macedonia take steps to have qualifying competent authority agreements in effect with jurisdictions of the Inclusive Framework that meet the confidentiality, consistency and appropriate use conditions and with which north Macedonia has an international exchange of information agreement in effect that allows for the automatic exchange of tax information.

5. It is recommended that North Macedonia take steps to implement processes or written procedures to ensure that the exchange of information is conducted in a manner consistent with the terms of reference (OECD, 2017[3]) relating to the exchange of information framework ahead of the first exchanges of information.

6. It is recommended that North Macedonia take steps to ensure that the appropriate use condition is met ahead of the first exchanges of information.

7. These recommendations remain in place since the 2018/2019 peer review.

Part A: The domestic legal and administrative framework

8 North Macedonia does not yet have legislation in place for implementing the BEPS Action 13 minimum standard.

(a) Parent entity filing obligation

(b) Scope and timing of parent entity filing

(c) Limitation on local filing obligation

(d) Limitation on local filing in case of surrogate filing

(e) Effective implementation

Conclusion

9. It is recommended that North Macedonia take steps to implement a domestic legal and administrative framework to impose and enforce CbC reporting requirements as soon as possible. This recommendation remains unchanged since the 2018/2019 peer review.

Part B: The exchange of information framework

(a) Exchange of information framework

10. As of 31 March 2020, North Macedonia has no bilateral relationships in place for the exchange of CbC reports. It is recommended that North Macedonia take steps to have qualifying competent authority agreements in effect with jurisdictions of the Inclusive Framework that meet the confidentiality, consistency and appropriate use conditions and with which North Macedonia has an international exchange of information agreement in effect that allows for the automatic exchange of tax information. This recommendation remains unchanged since the 2018/2019 peer review.

(b) Content of information exchanged

11. No changes were identified.

(c) Completeness of exchanges

12. No changes were identified.

(d) Timeliness of exchanges

13. No changes were identified.

(e) Temporary suspension of exchange or termination of QCAA

14. No changes were identified.

(f) Consultation with other Competent Authority before determining systemic failure or significant non-compliance

15. No changes were identified.

(g) Format for information exchange

16. No changes were identified.

(h) Method for transmission

17. No changes were identified.

Conclusion

18. It is recommended that North Macedonia take steps to have qualifying competent authority agreements in effect with jurisdictions of the Inclusive Framework that meet the confidentiality, consistency and appropriate use conditions and with which North Macedonia has an international exchange of information agreement in effect that allows for the automatic exchange of tax information. This recommendation remains unchanged since the 2018/2019 peer review.

19. it is recommended that North Macedonia take steps to implement processes or written procedures to ensure that the exchange of information is conducted in a manner consistent with the terms of reference relating to the exchange of information framework ahead of its first exchanges of information. This recommendation remains unchanged since the 2018/2019 peer review.

Part C: Appropriate use

Appropriate use

20. No changes were identified.

Conclusion

21. It is recommended that North Macedonia take steps to ensure that the appropriate use condition is met ahead of its first exchanges of information. This recommendation remains unchanged since the 2018/2019 peer review.

Summary of recommendations on the implementation of Country-by-Country Reporting

Aspect of the implementation that should be improved		Recommendation for improvement
Part A	Domestic legal and administrative framework	It is recommended that North Macedonia take steps to implement a domestic legal and administrative framework to impose and enforce CbC requirements as soon as possible.
Part B	Exchange of information framework	It is recommended that North Macedonia take steps to put in place an exchange of information framework that allows Automatic Exchange of Information and have QCAAs in effect with jurisdictions of the Inclusive Framework which meet the confidentiality, consistency and appropriate use prerequisites and with which they have an international exchange of information agreement in effect that allows for the automatic exchange of tax information
Part B	Exchange of information framework	It is recommended that North Macedonia take steps to implement the necessary processes or written procedures to ensure that the exchange of information is conducted in a manner consistent with the terms of reference relating to the exchange of information framework.
Part C	Appropriate use	It is recommended that North Macedonia take steps to ensure that the appropriate use condition is met ahead of the first exchanges of information.

References

OECD (2018), *Country-by-Country Reporting – Compilation of Peer Review Reports (Phase 1): Inclusive Framework on BEPS: Action 13*, OECD/G20 Base Erosion and Profit Shifting Project, OECD Publishing, Paris, https://dx.doi.org/10.1787/9789264300057-en. [2]

OECD (2017), *Terms of reference for the conduct of peer review of the Action 13 minimum standard on country-by-country reporting*, OECD Publishing, https://www.oecd.org/tax/beps/beps-action-13-on-country-by-country-reporting-peer-review-documents.pdf. [3]

Norway

1. Norway was reviewed as part of the 2017/2018 and the 2018/2019 peer reviews. This report is supplementary to those previous reports (OECD, 2019[1]) (OECD, 2018[2]).

2. The first filing obligation for a CbC report in Norway applies to reporting fiscal years commencing on or after 1 January 2016.

Summary of key findings

3. Norway's implementation of the Action 13 minimum standard meets all applicable terms of reference (OECD, 2017[3]).

Part A: The domestic legal and administrative framework

4. Norway has legislation in place to implement the BEPS Action 13 minimum standard.

(a) Parent entity filing obligation

5. No changes were identified.

(b) Scope and timing of parent entity filing

6. No changes were identified.

(c) Limitation on local filing obligation

7. No changes were identified.[1]

(d) Limitation on local filing in case of surrogate filing

8. No changes were identified.

(e) Effective implementation

9. No changes were identified.

Conclusion

10. Norway meets all the terms of reference relating to the domestic legal and administrative framework.

Part B: The exchange of information framework

(a) Exchange of information framework

11. As of 31 March 2020, Norway has 73 bilateral relationships in place, including those activated under the CbC MCAA, and under bilateral CAAs. Within the context of its international exchange of information agreements that allow automatic exchange of information, Norway has taken steps to have qualifying competent authority agreements in effect with jurisdictions of the Inclusive Framework that meet

the confidentiality, consistency and appropriate use conditions.[2] Regarding Norway's exchange of information framework, no inconsistencies with the terms of reference were identified.

(b) Content of information exchanged

12. No changes were identified.

(c) Completeness of exchanges

13. No changes were identified.

(d) Timeliness of exchanges

14. No changes were identified.

(e) Temporary suspension of exchange or termination of QCAA

15. No changes were identified.

(f) Consultation with other Competent Authority before determining systemic failure or significant non-compliance

16. No changes were identified.

(g) Format for information exchange

17. No changes were identified.

(h) Method for transmission

18. No changes were identified.

Conclusion

19. Norway meets all the terms of reference regarding the exchange of information.

Part C: Appropriate use

Appropriate use

20. No changes were identified.

Conclusion

21. Norway meets all the terms of reference relating to appropriate use of CbC reports.

Summary of recommendations on the implementation of country-by-country reporting

Aspect of the implementation that should be improved		Recommendation for improvement
Part A	Domestic legal and administrative framework	-
Part B	Exchange of information framework	-
Part C	Appropriate use	-

References

OECD (2019), *Country-by-Country Reporting – Compilation of Peer Review Reports (Phase 2): Inclusive Framework on BEPS: Action 13*, OECD/G20 Base Erosion and Profit Shifting Project, OECD Publishing, Paris, https://dx.doi.org/10.1787/f9bf1157-en. [1]

OECD (2018), *Country-by-Country Reporting – Compilation of Peer Review Reports (Phase 1): Inclusive Framework on BEPS: Action 13*, OECD/G20 Base Erosion and Profit Shifting Project, OECD Publishing, Paris, https://dx.doi.org/10.1787/9789264300057-en. [2]

OECD (2017), *Terms of reference for the conduct of peer review of the Action 13 minimum standard on country-by-country reporting*, OECD Publishing, https://www.oecd.org/tax/beps/beps-action-13-on-country-by-country-reporting-peer-review-documents.pdf. [3]

Notes

[1] Norway's 2017/2018 peer review included a monitoring point relating to the interpretation of the concept of "System Failure". This monitoring point remains in place.

[2] No inconsistency with the terms of reference will be identified where a QCAA is not in effect with one or more jurisdictions of the Inclusive Framework that meet the confidentiality, consistency and appropriate use conditions, but this is due to circumstances that are not under the control of the reviewed jurisdiction. This may include, for example, where the other jurisdiction intends to exchange CbC reports using the MCAA but it does not have the Convention in effect for the relevant fiscal period, or where the other jurisdiction has declined to have a QCAA in effect with the reviewed jurisdiction.

Oman

1. Oman was first reviewed during the 2018/2019 peer review. This report is supplementary to that previous report (OECD, 2018[2]).

2. There is no filing obligation for a CbC report in Oman yet.

Summary of key findings

3. Oman does not yet have legislation in place for implementing the BEPS Action 13 minimum standard. It is recommended that Oman take steps to implement a domestic legal and administrative framework to impose and enforce CbC reporting requirements as soon as possible. This recommendation remains unchanged since the 2018/2019 peer review.

4. It is recommended that Oman take steps to put in place QCAAs in effect with jurisdictions of the Inclusive Framework which meet the confidentiality, consistency and appropriate use prerequisites and with which they have an international exchange of information agreement in effect that allows for the automatic exchange of tax information. This recommendation remains unchanged since the 2018/2019 peer review.

5. It is recommended that Oman take steps to implement processes or written procedures to ensure that the exchange of information is conducted in a manner consistent with the terms of reference (OECD, 2017[3]) relating to the exchange of information framework ahead of the first exchanges of information. This recommendation remains unchanged since the 2018/2019 peer review.

6. It is recommended that Oman take steps to ensure that the appropriate use condition is met ahead of the first exchanges of information. This recommendation remains unchanged since the 2018/2019 peer review.

Part A: The domestic legal and administrative framework

7. Oman does not yet have legislation in place for implementing the BEPS Action 13 minimum standard.

(a) Parent entity filing obligation

(b) Scope and timing of parent entity filing

(c) Limitation on local filing obligation

(d) Limitation on local filing in case of surrogate filing

(e) Effective implementation

8. It is recommended that Oman take steps to implement a domestic legal and administrative framework to impose and enforce CbC reporting requirements as soon as possible.

Conclusion

9. It is recommended that Oman take steps to implement a domestic legal and administrative framework to impose and enforce CbC reporting requirements as soon as possible.

Part B: The exchange of information framework

(a) Exchange of information framework

10. As of 31 March 2020, Oman has no bilateral relationships in place for the exchange of CbC reports. It is recommended that Oman take steps to have qualifying competent authority agreements in effect with jurisdictions of the Inclusive Framework that meet the confidentiality, consistency and appropriate use conditions and with which Oman has an international exchange of information agreement in effect that allows for the automatic exchange of tax information. This recommendation remains unchanged since the 2018/2019 peer review.

(b) Content of information exchanged

11. No changes were identified.

(c) Completeness of exchanges

12. No changes were identified.

(d) Timeliness of exchanges

13. No changes were identified

(e) Temporary suspension of exchange or termination of QCAA

14. No changes were identified.

(f) Consultation with other Competent Authority before determining systemic failure or significant non-compliance

15. No changes were identified.

(g) Format for information exchange

16. No changes were identified.

(h) Method for transmission

17. No changes were identified.

Conclusion

18. It is recommended that Oman take steps to put in place an exchange of information framework that allows automatic exchange of information and have QCAAs in effect with jurisdictions of the Inclusive Framework which meet the confidentiality, consistency and appropriate use prerequisites and with which Oman has an international exchange of information agreement in effect that allows for the automatic exchange of tax information. This recommendation remains unchanged since the 2018/2019 peer review.

19. It is recommended that Oman take steps to implement processes or written procedures to ensure that the exchange of information is conducted in a manner consistent with the terms of reference relating to the exchange of information framework ahead of its first exchanges of information. This recommendation remains unchanged since the 2018/2019 peer review.

Part C: Appropriate use

Appropriate use

20. No changes were identified.

Conclusion

21. It is recommended that Oman take steps to ensure that the appropriate use condition is met ahead of its first exchanges of information. This recommendation remains unchanged since the 2018/2019 peer review.

Summary of recommendations on the implementation of Country-by-Country Reporting

Aspect of the implementation that should be improved		Recommendation for improvement
Part A	Domestic legal and administrative framework	It is recommended that Oman take steps to implement a domestic legal and administrative framework to impose and enforce CbC requirements as soon as possible.
Part B	Exchange of information framework	It is recommended that Oman take steps to put in place an exchange of information framework that allows Automatic Exchange of Information and have QCAAs in effect with jurisdictions of the Inclusive Framework which meet the confidentiality, consistency and appropriate use prerequisites and with which they have an international exchange of information agreement in effect that allows for the automatic exchange of tax information
Part B	Exchange of information framework	It is recommended that Oman take steps to implement the necessary processes or written procedures to ensure that the exchange of information is conducted in a manner consistent with the terms of reference relating to the exchange of information framework.
Part C	Appropriate use	It is recommended that Oman take steps to ensure that the appropriate use condition is met ahead of the first exchanges of information.

References

OECD (2018), *Country-by-Country Reporting – Compilation of Peer Review Reports (Phase 1): Inclusive Framework on BEPS: Action 13*, OECD/G20 Base Erosion and Profit Shifting Project, OECD Publishing, Paris, https://dx.doi.org/10.1787/9789264300057-en. [2]

OECD (2017), *Terms of reference for the conduct of peer review of the Action 13 minimum standard on country-by-country reporting*, OECD Publishing, https://www.oecd.org/tax/beps/beps-action-13-on-country-by-country-reporting-peer-review-documents.pdf. [3]

Pakistan

1. Pakistan was reviewed as part of the 2017/2018 and the 2018/2019 peer reviews. This report is supplementary to those previous reports (OECD, 2019[1]) (OECD, 2018[2]).

2. The first filing obligation for a CbC report in Pakistan commences in respect of financial years beginning on or after 1 January 2016.

Summary of key findings

3. Pakistan's implementation of Action 13 minimum standard meets all applicable terms of reference (OECD, 2017[3]) relating to the domestic legal and administrative framework.

4. It is recommended that Pakistan take steps to implement processes or written procedures to ensure that the exchange of information is conducted in a manner consistent with the terms of reference relating to the exchange of information framework. This recommendation remains unchanged since the 2018/2019 peer review.

5. Pakistan's previous peer reviews recommended that Pakistan take steps to ensure that the appropriate use condition is met. The steps have now been taken and the recommendation is removed.

Part A: The domestic legal and administrative framework

6. Pakistan has legislation in place to implement the BEPS Action 13 minimum standard, establishing the necessary requirements, including the filing and reporting obligations.

(a) Parent entity filing obligation

7. No changes were identified.

(b) Scope and timing of parent entity filing

8. No changes were identified.

(c) Limitation on local filing obligation

9. No changes were identified.

(d) Limitation on local filing in case of surrogate filing

10. No changes were identified.

(e) Effective implementation

11. No changes were identified.

Conclusion

12. Pakistan meets all the terms of reference relating to the domestic legal and administrative framework.

Part B: The exchange of information framework

(a) Exchange of information framework

13. As at 31 March 2020, Pakistan has 61 bilateral relationships activated under the CbC MCAA. Within the context of its international exchange of information agreements that allow automatic exchange of information, Pakistan has taken steps to have qualifying competent authority agreements in effect with jurisdictions of the Inclusive Framework that meet the confidentiality, consistency and appropriate use conditions.[1]

(b) Content of information exchanged

14. Pakistan does not have a process or written procedures in place that are intended to ensure that each of the mandatory fields of information required in the CbC reporting template are present in the information exchanged.

(c) Completeness of exchanges

15. Pakistan does not have processes in place that are intended to ensure that CbC reports are exchanged with all tax jurisdictions listed in Table 1 of a CbC report with which it should exchange information as per the relevant QCAA.

(d) Timeliness of exchanges

16. Pakistan does not have processes or written procedures in place that are intended to ensure that the information to be exchanged is transmitted to the relevant jurisdictions in accordance with the timelines provided for in the relevant QCAAs.

(e) Temporary suspension of exchange or termination of QCAA

17. Pakistan does not have processes in place that are intended to ensure that a temporary suspension of the exchange of information or termination of a relevant QCAA would be carried out only as per the conditions set out in the relevant QCAA.

(f) Consultation with other Competent Authority before determining systemic failure or significant non-compliance

18. Pakistan does not have processes in place that are intended to ensure that its Competent Authority consults with the other Competent Authority before making a determination of systemic failure or significant non-compliance with the terms of the relevant QCAA by that other Competent Authority.

(g) Format for information exchange

19. Pakistan has not confirmed the format that will be used for the international exchange of CbC reports.

(h) Method for transmission

20. Pakistan has not indicated that it uses the Common Transmission System, or any other mechanism, to exchange CbC reports.

Conclusion

21. Pakistan does not have in place the necessary processes and written procedures to ensure that the exchange of information is conducted in a manner consistent with the terms of reference relating to the information framework. It is recommended that Pakistan take steps to implement processes or written

procedures to ensure that the exchange of information is conducted in a manner consistent with the terms of reference relating to the exchange of information framework.

Part C: Appropriate use

Appropriate use

22. Pakistan's previous peer reviews recommended that Pakistan take steps to ensure that the appropriate use condition is met. The steps have now been taken and the recommendation is removed.

Conclusion

23. Pakistan meets all the terms of reference on appropriate use.

Summary of recommendations on the implementation of Country-by-Country Reporting

Aspect of the implementation that should be improved		Recommendation for improvement
Part A	Domestic legal and administrative framework	-
Part A	Exchange of information framework	It is recommended that Pakistan take steps to implement processes or written procedures to ensure that the exchange of information is conducted in a manner consistent with the terms of reference relating to the exchange of information framework.
Part C	Appropriate Use	

References

OECD (2019), *Country-by-Country Reporting – Compilation of Peer Review Reports (Phase 2): Inclusive Framework on BEPS: Action 13*, OECD/G20 Base Erosion and Profit Shifting Project, OECD Publishing, Paris, https://dx.doi.org/10.1787/f9bf1157-en. [1]

OECD (2018), *Country-by-Country Reporting – Compilation of Peer Review Reports (Phase 1): Inclusive Framework on BEPS: Action 13*, OECD/G20 Base Erosion and Profit Shifting Project, OECD Publishing, Paris, https://dx.doi.org/10.1787/9789264300057-en. [2]

OECD (2017), *Terms of reference for the conduct of peer review of the Action 13 minimum standard on country-by-country reporting*, OECD Publishing, https://www.oecd.org/tax/beps/beps-action-13-on-country-by-country-reporting-peer-review-documents.pdf. [3]

Note

[1] No inconsistency with the terms of reference will be identified where a QCAA is not in effect with one or more jurisdictions of the Inclusive Framework that meet the confidentiality, consistency and appropriate use conditions, but this is due to circumstances that are not under the control of the reviewed jurisdiction. This may include, for example, where the other jurisdiction intends to exchange CbC reports using the MCAA but it does not have the Convention in effect for the relevant fiscal period, or where the other jurisdiction has declined to have a QCAA in effect with the reviewed jurisdiction.

Panama

1. Panama was reviewed as part of the 2017/2018 and the 2018/2019 peer reviews. This report is supplementary to those previous reports (OECD, 2019[1]) (OECD, 2018[2]).

2. The first filing obligation for a CbC report in Panama applies to reporting fiscal years commencing on or after 1 January 2018.

Summary of key findings

3. Panama's implementation of the Action 13 minimum standard meets all the applicable terms of reference (OECD, 2017[3]) relating to the domestic legal and administrative framework, with the exception that:

- It is recommended that Panama take steps to implement a penalty regime in order to enforce the timely and accurate filing of CbC reports.

4. Previous peer reviews recommended that Panama take steps to have QCAAs in effect with jurisdictions of the Inclusive Framework which meet the confidentiality, consistency and appropriate use prerequisites and with which Panama has an international exchange of information agreement in effect that allows for the automatic exchange of tax information. These steps have been taken and the recommendation is removed.

5. It is recommended that Panama take steps to implement processes or written procedures to ensure that the exchange of information is conducted in a manner consistent with the terms of reference (OECD, 2017[3]) relating to the exchange of information framework ahead of the first exchanges of information.

6. It is recommended that Panama take steps to ensure that the appropriate use condition is met ahead of the first exchanges of information. This recommendation remains unchanged since the 2017/2018 peer review.

Part A: The domestic legal and administrative framework

7. Panama has legislation in effect which imposes a CbC requirement for fiscal years commencing on or after 1 January 2018.

(a) Parent entity filing obligation

8. Panama has introduced a filing requirement which applies to all Ultimate Parent Entities of MNE Groups above a certain threshold and which inclusion of all constituent entities.

(b) Scope and timing of parent entity filing

9. The filing requirements of MNE Groups in Panama apply for fiscal years commencing on or after 1 January 2018. Filing is required within 12 months after the reporting year end.

(c) Limitation on local filing obligation

10. Panama does not have a requirement for local filing.

(d) Limitation of local filing in case of surrogate filing

11. Panama does not have a requirement for local filing and does not allow surrogate filing.

(e) Effective implementation

12. Panama has notification requirements for resident entities of MNE Groups who are required to file a CbC report.

13. It is recommended that Panama take steps to implement a penalty regime in order to enforce the timely and accurate filing of CbC reports.

Conclusion

14. Panama's legal framework meets all the terms of reference except for the following:

- It is recommended that Panama take steps to implement a penalty regime in order to enforce the timely and accurate filing of CbC reports.

Part B: The exchange of information framework

(a) Exchange of information framework

15. Previous peer reviews recommended that Panama take steps to have QCAAs in effect with jurisdictions of the Inclusive Framework which meet the confidentiality, consistency and appropriate use prerequisites and with which Panama has an international exchange of information agreement in effect that allows for the automatic exchange of tax information. These steps have been taken and the recommendation is removed.

16. As of 31 March 2020, Panama has 57 bilateral relationships in place for the exchange of CbC reports. Within the context of its international exchange of information agreements that allow automatic exchange of information, Panama has taken steps to have qualifying competent authority agreements in effect with jurisdictions of the Inclusive Framework that meet the confidentiality, consistency and appropriate use conditions. Regarding Panama's exchange of information framework, no inconsistencies with the terms of reference were identified. [1]

(b) Content of information exchanged

17. No changes were identified.

(c) Completeness of exchanges

18. No changes were identified.

(d) Timeliness of exchanges

19. No changes were identified.

(e) Temporary suspension of exchange or termination of QCAA

20. No changes were identified.

(f) Consultation with other Competent Authority before determining systemic failure or significant non-compliance

21. No changes were identified.

(g) Format for information exchange

22. Panama intends to require filing using the OECD XML Schema.

(h) Method for transmission

23. No changes were identified.

Conclusion

24. Previous peer reviews recommended that Panama take steps to have QCAAs in effect with jurisdictions of the Inclusive Framework which meet the confidentiality, consistency and appropriate use prerequisites and with which Panama has an international exchange of information agreement in effect that allows for the automatic exchange of tax information. These steps have been taken and the recommendation is removed.

25. It is recommended that Panama take steps to implement processes or written procedures to ensure that the exchange of information is conducted in a manner consistent with the terms of reference relating to the exchange of information framework ahead of its first exchanges of information. This recommendation remains unchanged since the 2018/2019 peer review.

Part C: Appropriate use

Appropriate use

26. No changes were identified.

Conclusion

27. It is recommended that Panama take steps to ensure that the appropriate use condition is met ahead of the first exchanges of information. This recommendation remains unchanged since the 2017/2018 peer review.

Summary of recommendations on the implementation of Country-by-Country Reporting

Aspect of the implementation that should be improved		Recommendation for improvement
Part A	Domestic legal and administrative framework	It is recommended that Panama take steps to implement a penalty regime in order to enforce the timely and accurate filing of CbC reports.
Part B	Exchange of information framework	
Part B	Exchange of information framework	It is recommended that Panama take steps to implement the necessary processes or written procedures to ensure that the exchange of information is conducted in a manner consistent with the terms of reference relating to the exchange of information framework.
Part C	Appropriate use	It is recommended that Panama take steps to ensure that the appropriate use condition is met ahead of the first exchanges of information.

References

OECD (2019), *Country-by-Country Reporting – Compilation of Peer Review Reports (Phase 2): Inclusive Framework on BEPS: Action 13*, OECD/G20 Base Erosion and Profit Shifting Project, OECD Publishing, Paris, https://dx.doi.org/10.1787/f9bf1157-en. [1]

OECD (2018), *Country-by-Country Reporting – Compilation of Peer Review Reports (Phase 1): Inclusive Framework on BEPS: Action 13*, OECD/G20 Base Erosion and Profit Shifting Project, OECD Publishing, Paris, https://dx.doi.org/10.1787/9789264300057-en. [2]

OECD (2017), *Terms of reference for the conduct of peer review of the Action 13 minimum standard on country-by-country reporting*, OECD Publishing, https://www.oecd.org/tax/beps/beps-action-13-on-country-by-country-reporting-peer-review-documents.pdf. [3]

Papua New Guinea

1. Papua New Guinea was first reviewed during the 2018/2019 peer review. This report is supplementary to that previous report (OECD, 2018[2]).

2. The first filing obligation for a CbC report in Papua New Guinea applies to reporting fiscal years commencing on or after 1 January 2017. Papua New Guinea also allows its MNE groups to file a CbC report on a voluntary basis for reporting fiscal years beginning between 1 January 2016 and 31 December 2016.

Summary of key findings

3. Papua New Guinea's implementation of the Action 13 minimum standard meets all applicable terms of reference (OECD, 2017[3]), except that:

- It is recommended that Papua New Guinea take steps to amend its legislation or otherwise alter the threshold condition to bring it in line with the Action 13 minimum standard. This recommendation remains in place since the 2018/2019 peer review.
- It is recommended that Papua New Guinea amend its legislation or otherwise take steps to ensure that provisions to enforce the effective implementation of CbC reporting requirements are provided for. This recommendation remains in place since the 2018/2019 peer review.

4. It is recommended that Papua New Guinea take steps to put in place an exchange of information framework that allows automatic exchange of information and have QCAAs in effect with jurisdictions of the Inclusive Framework which meet the confidentiality, consistency and appropriate use prerequisites and with which they have an international exchange of information agreement in effect that allows for the automatic exchange of tax information. This recommendation remains in place since the 2018/2019 peer review.

5. It is recommended that Papua New Guinea take steps to implement processes or written procedures to ensure that the exchange of information is conducted in a manner consistent with the terms of reference relating to the exchange of information framework ahead of the first exchanges of information. This recommendation remains in place since the 2018/2019 peer review.

6. It is recommended that Papua New Guinea take steps to ensure that the appropriate use condition is met ahead of the first exchanges of information. This recommendation remains in place since the 2018/2019 peer review.

Part A: The domestic legal and administrative framework

7. Papua New Guinea has legislation in place to implement the BEPS Action 13 minimum standard.

(a) Parent entity filing obligation

8. No changes were identified.

(b) Scope and timing of parent entity filing

9. No changes were identified.

(c) Limitation on local filing obligation

10. No changes were identified.

(d) Limitation on local filing in case of surrogate filing

11. No changes were identified.

(e) Effective implementation

12. No changes were identified.

Conclusion

13. It is recommended that Papua New Guinea take steps to amend its legislation or otherwise alter the threshold condition to bring it in line with the Action 13 minimum standard.

14. It is recommended that Papua New Guinea amend its legislation or otherwise take steps to ensure that enforcement provisions relating to the CbCR's effective implementation are provided for.

Part B: The exchange of information framework

(a) Exchange of information framework

15. As of 31 March 2020, Papua New Guinea has no bilateral relationships in place for the exchange of CbC reports. It is recommended that Papua New Guinea take steps to have qualifying competent authority agreements in effect with jurisdictions of the Inclusive Framework that meet the confidentiality, consistency and appropriate use conditions and with which Papua New Guinea has an international exchange of information agreement in effect that allows for the automatic exchange of tax information.

(b) Content of information exchanged

16. No changes were identified.

(c) Completeness of exchanges

17. No changes were identified.

(d) Timeliness of exchanges

18. No changes were identified.

(e) Temporary suspension of exchange or termination of QCAA

19. No changes were identified.

(f) Consultation with other Competent Authority before determining systemic failure or significant non-compliance

20. No changes were identified.

(g) Format for information exchange

21. No changes were identified.

(h) Method for transmission

22. No changes were identified.

Conclusion

23. It is recommended that Papua New Guinea take steps to have QCAAs in effect with jurisdictions of the Inclusive Framework which meet the confidentiality, consistency and appropriate use prerequisites and with which Papua New Guinea has an international exchange of information agreement in effect that allows for the automatic exchange of tax information. This recommendation remains in place since the 2018/2019 peer review.

24. It is recommended that Papua New Guinea take steps to implement processes or written procedures to ensure that the exchange of information is conducted in a manner consistent with the terms of reference relating to the exchange of information framework ahead of its first exchanges of information. This recommendation remains in place since the 2018/2019 peer review.

Part C: Appropriate use

Appropriate use

25. No changes were identified.

Conclusion

26. It is recommended that Papua New Guinea take steps to ensure that the appropriate use condition is met ahead of its first exchanges of information.

Summary of recommendations on the implementation of Country-by-Country Reporting

Aspect of the implementation that should be improved		Recommendation for improvement
Part A	Domestic legal and administrative framework	It is recommended that Papua New Guinea take steps to amend its legislation or otherwise alter the threshold condition to bring it in line with the Action 13 minimum standard.
Part A	Domestic legal and administrative framework	It is recommended that Papua New Guinea amend its legislation or otherwise take steps to ensure that enforcement provisions relating to the CbCR's effective implementation are provided for as required by the terms of reference as soon as possible.
Part B	Domestic legal and administrative framework	It is recommended that Papua New Guinea take steps to put in place an exchange of information framework that allows Automatic Exchange of Information and have QCAAs in effect with jurisdictions of the Inclusive Framework which meet the confidentiality, consistency and appropriate use prerequisites and with which they have an international exchange of information agreement in effect that allows for the automatic exchange of tax information
Part B	Exchange of information framework	It is recommended that Papua New Guinea take steps to implement processes or written procedures to ensure that the exchange of information is conducted in a manner consistent with the terms of reference relating to the exchange of information framework ahead of the first exchanges of information.
Part C	Appropriate use	It is recommended that Papua New Guinea take steps to ensure that the appropriate use condition is met ahead of the first exchanges of information.

References

OECD (2018), *Country-by-Country Reporting – Compilation of Peer Review Reports (Phase 1): Inclusive Framework on BEPS: Action 13*, OECD/G20 Base Erosion and Profit Shifting Project, OECD Publishing, Paris, https://dx.doi.org/10.1787/9789264300057-en. [2]

OECD (2017), *Terms of reference for the conduct of peer review of the Action 13 minimum standard on country-by-country reporting*, OECD Publishing, https://www.oecd.org/tax/beps/beps-action-13-on-country-by-country-reporting-peer-review-documents.pdf. [3]

Paraguay

1. Paraguay was reviewed as part of the 2017/2018 and the 2018/2019 peer reviews. This report is supplementary to those previous reports (OECD, 2019[1]) (OECD, 2018[2]).

2. There is no filing obligation for a CbC report in Paraguay yet.

Summary of key findings

3. Paraguay does not yet have legislation in place for implementing the BEPS Action 13 minimum standard. It is recommended that Paraguay take steps to implement a domestic legal and administrative framework to impose and enforce CbC reporting requirements as soon as possible. This recommendation remains unchanged since the 2017/2018 peer review.

4. It is recommended that Paraguay take steps to put in place an exchange of information framework that allows automatic exchange of information and have QCAAs in effect with jurisdictions of the Inclusive Framework which meet the confidentiality, consistency and appropriate use prerequisites and with which it has international agreements which allow for the automatic exchange of information. This recommendation remains unchanged since the 2017/2018 peer review.

5. It is recommended that Paraguay take steps to implement processes or written procedures to ensure that the exchange of information is conducted in a manner consistent with the terms of reference (OECD, 2017[3]) relating to the exchange of information framework ahead of the first exchanges of information. This recommendation remains unchanged since the 2018/2019 peer review.

6. It is recommended that Paraguay take steps to ensure that the appropriate use condition is met ahead of the first exchanges of information. This recommendation remains unchanged since the 2017/2018 peer review.

Part A: The domestic legal and administrative framework

7. Paraguay does not yet have legislation in place for implementing the BEPS Action 13 minimum standard.

(a) Parent entity filing obligation

8. No changes were identified.

(b) Scope and timing of parent entity filing

9. No changes were identified.

(c) Limitation on local filing obligation

10. No changes were identified.

(d) Limitation on local filing in case of surrogate filing

11. No changes were identified.

(e) Effective implementation

12. No changes were identified.

Conclusion

13. It is recommended that Paraguay take steps to implement a domestic legal and administrative framework to impose and enforce CbC reporting requirements as soon as possible, remains in place. This recommendation remains unchanged since the 2017/2018 peer review.

Part B: The exchange of information framework

(a) Exchange of information framework

14. As of 31 March 2020, Paraguay has no bilateral relationships in place for the exchange of CbC reports. It is recommended that Paraguay take steps to have qualifying competent authority agreements in effect with jurisdictions of the Inclusive Framework that meet the confidentiality, consistency and appropriate use conditions and with which Paraguay has an international exchange of information agreement in effect that allows for the automatic exchange of tax information.

(b) Content of information exchanged

15. No changes were identified.

(c) Completeness of exchanges

16. No changes were identified.

(d) Timeliness of exchanges

17. No changes were identified.

(e) Temporary suspension of exchange or termination of QCAA

18. No changes were identified.

(f) Consultation with other Competent Authority before determining systemic failure or significant non-compliance

19. No changes were identified.

(g) Format for information exchange

20. No changes were identified.

(h) Method for transmission

21. No changes were identified.

Conclusion

22. It is recommended that Paraguay take steps to have QCAAs in effect with jurisdictions of the Inclusive Framework which meet the confidentiality, consistency and appropriate use prerequisites and which Paraguay has an international exchange of information agreement in effect with that allows for the automatic exchange of information remains in place. This recommendation remains unchanged since the 2017/2018 peer review.

23. It is recommended that Paraguay take steps to implement processes or written procedures to ensure that the exchange of information is conducted in a manner consistent with the terms of reference relating to the exchange of information framework ahead of its first exchanges of information. This recommendation remains unchanged since the 2018/2019 peer review.

Part C: Appropriate use

Appropriate use

24. No changes were identified.

Conclusion

25. It is recommended that Paraguay take steps to ensure that the appropriate use condition is met ahead of its first exchanges of information. This recommendation remains unchanged since the 2018/2019 peer review.

Summary of recommendations on the implementation of Country-by-Country Reporting

Aspect of the implementation that should be improved		Recommendation for improvement
Part A	Domestic legal and administrative framework	It is recommended that Paraguay take steps to implement a domestic legal and administrative framework to impose and enforce CbC requirements as soon as possible.
Part B	Exchange of information framework	It is recommended that Paraguay take steps to put in place an exchange of information framework that allows Automatic Exchange of Information and have QCAAs in effect with jurisdictions of the Inclusive Framework which meet the confidentiality, consistency and appropriate use prerequisite and with which it has an international exchange of information agreement in effect that allows for the automatic exchange of tax information s
Part B	Exchange of information framework	It is recommended that Paraguay take steps to implement the necessary processes or written procedures to ensure that the exchange of information is conducted in a manner consistent with the terms of reference relating to the exchange of information framework.
Part C	Appropriate use	It is recommended that Paraguay take steps to ensure that the appropriate use condition is met ahead of the first exchanges of information.

References

OECD (2019), *Country-by-Country Reporting – Compilation of Peer Review Reports (Phase 2): Inclusive Framework on BEPS: Action 13*, OECD/G20 Base Erosion and Profit Shifting Project, OECD Publishing, Paris, https://dx.doi.org/10.1787/f9bf1157-en. [1]

OECD (2018), *Country-by-Country Reporting – Compilation of Peer Review Reports (Phase 1): Inclusive Framework on BEPS: Action 13*, OECD/G20 Base Erosion and Profit Shifting Project, OECD Publishing, Paris, https://dx.doi.org/10.1787/9789264300057-en. [2]

OECD (2017), *Terms of reference for the conduct of peer review of the Action 13 minimum standard on country-by-country reporting*, OECD Publishing, https://www.oecd.org/tax/beps/beps-action-13-on-country-by-country-reporting-peer-review-documents.pdf. [3]

Peru

1. Peru was reviewed as part of the 2017/2018 and the 2018/2019 peer reviews. This report is supplementary to those previous reports (OECD, 2019[1]) (OECD, 2018[2]).

2. The first filing obligation for CbC reporting in Peru commences in respect of periods commencing on or after 1 January 2017.

Summary of key findings

3. Peru's implementation of the Action 13 minimum standard meets all applicable terms of reference (OECD, 2017[3]), except that it is recommended that Peru take steps to have the necessary processes and written procedures in place to ensure that the exchange of information is conducted in a manner consistent with the terms of reference relating to the exchange of information framework. This recommendation remains unchanged since the 2018/2019 peer review.

Part A: The domestic legal and administrative framework

4. Peru has legislation in place to implement the BEPS Action 13 minimum standard, establishing the necessary requirements, including the filing and reporting obligations.

(a) Parent entity filing obligation

5. No changes were identified.

(b) Scope and timing of parent entity filing

6. No changes were identified.

(c) Limitation on local filing obligation

7. No changes were identified.

(d) Limitation on local filing in case of surrogate filing

8. No changes were identified.

(e) Effective implementation

9. No changes were identified.[2]

Conclusion

10. Peru meets all the terms of reference relating to the domestic legal and administrative framework.

Part B: The exchange of information framework

(a) Exchange of information framework

11. As of 31 March 2020, Peru has 45 bilateral relationships in place for the exchange of CbC reports, including those activated under the CbC MCAA. Within the context of its international exchange of information agreements that allow automatic exchange of tax information, Peru has taken steps to have qualifying competent authority agreements in effect with jurisdictions of the Inclusive Framework that currently meet the confidentiality, consistency and appropriate use conditions. Regarding Peru's exchange of information framework, no inconsistencies with the terms of reference were identified.[3]

(b) Content of information exchanged

12. No changes were identified.

(c) Completeness of exchanges

13. No changes were identified.

(d) Timeliness of exchanges

14. No changes were identified.

(e) Temporary suspension of exchange or termination of QCAA

15. No changes were identified.

(f) Consultation with other Competent Authority before determining systemic failure or significant non-compliance

16. No changes were identified.

(g) Format for information exchange

17. No changes were identified.

(h) Method for transmission

18. No changes were identified.

Conclusion

19. It is recommended that Peru take steps to implement such processes and written procedures to ensure that the exchange of information is conducted in a manner consistent with the terms of reference relating to the exchange of information framework.

Part C: Appropriate use

Appropriate use

20. No changes were identified.

Conclusion

21. Peru is a non-reciprocal jurisdiction and, as such, will not receive CbC reports submitted to tax authorities in other jurisdictions, and will not apply local filing. It is not necessary for this peer review

evaluation to reach any conclusion with respect to Peru's compliance with the terms of reference on appropriate use.

Summary of recommendations on the implementation of country-by-country reporting

Aspect of the implementation that should be improved		Recommendation for improvement
Part A	Domestic legal and administrative framework	-
Part B	Exchange of information framework	it is recommended that Peru take steps to have the necessary processes and written procedures in place to ensure that the exchange of information is conducted in a manner consistent with the terms of reference relating to the exchange of information framework
Part C	Appropriate use	-

References

OECD (2019), *Country-by-Country Reporting – Compilation of Peer Review Reports (Phase 2): Inclusive Framework on BEPS: Action 13*, OECD/G20 Base Erosion and Profit Shifting Project, OECD Publishing, Paris, https://dx.doi.org/10.1787/f9bf1157-en. [1]

OECD (2018), *Country-by-Country Reporting – Compilation of Peer Review Reports (Phase 1): Inclusive Framework on BEPS: Action 13*, OECD/G20 Base Erosion and Profit Shifting Project, OECD Publishing, Paris, https://dx.doi.org/10.1787/9789264300057-en. [2]

OECD (2017), *Terms of reference for the conduct of peer review of the Action 13 minimum standard on country-by-country reporting*, OECD Publishing, https://www.oecd.org/tax/beps/beps-action-13-on-country-by-country-reporting-peer-review-documents.pdf. [3]

Notes

[1] No inconsistency with the terms of reference will be identified where a QCAA is not in effect with one or more jurisdictions of the Inclusive Framework that meet the confidentiality, consistency and appropriate use conditions, but this is due to circumstances that are not under the control of the reviewed jurisdiction. This may include, for example, where the other jurisdiction intends to exchange CbC reports using the MCAA but it does not have the Convention in effect for the relevant fiscal period, or where the other jurisdiction has declined to have a QCAA in effect with the reviewed jurisdiction.

[2] Peru's 2017/2018 peer review included a monitoring point relating to the absence of specific processes in place that would allow Peru to take appropriate measures in case it is notified by another jurisdiction that such other jurisdiction has reason to believe that an error may have led to incorrect or incomplete information reporting by a Reporting Entity or that there is non-compliance of a Reporting Entity with respect to its obligation to file a CbC report. This aspect will be further monitored once the actual exchanges of CbC reports will commence. This monitoring point remains in place.

[3] No inconsistency with the terms of reference will be identified where a QCAA is not in effect with one or more jurisdictions of the Inclusive Framework that meet the confidentiality, consistency and appropriate use conditions, but this is due to circumstances that are not under the control of the reviewed jurisdiction. This may include, for example, where the other jurisdiction intends to exchange CbC reports using the MCAA but it does not have the Convention in effect for the relevant fiscal period, or where the other jurisdiction has declined to have a QCAA in effect with the reviewed jurisdiction.

Poland

1. Poland was reviewed as part of the 2017/2018 and the 2018/2019 peer reviews. This report is supplementary to those previous reports (OECD, 2019[1]) (OECD, 2018[2]).

2. The first filing obligation for a CbC report in Poland commences in respect of periods commencing on or after 1 January 2016.

Summary of key findings

3. Poland's implementation of the Action 13 minimum standard meets all applicable terms of reference (OECD, 2017[3]).

Part A: The domestic legal and administrative framework

4. Poland has legislation in place to implement the BEPS Action 13 minimum standard, establishing the necessary requirements including the filing and reporting obligations.

(a) Parent entity filing obligation

5. No changes were identified.

(b) Scope and timing of parent entity filing

6. No changes were identified.

(c) Limitation on local filing obligation

7. No changes were identified.

(d) Limitation on local filing in case of surrogate filing

8. No changes were identified.

(e) Effective implementation

9. No changes were identified.

Conclusion

10. Poland meets all the terms of reference relating to the domestic legal and administrative framework.

Part B: The exchange of information framework

(a) Exchange of information framework

11. As of 31 March 2020, Poland has 75 bilateral relationships, including those activated under the CbC MCAA, under bilateral CAAs and under the EU Council Directive (2016/881/EU). Within the context of its international exchange of information agreements that allow automatic exchange of information, Poland has taken steps to have qualifying competent authority agreements in effect with jurisdictions of

the Inclusive Framework that meet the confidentiality, consistency and appropriate use conditions. Regarding Poland's exchange of information framework, no inconsistencies with the terms of reference were identified.[1]

(b) Content of information exchanged

12. No changes were identified.

(c) Completeness of exchanges

13. No changes were identified.

(d) Timeliness of exchanges

14. No changes were identified.

(e) Temporary suspension of exchange or termination of QCAA

15. No changes were identified

(f) Consultation with other Competent Authority before determining systemic failure or significant non-compliance

16. No changes were identified.

(g) Format for information exchange

17. No changes were identified.

(h) Method for transmission

18. No changes were identified.

Conclusion

19. Poland meets all the terms of reference regarding the exchange of information.

Part C: Appropriate use

Appropriate use

20. No changes were identified.

Conclusion

21. Poland meets all the terms of reference relating to appropriate use of CbC reports.

Summary of recommendations on the implementation of country-by-country reporting

Aspect of the implementation that should be improved		Recommendation for improvement
Part A	Domestic legal and administrative framework	-
Part B	Exchange of information framework	-
Part C	Appropriate use	-

References

OECD (2019), *Country-by-Country Reporting – Compilation of Peer Review Reports (Phase 2): Inclusive Framework on BEPS: Action 13*, OECD/G20 Base Erosion and Profit Shifting Project, OECD Publishing, Paris, https://dx.doi.org/10.1787/f9bf1157-en. [1]

OECD (2018), *Country-by-Country Reporting – Compilation of Peer Review Reports (Phase 1): Inclusive Framework on BEPS: Action 13*, OECD/G20 Base Erosion and Profit Shifting Project, OECD Publishing, Paris, https://dx.doi.org/10.1787/9789264300057-en. [2]

OECD (2017), *Terms of reference for the conduct of peer review of the Action 13 minimum standard on country-by-country reporting*, OECD Publishing, https://www.oecd.org/tax/beps/beps-action-13-on-country-by-country-reporting-peer-review-documents.pdf. [3]

Note

[1] No inconsistency with the terms of reference will be identified where a QCAA is not in effect with one or more jurisdictions of the Inclusive Framework that meet the confidentiality, consistency and appropriate use conditions, but this is due to circumstances that are not under the control of the reviewed jurisdiction. This may include, for example, where the other jurisdiction intends to exchange CbC reports using the MCAA but it does not have the Convention in effect for the relevant fiscal period, or where the other jurisdiction has declined to have a QCAA in effect with the reviewed jurisdiction.

Portugal

1. Portugal was reviewed as part of the 2017/2018 and the 2018/2019 peer reviews. This report is supplementary to those previous reports (OECD, 2019[1]) (OECD, 2018[2]).

2. The first filing obligation for a CbC report in Portugal commences in respect of financial years beginning on or after 1 January 2016.

Summary of key findings

3. Portugal's implementation of the Action 13 minimum standard meets all applicable terms of reference (OECD, 2017[3]) for the year in review.

Part A: The domestic legal and administrative framework

4. Portugal has legislation in place to implement the BEPS Action 13 minimum standard.

(a) Parent entity filing obligation

5. No changes were identified.

(b) Scope and timing of parent entity filing

6. No changes were identified.

(c) Limitation on local filing obligation

7. No changes were identified.

(d) Limitation on local filing in case of surrogate filing

8. No changes were identified.

(e) Effective implementation

9. No changes were identified.

Conclusion

10. Portugal meets all the terms of reference relating to the domestic legal and administrative framework.

Part B: The exchange of information framework

(a) Exchange of information framework

11. As of 31 March 2020, Portugal has 67 bilateral relationships in place, including those activated under the CbC MCAA, under bilateral CAAs and under the EU Council Directive (2016/881/EU). Within the context of its international exchange of information agreements that allow automatic exchange of information, Portugal has taken steps to have qualifying competent authority agreements in effect with jurisdictions of the Inclusive Framework that meet the confidentiality, consistency and appropriate use

conditions.[1] Regarding Portugal's exchange of information framework, no inconsistencies with the terms of reference were identified.

(b) Content of information exchanged

12. No changes were identified.

(c) Completeness of exchanges

13. No changes were identified.

(d) Timeliness of exchanges

14. No changes were identified.

(e) Temporary suspension of exchange or termination of QCAA

15. No changes were identified.

(f) Consultation with other Competent Authority before determining systemic failure or significant non-compliance

16. No changes were identified.

(g) Format for information exchange

17. No changes were identified.

(h) Method for transmission

18. No changes were identified.

Conclusion

19. Portugal meets all the terms of reference regarding the exchange of information.

Part C: Appropriate use

Appropriate use

20. No changes were identified

Conclusion

21. Portugal meets all the terms of reference relating to appropriate use of CbC reports.

Summary of recommendations on the implementation of country-by-country reporting

Aspect of the implementation that should be improved		Recommendation for improvement
Part A	Domestic legal and administrative framework	.
Part B	Exchange of information framework	-
Part C	Appropriate use	-

References

OECD (2019), *Country-by-Country Reporting – Compilation of Peer Review Reports (Phase 2): Inclusive Framework on BEPS: Action 13*, OECD/G20 Base Erosion and Profit Shifting Project, OECD Publishing, Paris, https://dx.doi.org/10.1787/f9bf1157-en. [1]

OECD (2018), *Country-by-Country Reporting – Compilation of Peer Review Reports (Phase 1): Inclusive Framework on BEPS: Action 13*, OECD/G20 Base Erosion and Profit Shifting Project, OECD Publishing, Paris, https://dx.doi.org/10.1787/9789264300057-en. [2]

OECD (2017), *Terms of reference for the conduct of peer review of the Action 13 minimum standard on country-by-country reporting*, OECD Publishing, https://www.oecd.org/tax/beps/beps-action-13-on-country-by-country-reporting-peer-review-documents.pdf. [3]

Note

[1] No inconsistency with the terms of reference will be identified where a QCAA is not in effect with one or more jurisdictions of the Inclusive Framework that meet the confidentiality, consistency and appropriate use conditions, but this is due to circumstances that are not under the control of the reviewed jurisdiction. This may include, for example, where the other jurisdiction intends to exchange CbC reports using the MCAA but it does not have the Convention in effect for the relevant fiscal period, or where the other jurisdiction has declined to have a QCAA in effect with the reviewed jurisdiction

Qatar

1. Qatar was reviewed as part of the 2017/2018 and the 2018/2019 peer reviews. This report is supplementary to those previous reports (OECD, 2019[1]) (OECD, 2018[2]).

2. The first filing obligation for a CbC report in Qatar applies to reporting fiscal years commencing on or after 1 January 2018.[1]

Summary of key findings

3. Qatar's implementation of the Action 13 minimum standard meets all applicable terms of reference (OECD, 2017[3]).

4. The 2018/2019 peer review recommended that Qatar take steps to implement processes or written procedures to ensure that the exchange of information is conducted in a manner consistent with the terms of reference relating to the exchange of information framework ahead of its first exchanges of information. The processes are in place and the recommendation is removed.

Part A: The domestic legal and administrative framework

5. Qatar has legislation in place to implement the BEPS Action 13 minimum standard.

(a) Parent entity filing obligation

6. Qatar indicates that any Ultimate Parent Entity of MNE groups that is resident in Qatar is not required to file a CbC report with the Qatari tax administration for fiscal year starting on 1 January 2017, if the MNE groups files a CbC report for that year through a surrogate parent entity with the tax authority of the country of its tax residence. An obligation to file a CbC report in Qatar applies for fiscal years commencing on or after 1 January 2018.

7. No changes were identified.[2]

(b) Scope and timing of parent entity filing

8. No changes were identified.

(c) Limitation on local filing obligation

9. No changes were identified.

(d) Limitation on local filing in case of surrogate filing

10. No changes were identified.

(e) Effective implementation

11. No changes were identified.

Conclusion

12. Qatar meets all the terms of reference relating to the domestic legal and administrative framework.

Part B: The exchange of information framework (a) Exchange of information framework

13. As of 31 March 2020, Qatar has 54 bilateral relationships in place for the exchange of CbC reports, including those activated under the CbC MCAA. Within the context of its international exchange of information agreements that allow automatic exchange of tax information, Qatar has taken steps to have qualifying competent authority agreements in effect with jurisdictions of the Inclusive Framework that currently meet the confidentiality, consistency and appropriate use conditions. Regarding Qatar's exchange of information framework, no inconsistencies with the terms of reference were identified.

(b) Content of information exchanged

14. Qatar has processes in place that are intended to ensure that each of the mandatory fields of information as required in the CbC template are present in the information exchanged. It has provided details in relation to these processes and written procedures.

(c) Completeness of exchanges

15. Qatar has processes and written procedures in place that are intended to ensure that CbC reports are exchanged with all tax jurisdictions listed in Table 1 of a CbC reporting template with which it should exchange information as per the relevant QCAAs. It has provided details in relation to these processes and written procedures.

(d) Timeliness of exchanges

16. Qatar has processes and written procedures in place that are intended to ensure that the information to be exchanged is transmitted to the relevant jurisdictions in accordance with the timelines provided for in the relevant QCAAs and terms of reference. It has provided details in relation to these processes and written procedures.

(e) Temporary suspension of exchange or termination of QCAA

17. Qatar has processes in place that are intended to ensure that a temporary suspension of the exchange of information or termination of a relevant QCAA be carried out only as per the conditions set out in the QCAA. It has provided details in relation to those processes.

(f) Consultation with other Competent Authority before determining systemic failure or significant non-compliance

18. Qatar has processes in place that are intended to ensure that the Competent Authority consults with the other Competent Authority prior to making a determination that there is or has been significant non-compliance with the terms of the relevant QCAA or that the other Competent Authority has caused a systemic failure. It has provided details in relation to those processes.

(g) Format for information exchange

19. Qatar confirms that it will use the OECD XML Schema and User Guide for the international exchange of CbC reports.

(h) Method for transmission

20. Qatar confirms that it will use the Common Transmission System for the exchange of CbC reports.

Conclusion

21. The 2018/2019 peer review recommended that Qatar take steps to implement processes or written procedures to ensure that the exchange of information is conducted in a manner consistent with the terms of reference relating to the exchange of information framework ahead of its first exchanges of information. The processes are in place and the recommendation is removed.

Part C: Appropriate use

Appropriate use

22. No changes were identified.

Conclusion

23. Qatar is a non-reciprocal jurisdiction and, as such, will not receive CbC reports submitted to tax authorities in other jurisdictions, and will not apply local filing. It is not necessary for this peer review evaluation to reach any conclusion with respect to Qatar's compliance with the terms of reference on appropriate use.

Summary of recommendations on the implementation of Country-by-Country Reporting

Aspect of the implementation that should be improved		Recommendation for improvement
Part A	Domestic legal and administrative framework	-
Part B	Exchange of information framework	-
Part C	Appropriate use	-

References

OECD (2019), *Country-by-Country Reporting – Compilation of Peer Review Reports (Phase 2): Inclusive Framework on BEPS: Action 13*, OECD/G20 Base Erosion and Profit Shifting Project, OECD Publishing, Paris, https://dx.doi.org/10.1787/f9bf1157-en. [1]

OECD (2018), *Country-by-Country Reporting – Compilation of Peer Review Reports (Phase 1): Inclusive Framework on BEPS: Action 13*, OECD/G20 Base Erosion and Profit Shifting Project, OECD Publishing, Paris, https://dx.doi.org/10.1787/9789264300057-en. [2]

OECD (2017), *Terms of reference for the conduct of peer review of the Action 13 minimum standard on country-by-country reporting*, OECD Publishing, https://www.oecd.org/tax/beps/beps-action-13-on-country-by-country-reporting-peer-review-documents.pdf. [3]

Notes

[1] In principle, an Ultimate Parent Entity of an MNE Group that is resident in Qatar is required to file a CbC report in Qatar for fiscal years commencing between 1 January 2017 and 31 December 2017. However, this obligation is waived in circumstances where the MNE Group files a CbC report for the fiscal year in another jurisdiction via a surrogate parent entity in that jurisdiction, and certain conditions are met.

[2] Qatar's 2017/2018 peer review included a monitoring point relating to the definition of "Excluded MNE group". This monitoring point remains in place.

Romania

1. Romania was reviewed as part of the 2017/2018 and the 2018/2019 peer reviews. This report is supplementary to those previous reports (OECD, 2019[1]) (OECD, 2018[2]).

2. The first filing obligation for a CbC report in Romania commences in respect of fiscal years commencing on or after 1 January 2016.

Summary of key findings

3. Romania's implementation of the Action 13 minimum standard meets all the applicable terms of reference (OECD, 2017[3]) relating to the domestic legal and administrative framework, with the exception that :

- It is recommended that Romania take steps to align its local filing implementation with that required by the Action 13 minimum standard.

4. It is recommended that Romania take steps to implement processes or written procedures to ensure that the exchange of information is conducted in a manner consistent with the terms of reference relating to the exchange of information framework. This recommendation remains unchanged since the 2018/2019 peer review.

5. It is recommended that Romania take steps to ensure that the appropriate use condition is met ahead of the first exchanges of information. This recommendation remains unchanged since the 2017/2018 peer review.

Part A: The domestic legal and administrative framework

6. Romania has legislation in place to implement the BEPS Action 13 minimum standard.

(a) Parent entity filing obligation

7. No changes were identified.

(b) Scope and timing of parent entity filing

8. No changes were identified

(c) Limitation on local filing obligation

9. It is recommended that Romania take steps to align its local filing implementation with that required by the Action 13 minimum standard.

(d) Limitation on local filing in case of surrogate filing

10. No changes were identified.

(e) Effective implementation

11. No changes were identified.

Conclusion

12. It is recommended that Romania take steps to align its local filing implementation with that required by the Action 13 minimum standard.

Part B: The exchange of information framework

(a) Exchange of information framework

13. As at 31 March 2020 Romania has 62 bilateral relationships activated under the MCAA and the EU Directive on exchange of Information (EU Directive 2016/881/EU). Within the context of its international exchange of information agreements that allow automatic exchange of tax information, Romania has taken steps to have qualifying competent authority agreements in effect with jurisdictions of the Inclusive Framework that currently meet the confidentiality, consistency and appropriate use conditions. Regarding Romania's exchange of information framework, no inconsistencies with the terms of reference were identified.[1]

(b) Content of information exchanged

14. No changes were identified.

(c) Completeness of exchanges

15. No changes were identified.

(d) Timeliness of exchanges

16. No changes were identified.

(e) Temporary suspension of exchange or termination of QCAA

17. No changes were identified.

(f) Consultation with other Competent Authority before determining systemic failure or significant non-compliance

18. No changes were identified.

(g) Format for information exchange

19. No changes were identified.

(h) Method for transmission

20. No changes were identified.

Conclusion

21. It is recommended that Romania take steps to implement processes or written procedures to ensure that the exchange of information is conducted in a manner consistent with the terms of reference relating to the exchange of information framework as soon as possible. This recommendation remains unchanged since the 2018/2019 peer review.

Part C: Appropriate use

Appropriate use

22. No changes were identified.

Conclusion

23. Romania has notified under the CbC MCAA as a non-reciprocal jurisdiction and, as such, will not receive CbC reports submitted to tax authorities in other jurisdictions but does have a legislative requirement for local filing. It is therefore recommended that Romania take steps to ensure that the appropriate use condition is met as soon as possible.

Summary of recommendations on the implementation of Country-by-Country Reporting

Aspect of the implementation that should be improved		Recommendation for improvement
Part A	Domestic legal and administrative framework	It is recommended that Romania take steps to align its local filing implementation with that required by the Action 13 minimum standard.
Part B	Exchange of information framework	It is recommended that Romania take steps to implement the necessary processes or written procedures to ensure that the exchange of information is conducted in a manner consistent with the terms of reference relating to the exchange of information framework.
Part C	Appropriate use	It is recommended that Romania take steps to ensure that the appropriate use condition is met as soon as possible.

References

OECD (2019), *Country-by-Country Reporting – Compilation of Peer Review Reports (Phase 2): Inclusive Framework on BEPS: Action 13*, OECD/G20 Base Erosion and Profit Shifting Project, OECD Publishing, Paris, https://dx.doi.org/10.1787/f9bf1157-en. [1]

OECD (2018), *Country-by-Country Reporting – Compilation of Peer Review Reports (Phase 1): Inclusive Framework on BEPS: Action 13*, OECD/G20 Base Erosion and Profit Shifting Project, OECD Publishing, Paris, https://dx.doi.org/10.1787/9789264300057-en. [2]

OECD (2017), *Terms of reference for the conduct of peer review of the Action 13 minimum standard on country-by-country reporting*, OECD Publishing, https://www.oecd.org/tax/beps/beps-action-13-on-country-by-country-reporting-peer-review-documents.pdf. [3]

Note

[1] No inconsistency with the terms of reference will be identified where a QCAA is not in effect with one or more jurisdictions of the Inclusive Framework that meet the confidentiality, consistency and appropriate use conditions, but this is due to circumstances that are not under the control of the reviewed jurisdiction. This may include, for example, where the other jurisdiction intends to exchange CbC reports using the MCAA but it does not have the Convention in effect for the relevant fiscal period, or where the other jurisdiction has declined to have a QCAA in effect with the reviewed jurisdiction.

Russian Federation

1. The Russian Federation (Russia) was reviewed as part of the 2017/2018 and the 2018/2019 peer reviews. This report is supplementary to those previous reports (OECD, 2019[1]) (OECD, 2018[2]).

2. The first filing obligation for a CbC report in Russia commences in respect of financial years beginning on or after 1 January 2017. Russia also allowed its MNE groups to file a CbC report on a voluntary basis, for reporting fiscal years beginning between 1 January 2016 and 31 December 2016.

Summary of key findings

3. Russia's implementation of Action 13 minimum standard meets all applicable terms of reference (OECD, 2017[3]) relating to the domestic legal and administrative framework, with the exception of:

- the recommendation that Russia amend its legislation or otherwise takes steps to ensure that local filing is only required in the circumstances contained in the terms of reference. This recommendation remains unchanged since the 2017/2018 peer review.
- the recommendation that Russia amend its legislation or otherwise take steps to ensure that enforcement provisions and monitoring relating to the CbCR's effective implementation are provided for as contained in the terms of reference as from the first reporting period. This recommendation remains unchanged since the 2017/2018 peer review.

Part A: The domestic legal and administrative framework

4. Russia has legislation in place to implement the BEPS Action 13 minimum standard.

(a) Parent entity filing obligation

5. No changes were identified.

(b) Scope and timing of parent entity filing

6. No changes were identified.

(c) Limitation on local filing obligation

7. Russia's 2017/2018 peer review included a recommendation that Russia amend its legislation or otherwise takes steps to ensure that local filing is only required in the circumstances contained in the terms of reference. This recommendation remains in place.

(d) Limitation on local filing in case of surrogate filing

8. No changes were identified.

(e) Effective implementation

9. Russia's 2017/2018 peer review included a recommendation that Russia amend its legislation or otherwise take steps to ensure that enforcement provisions and monitoring relating to the CbCR's effective implementation are provided for. This recommendation remain in place.

Conclusion

10. It is recommended that Russia amend its legislation or otherwise takes steps to ensure that local filing is only required in the circumstances contained in the terms of reference. This recommendation remains unchanged since the 2017/2018 peer review.

11. It is recommended that Russia amend its legislation or otherwise take steps to ensure that enforcement provisions and monitoring relating to the CbCR's effective implementation are provided for as contained in the terms of reference. This recommendation remains unchanged since the 2017/2018 peer review.

Part B: The exchange of information framework

(a) Exchange of information framework

12. As at 31 March 2020, Russia has 70 bilateral relationships activated under the CbC MCAA. Within the context of its international exchange of information agreements that allow automatic exchange of information, Russia has taken steps to have qualifying competent authority agreements in effect with jurisdictions of the Inclusive Framework that meet the confidentiality, consistency and appropriate use conditions. Regarding Russia's exchange of information framework, no inconsistencies with the terms of reference were identified.[1]

(b) Content of information exchanged

13. No changes were identified.

(c) Completeness of exchanges

14. No changes were identified.

(d) Timeliness of exchanges

15. No changes were identified.

(e) Temporary suspension of exchange or termination of QCAA

16. No changes were identified.

(f) Consultation with other Competent Authority before determining systemic failure or significant non-compliance

17. No changes were identified.

(g) Format for information exchange

18. No changes were identified.

(h) Method for transmission

19. No changes were identified.

Conclusion

20. Russia meets all the terms of reference regarding the exchange of information.

Part C: Appropriate use

Appropriate use

21. No changes were identified.

Conclusion

22. Russia meets all the terms of reference relating to appropriate use of CbC reports.

Summary of recommendations on the implementation of Country-by-Country Reporting

Aspect of the implementation that should be improved		Recommendation for improvement
Part A	Domestic legal and administrative framework	It is recommended that Russia amend its legislation or otherwise take steps to ensure that local filing is only required in the circumstances contained in the terms of reference.
Part A	Domestic legal and administrative framework	It is recommended that Russia amends its legislation or otherwise take steps to ensure that enforcement provisions and monitoring relating to the CbCR's effective implementation are provided for as contained in the terms of reference as from the first reporting period.
Part B	Exchange of information framework	-
Part C	Appropriate use	-

References

OECD (2019), *Country-by-Country Reporting – Compilation of Peer Review Reports (Phase 2): Inclusive Framework on BEPS: Action 13*, OECD/G20 Base Erosion and Profit Shifting Project, OECD Publishing, Paris, https://dx.doi.org/10.1787/f9bf1157-en. [1]

OECD (2018), *Country-by-Country Reporting – Compilation of Peer Review Reports (Phase 1): Inclusive Framework on BEPS: Action 13*, OECD/G20 Base Erosion and Profit Shifting Project, OECD Publishing, Paris, https://dx.doi.org/10.1787/9789264300057-en. [2]

OECD (2017), *Terms of reference for the conduct of peer review of the Action 13 minimum standard on country-by-country reporting*, OECD Publishing, https://www.oecd.org/tax/beps/beps-action-13-on-country-by-country-reporting-peer-review-documents.pdf. [3]

Note

[1] No inconsistency with the terms of reference will be identified where a QCAA is not in effect with one or more jurisdictions of the Inclusive Framework that meet the confidentiality, consistency and appropriate use conditions, but this is due to circumstances that are not under the control of the reviewed jurisdiction. This may include, for example, where the other jurisdiction intends to exchange CbC reports using the MCAA but it does not have the Convention in effect for the relevant fiscal period, or where the other jurisdiction has declined to have a QCAA in effect with the reviewed jurisdiction

Saint Lucia

1. Saint Lucia was first reviewed during the 2018/2019 peer review. This report is supplementary to that previous report (OECD, 2018[2]).

2. There is no filing obligation for a CbC report in Saint Lucia yet.

Summary of key findings

3. Saint Lucia does not yet have legislation in place for implementing the BEPS Action 13 minimum standard. It is recommended that Saint Lucia take steps to implement a domestic legal and administrative framework to impose and enforce CbC reporting requirements as soon as possible. This recommendation remains unchanged since the 2018/2019 peer review.

4. It is recommended that Saint Lucia take steps to put QCAAs in effect with jurisdictions of the Inclusive Framework which meet the confidentiality, consistency and appropriate use prerequisites and with which Saint Lucia has an international exchange of information agreement in effect that allows for the automatic exchange of tax information. This recommendation remains unchanged since the 2018/2019 peer review.

5. It is recommended that Saint Lucia take steps to implement processes or written procedures to ensure that the exchange of information is conducted in a manner consistent with the terms of reference (OECD, 2017[3]) relating to the exchange of information framework ahead of the first exchanges of information. This recommendation remains unchanged since the 2018/2019 peer review.

6. It is recommended that Saint Lucia take steps to ensure that the appropriate use condition is met ahead of the first exchanges of information. This recommendation remains unchanged since the 2018/2019 peer review.

Part A: The domestic legal and administrative framework

7. Saint Lucia does not yet have legislation in place for implementing the BEPS Action 13 minimum standard.

(a) Parent entity filing obligation

(b) Scope and timing of parent entity filing

(c) Limitation on local filing obligation

(d) Limitation on local filing in case of surrogate filing

(e) Effective implementation

8. No changes were identified.

Conclusion

9. It is recommended that Saint Lucia take steps to implement a domestic legal and administrative framework to impose and enforce CbC reporting requirements as soon as possible.

Part B: The exchange of information framework

(a) Exchange of information framework

10. As of 31 March 2020, Saint Lucia no bilateral relationships in place for the exchange of CbC reports. It is recommended that Saint Lucia take steps to have qualifying competent authority agreements in effect with jurisdictions of the Inclusive Framework that meet the confidentiality, consistency and appropriate use conditions and with which Saint Lucia has an international exchange of information agreement in effect that allows for the automatic exchange of tax information.

(b) Content of information exchanged

11. No changes were identified.

(c) Completeness of exchanges

12. No changes were identified.

(d) Timeliness of exchanges

13. No changes were identified.

(e) Temporary suspension of exchange or termination of QCAA

14. No changes were identified.

(f) Consultation with other Competent Authority before determining systemic failure or significant non-compliance

15. No changes were identified

(g) Format for information exchange

16. No changes were identified.

(h) Method for transmission

17. No changes were identified.

Conclusion

18. It is recommended that Saint Lucia take steps take steps to have qualifying competent authority agreements in effect with jurisdictions of the Inclusive Framework that meet the confidentiality, consistency and appropriate use conditions and with which Saint Lucia has an international exchange of information agreement in effect that allows for the automatic exchange of tax information. This recommendation remains unchanged since the 2018/2019 peer review.

19. It is recommended that Saint Lucia take steps to implement processes or written procedures to ensure that the exchange of information is conducted in a manner consistent with the terms of reference relating to the exchange of information framework ahead of its first exchanges of information. This recommendation remains unchanged since the 2018/2019 peer review.

Part C: Appropriate use

Appropriate use

20. No changes were identified.

Conclusion

21. It is recommended that Saint Lucia take steps to ensure that the appropriate use condition is met ahead of its first exchanges of information. This recommendation remains unchanged since the 2018/2019 peer review.

Summary of recommendations on the implementation of Country-by-Country Reporting

Aspect of the implementation that should be improved		Recommendation for improvement
Part A	Domestic legal and administrative framework	It is recommended that Saint Lucia take steps to implement a domestic legal and administrative framework to impose and enforce CbC requirements as soon as possible.
Part B	Exchange of information framework	It is recommended that Saint Lucia take steps have QCAAs in effect with jurisdictions of the Inclusive Framework which meet the confidentiality, consistency and appropriate use prerequisites and with which they have an international exchange of information agreement in effect that allows for the automatic exchange of tax information.
Part B	Exchange of information framework	It is recommended that Saint Lucia take steps to implement the necessary processes or written procedures to ensure that the exchange of information is conducted in a manner consistent with the terms of reference relating to the exchange of information framework.
Part C	Appropriate use	It is recommended that Saint Lucia take steps to ensure that the appropriate use condition is met ahead of the first exchanges of information.

References

OECD (2018), *Country-by-Country Reporting – Compilation of Peer Review Reports (Phase 1): Inclusive Framework on BEPS: Action 13*, OECD/G20 Base Erosion and Profit Shifting Project, OECD Publishing, Paris, https://dx.doi.org/10.1787/9789264300057-en. [2]

OECD (2017), *Terms of reference for the conduct of peer review of the Action 13 minimum standard on country-by-country reporting*, OECD Publishing, https://www.oecd.org/tax/beps/beps-action-13-on-country-by-country-reporting-peer-review-documents.pdf. [3]

Saint Vincent and the Grenadines

1. This report is Saint Vincent and the Grenadines' first annual peer review report. Consistent with the agreed methodology this report covers: (i) the domestic legal and administrative framework, (ii) the exchange of information framework as well as (iii) the appropriate use of CbC reports.

2. There is no filing obligation for a CbC report in Saint Vincent and the Grenadines yet.

Summary of key findings

3. Saint Vincent and the Grenadines does not yet have legislation in place for implementing the BEPS Action 13 minimum standard.

4. It is recommended that Saint Vincent and the Grenadines take steps to implement a domestic legal and administrative framework to impose and enforce CbC reporting requirements as soon as possible.

5. It is recommended that Saint Vincent and the Grenadines take steps to put in place an exchange of information framework that allows automatic exchange of information and have QCAAs in effect with jurisdictions of the Inclusive Framework which meet the confidentiality, consistency and appropriate use prerequisites and with which Saint Vincent and the Grenadines has an international exchange of information agreement in effect that allows for the automatic exchange of tax information.

6. It is recommended that Saint Vincent and the Grenadines take steps to implement processes or written procedures to ensure that the exchange of information is conducted in a manner consistent with the terms of reference (OECD, 2017[3]) relating to the exchange of information framework ahead of the first exchanges of information.

7. It is recommended that Saint Vincent and the Grenadines take steps to ensure that the appropriate use condition is met ahead of the first exchanges of information.

Part A: The domestic legal and administrative framework

8. Saint Vincent and the Grenadines does not yet have legislation in place for implementing the BEPS Action 13 minimum standard.

(a) Parent entity filing obligation

(b) Scope and timing of parent entity filing

(c) Limitation on local filing obligation

(d) Limitation on local filing in case of surrogate filing

(e) Effective implementation

Conclusion

9. It is recommended that Saint Vincent and the Grenadines take steps to implement a domestic legal and administrative framework to impose and enforce CbC reporting requirements as soon as possible.

Part B: The exchange of information framework

(a) Exchange of information framework

10. As of 31 March 2020, Saint Vincent and the Grenadines has no bilateral relationships in place for the exchange of CbC reports. It is recommended that Saint Vincent and the Grenadines take steps to have qualifying competent authority agreements in effect with jurisdictions of the Inclusive Framework that meet the confidentiality, consistency and appropriate use conditions and with which Saint Vincent and the Grenadines has an international exchange of information agreement in effect that allows for the automatic exchange of tax information.

(b) Content of information exchanged

11. Saint Vincent and the Grenadines does not have processes or written procedures in place that are intended to ensure that each of the mandatory fields of information required in the CbC reporting template are present in the information exchanged.

(c) Completeness of exchanges

12. Saint Vincent and the Grenadines does not have processes or written procedures in place that are intended to ensure that CbC reports are exchanged with all tax jurisdictions listed in Table 1 of a CbC report with which it should exchange information as per the relevant QCAA.

(d) Timeliness of exchanges

13. Saint Vincent and the Grenadines does not have processes or written procedures in place that are intended to ensure that the information to be exchanged is transmitted to the relevant jurisdictions in accordance with the timelines provided for in the relevant QCAAs.

(e) Temporary suspension of exchange or termination of QCAA

14. Saint Vincent and the Grenadines does not have processes or written procedures in place that are intended to ensure that a temporary suspension of the exchange of information or termination of a relevant QCAA would be carried out only as per the conditions set out in the relevant QCAA.

(f) Consultation with other Competent Authority before determining systemic failure or significant non-compliance

15. Saint Vincent and the Grenadines does not have processes or written procedures in place that are intended to ensure that its Competent Authority consults with the other Competent Authority before making a determination of systemic failure or significant non-compliance with the terms of the relevant QCAA by that other Competent Authority.

(g) Format for information exchange

16. Saint Vincent and the Grenadines has not confirmed the format that will be used for the international exchange of CbC reports.

(h) Method for transmission

17. Saint Vincent and the Grenadines has not confirmed the mechanism that it will use to exchange CbC reports.

Conclusion

18. It is recommended that Saint Vincent and the Grenadines take steps to have qualifying competent authority agreements in effect with jurisdictions of the Inclusive Framework that meet the confidentiality, consistency and appropriate use conditions and with which Saint Vincent and the Grenadines has an international exchange of information agreement in effect that allows for the automatic exchange of tax information.

19. It is recommended that Saint Vincent and the Grenadines take steps to implement processes or written procedures to ensure that the exchange of information is conducted in a manner consistent with the terms of reference (OECD, 2017[3]) relating to the exchange of information framework ahead of its first exchanges of information.

Part C: Appropriate use

Appropriate use

20. Saint Vincent and the Grenadines does not yet have measures in place relating to appropriate use.

21. It is recommended that Saint Vincent and the Grenadines take steps to have measures in place relating to appropriate use ahead of the first exchanges of information remains in place.

Conclusion

22. It is recommended that Saint Vincent and the Grenadines take steps to ensure that the appropriate use condition is met ahead of its first exchanges of information.

Summary of recommendations on the implementation of Country-by-Country Reporting

Aspect of the implementation that should be improved		Recommendation for improvement
Part A	Domestic legal and administrative framework	It is recommended that Saint Vincent and the Grenadines take steps to implement a domestic legal and administrative framework to impose and enforce CbC requirements as soon as possible.
Part B	Exchange of information framework	It is recommended that Saint Vincent and the Grenadines take steps to put in place an exchange of information framework that allows Automatic Exchange of Information and have QCAAs in effect with jurisdictions of the Inclusive Framework which meet the confidentiality, consistency and appropriate use prerequisites and with which Saint Vincent and the Grenadines has an international exchange of information agreement in effect that allows for the automatic exchange of tax information.
Part B	Exchange of information framework	It is recommended that Saint Vincent and the Grenadines take steps to implement the necessary processes or written procedures to ensure that the exchange of information is conducted in a manner consistent with the terms of reference relating to the exchange of information framework.
Part C	Appropriate use	It is recommended that Saint Vincent and the Grenadines take steps to ensure that the appropriate use condition is met ahead of the first exchanges of information.

References

OECD (2019), *Country-by-Country Reporting – Compilation of Peer Review Reports (Phase 2): Inclusive Framework on BEPS: Action 13*, OECD/G20 Base Erosion and Profit Shifting Project, OECD Publishing, Paris, https://dx.doi.org/10.1787/f9bf1157-en. [1]

San Marino

1. San Marino was reviewed as part of the 2017/2018 and the 2018/2019 peer reviews. This report is supplementary to those previous reports (OECD, 2019[1]) (OECD, 2018[2]).

2. The filing obligation for a CbC report in San Marino applies to reporting fiscal years commencing on or after 1 January 2019.

Summary of key findings

3. San Marino's implementation of the Action 13 minimum standard meets all applicable terms of reference (OECD, 2017[3]).

Part A: The domestic legal and administrative framework

4. San Marino has primary law in place to implement the BEPS Action 13 minimum standard, establishing the necessary requirements including the filing and reporting obligations.

(a) Parent entity filing obligation

5. No changes were identified.

(b) Scope and timing of parent entity filing

6. No changes were identified.

(c) Limitation on local filing obligation

7. No changes were identified.

(d) Limitation on local filing in case of surrogate filing

8. No changes were identified.

(e) Effective implementation

9. No changes were identified.

Conclusion

10. San Marino meets all the terms of reference relating to the domestic legal and administrative framework.

Part B: The exchange of information framework

(a) Exchange of information framework

11. As of 31 March 2020, San Marino has 65 bilateral relationships in place for the exchange of CbC reports under the CbC MCAA. In the context of its international exchange of information agreements that allow automatic exchange of tax information, San Marino has taken steps to have qualifying competent authority agreements in effect with jurisdictions of the Inclusive Framework that currently meet the

confidentiality, consistency and appropriate use conditions. Regarding San Marino's exchange of information framework, no inconsistencies with the terms of reference were identified.[1]

(b) Content of information exchanged

12. No changes were identified.

(c) Completeness of exchanges

13. No changes were identified.

(d) Timeliness of exchanges

14. No changes were identified.

(e) Temporary suspension of exchange or termination of QCAA

15. No changes were identified.

(f) Consultation with other Competent Authority before determining systemic failure or significant non-compliance

16. No changes were identified.

(g) Format for information exchange

17. No changes were identified.

(h) Method for transmission

18. No changes were identified.

Conclusion

19. San Marino meets all the terms of reference regarding the exchange of information.

Part C: Appropriate use

Appropriate use

20. No changes were identified.

Conclusion

21. San Marino meets all the terms of reference relating to appropriate use of CbC reports.

Summary of recommendations on the implementation of Country-by-Country Reporting

Aspect of the implementation that should be improved		Recommendation for improvement
Part A	Domestic legal and administrative framework	-
Part B	Exchange of information framework	-
Part C	Appropriate use	-

References

OECD (2019), *Country-by-Country Reporting – Compilation of Peer Review Reports (Phase 2): Inclusive Framework on BEPS: Action 13*, OECD/G20 Base Erosion and Profit Shifting Project, OECD Publishing, Paris, https://dx.doi.org/10.1787/f9bf1157-en. [1]

OECD (2018), *Country-by-Country Reporting – Compilation of Peer Review Reports (Phase 1): Inclusive Framework on BEPS: Action 13*, OECD/G20 Base Erosion and Profit Shifting Project, OECD Publishing, Paris, https://dx.doi.org/10.1787/9789264300057-en. [2]

OECD (2017), *Terms of reference for the conduct of peer review of the Action 13 minimum standard on country-by-country reporting*, OECD Publishing, https://www.oecd.org/tax/beps/beps-action-13-on-country-by-country-reporting-peer-review-documents.pdf. [3]

Note

[1] No inconsistency with the terms of reference will be identified where a QCAA is not in effect with one or more jurisdictions of the Inclusive Framework that meet the confidentiality, consistency and appropriate use conditions, but this is due to circumstances that are not under the control of the reviewed jurisdiction. This may include, for example, where the other jurisdiction intends to exchange CbC reports using the MCAA but it does not have the Convention in effect for the relevant fiscal period, or where the other jurisdiction has declined to have a QCAA in effect with the reviewed jurisdiction.

Saudi Arabia

1. Saudi Arabia was reviewed as part of the 2017/2018 and the 2018/2019 peer reviews. This report is supplementary to those previous reports (OECD, 2019[1]) (OECD, 2018[2]).

2. The first filing obligation for a CbC report in Saudi Arabia applies to reporting fiscal years beginning on or after 1 January 2018.

Summary of key findings

3. Saudi Arabia's previous peer reviews recommended that Saudi Arabia take steps to implement a domestic legal and administrative framework to impose and enforce CbC reporting requirements as soon as possible. Legislation is now in effect and this recommendation is removed.

4. Saudi Arabia's previous peer reviews recommended that Saudi Arabia take steps to have QCAAs in effect with jurisdictions of the Inclusive Framework which meet the confidentiality, consistency and appropriate use prerequisites and with which Saudi Arabia has an international exchange of information agreement in effect that allows for the automatic exchange of tax information. Steps have been taken and this recommendation is removed.

5. Saudi Arabia's previous peer reviews recommended that Saudi Arabia take steps to implement processes or written procedures to ensure that the exchange of information is conducted in a manner consistent with the terms of reference (OECD, 2017[3]) relating to the exchange of information framework ahead of the first exchanges of information. Steps have been taken and the recommendation is removed.

6. Saudi Arabia's previous peer reviews recommended that Saudi Arabia take steps to ensure that the appropriate use condition is met ahead of the first exchanges of information. Steps have been taken and the recommendation is removed

Part A: The domestic legal and administrative framework

7. Saudi Arabia has published guidelines for transfer pricing that impose and enforce a CbC filing requirement for fiscal years commencing on or after 1 January 2018[1].

(a) Parent entity filing obligation

8. Saudi Arabia has introduced a filing requirement which applies to all Ultimate Parent Entities of MNE Groups above a certain threshold and which requires inclusion of all constituent entities.

9. No inconsistencies were identified.

(b) Scope and timing of parent entity filing

10. The first filing requirements for MNE Groups in Saudi Arabia enforce a CbC filing requirement for fiscal years commencing on or after 1 January 2018 and filing is required 12 months after the reporting year end.

11. No inconsistencies were identified.

(c) Limitation on local filing obligation

12. Saudi Arabia has introduced a local filing requirement which is in line with the terms of reference with regard to the circumstances in which a local filing requirement can be imposed.

13. No inconsistencies were identified.

(d) Limitation on local filing in case of surrogate filing

14. Saudi Arabia's local filing requirements will not apply if there is surrogate filing in another jurisdiction.

15. No inconsistencies were identified.

(e) Effective implementation

16. Saudi Arabia has notification requirements and a penalty regime which penalises businesses who do not meet their filing commitments by withdrawing certification required to do business in Saudi Arabia.

17. No inconsistencies were identified.

Conclusion

18. Saudi Arabia's legal framework meets all the terms of reference.

Part B: The exchange of information framework

(a) Exchange of information framework

19. Saudi Arabia's previous peer reviews recommended that Saudi Arabia take steps to have qualifying competent authority agreements in effect with jurisdictions of the Inclusive Framework that meet the confidentiality, consistency and appropriate use conditions and with which it has an international exchange of information agreement in effect that allows for the automatic exchange of tax information. These steps have been taken and the recommendation is removed.

20. As of 31 March 2020, Saudi Arabia has 58 bilateral relationships activated under the CbC MCAA. Within the context of its international exchange of information agreements that allow automatic exchange of information, Saudi Arabia has taken steps to have qualifying competent authority agreements in effect with jurisdictions of the Inclusive Framework that meet the confidentiality, consistency and appropriate use conditions.[2] Regarding Saudi Arabia's exchange of information framework, no inconsistencies with the terms of reference were identified

(b) Content of information exchanged

21. Saudi Arabia has processes and written procedures in place that are intended to ensure that each of the mandatory fields of information as required in the CbC template are present in the information exchanged. It has provided details in relation to these processes and written procedures.

(c) Completeness of exchanges

22. Saudi Arabia has processes and written procedures in place that are intended to ensure that CbC reports are exchanged with all tax jurisdictions listed in Table 1 of a CbC reporting template with which it should exchange information as per the relevant QCAAs. It has provided details in relation to these processes and written procedures.

(d) Timeliness of exchanges

23. Saudi Arabia has processes and written procedures in place that are intended to ensure that the information to be exchanged is transmitted to the relevant jurisdictions in accordance with the timelines provided for in the relevant QCAAs and terms of reference. It has provided details in relation to these processes and written procedures.

(e) Temporary suspension of exchange or termination of QCAA

24. Saudi Arabia has processes in place that are intended to ensure that a temporary suspension of the exchange of information or termination of a relevant QCAA be carried out only as per the conditions set out in the QCAA. It has provided details in relation to those processes.

(f) Consultation with other Competent Authority before determining systemic failure or significant non-compliance

25. Saudi Arabia has processes in place that are intended to ensure that the Competent Authority consults with the other Competent Authority prior to making a determination that there is or has been significant non-compliance with the terms of the relevant QCAA or that the other Competent Authority has caused a systemic failure. It has provided details in relation to those processes.

(g) Format for information exchange

26. Saudi Arabia confirms that it uses the OECD XML Schema and User Guide for the international exchange of CbC reports.

(h) Method for transmission

27. Saudi Arabia confirms that it uses the Common Transmission System for the international exchange of CbC reports.

Conclusion

28. Saudi Arabia's previous peer reviews recommended that Saudi Arabia take steps to have qualifying competent authority agreements in effect with jurisdictions of the Inclusive Framework that meet the confidentiality, consistency and appropriate use conditions and with which it has an international exchange of information agreement in effect that allows for the automatic exchange of tax information. These steps have been taken and the recommendation is removed.

29. Saudi Arabia's previous peer review recommended that Saudi Arabia take steps to implement processes or written procedures to ensure that the exchange of information is conducted in a manner consistent with the terms of reference relating to the exchange of information framework ahead of its first exchanges of information. These steps have been taken and the recommendation is removed.

Part C: Appropriate use

Appropriate use

30. Saudi Arabia's previous peer review recommended that Saudi Arabia take steps to ensure that the appropriate use condition is met. These steps have been taken and the recommendation is removed.

Conclusion

31. Saudi Arabia meets all of the terms and conditions with regard to the appropriate use of CbC reports.

Summary of recommendations on the implementation of Country-by-Country Reporting

Aspect of the implementation that should be improved		Recommendation for improvement
Part A	Domestic legal and administrative framework	-
Part B	Exchange of information framework	-
Part C	Appropriate use	-

References

OECD (2019), *Country-by-Country Reporting – Compilation of Peer Review Reports (Phase 2): Inclusive Framework on BEPS: Action 13*, OECD/G20 Base Erosion and Profit Shifting Project, OECD Publishing, Paris, https://dx.doi.org/10.1787/f9bf1157-en. [1]

OECD (2018), *Country-by-Country Reporting – Compilation of Peer Review Reports (Phase 1): Inclusive Framework on BEPS: Action 13*, OECD/G20 Base Erosion and Profit Shifting Project, OECD Publishing, Paris, https://dx.doi.org/10.1787/9789264300057-en. [2]

OECD (2017), *Terms of reference for the conduct of peer review of the Action 13 minimum standard on country-by-country reporting*, OECD Publishing, https://www.oecd.org/tax/beps/beps-action-13-on-country-by-country-reporting-peer-review-documents.pdf. [3]

Notes

[1] https://gazt.gov.sa/en/RulesRegulations/Taxes/Pages/transfer-pricing.aspx; (accessed on 24 August 2020).

https://gazt.gov.sa/en/HelpCenter/guidelines/Documents/Transfer%20Pricing%20Guidelines_Final_Manual.pdf (accessed on 24 August 2020).

[2] No inconsistency with the terms of reference will be identified where a QCAA is not in effect with one or more jurisdictions of the Inclusive Framework that meet the confidentiality, consistency and appropriate use conditions, but this is due to circumstances that are not under the control of the reviewed jurisdiction. This may include, for example, where the other jurisdiction intends to exchange CbC reports using the MCAA but it does not have the Convention in effect for the relevant fiscal period, or where the other jurisdiction has declined to have a QCAA in effect with the reviewed jurisdiction.

Senegal

1. Senegal was reviewed as part of the 2017/2018 and the 2018/2019 peer reviews. This report is supplementary to those previous reports (OECD, 2019[1]) (OECD, 2018[2]).

2. The first filing obligation for a CbC report in Senegal commences in respect of financial years beginning on or after 1 January 2018.

Summary of key findings

3. Senegal's implementation of the Action 13 minimum standard meets all applicable terms of reference (OECD, 2017[3]), except for the following:

- It is recommended that Senegal define the concepts of an "Ultimate Parent Entity", "MNE Group", "Group" and "Constituent Entity" in a manner consistent with the terms of reference,
- It is recommended that Senegal publish the content and format of a CbC report,
- It is recommended that Senegal amend or otherwise clarify the annual consolidated revenue threshold calculation rule in respect of MNE Groups whose Ultimate Parent Entity is located in a jurisdiction other than Senegal which may deviate from the guidance issued by the OECD.
- It is recommended that Senegal amend the conditions for local filing or otherwise take steps to ensure that local filing can only be required in the circumstances contained in the terms of reference,
- It is recommended that Senegal have enforcement measures in case of an incomplete or erroneous filing of a CbC report.

These recommendations remain in place since the 2018/2019 peer review.

4. It is recommended that Senegal take steps to have QCAAs in effect with jurisdictions of the Inclusive Framework that meet the confidentiality, consistency and appropriate use prerequisites and with which Senegal has an international exchange of information agreement in effect that allows for the automatic exchange of tax information. This recommendation remains unchanged since the 2017/2018 peer review.

5. It is recommended that Senegal have in place the necessary processes or written procedures to ensure that the exchange of information is conducted in a manner consistent with the terms of reference relating to the exchange of information framework.

6. It is recommended that Senegal take steps to ensure that the appropriate use condition is met ahead of the first exchanges of information. This recommendation remains unchanged since the 2017/2018 peer review.

Part A: The domestic legal and administrative framework

7. Senegal has introduced primary legislation in 2018 to implement the BEPS Action 13 minimum standard. Secondary law and / or guidance have not been published.

(a) Parent entity filing obligation

8. It is recommended that Senegal complete the definition of an "Ultimate Parent Entity" in a manner consistent with the terms of reference. This recommendation remains unchanged since the 2018/2019 peer review.

9. It is recommended that Senegal introduce definitions of "MNE Group", "Group" and "Constituent Entity" in its domestic legal and administrative framework. This recommendation remain in place since the 2018/2019 peer review.

(b) Scope and timing of parent entity filing

10. It is recommended that Senegal prescribe the contents of a CbC report. This recommendation remains unchanged since the2018/2019 peer review.

11. It is recommended that Senegal amend or otherwise clarify that its threshold rule would apply in a manner consistent with the OECD guidance on currency fluctuations in respect of an MNE Group whose Ultimate Parent Entity is located in a jurisdiction other than Senegal. This recommendation remains in place form the 2018/2019 peer review.

(c) Limitation on local filing obligation

12. It is recommended that Senegal amend its primary law or otherwise ensure that local filing only occurs in the circumstances permitted under the minimum standard and set out in the terms of reference, in particular to prevent local filing in the absence on an international agreement. This recommendation remain in place since the 2018/2019 peer review.

13. It is recommended that Senegal amend its primary legislation or otherwise clarify that local filing will only apply if there is a "Systemic Failure". This recommendation remains unchanged since the 2018/2019 peer review.

(d) Limitation on local filing in case of surrogate filing

14. No changes were identified.[1]

(e) Effective implementation

15. It is recommended that Senegal implement enforcement measures in case of incomplete or erroneous filing of a CbC report. This recommendation remains in place form the 2018/2019 peer review.[2]

Conclusion

16. It is recommended that Senegal:

- introduce or complete the definitions of an "Ultimate Parent Entity", "MNE Group", "Group" and "Constituent Entity" in a manner that is consistent with the terms of reference;
- publish the content and format of a CbC report;
- amend or otherwise clarify the annual consolidated revenue threshold calculation rule in respect of MNE Groups whose Ultimate Parent Entity is located in a jurisdiction other than Senegal which may deviate from the guidance issued by the OECD;
- amend the conditions for local filing or otherwise take steps to ensure that local filing can only be required in the circumstances contained in the terms of reference; and
- have enforcement measures in place in case of incomplete or erroneous filing.

Part B: The exchange of information framework

(a) Exchange of information framework

17. As of 31 March 2020, Senegal has no bilateral relationships in place for the exchange of CbC reports. It is recommended that Senegal take steps to have qualifying competent authority agreements in effect with jurisdictions of the Inclusive Framework that meet the confidentiality, consistency and appropriate use conditions and with which Senegal has an international exchange of information agreement in effect that allows for the automatic exchange of tax information. This recommendation remains unchanged since the 2017/2018 peer review.

(b) Content of information exchanged

18. No changes were identified.

(c) Completeness of exchanges

19. No changes were identified.

(d) Timeliness of exchanges

20. No changes were identified.

(e) Temporary suspension of exchange or termination of QCAA

21. No changes were identified.

(f) Consultation with other Competent Authority before determining systemic failure or significant non-compliance

22. No changes were identified.

(g) Format for information exchange

23. No changes were identified.

(h) Method for transmission

24. No changes were identified.

Conclusion

25. It is recommended that Senegal take steps to have QCAAs in effect with jurisdictions of the Inclusive Framework which meet the confidentiality, consistency and appropriate use prerequisites and with which it has an international exchange of information agreement in effect that allows for the automatic exchange of tax information. This recommendation remains in place since the 2017/2018 peer review

26. It is recommended that Senegal has the necessary processes or written procedures to ensure that the exchange of information is conducted in a manner consistent with the terms of reference relating to the exchange of information framework in place ahead of its first exchanges of information. Tis recommendation remains in place form the the 2017/2018 peer review.

Part C: Appropriate use

Appropriate use

27. No changes were identified.

Conclusion

28. It is recommended that Senegal take steps to ensure that the appropriate use condition is met ahead of its first exchanges of information. This recommendation remains in place since the 2017/2018 peer review.

Summary of recommendations on the implementation of Country-by-Country Reporting

Aspect of the implementation that should be improved		Recommendation for improvement
Part A	Domestic legal and administrative framework	It is recommended that Senegal finalise its domestic legal and administrative framework as soon as possible. Specifically, it is recommended that Senegal: - introduce or complete the definitions of an "Ultimate Parent Entity", "MNE Group", "Group" and "Constituent Entity" in a manner that is consistent with the terms of reference; - publish the content and format of a CbC report; - amend or otherwise clarify the annual consolidated revenue threshold calculation rule in respect of MNE Groups whose Ultimate Parent Entity is located in a jurisdiction other than Senegal which may deviate from the guidance issued by the OECD; - amend the conditions for local filing or otherwise take steps to ensure that local filing can only be required in the circumstances contained in the terms of reference; - have enforcement measures in place in case of incomplete or erroneous filing.
Part B	Exchange of information framework	It is recommended that Senegal take steps to have QCAAs in effect with jurisdictions of the Inclusive Framework which meet the confidentiality, consistency and appropriate use prerequisites and with which Senegal has an international exchange of information agreement in effect that allows for the automatic exchange of tax information.
Part B	Exchange of information framework	It is recommended that Senegal have in place the necessary processes or written procedures to ensure that the exchange of information is conducted in a manner consistent with the terms of reference relating to the exchange of information framework.
Part C	Appropriate use	It is recommended that Senegal take steps to ensure that the appropriate use condition is met ahead of the first exchanges of information.

References

OECD (2019), *Country-by-Country Reporting – Compilation of Peer Review Reports (Phase 2): Inclusive Framework on BEPS: Action 13*, OECD/G20 Base Erosion and Profit Shifting Project, OECD Publishing, Paris, https://dx.doi.org/10.1787/f9bf1157-en. [1]

OECD (2018), *Country-by-Country Reporting – Compilation of Peer Review Reports (Phase 1): Inclusive Framework on BEPS: Action 13*, OECD/G20 Base Erosion and Profit Shifting Project, OECD Publishing, Paris, https://dx.doi.org/10.1787/9789264300057-en. [2]

OECD (2017), *Terms of reference for the conduct of peer review of the Action 13 minimum standard on country-by-country reporting*, OECD Publishing, https://www.oecd.org/tax/beps/beps-action-13-on-country-by-country-reporting-peer-review-documents.pdf. [3]

Notes

[1] Senegal's local filing requirements will not apply if there is surrogate filing in another jurisdiction which is listed in a list of states or territories which have adopted regulations imposing the filing of a CbC report similar to that required in Senegal, which have concluded an agreement with Senegal for the automatic exchange of CbC reports and which comply with the obligations arising from such agreement. It is unclear whether local filing would be "deactivated" in respect of jurisdictions which allow voluntary parent surrogate filing, being noted that the list mentioned above has not yet been published at this point in time. A monitoring point on this remains in place since the 2018/2019 peer review.

[2] There are no specific processes in place that would allow Senegal to take appropriate measures in case it is notified by another jurisdiction that such other jurisdiction has reason to believe that an error may have led to incorrect or incomplete information reporting by a Reporting Entity or that there is non-compliance of a Reporting Entity with respect to its obligation to file a CbC report. As no exchange of CbC reports has yet occurred, this aspect is being monitored. This monitoring point remains in place form the 2018/2019 peer review.

Serbia

1. Serbia was first reviewed during the 2018/2019 peer review. This report is supplementary to that previous report (OECD, 2018[2]).

2. There is no filing obligation for a CbC report in Serbia yet.

Summary of key findings

3. Serbia does not yet have legislation in place for implementing the BEPS Action 13 minimum standard.

4. It is recommended that Serbia take steps to implement a domestic legal and administrative framework to impose and enforce CbC reporting requirements as soon as possible. This recommendation remains in place form the 2018/2019 peer review.

5. It is recommended that Serbia take steps to have qualifying competent authority agreements in effect with jurisdictions of the Inclusive Framework that meet the confidentiality, consistency and appropriate use conditions and with which Serbia has an international exchange of information agreement in effect that allows for the automatic exchange of tax information. This recommendation remains in place since the 2018/2019 peer review

6. It is recommended that Serbia take steps to implement processes or written procedures to ensure that the exchange of information is conducted in a manner consistent with the terms of reference (OECD, 2017[3]) relating to the exchange of information framework ahead of the first exchanges of information. This recommendation remains in place form the 2018/2019 peer review

7. It is recommended that Serbia take steps to ensure that the appropriate use condition is met ahead of the first exchanges of information. This recommendation remains in place form the 2018/2019 peer review

Part A: The domestic legal and administrative framework

8. Serbia does not yet have legislation in place for implementing the BEPS Action 13 minimum standard.

(a) Parent entity filing obligation

(b) Scope and timing of parent entity filing

(c) Limitation on local filing obligation

(d) Limitation on local filing in case of surrogate filing

(e) Effective implementation

Conclusion

9. It is recommended that Serbia take steps to implement a domestic legal and administrative framework to impose and enforce CbC reporting requirements as soon as possible.

Part B: The exchange of information framework

(a) Exchange of information framework

10. As of 31 March 2020, Serbia has no bilateral relationships in place for the exchange of CbC reports. It is recommended that Serbia take steps to have qualifying competent authority agreements in effect with jurisdictions of the Inclusive Framework that meet the confidentiality, consistency and appropriate use conditions and with which Serbia has an international exchange of information agreement in effect that allows for the automatic exchange of tax information. This recommendation remains in place form the 2018/2019 peer review

(b) Content of information exchanged

11. No change is identified.

(c) Completeness of exchanges

12. No change is identified.

(d) Timeliness of exchanges

13. No change is identified.

(e) Temporary suspension of exchange or termination of QCAA

14. No change is identified.

(f) Consultation with other Competent Authority before determining systemic failure or significant non-compliance

15. No change is identified.

(g) Format for information exchange

16. No change is identified.

(h) Method for transmission

17. No change is identified.

Conclusion

18. It is recommended that Serbia take steps to have qualifying competent authority agreements in effect with jurisdictions of the Inclusive Framework that meet the confidentiality, consistency and appropriate use conditions and with which Serbia has an international exchange of information agreement in effect that allows for the automatic exchange of tax information. This recommendation remains in place since the 2018/2019 peer review

19. It is recommended that Serbia take steps to implement processes or written procedures to ensure that the exchange of information is conducted in a manner consistent with the terms of reference relating to the exchange of information framework ahead of its first exchanges of information. This recommendation remains in place from the 2018/2019 peer review.

Part C: Appropriate use

Appropriate use

20. No change was identified.

Conclusion

21. It is recommended that Serbia take steps to ensure that the appropriate use condition is met ahead of its first exchanges of information. This recommendation remains in place form the 2018/2019 peer review/

Summary of recommendations on the implementation of country-by-country reporting

Aspect of the implementation that should be improved		Recommendation for improvement
Part A	Domestic legal and administrative framework	It is recommended that Serbia take steps to implement a domestic legal and administrative framework to impose and enforce CbC requirements as soon as possible.
Part B	Exchange of information framework	It is recommended that Serbia take steps to put in place an exchange of information framework that allows Automatic Exchange of Information and have QCAAs in effect with jurisdictions of the Inclusive Framework which meet the confidentiality, consistency and appropriate use prerequisites and with which it has an international exchange of information agreement in effect that allows for the automatic exchange of tax information.
Part B	Exchange of information framework	It is recommended that Serbia take steps to implement the necessary processes or written procedures to ensure that the exchange of information is conducted in a manner consistent with the terms of reference relating to the exchange of information framework.
Part C	Appropriate use	It is recommended that Serbia take steps to ensure that the appropriate use condition is met ahead of the first exchanges of information.

References

OECD (2018), *Country-by-Country Reporting – Compilation of Peer Review Reports (Phase 1): Inclusive Framework on BEPS: Action 13*, OECD/G20 Base Erosion and Profit Shifting Project, OECD Publishing, Paris, https://dx.doi.org/10.1787/9789264300057-en. [2]

OECD (2017), *Terms of reference for the conduct of peer review of the Action 13 minimum standard on country-by-country reporting*, OECD Publishing, https://www.oecd.org/tax/beps/beps-action-13-on-country-by-country-reporting-peer-review-documents.pdf. [3]

Seychelles

1. The Seychelles was reviewed as part of the 2017/2018 and the 2018/2019 peer reviews. This report is supplementary to those previous reports (OECD, 2019[1]) (OECD, 2018[2]).

2. The first filing obligation for a CbC report in the Seychelles applies to reporting fiscal years ending on or after the 31 December 2019.

Summary of key findings

3. The Seychelles' implementation of the Action 13 minimum standard meets all applicable terms of reference (OECD, 2017[3]) with the exception that:

- It is recommended that the Seychelles take steps to implement processes or written procedures to ensure that the exchange of information is conducted in a manner consistent with the terms of reference relating to the exchange of information framework ahead of its first exchanges of information. This recommendation remains unchanged since the 2018/2019 peer review.
- It is recommended that the Seychelles take steps to ensure that the appropriate use condition is met ahead of its first exchanges of information. This recommendation remains unchanged since the 2017/2018 peer review.

Part A: The domestic legal and administrative framework

4. The Seychelles has legislation in place to implement the BEPS Action 13 minimum standard.

(a) Parent entity filing obligation

(b) Scope and timing of parent entity filing

(c) Limitation on local filing obligation

(d) Limitation on local filing in case of surrogate filing

(e) Effective implementation

Conclusion

5. The Seychelles meets all the terms of reference with regard to its domestic and legal framework.

Part B: The exchange of information framework

(a) Exchange of information framework

6. The Seychelles' previous peer reviews recommended that the Seychelles take steps to have qualifying competent authority agreements in effect with jurisdictions of the Inclusive Framework that meet the confidentiality, consistency and appropriate use conditions and with which the Seychelles has an international exchange of information agreement in effect that allows for the automatic exchange of tax information. These steps have been taken and the recommendation is removed.

7. As of 31 March 2020, Seychelles has 59 bilateral relationships activated under the CbC MCAA. Within the context of its international exchange of information agreements that allow automatic exchange of information, the Seychelles has taken steps to have qualifying competent authority agreements in effect with jurisdictions of the Inclusive Framework that meet the confidentiality, consistency and appropriate use conditions.[1] Regarding the Seychelles' exchange of information framework, no inconsistencies with the terms of reference were identified

(b) Content of information exchanged

8. No changes were identified.

(c) Completeness of exchanges

9. No changes were identified.

(d) Timeliness of exchanges

10. No changes were identified.

(e) Temporary suspension of exchange or termination of QCAA

11. No changes were identified.

(f) Consultation with other Competent Authority before determining systemic failure or significant non-compliance

12. No changes were identified

(g) Format for information exchange

13. No changes were identified.

(h) Method for transmission

14. No changes were identified.

Conclusion

15. The Seychelles' previous peer reviews recommended that the Seychelles take steps to have qualifying competent authority agreements in effect with jurisdictions of the Inclusive Framework that meet the confidentiality, consistency and appropriate use conditions and with which the Seychelles has an international exchange of information agreement in effect that allows for the automatic exchange of tax information. These steps have been taken and the recommendation is removed.

16. It is recommended that the Seychelles take steps to implement processes or written procedures to ensure that the exchange of information is conducted in a manner consistent with the terms of reference relating to the exchange of information framework ahead of its first exchanges of information. This recommendation remains unchanged since the 2018/2019 peer review.

Part C: Appropriate use

Appropriate use

17. No changes were identified.

Conclusion

18. It is recommended that the Seychelles take steps to ensure that the appropriate use condition is met ahead of its first exchanges of information. This recommendation remains unchanged since the 2017/2018 peer review.

Summary of recommendations on the implementation of Country-by-Country Reporting

Aspect of the implementation that should be improved		Recommendation for improvement
Part A	Domestic legal and administrative framework	-
Part B	Exchange of information framework	It is recommended that the Seychelles take steps to implement the necessary processes or written procedures to ensure that the exchange of information is conducted in a manner consistent with the terms of reference relating to the exchange of information framework.
Part C	Appropriate use	It is recommended that the Seychelles take steps to ensure that the appropriate use condition is met ahead of the first exchanges of information.

References

OECD (2019), *Country-by-Country Reporting – Compilation of Peer Review Reports (Phase 2): Inclusive Framework on BEPS: Action 13*, OECD/G20 Base Erosion and Profit Shifting Project, OECD Publishing, Paris, https://dx.doi.org/10.1787/f9bf1157-en. [1]

OECD (2018), *Country-by-Country Reporting – Compilation of Peer Review Reports (Phase 1): Inclusive Framework on BEPS: Action 13*, OECD/G20 Base Erosion and Profit Shifting Project, OECD Publishing, Paris, https://dx.doi.org/10.1787/9789264300057-en. [2]

OECD (2017), *Terms of reference for the conduct of peer review of the Action 13 minimum standard on country-by-country reporting*, OECD Publishing, https://www.oecd.org/tax/beps/beps-action-13-on-country-by-country-reporting-peer-review-documents.pdf. [3]

Note

[1] No inconsistency with the terms of reference will be identified where a QCAA is not in effect with one or more jurisdictions of the Inclusive Framework that meet the confidentiality, consistency and appropriate use conditions, but this is due to circumstances that are not under the control of the reviewed jurisdiction. This may include, for example, where the other jurisdiction intends to exchange CbC reports using the MCAA but it does not have the Convention in effect for the relevant fiscal period, or where the other jurisdiction has declined to have a QCAA in effect with the reviewed jurisdiction.

Sierra Leone

1. Sierra Leone was first reviewed during the 2018/2019 peer review. This report is supplementary to that previous report (OECD, 2018[2]).

2. There is no filing obligation for a CbC report in Sierra Leone yet.

Summary of key findings

3. Sierra Leone does not yet have legislation in place for implementing the BEPS Action 13 minimum standard. It is recommended that Sierra Leone take steps to implement a domestic legal and administrative framework to impose and enforce CbC reporting requirements as soon as possible.

4. It is recommended that Sierra Leone take steps to have qualifying competent authority agreements in effect with jurisdictions of the Inclusive Framework that meet the confidentiality, consistency and appropriate use conditions and with which Sierra Leone has an international exchange of information agreement in effect that allows for the automatic exchange of tax information.

5. It is recommended that Sierra Leone take steps to implement processes or written procedures to ensure that the exchange of information is conducted in a manner consistent with the terms of reference (OECD, 2017[3]) relating to the exchange of information framework ahead of the first exchanges of information.

6. It is recommended that Sierra Leone take steps to ensure that the appropriate use condition is met ahead of the first exchanges of information.

Part A: The domestic legal and administrative framework

7. Sierra Leone does not yet have legislation in place for implementing the BEPS Action 13 minimum standard.

(a) Parent entity filing obligation

(b) Scope and timing of parent entity filing

(c) Limitation on local filing obligation

(d) Limitation on local filing in case of surrogate filing

(e) Effective implementation

Conclusion

8. It is recommended that Sierra Leone take steps to implement a domestic legal and administrative framework to impose and enforce CbC reporting requirements as soon as possible. This recommendation remains unchanged since the 2018/2019 peer review.

Part B: The exchange of information framework

(a) Exchange of information framework

9. As of 31 March 2020, Sierra Leone has no bilateral relationships in place for the exchange of CbC reports. It is recommended that Sierra Leone take steps to have qualifying competent authority agreements in effect with jurisdictions of the Inclusive Framework that meet the confidentiality, consistency and appropriate use conditions and with which sierra Leone has an international exchange of information agreement in effect that allows for the automatic exchange of tax information. This recommendation remains unchanged since the 2018/2019 peer review.

(b) Content of information exchanged

10. No changes were identified.

(c) Completeness of exchanges

11. No changes were identified.

(d) Timeliness of exchanges

12. No changes were identified.

(e) Temporary suspension of exchange or termination of QCAA

13. No changes were identified

(f) Consultation with other Competent Authority before determining systemic failure or significant non-compliance

14. No changes were identified.

(g) Format for information exchange

15. No changes were identified.

(h) Method for transmission

16. No changes were identified.

Conclusion

17. It is recommended that Sierra Leone take steps to have qualifying competent authority agreements in effect with jurisdictions of the Inclusive Framework that meet the confidentiality, consistency and appropriate use conditions and with which Sierra Leone has an international exchange of information agreement in effect that allows for the automatic exchange of tax information. This recommendation remains unchanged since the 2018/2019 peer review.

18. It is recommended that Sierra Leone take steps to implement processes or written procedures to ensure that the exchange of information is conducted in a manner consistent with the terms of reference relating to the exchange of information framework ahead of its first exchanges of information. This recommendation remains unchanged since the 2018/2019 peer review.

Part C: Appropriate use

Appropriate use

19. No changes were identified.

Conclusion

20. It is recommended that Sierra Leone take steps to ensure that the appropriate use condition is met ahead of its first exchanges of information. This recommendation remains unchanged since the 2018/2019 peer review.

Summary of recommendations on the implementation of Country-by-Country Reporting

Aspect of the implementation that should be improved		Recommendation for improvement
Part A	Domestic legal and administrative framework	It is recommended that Sierra Leone take steps to implement a domestic legal and administrative framework to impose and enforce CbC requirements as soon as possible.
Part B	Exchange of information framework	It is recommended that Sierra Leone take steps to have QCAAs in effect with jurisdictions of the Inclusive Framework which meet the confidentiality, consistency and appropriate use prerequisites and with which Sierra Leone has an international exchange of information agreement in effect that allows for the automatic exchange of tax information
Part B	Exchange of information framework	It is recommended that Sierra Leone take steps to implement the necessary processes or written procedures to ensure that the exchange of information is conducted in a manner consistent with the terms of reference relating to the exchange of information framework.
Part C	Appropriate use	It is recommended that Sierra Leone take steps to ensure that the appropriate use condition is met ahead of the first exchanges of information.

References

OECD (2018), *Country-by-Country Reporting – Compilation of Peer Review Reports (Phase 1): Inclusive Framework on BEPS: Action 13*, OECD/G20 Base Erosion and Profit Shifting Project, OECD Publishing, Paris, https://dx.doi.org/10.1787/9789264300057-en. [2]

OECD (2017), *Terms of reference for the conduct of peer review of the Action 13 minimum standard on country-by-country reporting*, OECD Publishing, https://www.oecd.org/tax/beps/beps-action-13-on-country-by-country-reporting-peer-review-documents.pdf. [3]

Singapore

1. Singapore was reviewed as part of the 2017/2018 and the 2018/2019 peer reviews. This report is supplementary to those previous reports (OECD, 2019[1]) (OECD, 2018[2]).

2. The first filing obligation for a CbC report in Singapore applies in respect of financial years beginning on or after 1 January 2017. Singapore also allows its MNE groups to file a CbC report on a voluntary basis, for reporting fiscal years beginning between 1 January 2016 and 31 December 2016.

Summary of key findings

3. Singapore's implementation of the Action 13 minimum standard meets all applicable terms of reference (OECD, 2017[3]).

Part A: The domestic legal and administrative framework

4. Singapore has legislation in place to implement the BEPS Action 13 minimum standard. Guidance has been published.

(a) Parent entity filing obligation

5. No changes were identified.[1]

(b) Scope and timing of parent entity filing

6. No changes were identified.[2]

(c) Limitation on local filing obligation

7. No changes were identified.[3]

(d) Limitation on local filing in case of surrogate filing

8. No changes were identified.[4]

(e) Effective implementation

9. No changes were identified.

Conclusion

10. Singapore meets all the terms of reference relating to the domestic legal and administrative framework.

Part B: The exchange of information framework

(a) Exchange of information framework

11. As of 31 March 2020, Singapore has 64 bilateral relationships activated under the CbC MCAA. Within the context of its international exchange of information agreements that allow automatic exchange

of information, Singapore has taken steps to have qualifying competent authority agreements in effect with jurisdictions of the Inclusive Framework that meet the confidentiality, consistency and appropriate use conditions.[5]

(b) Content of information exchanged

12. No changes were identified.

(c) Completeness of exchanges

13. No changes were identified.

(d) Timeliness of exchanges

14. No changes were identified.

(e) Temporary suspension of exchange or termination of QCAA

15. No changes were identified.

(f) Consultation with other Competent Authority before determining systemic failure or significant non-compliance

16. No changes were identified.

(g) Format for information exchange

17. No changes were identified.

(h) Method for transmission

18. No changes were identified.

Conclusion

19. Singapore meets all the terms of reference regarding the exchange of information.

Part C: Appropriate use

Appropriate use

20. No changes were identified.

Conclusion

21. Singapore meets all the terms of reference relating to appropriate use of CbC reports.

Summary of recommendations on the implementation of country-by-country reporting

Aspect of the implementation that should be improved		Recommendation for improvement
Part A	Domestic legal and administrative framework	-
Part B	Exchange of information framework	-
Part C	Appropriate use	-

References

OECD (2019), *Country-by-Country Reporting – Compilation of Peer Review Reports (Phase 2): Inclusive Framework on BEPS: Action 13*, OECD/G20 Base Erosion and Profit Shifting Project, OECD Publishing, Paris, https://dx.doi.org/10.1787/f9bf1157-en. [1]

OECD (2018), *Country-by-Country Reporting – Compilation of Peer Review Reports (Phase 1): Inclusive Framework on BEPS: Action 13*, OECD/G20 Base Erosion and Profit Shifting Project, OECD Publishing, Paris, https://dx.doi.org/10.1787/9789264300057-en. [2]

OECD (2017), *Terms of reference for the conduct of peer review of the Action 13 minimum standard on country-by-country reporting*, OECD Publishing, https://www.oecd.org/tax/beps/beps-action-13-on-country-by-country-reporting-peer-review-documents.pdf. [3]

Notes

[1] Singapore's 2017/2018 peer review included a monitoring point in relation to a "designation provision". This monitoring point remains in place.

[2] Singapore's 2017/2018 peer review included a monitoring point in relation to the ability of the Comptroller to allow a CbC report to be filed later than the filing deadline as set in the regulations. This monitoring point remains in place.

[3] Singapore's 2017/2018 peer review included a monitoring point whereby if local filing requirements were introduced, these requirements should comply with the terms of reference under paragraph 8 (c). This monitoring point remains in place.

[4] Singapore's 2017/2018 peer review included a monitoring point whereby if local filing requirements were introduced, these requirements should be deactivated in case of surrogate filing in a manner consistent with the terms of reference under paragraph 8 (d). This monitoring point remains in place.

[5] No inconsistency with the terms of reference will be identified where a QCAA is not in effect with one or more jurisdictions of the Inclusive Framework that meet the confidentiality, consistency and appropriate use conditions, but this is due to circumstances that are not under the control of the reviewed jurisdiction. This may include, for example, where the other jurisdiction intends to exchange CbC reports using the MCAA but it does not have the Convention in effect for the relevant fiscal period, or where the other jurisdiction has declined to have a QCAA in effect with the reviewed jurisdiction

Slovak Republic

1. The Slovak Republic was reviewed as part of the 2017/2018 and the 2018/2019 peer reviews. This report is supplementary to those previous reports (OECD, 2019[1]) (OECD, 2018[2]).

2. The first filing obligation for a CbC report in the Slovak Republic applies to reporting fiscal years commencing on or after 1 January 2016.

Summary of key findings

3. The Slovak Republic's implementation of the Action 13 minimum standard meets all applicable terms of reference (OECD, 2017[3]).

Part A: The domestic legal and administrative framework

4. The Slovak Republic has law in place for implementing the BEPS Action 13 minimum standard.

(a) Parent entity filing obligation

5. No changes were identified.

(b) Scope and timing of parent entity filing

6. No changes were identified.

(c) Limitation on local filing obligation

7. No changes were identified.

(d) Limitation on local filing in case of surrogate filing

8. No changes were identified.

(e) Effective implementation

9. No changes were identified.

Conclusion

10. The Slovak Republic meets all the terms of reference relating to the domestic legal and administrative framework.

Part B: The exchange of information framework

(a) Exchange of information framework

11. As of 31 March 2020, the Slovak Republic has 67 bilateral relationships in place for the exchange of CbC reports, including those activated under the CbC MCAA, under bilateral CAAs and under the EU Council Directive (2016/881/EU). Within the context of its international exchange of information agreements that allow automatic exchange of tax information, Slovak Republic has taken steps to have

qualifying competent authority agreements in effect with jurisdictions of the Inclusive Framework that currently meet the confidentiality, consistency and appropriate use conditions. Regarding the Slovak Republic's exchange of information framework, no inconsistencies with the terms of reference were identified.[1]

(b) Content of information exchanged

12. No changes were identified.

(c) Completeness of exchanges

13. No changes were identified.

(d) Timeliness of exchanges

14. No changes were identified.

(e) Temporary suspension of exchange or termination of QCAA

15. No changes were identified.

(f) Consultation with other Competent Authority before determining systemic failure or significant non-compliance

16. No changes were identified.

(g) Format for information exchange

17. No changes were identified.

(h) Method for transmission

18. No changes were identified.

Conclusion

19. The Slovak Republic meets all the terms of reference regarding the exchange of information.

Part C: Appropriate use

Appropriate use

20. No changes were identified.

Conclusion

21. The Slovak Republic meets all the terms of reference relating to appropriate use of CbC reports.

Summary of recommendations on the implementation of country-by-country reporting

Aspect of the implementation that should be improved		Recommendation for improvement
Part A	Domestic legal and administrative framework	-
Part B	Exchange of information framework	-
Part C	Appropriate use	-

References

OECD (2019), *Country-by-Country Reporting – Compilation of Peer Review Reports (Phase 2): Inclusive Framework on BEPS: Action 13*, OECD/G20 Base Erosion and Profit Shifting Project, OECD Publishing, Paris, https://dx.doi.org/10.1787/f9bf1157-en. [1]

OECD (2018), *Country-by-Country Reporting – Compilation of Peer Review Reports (Phase 1): Inclusive Framework on BEPS: Action 13*, OECD/G20 Base Erosion and Profit Shifting Project, OECD Publishing, Paris, https://dx.doi.org/10.1787/9789264300057-en. [2]

OECD (2017), *Terms of reference for the conduct of peer review of the Action 13 minimum standard on country-by-country reporting*, OECD Publishing, https://www.oecd.org/tax/beps/beps-action-13-on-country-by-country-reporting-peer-review-documents.pdf. [3]

Note

[1] No inconsistency with the terms of reference will be identified where a QCAA is not in effect with one or more jurisdictions of the Inclusive Framework that meet the confidentiality, consistency and appropriate use conditions, but this is due to circumstances that are not under the control of the reviewed jurisdiction. This may include, for example, where the other jurisdiction intends to exchange CbC reports using the MCAA but it does not have the Convention in effect for the relevant fiscal period, or where the other jurisdiction has declined to have a QCAA in effect with the reviewed jurisdiction.

Slovenia

1. Slovenia was reviewed as part of the 2017/2018 and the 2018/2019 peer reviews. This report is supplementary to those previous reports (OECD, 2019[1]) (OECD, 2018[2]).

2. The first filing obligation for a CbC report in Slovenia applies to reporting fiscal years commencing on or after 1 January 2016.

Summary of key findings

3. Slovenia's implementation of the Action 13 minimum standard meets all applicable terms of reference (OECD, 2017[3]).

Part A: The domestic legal and administrative framework

4. Slovenia has laws in place for implementing the BEPS Action 13 minimum standard.

(a) Parent entity filing obligation

5. No changes were identified.

(b) Scope and timing of parent entity filing

6. No changes were identified.

(c) Limitation on local filing obligation

7. No changes were identified.

(d) Limitation on local filing in case of surrogate filing

8. No changes were identified.

(e) Effective implementation

9. No changes were identified.[1]

Conclusion

10. There is no change to the conclusion in relation to the domestic legal and administration framework for Slovenia since the previous peer review. Slovenia meets all the terms of reference relating to the domestic legal and administrative framework.

Part B: The exchange of information framework

(a) Exchange of information framework

11. As of 31 March 2020, Slovenia has 75 bilateral relationships in place, including those activated under the CbC MCAA, under bilateral CAAs and under the EU Council Directive (2016/881/EU). Within the context of its international exchange of information agreements that allow automatic exchange of

information, Slovenia has taken steps to have qualifying competent authority agreements in effect with jurisdictions of the Inclusive Framework that meet the confidentiality, consistency and appropriate use conditions. Regarding Slovenia's exchange of information framework, no inconsistencies with the terms of reference were identified.[2]

(b) Content of information exchanged

12. No changes were identified.

(c) Completeness of exchanges

13. No changes were identified.

(d) Timeliness of exchanges

14. No changes were identified.

(e) Temporary suspension of exchange or termination of QCAA

15. No changes were identified.

(f) Consultation with other Competent Authority before determining systemic failure or significant non-compliance

16. No changes were identified.

(g) Format for information exchange

17. No changes were identified.

(h) Method for transmission

18. No changes were identified.

Conclusion

19. Slovenia meets all the terms of reference regarding the exchange of information.

Part C: Appropriate use

Appropriate use

20. No changes were identified

Conclusion

21. Slovenia meets all the terms of reference relating to appropriate use of CbC reports.

Summary of recommendations on the implementation of country-by-country reporting

Aspect of the implementation that should be improved		Recommendation for improvement
Part A	Domestic legal and administrative framework	-
Part B	Exchange of information framework	-
Part C	Appropriate use	-

References

OECD (2019), *Country-by-Country Reporting – Compilation of Peer Review Reports (Phase 2): Inclusive Framework on BEPS: Action 13*, OECD/G20 Base Erosion and Profit Shifting Project, OECD Publishing, Paris, https://dx.doi.org/10.1787/f9bf1157-en. [1]

OECD (2018), *Country-by-Country Reporting – Compilation of Peer Review Reports (Phase 1): Inclusive Framework on BEPS: Action 13*, OECD/G20 Base Erosion and Profit Shifting Project, OECD Publishing, Paris, https://dx.doi.org/10.1787/9789264300057-en. [2]

OECD (2017), *Terms of reference for the conduct of peer review of the Action 13 minimum standard on country-by-country reporting*, OECD Publishing, https://www.oecd.org/tax/beps/beps-action-13-on-country-by-country-reporting-peer-review-documents.pdf. [3]

Notes

[1] Slovenia's 2017/2018 peer review included a general monitoring point relating to a specific process to that would allow to take appropriate measures in case Slovenia is notified by another jurisdiction that such other jurisdiction has reason to believe that an error may have led to incorrect or incomplete information reporting by a Reporting Entity or that there is non-compliance of a Reporting Entity with respect to its obligation to file a CbC report. This monitoring point remains in place.

[2] No inconsistency with the terms of reference will be identified where a QCAA is not in effect with one or more jurisdictions of the Inclusive Framework that meet the confidentiality, consistency and appropriate use conditions, but this is due to circumstances that are not under the control of the reviewed jurisdiction. This may include, for example, where the other jurisdiction intends to exchange CbC reports using the MCAA but it does not have the Convention in effect for the relevant fiscal period, or where the other jurisdiction has declined to have a QCAA in effect with the reviewed jurisdiction.

South Africa

1. South Africa was reviewed as part of the 2017/2018 and the 2018/2019 peer reviews. This report is supplementary to those previous reports (OECD, 2019[1]) (OECD, 2018[2]).

2. The first filing obligation for a CbC report in South Africa applies to reporting fiscal years commencing on or after 1 January 2016.

Summary of key findings

3. South Africa's implementation of the Action 13 minimum standard meets all applicable terms of reference (OECD, 2017[3]).

Part A: The domestic legal and administrative framework *Approved*

4. South Africa has legislation in place which implements the BEPS Action 13 minimum standard, establishing the necessary requirements[1].

(a) Parent entity filing obligation

5. No changes were identified.

(b) Scope and timing of parent entity filing

6. No changes were identified.

(c) Limitation on local filing obligation

7. No changes were identified.

(d) Limitation on local filing in case of surrogate filing

8. No changes were identified.

(e) Effective implementation

9. No changes were identified.

Conclusion

10. South Africa meets all the terms of reference relating to the domestic legal and administrative framework.

Part B: The exchange of information framework

(a) Exchange of information framework

11. As of 31 March 2020, South Africa has 72 bilateral relationships in place, including those activated under the CbC MCAA and under a bilateral CAA. Within the context of its international exchange of information agreements that allow automatic exchange of tax information, South Africa has taken steps to

have qualifying competent authority agreements in effect with jurisdictions of the Inclusive Framework that meet the confidentiality, consistency and appropriate use conditions. Regarding South Africa's exchange of information framework, no inconsistencies with the terms of reference were identified.[2]

(b) Content of information exchanged

12. No changes were identified.

(c) Completeness of exchanges

13. No changes were identified.

(d) Timeliness of exchanges

14. No changes were identified.

(e) Temporary suspension of exchange or termination of QCAA

15. No changes were identified.

(f) Consultation with other Competent Authority before determining systemic failure or significant non-compliance

16. No changes were identified.

(g) Format for information exchange

17. No changes were identified.

(h) Method for transmission

18. No changes were identified.

Conclusion

19. South Africa meets all the terms of reference regarding the exchange of information.

Part C: Appropriate use

Appropriate use

20. No changes were identified.

Conclusion

21. South Africa meets all the terms of reference relating to appropriate use of CbC reports.

Summary of recommendations on the implementation of country-by-country reporting

Aspect of the implementation that should be improved		Recommendation for improvement
Part A	Domestic legal and administrative framework	-
Part B	Exchange of information framework	-
Part C	Appropriate use	-

References

OECD (2019), *Country-by-Country Reporting – Compilation of Peer Review Reports (Phase 2): Inclusive Framework on BEPS: Action 13*, OECD/G20 Base Erosion and Profit Shifting Project, OECD Publishing, Paris, https://dx.doi.org/10.1787/f9bf1157-en. [1]

OECD (2018), *Country-by-Country Reporting – Compilation of Peer Review Reports (Phase 1): Inclusive Framework on BEPS: Action 13*, OECD/G20 Base Erosion and Profit Shifting Project, OECD Publishing, Paris, https://dx.doi.org/10.1787/9789264300057-en. [2]

OECD (2017), *Terms of reference for the conduct of peer review of the Action 13 minimum standard on country-by-country reporting*, OECD Publishing, https://www.oecd.org/tax/beps/beps-action-13-on-country-by-country-reporting-peer-review-documents.pdf. [3]

Notes

[1] South Africa's 2017/2018 peer review included a monitoring point for South Africa to issue an updated interpretation or clarification of the definitions of "Revenues – Unrelated Party" and "Revenues – Related Party" within a reasonable timeframe to ensure consistency with OECD guidance. This monitoring point remains in place

[2] No inconsistency with the terms of reference will be identified where a QCAA is not in effect with one or more jurisdictions of the Inclusive Framework that meet the confidentiality, consistency and appropriate use conditions, but this is due to circumstances that are not under the control of the reviewed jurisdiction. This may include, for example, where the other jurisdiction intends to exchange CbC reports using the MCAA but it does not have the Convention in effect for the relevant fiscal period, or where the other jurisdiction has declined to have a QCAA in effect with the reviewed jurisdiction.

Spain

1. Spain was reviewed as part of the 2017/2018 and the 2018/2019 peer reviews. This report is supplementary to those previous reports (OECD, 2019[1]) (OECD, 2018[2]).

2. The first filing obligation for a CbC report in Spain applies to reporting fiscal years commencing on or after 1 January 2016.

Summary of key findings

3. Spain's implementation of the Action 13 minimum standard meets all applicable terms of reference (OECD, 2017[3]), except for the following:

- It is recommended that Spain amend its legislation or otherwise clarify that the annual consolidated group revenue threshold calculation applies in a manner consistent with the OECD guidance on currency fluctuations in respect of an MNE Group whose Ultimate Parent Entity is located in a jurisdiction other than Spain, when local filing requirements are applicable.
- It is recommended that Spain amend its legislation or otherwise clarify the definition of a Constituent Entity to be included in a CbC report in a manner consistent with the terms of reference.
- It is recommended that Spain amend its legislation or otherwise clarify that local filing is only required in the circumstances contained in the terms of reference.

These recommendations remain in place since the 2017/2018 peer review.

Part A: The domestic legal and administrative framework

4. Spain has legislation in place which implements the BEPS Action 13 minimum standard.

(a) Parent entity filing obligation

5. It is recommended that Spain amend its rule for the calculation of the annual consolidated group revenue threshold calculation so that it applies in a manner consistent with the OECD guidance on currency fluctuations in respect of an MNE Group whose Ultimate Parent Entity is located in a jurisdiction other than Spain, when local filing requirements are applicable. This recommendation remains in place since the 2017/2018 peer review.

6. It is recommended that Spain amend or otherwise clarify the definition of a Constituent Entity to include those excluded from consolidated financial accounts only on size or materiality grounds. This recommendation remains in place since the 2017/2018 peer review.[1]

(b) Scope and timing of parent entity filing

7. No changes were identified.[2]

(c) Limitation on local filing obligation

8. It is recommended that Spain amend its legislation or otherwise take steps to ensure that local filing is only required in the circumstances contained in the terms of reference. This recommendation remains unchanged since the 2017/2018 peer review[3].

(d) Limitation on local filing in case of surrogate filing

9. No changes were identified.

(e) Effective implementation

10. No changes were identified.

Conclusion

11. There is no change to the conclusion in relation to the domestic legal and administration framework for Spain since the previous peer review. Spain meets all the terms of reference relating to the domestic legal and administrative framework, with the following exceptions:

- It is recommended that Spain amend its legislation or otherwise clarify that the annual consolidated group revenue threshold calculation applies in a manner consistent with the OECD guidance on currency fluctuations in respect of an MNE Group whose Ultimate Parent Entity is located in a jurisdiction other than Spain, when local filing requirements are applicable.
- It is recommended that Spain amend its legislation or otherwise clarify the definition of a Constituent Entity to be included in a CbC report in a manner consistent with the terms of reference.
- It is recommended that Spain amend its legislation or otherwise clarify that local filing is only required in the circumstances contained in the terms of reference.

These recommendations remain unchanged since the 2017/2018 peer review.

Part B: The exchange of information framework

(a) Exchange of information framework

12. As of 31 March 2020, Spain has 75 bilateral relationships in place for the exchange of CbC reports, including those activated under the CbC MCAA, under bilateral CAAs[4] and under the EU Council Directive (2016/881/EU). Within the context of its international exchange of information agreements that allow automatic exchange of tax information, Spain has taken steps to have qualifying competent authority agreements in effect with jurisdictions of the Inclusive Framework that meet the confidentiality, consistency and appropriate use conditions. Regarding Spain's exchange of information framework, no inconsistencies with the terms of reference were identified.[5]

(b) Content of information exchanged

13. No changes were identified.

(c) Completeness of exchanges

14. No changes were identified.

(d) Timeliness of exchanges

15. No changes were identified.

(e) Temporary suspension of exchange or termination of QCAA

16. No changes were identified.

(f) Consultation with other Competent Authority before determining systemic failure or significant non-compliance

17. No changes were identified.

(g) Format for information exchange

18. No changes were identified.

(h) Method for transmission

19. No changes were identified.

Conclusion

20. Spain meets all the terms of reference regarding the exchange of information.

Part C: Appropriate use

Appropriate use

21. No changes were identified.

Conclusion

22. Spain meets all the terms of reference relating to appropriate use of CbC reports.

Summary of recommendations on the implementation of country-by-country reporting

Aspect of the implementation that should be improved		Recommendation for improvement
Part A	Domestic legal and administrative framework	It is recommended that Spain amend its legislation or otherwise clarify that the annual consolidated group revenue threshold calculation applies in a manner consistent with the OECD guidance on currency fluctuations in respect of an MNE Group whose Ultimate Parent Entity is located in a jurisdiction other than Spain, when local filing requirements are applicable.
Part A	Domestic legal and administrative framework	It is recommended that Spain amend its legislation or otherwise clarify the definition of a Constituent Entity to be included in a CbC report in a manner consistent with the terms of reference.
Part A	Domestic legal and administrative framework	It is recommended that Spain amend its legislation or otherwise clarify that local filing is only required in the circumstances contained in the terms of reference.
Part B	Exchange of information framework	-
Part C	Appropriate use	-

References

OECD (2019), *Country-by-Country Reporting – Compilation of Peer Review Reports (Phase 2): Inclusive Framework on BEPS: Action 13*, OECD/G20 Base Erosion and Profit Shifting Project, OECD Publishing, Paris, https://dx.doi.org/10.1787/f9bf1157-en. [1]

OECD (2018), *Country-by-Country Reporting – Compilation of Peer Review Reports (Phase 1): Inclusive Framework on BEPS: Action 13*, OECD/G20 Base Erosion and Profit Shifting Project, OECD Publishing, Paris, https://dx.doi.org/10.1787/9789264300057-en. [2]

OECD (2017), *Terms of reference for the conduct of peer review of the Action 13 minimum standard on country-by-country reporting*, OECD Publishing, https://www.oecd.org/tax/beps/beps-action-13-on-country-by-country-reporting-peer-review-documents.pdf. [3]

Notes

[1] Spain's 2017/2018 peer review included a monitoring point on the potential exclusion of companies which are not required to produce consolidated financial statements from the filing requirement with respect to the absence in the definition of a "dominant company" of the "deemed listing provision". This monitoring point remains in place

[2] Spain's 2017/2018 peer review included a monitoring point with respect to the absence of a provision relating to the "Source of data" to complete a CbC report. This monitoring point remains in place.

[3] Spain has draft legislative amendments to address this issue which are currently in the process to be put into effect.

[4] Spain signed a bilateral Competent Authority Agreement with the United Stated on 19 December 2017.

[5] No inconsistency with the terms of reference will be identified where a QCAA is not in effect with one or more jurisdictions of the Inclusive Framework that meet the confidentiality, consistency and appropriate use conditions, but this is due to circumstances that are not under the control of the reviewed jurisdiction. This may include, for example, where the other jurisdiction intends to exchange CbC reports using the MCAA but it does not have the Convention in effect for the relevant fiscal period, or where the other jurisdiction has declined to have a QCAA in effect with the reviewed jurisdiction.

Sri Lanka

1. Sri Lanka was reviewed as part of the 2017/2018 and the 2018/2019 peer reviews. This report is supplementary to those previous reports (OECD, 2019[1]) (OECD, 2018[2]).

2. The first filing obligation for a CbC report in Sri Lanka applies to reporting fiscal years commencing on or after 1 April 2018.

Summary of key findings

3. Sri Lanka meets all the terms of reference (OECD, 2017[3]) relating to the domestic legal and administrative framework, except for the following:

- It is recommended that Sri Lanka amend or otherwise clarify its threshold rule so that it would apply in a manner consistent with the OECD guidance on currency fluctuations in respect of an MNE Group whose Ultimate Parent entity is located in a jurisdiction other than Sri Lanka (OECD, 2018[5]).
- It is recommended that Sri Lanka take steps to align its local filing implementation with that required by the Action 13 minimum standard.

4. It is recommended that Sri Lanka take steps to have QCAAs in effect with jurisdictions of the Inclusive Framework which meet the confidentiality, consistency and appropriate use prerequisite and with which Sri Lanka has an international exchange of information agreement in effect that allows for the automatic exchange of tax information. This recommendation remains unchanged since the 2017/2018 peer review.

5. It is recommended that Sri Lanka take steps to implement processes or written procedures to ensure that the exchange of information is conducted in a manner consistent with the terms of reference relating to the exchange of information framework ahead of the first exchanges of information.

6. It is recommended that Sri Lanka take steps to ensure that the appropriate use condition is met ahead of the first exchanges of information. This recommendation remains unchanged since the 2017/2018 peer review.

Part A: The domestic legal and administrative framework

7. Sri Lanka has law in place to implement the BEPS Action 13 minimum standard.

(a) Parent entity filing obligation

8. It is recommended that Sri Lanka amend or otherwise clarify this rule so that it would apply in a manner consistent with the OECD guidance on currency fluctuations in respect of an MNE Group whose Ultimate Parent entity is located in a jurisdiction other than Sri Lanka. This recommendation remains unchanged since the 2017/2018 peer review.[1]

(b) Scope and timing of parent entity filing

9. No changes were identified.

(c) Limitation on local filing obligation

10. No changes were identified.

(d) Limitation on local filing in case of surrogate filing

11. No changes were identified.

(e) Effective implementation

12. No changes were identified.

Conclusion

13. It is recommended that Sri Lanka amend or otherwise clarify its threshold rule so that it would apply in a manner consistent with the OECD guidance on currency fluctuations in respect of an MNE Group whose Ultimate Parent entity is located in a jurisdiction other than Sri Lanka. This recommendation remains unchanged since the 2018/2019 peer review.

14. Sri Lanka requires local filing despite not meeting the conditions to apply this requirement. It is recommended that Sri Lanka take steps to change its legislation or issue guidance to cancel or suspend the local filing requirement until it meets the standards required. This recommendation remains unchanged since the 2018/2019 peer review.

Part B: The exchange of information framework

(a) Exchange of information framework

15. As of 31 March 2020, Sri Lanka has no bilateral relationships in place for the exchange of CbC reports. It is recommended that Sri Lanka take steps to have qualifying competent authority agreements in effect with jurisdictions of the Inclusive Framework that meet the confidentiality, consistency and appropriate use conditions and with which Sri Lanka has an international exchange of information agreement in effect that allows for the automatic exchange of tax information.

(b) Content of information exchanged

16. No changes were identified.

(c) Completeness of exchanges

17. No changes were identified.

(d) Timeliness of exchanges

18. No changes were identified.

(e) Temporary suspension of exchange or termination of QCAA

19. No changes were identified.

(f) Consultation with other Competent Authority before determining systemic failure or significant non-compliance

20. No changes were identified.

(g) Format for information exchange

21. No changes were identified.

(h) Method for transmission

22. No changes were identified.

Conclusion

23. It is recommended that Sri Lanka take steps to have QCAAs in effect with jurisdictions of the Inclusive Framework which meet the confidentiality, consistency and appropriate use prerequisites remains in place. This recommendation remains unchanged since the 2017/2018 peer review.

24. It is recommended that Sri Lanka take steps to implement processes or written procedures to ensure that the exchange of information is conducted in a manner consistent with the terms of reference relating to the exchange of information framework ahead of its first exchanges of information. This recommendation remains unchanged since the 2018/2019 peer review.

Part C: Appropriate use

Appropriate use

25. No changes were identified.

Conclusion

26. It is recommended that Sri Lanka take steps to ensure that the appropriate use condition is met ahead of its first exchanges of information. This recommendation remains unchanged since the 2017/2018 peer review.

Summary of recommendations on the implementation of Country-by-Country Reporting

Aspect of the implementation that should be improved		Recommendation for improvement
Part A	Domestic legal and administrative framework	It is recommended that Sri Lanka amend or otherwise clarify the annual consolidated group revenue threshold calculation rule applies in a manner consistent with the OECD guidance on currency fluctuations in respect of an MNE Group whose Ultimate Parent entity is located in a jurisdiction other than Sri Lanka.
Part A	Domestic legal and administrative framework	It is recommended that Sri Lanka take steps to change its legislation or issue guidance to suspend local filing until they have met the conditions.
Part B	Exchange of information framework	It is recommended that Sri Lanka take steps to have QCAAs in effect with jurisdictions of the Inclusive Framework which meet the confidentiality, consistency and appropriate use prerequisites and with which it has an international exchange of information agreement in effect that allows for the automatic exchange of tax information.
Part B	Exchange of information framework	It is recommended that Sri Lanka take steps to implement the necessary processes or written procedures to ensure that the exchange of information is conducted in a manner consistent with the terms of reference relating to the exchange of information framework.
Part C	Appropriate use	It is recommended that Sri Lanka take steps to ensure that the appropriate use condition is met ahead of the first exchanges of information.

References

OECD (2019), *Country-by-Country Reporting – Compilation of Peer Review Reports (Phase 2): Inclusive Framework on BEPS: Action 13*, OECD/G20 Base Erosion and Profit Shifting Project, OECD Publishing, Paris, https://dx.doi.org/10.1787/f9bf1157-en. [1]

OECD (2018), *Country-by-Country Reporting – Compilation of Peer Review Reports (Phase 1): Inclusive Framework on BEPS: Action 13*, OECD/G20 Base Erosion and Profit Shifting Project, OECD Publishing, Paris, https://dx.doi.org/10.1787/9789264300057-en. [2]

OECD (2018), *Guidance on the Implementation of Country-by-Country Reportings - BEPS Action 13, OECD/G20 Base Erosion and Profit Shifting Project*, OECD Publisher, http://www.oecd.org/tax/guidance-on-the-implementation-of-country-by-country-reporting-beps-action-13.pdf. [5]

OECD (2017), *Terms of reference for the conduct of peer review of the Action 13 minimum standard on country-by-country reporting*, OECD Publishing, https://www.oecd.org/tax/beps/beps-action-13-on-country-by-country-reporting-peer-review-documents.pdf. [3]

Note

[1] Sri Lanka's Regulations on Transfer Pricing refer to the responsibility to prepare and maintain transfer pricing documentation including the Country-by-Country Report applying to enterprises carrying out controlled transactions with associated enterprises subject to sections of Sri Lanka's primary legislation. This narrows the population of MNEs required to file a CbC report in Sri Lanka and apparently applies an exemption from reporting to MNEs who meet the threshold requirement but do not carry out controlled transactions with associated enterprises. In practice this is very unlikely to be the case for MNEs who would otherwise meet the requirement so no recommendation is made but the situation will be monitored. This monitoring point remains in place since the 2018/2019 peer review.

Sweden

1. Sweden was reviewed as part of the 2017/2018 and the 2018/2019 peer reviews. This report is supplementary to those previous reports (OECD, 2019[1]) (OECD, 2018[2]).

2. The first filing obligation for a CbC report in Sweden applies to reporting fiscal years commencing on or after 1 January 2016.

Summary of key findings

3. Sweden's implementation of the Action 13 minimum standard meets all applicable terms of reference (OECD, 2017[3]).

Part A: The domestic legal and administrative framework

4. Sweden has laws in place for implementing the BEPS Action 13 minimum standard establishing the necessary requirements.

(a) Parent entity filing obligation

5. No changes were identified.

(b) Scope and timing of parent entity filing

6. No changes were identified.

(c) Limitation on local filing obligation

7. No changes were identified.[1]

(d) Limitation on local filing in case of surrogate filing

8. No changes were identified.

(e) Effective implementation

9. No changes were identified.

Conclusion

10. Sweden meets all the terms of reference relating to the domestic legal and administrative framework.

Part B: The exchange of information framework

(a) Exchange of information framework

11. As of 31 March 2020, Sweden has 65 bilateral relationships, including those activated under the CbC MCAA, under bilateral CAAs and under the EU Council Directive (2016/881/EU). Within the context of its international exchange of information agreements that allow automatic exchange of information, Sweden has taken steps to have qualifying competent authority agreements in effect with jurisdictions of

the Inclusive Framework that meet the confidentiality, consistency and appropriate use conditions.[2] Regarding Sweden's exchange of information framework, no inconsistencies with the terms of reference were identified.

(b) Content of information exchanged

12. No changes were identified.

(c) Completeness of exchanges

13. No changes were identified.

(d) Timeliness of exchanges

14. No changes were identified.

(e) Temporary suspension of exchange or termination of QCAA

15. No changes were identified.

(f) Consultation with other Competent Authority before determining systemic failure or significant non-compliance

16. No changes were identified.

(g) Format for information exchange

17. No changes were identified.

(h) Method for transmission

18. No changes were identified.

Conclusion

19. Sweden meets all the terms of reference regarding the exchange of information.

Part C: Appropriate use

Appropriate use

20. No changes were identified.

Conclusion

21. Sweden meets all the terms of reference relating to appropriate use of CbC reports.

Summary of recommendations on the implementation of country-by-country reporting

Aspect of the implementation that should be improved		Recommendation for improvement
Part A	Domestic legal and administrative framework	-
Part B	Exchange of information framework	-
Part C	Appropriate use	-

References

OECD (2019), *Country-by-Country Reporting – Compilation of Peer Review Reports (Phase 2): Inclusive Framework on BEPS: Action 13*, OECD/G20 Base Erosion and Profit Shifting Project, OECD Publishing, Paris, https://dx.doi.org/10.1787/f9bf1157-en. [1]

OECD (2018), *Country-by-Country Reporting – Compilation of Peer Review Reports (Phase 1): Inclusive Framework on BEPS: Action 13*, OECD/G20 Base Erosion and Profit Shifting Project, OECD Publishing, Paris, https://dx.doi.org/10.1787/9789264300057-en. [2]

OECD (2017), *Terms of reference for the conduct of peer review of the Action 13 minimum standard on country-by-country reporting*, OECD Publishing, https://www.oecd.org/tax/beps/beps-action-13-on-country-by-country-reporting-peer-review-documents.pdf. [3]

Notes

[1] Sweden's 2017/2018 peer review included a monitoring point relating to the conditions under which local filing may be required (paragraph 8 (c) iv. b) of the terms of reference). This monitoring point remains in place.

[2] No inconsistency with the terms of reference will be identified where a QCAA is not in effect with one or more jurisdictions of the Inclusive Framework that meet the confidentiality, consistency and appropriate use conditions, but this is due to circumstances that are not under the control of the reviewed jurisdiction. This may include, for example, where the other jurisdiction intends to exchange CbC reports using the MCAA but it does not have the Convention in effect for the relevant fiscal period, or where the other jurisdiction has declined to have a QCAA in effect with the reviewed jurisdiction

Switzerland

1. Switzerland was reviewed as part of the 2017/2018 and the 2018/2019 peer reviews. This report is supplementary to those previous reports (OECD, 2019[1]) (OECD, 2018[2]).

2. The first filing obligation for a CbC report in Switzerland applies to reporting fiscal years commencing on or after 1 January 2018. Switzerland also allows Swiss MNE groups to file a CbC report on a voluntary basis, for reporting fiscal years beginning between 1 January 2016 and 31 December 2017.

Summary of key findings

3. Switzerland's implementation of the Action 13 minimum standard meets all applicable terms of reference (OECD, 2017[3]).

Part A: The domestic legal and administrative framework

4. Switzerland has law in place for implementing the BEPS Action 13 minimum standard.

(a) Parent entity filing obligation

5. No changes were identified.

(b) Scope and timing of parent entity filing

6. No changes were identified.

(c) Limitation on local filing obligation

7. No changes were identified.

(d) Limitation on local filing in case of surrogate filing

8. No changes were identified.

(e) Effective implementation

9. No changes were identified.

Conclusion

10. Switzerland meets all the terms of reference relating to the domestic legal and administrative framework.

Part B: The exchange of information framework

(a) Exchange of information framework

11. As of 31 March 2020, Switzerland has 63 bilateral relationships activated under the CbC MCAA. Within the context of its international exchange of information agreements that allow automatic exchange of information, Switzerland has taken steps to have QCAAs in effect with jurisdictions of the Inclusive

Framework that meet the confidentiality, consistency, and appropriate use conditions.[1] Regarding Switzerland's exchange of information framework, no inconsistencies with the terms of reference were identified.

(b) Content of information exchanged

12. No changes were identified.

(c) Completeness of exchanges

13. No changes were identified.

(d) Timeliness of exchanges

14. No changes were identified.

(e) Temporary suspension of exchange or termination of QCAA

15. No changes were identified.

(f) Consultation with other Competent Authority before determining systemic failure or significant non-compliance

16. No changes were identified.

(g) Format for information exchange

17. No changes were identified.

(h) Method for transmission

18. No changes were identified.

Conclusion

19. Switzerland meets all the terms of reference regarding the exchange of information.[2]

Part C: Appropriate use

Appropriate use

20. No changes were identified.

Conclusion

21. Switzerland meets all the terms of reference relating to appropriate use of CbC reports.

Summary of recommendations on the implementation of country-by-country reporting

Aspect of the implementation that should be improved		Recommendation for improvement
Part A	Domestic legal and administrative framework	-
Part B	Exchange of information framework	-
Part C	Appropriate use	-

References

OECD (2019), *Country-by-Country Reporting – Compilation of Peer Review Reports (Phase 2): Inclusive Framework on BEPS: Action 13*, OECD/G20 Base Erosion and Profit Shifting Project, OECD Publishing, Paris, https://dx.doi.org/10.1787/f9bf1157-en. [1]

OECD (2018), *Country-by-Country Reporting – Compilation of Peer Review Reports (Phase 1): Inclusive Framework on BEPS: Action 13*, OECD/G20 Base Erosion and Profit Shifting Project, OECD Publishing, Paris, https://dx.doi.org/10.1787/9789264300057-en. [2]

OECD (2017), *Terms of reference for the conduct of peer review of the Action 13 minimum standard on country-by-country reporting*, OECD Publishing, https://www.oecd.org/tax/beps/beps-action-13-on-country-by-country-reporting-peer-review-documents.pdf. [3]

Notes

[1] It is noted that a few Qualifying Competent Authority agreements are not in effect with jurisdictions of the Inclusive Framework that meet the confidentiality condition and have legislation in place: this may be because the partner jurisdictions considered do not have the Convention in effect for the first reporting period, or may not have listed the reviewed jurisdiction in their notifications under Section 8 of the CbC MCAA.

[2] The CbC Reporting Group will monitor Switzerland to ensure that these processes continue to apply when it starts exchanging reports via the Common Transmission System in 2020.

Thailand

1. Thailand was reviewed as part of the 2017/2018 and the 2018/2019 peer reviews. This report is supplementary to those previous reports (OECD, 2019[1]) (OECD, 2018[2]).

2. There is no filing obligation for a CbC report in Thailand yet.

Summary of key findings

3. It is recommended that Thailand take steps to implement a domestic legal and administrative framework to impose and enforce CbC reporting requirements as soon as possible. This recommendation remains unchanged since the 2017/2018 peer review.

4. It is recommended that Thailand take steps to have QCAAs in effect with jurisdictions of the Inclusive Framework which meet the confidentiality, consistency and appropriate use prerequisites and with which Thailand has an international exchange of information agreement in effect that allows for the automatic exchange of tax information. This recommendation remains unchanged since the 2017/2018 peer review.

5. It is recommended that Thailand take steps to implement processes or written procedures to ensure that the exchange of information is conducted in a manner consistent with the terms of reference (OECD, 2017[3]) relating to the exchange of information framework ahead of the first exchanges of information. This recommendation remains unchanged since the 2018/2019 peer review.

6. It is recommended that Thailand take steps to ensure that the appropriate use condition is met ahead of the first exchanges of information. This recommendation remains unchanged since the 2017/2018 peer review.

Part A: The domestic legal and administrative framework

7. Thailand does not yet have legislation in place for implementing the BEPS Action 13 minimum standard.

(a) Parent entity filing obligation

(b) Scope and timing of parent entity filing

(c) Limitation on local filing obligation

(d) Limitation on local filing in case of surrogate filing

(e) Effective implementation

Conclusion

8. It is recommended that Thailand take steps to implement a domestic legal and administrative framework to impose and enforce CbC reporting requirements as soon as possible. This recommendation remains unchanged since the 2017/2018 peer review.

Part B: The exchange of information framework

(a) Exchange of information framework

9. As of 31 March 2020, Thailand has no bilateral relationships in place for the exchange of CbC reports. It is recommended that Thailand take steps to have qualifying competent authority agreements in effect with jurisdictions of the Inclusive Framework that meet the confidentiality, consistency and appropriate use conditions and with which Thailand has an international exchange of information agreement in effect that allows for the automatic exchange of tax information.

(b) Content of information exchanged

10. No changes were identified.

(c) Completeness of exchanges

11. No changes were identified.

(d) Timeliness of exchanges

12. No changes were identified.

(e) Temporary suspension of exchange or termination of QCAA

13. No changes were identified.

(f) Consultation with other Competent Authority before determining systemic failure or significant non-compliance

14. No changes were identified.

(g) Format for information exchange

15. No changes were identified.

(h) Method for transmission

16. No changes were identified.

Conclusion

17. It is recommended that Thailand take steps to have QCAAs in effect with jurisdictions of the Inclusive Framework which meet the confidentiality, consistency and appropriate use prerequisites and with which Thailand has an international exchange of information agreement in effect that allows for the automatic exchange of tax information. This recommendation remains unchanged since the 2017/2018 peer review.

18. It is recommended that Thailand take steps to implement processes or written procedures to ensure that the exchange of information is conducted in a manner consistent with the terms of reference relating to the exchange of information framework ahead of its first exchanges of information. This recommendation remains unchanged since the 2018/2019 peer review.

Part C: Appropriate use

Appropriate use

19. No changes were identified.

Conclusion

20. It is recommended that Thailand take steps to ensure that the appropriate use condition is met ahead of its first exchanges of information. This recommendation remains unchanged since the 2017/2018 peer review.

Summary of recommendations on the implementation of Country-by-Country Reporting

Aspect of the implementation that should be improved		Recommendation for improvement
Part A	Domestic legal and administrative framework	It is recommended that Thailand take steps to implement a domestic legal and administrative framework to impose and enforce CbC requirements as soon as possible.
Part B	Exchange of information framework	It is recommended that Thailand take steps to have QCAAs in effect with jurisdictions of the Inclusive Framework which meet the confidentiality, consistency and appropriate use prerequisites and with which Thailand has an international exchange of information agreement in effect that allows for the automatic exchange of tax information.
Part B	Exchange of information framework	It is recommended that Thailand take steps to implement the necessary processes or written procedures to ensure that the exchange of information is conducted in a manner consistent with the terms of reference relating to the exchange of information framework.
Part C	Appropriate use	It is recommended that Thailand take steps to ensure that the appropriate use condition is met ahead of the first exchanges of information.

References

OECD (2019), *Country-by-Country Reporting – Compilation of Peer Review Reports (Phase 2): Inclusive Framework on BEPS: Action 13*, OECD/G20 Base Erosion and Profit Shifting Project, OECD Publishing, Paris, https://dx.doi.org/10.1787/f9bf1157-en. [1]

OECD (2018), *Country-by-Country Reporting – Compilation of Peer Review Reports (Phase 1): Inclusive Framework on BEPS: Action 13*, OECD/G20 Base Erosion and Profit Shifting Project, OECD Publishing, Paris, https://dx.doi.org/10.1787/9789264300057-en. [2]

OECD (2017), *Terms of reference for the conduct of peer review of the Action 13 minimum standard on country-by-country reporting*, OECD Publishing, https://www.oecd.org/tax/beps/beps-action-13-on-country-by-country-reporting-peer-review-documents.pdf. [3]

Trinidad and Tobago

1. Trinidad and Tobago was first reviewed during the 2018/2019 peer review. This report is supplementary to that previous report (OECD, 2018[2]).

2. There is no filing obligation for a CbC report in Trinidad and Tobago yet.

Summary of key findings

3. It is recommended that Trinidad and Tobago take steps to implement a domestic legal and administrative framework to impose and enforce CbC reporting requirements as soon as possible.

4. It is recommended that Trinidad and Tobago take steps to have QCAAs in effect with jurisdictions of the Inclusive Framework which meet the confidentiality, consistency and appropriate use prerequisites and with which Trinidad and Tobago has an international exchange of information agreement in effect that allows for the automatic exchange of tax information.

5. It is recommended that Trinidad and Tobago take steps to implement processes or written procedures to ensure that the exchange of information is conducted in a manner consistent with the terms of reference (OECD, 2017[3]) relating to the exchange of information framework ahead of the first exchanges of information.

6. It is recommended that Trinidad and Tobago take steps to ensure that the appropriate use condition is met ahead of the first exchanges of information.

Part A: The domestic legal and administrative framework

7. Trinidad and Tobago does not yet have legislation in place for implementing the BEPS Action 13 minimum standard.

(a) Parent entity filing obligation

(b) Scope and timing of parent entity filing

(c) Limitation on local filing obligation

(d) Limitation on local filing in case of surrogate filing

(e) Effective implementation

Conclusion

8. It is recommended that Trinidad and Tobago take steps to implement a domestic legal and administrative framework to impose and enforce CbC reporting requirements as soon as possible.

Part B: The exchange of information framework

(a) Exchange of information framework

9. As of 31 March 2020, Trinidad and Tobago has no bilateral relationships activated under the CbC MCAA or bilateral QCAAs. It is recommended that Trinidad and Tobago take steps to have QCAAs in effect with jurisdictions of the Inclusive Framework which meet the confidentiality, consistency and appropriate use prerequisites and with which Trinidad and Tobago has an international exchange of information agreement in effect that allows for the automatic exchange of tax information.

(b) Content of information exchanged

10. No changes were identified.

(c) Completeness of exchanges

11. No changes were identified.

(d) Timeliness of exchanges

12. No changes were identified.

(e) Temporary suspension of exchange or termination of QCAA

13. No changes were identified.

(f) Consultation with other Competent Authority before determining systemic failure or significant non-compliance

14. No changes were identified.

(g) Format for information exchange

15. No changes were identified.

(h) Method for transmission

16. No changes were identified.

Conclusion

17. It is recommended that Trinidad and Tobago take steps to put QCAAs in effect with jurisdictions of the Inclusive Framework which meet the confidentiality, consistency and appropriate use prerequisites and with which Trinidad and Tobago has an international exchange of information agreement in effect that allows for the automatic exchange of tax information.

18. It is recommended that Trinidad and Tobago take steps to implement processes or written procedures to ensure that the exchange of information is conducted in a manner consistent with the terms of reference relating to the exchange of information framework ahead of its first exchanges of information.

Part C: Appropriate use

Appropriate use

19. No changes were identified.

Conclusion

20. It is recommended that Trinidad and Tobago take steps to ensure that the appropriate use condition is met ahead of its first exchanges of information.

Summary of recommendations on the implementation of Country-by-Country Reporting

Aspect of the implementation that should be improved		Recommendation for improvement
Part A	Domestic legal and administrative framework	It is recommended that Trinidad and Tobago take steps to implement a domestic legal and administrative framework to impose and enforce CbC requirements as soon as possible.
Part B	Exchange of information framework	It is recommended that Trinidad and Tobago take steps to put QCAAs in effect with jurisdictions of the Inclusive Framework which meet the confidentiality, consistency and appropriate use prerequisites and with which it has an international exchange of information agreement in effect that allows for the automatic exchange of tax information.
Part B	Exchange of information framework	It is recommended that Trinidad and Tobago take steps to implement the necessary processes or written procedures to ensure that the exchange of information is conducted in a manner consistent with the terms of reference relating to the exchange of information framework.
Part C	Appropriate use	It is recommended that Trinidad and Tobago take steps to ensure that the appropriate use condition is met ahead of its first exchanges of information.

References

OECD (2018), *Country-by-Country Reporting – Compilation of Peer Review Reports (Phase 1): Inclusive Framework on BEPS: Action 13*, OECD/G20 Base Erosion and Profit Shifting Project, OECD Publishing, Paris, https://dx.doi.org/10.1787/9789264300057-en. [2]

OECD (2017), *Terms of reference for the conduct of peer review of the Action 13 minimum standard on country-by-country reporting*, OECD Publishing, https://www.oecd.org/tax/beps/beps-action-13-on-country-by-country-reporting-peer-review-documents.pdf. [3]

Tunisia

1. Tunisia' was first reviewed during the 2018/2019 peer review. This report is supplementary to that previous report (OECD, 2018[2]).

2. The first filing obligation for a CbC report in Tunisia commences in respect of periods commencing on or after 1 January 2017.

Summary of key findings

3. Tunisia's domestic legal and administrative framework meets all applicable terms of reference (OECD, 2017[3]), except for the following:

- It is recommended that Tunisia introduce or complete the definitions of "Group", "MNE Group", "Constituent Entity", "Consolidated Financial Statements", "Fiscal Year", "Reporting Fiscal Year", "Qualifying Competent Authority Agreement" and "International Agreement" in a manner that is consistent with the terms of reference;
- It is recommended that Tunisia take steps to ensure that the annual consolidated group revenue threshold calculation rule is applied in a manner consistent with the OECD guidance on currency fluctuations;
- It is recommended that Tunisia take steps to amend the conditions for local filing or otherwise take steps to ensure that local filing can only be required in the circumstances contained in the terms of reference.

4. It is recommended that Tunisia take steps to have QCAAs in effect with jurisdictions of the Inclusive Framework which meet the confidentiality, consistency and appropriate use prerequisites and with which Tunisia has an international exchange of information agreement in effect that allows for the automatic exchange of tax information.

5. It is recommended that Tunisia take steps to implement processes or written procedures to ensure that the exchange of information is conducted in a manner consistent with the terms of reference relating to the exchange of information framework ahead of the first exchanges of information.

6. It is recommended that Tunisia take steps to ensure that the appropriate use condition is met ahead of the first exchanges of information.

Part A: The domestic legal and administrative framework

7. Tunisia has law in place for implementing the BEPS Action 13 minimum standard.

(a) Parent entity filing obligation

8. It is recommended that Tunisia introduce or complete the definitions of "Group", "MNE Group", "Constituent Entity", "Consolidated Financial Statements", "Fiscal Year", "Reporting Fiscal Year", "Qualifying Competent Authority Agreement" and "International Agreement" in its domestic legal and administrative framework. Tunisia notes that intends to introduce all these definitions when finalizing its legal framework.

9. It is recommended that Tunisia amend its rule for the calculation of the annual consolidated group revenue threshold calculation so that it applies in a manner consistent with the OECD guidance on currency

fluctuations in respect of an MNE Group whose Ultimate Parent Entity is located in a jurisdiction other than Tunisia, when local filing requirements are applicable.

(b) Scope and timing of parent entity filing

10. No changes were identified.

(c) Limitation on local filing obligation

11. It is recommended that Tunisia take steps to amend the conditions for local filing or otherwise take steps to ensure that local filing can only be required in the circumstances contained in the terms of reference

(d) Limitation on local filing in case of surrogate filing

12. No changes were identified.

(e) Effective implementation

13. No changes were identified.[1]

Conclusion

14. Tunisia's domestic legal and administrative framework meets all applicable terms of reference, except for the following:

- It is recommended that Tunisia introduce or complete the definitions of a " "Group", "MNE Group", "Constituent Entity", "Consolidated Financial Statements", "Fiscal Year", "Reporting Fiscal Year", "Qualifying Competent Authority Agreement" and "International Agreement" in a manner that is consistent with the terms of reference;
- It is recommended that Tunisia take steps to ensure that the annual consolidated group revenue threshold calculation rule is applied in a manner consistent with the OECD guidance on currency fluctuations;
- It is recommended that Tunisia take steps to amend the conditions for local filing or otherwise take steps to ensure that local filing can only be required in the circumstances contained in the terms of reference.

Part B: The exchange of information framework

(a) Exchange of information framework

15. As of 31 March 2020, Tunisia has no bilateral relationships in place for the exchange of CbC reports. It is recommended that Tunisia take steps to have qualifying competent authority agreements in effect with jurisdictions of the Inclusive Framework that meet the confidentiality, consistency and appropriate use conditions and with which Tunisia has an international exchange of information agreement in effect that allows for the automatic exchange of tax information.

(b) Content of information exchanged

16. No changes were identified.

(c) Completeness of exchanges

17. No changes were identified.

(d) Timeliness of exchanges

18. No changes were identified.

(e) Temporary suspension of exchange or termination of QCAA

19. No changes were identified.

(f) Consultation with other Competent Authority before determining systemic failure or significant non-compliance

20. No changes were identified.

(g) Format for information exchange

21. No changes were identified.

(h) Method for transmission

22. No changes were identified.

Conclusion

23. It is recommended that Tunisia take steps to have QCAAs in effect with jurisdictions of the Inclusive Framework which meet the confidentiality, consistency and appropriate use prerequisites and with which Tunisia has an international exchange of information agreement in effect that allows for the automatic exchange of tax information. This recommendation remains unchanged since the 2018/2019 peer review.

24. it is recommended that Tunisia take steps to implement processes or written procedures to ensure that the exchange of information is conducted in a manner consistent with the terms of reference relating to the exchange of information framework ahead of its first exchanges of information. This recommendation remains unchanged since the 2018/2019 peer review.

Part C: Appropriate use

Appropriate use

25. No changes were identified.

Conclusion

26. It is recommended that Tunisia take steps to ensure that the appropriate use condition is met ahead of its first exchanges of information.

Summary of recommendations on the implementation of country-by-country reporting

Aspect of the implementation that should be improved		Recommendation for improvement
Part A	Domestic legal and administrative framework	It is recommended that Tunisia introduce or complete the definitions of a " "Group", "MNE Group", "Constituent Entity", "Consolidated Financial Statements", "Fiscal Year", "Reporting Fiscal Year", "Qualifying Competent Authority Agreement" and "International Agreement" in a manner that is consistent with the terms of reference;
Part A	Domestic legal and administrative framework	It is recommended that Tunisia take steps to ensure that the annual consolidated group revenue threshold calculation rule is applied in a manner consistent with the OECD guidance on currency fluctuations;
Part A	Domestic legal and administrative framework	It is recommended that Tunisia amend the conditions for local filing or otherwise take steps to ensure that local filing can only be required in the circumstances contained in the terms of reference
Part A	Domestic legal and administrative framework	It is recommended that Tunisia implement a provision whereby a single Constituent Entity of the same MNE Group may be designated to file the CbC report which would satisfy the local filing requirement of all the Constituent Entities in Tunisia.
Part B	Exchange of information framework	It is recommended that Tunisia take steps to have qualifying competent authority agreements in effect with jurisdictions of the Inclusive Framework that meet the confidentiality, consistency and appropriate use conditions and with which Tunisia has an international exchange of information agreement in effect that allows for the automatic exchange of tax information.
Part B	Exchange of information framework	It is recommended that Tunisia take steps to implement the necessary processes or written procedures to ensure that the exchange of information is conducted in a manner consistent with the terms of reference relating to the exchange of information framework.
Part C	Appropriate use	It is recommended that Tunisia take steps to ensure that the appropriate use condition is met ahead of the first exchanges of information.

References

OECD (2018), *Country-by-Country Reporting – Compilation of Peer Review Reports (Phase 1): Inclusive Framework on BEPS: Action 13*, OECD/G20 Base Erosion and Profit Shifting Project, OECD Publishing, Paris, https://dx.doi.org/10.1787/9789264300057-en. [2]

OECD (2017), *Terms of reference for the conduct of peer review of the Action 13 minimum standard on country-by-country reporting*, OECD Publishing, https://www.oecd.org/tax/beps/beps-action-13-on-country-by-country-reporting-peer-review-documents.pdf. [3]

Note

[1] There are no specific processes in place that would allow Tunisia to take appropriate measures in case of notification by another jurisdiction that such other jurisdiction has reason to believe that an error may have led to incorrect or incomplete information reporting by a Reporting Entity or that there is non-compliance of a Reporting Entity with respect to CbC reporting obligations. As no exchange of CbC reports has yet occurred, no recommendation is made but this aspect will be further monitored. This monitoring point remains in place form the 2018/2019 peer review.

Turkey

1. Turkey was reviewed as part of the 2017/2018 and the 2018/2019 peer reviews. This report is supplementary to those previous reports (OECD, 2019[1]) (OECD, 2018[2]).

2. The first filing obligation for a CbC report in Turkey commences in respect of fiscal periods commencing on or after 1 January 2019.

Summary of key findings

3. Turkey has legislation to impose and enforce a CbC filing requirement that meets all of the terms of reference, with the exception that:

- It is recommended that Turkey take steps to amend its legislation or otherwise bring the definition of Constituent Entity in line with the standard.
- It is recommended that Turkey clarify that the annual consolidated group revenue threshold calculation rule applies in line with the OECD guidance on currency fluctuations in respect of an MNE Group whose Ultimate Parent Entity is located in a jurisdiction other than Turkey.

4. It is recommended that Turkey take steps to have qualifying competent authority agreements in effect with jurisdictions of the Inclusive Framework that meet the confidentiality, consistency and appropriate use conditions and with which Turkey has an international exchange of information agreement in effect that allows for the automatic exchange of tax information. This recommendation remains unchanged since the 2017/2018 peer review.

5. It is recommended that Turkey take steps to implement processes or written procedures to ensure that the exchange of information is conducted in a manner consistent with the terms of reference (OECD, 2017[3]) relating to the exchange of information framework ahead of the first exchanges of information. This recommendation remains unchanged since the 2018/2019 peer review.

6. It is recommended that Turkey take steps to ensure that the appropriate use condition is met ahead of the first exchanges of information. This remains unchanged since the 2017/2018 peer review.

7. Turkey's previous peer reviews recommended that Turkey take steps to implement a domestic legal and administrative framework to impose and enforce CbC reporting requirements as soon as possible. Legislation is now in effect and this recommendation is removed.

8. Turkey's previous peer reviews recommended that Turkey amend the conditions for local filing or otherwise take steps to ensure that the CbC reporting local filing obligations will only apply in the circumstances contained in the terms of reference. This amendment is in effect and the recommendation is removed.

Part A: The domestic legal and administrative framework

9. Turkey has legislation in place for implementing the BEPS Action 13 minimum standard.

(a) Parent entity filing obligation

10. Turkey has introduced a filing requirement which applies to all Ultimate Parent Entities of MNE Groups above a certain threshold and which requires inclusion of all constituent entities.

11. Turkey defines a Constituent Entity as any separate business unit or permanent establishment that is included in consolidated statements of the group. This is narrower than the Action 13 definition, which also includes any separate business unit excluded from consolidation solely on grounds of size or materiality, and any permanent establishment for which separate account are produced for any purpose. Because the narrower definition in Turkey's legislation may result in business units and permanent establishments not being included in the filed report it is recommended that turkey take steps to amend its legislation or otherwise bring the definition of Constituent Entity in line with the standard.

(b) Scope and timing of parent entity filing

12. The first filing requirements for MNE Groups in Turkey enforce a CbC filing requirement for fiscal years commencing on or after 1 January 2019 and filing is required 12 months after the reporting year end.

13. With respect to the annual consolidated group revenue threshold where the MNE Group draws up, or would draw up, its Consolidated Financial Statements in a currency other than that specified by Turkey, the reference to Turkey's threshold has the effect as if it were a reference to the equivalent in that currency at the average exchange rate for the accounting period. While this provision would not create an issue for MNE Groups whose Ultimate Parent Entity is a tax resident in Turkey, it may be incompatible with the guidance on currency fluctuations for MNE Groups whose Ultimate Parent Entity is located in another jurisdiction, if local filing requirements were applied in respect of a Constituent Entity (which is a Turkey tax resident) of an MNE Group which does not reach the threshold as determined in the jurisdiction of the Ultimate Parent Entity of such a Group

14. This is an unintended consequence of having a local filing requirement and it its therefore recommended that Turkey clarify that the annual consolidated group revenue threshold calculation rule applies in line with the OECD guidance on currency fluctuations in respect of an MNE Group whose Ultimate Parent Entity is located in a jurisdiction other than Turkey.

(c) Limitation on local filing obligations

15. Turkey has introduced a local filing requirement which is in line with the terms of reference with regard to the circumstances in which a local filing requirement can be imposed.

16. No inconsistencies were identified

(d) Limitation on local filing in case of surrogate filing

17. Turkey's local filing requirements will not apply if there is surrogate filing in another jurisdiction.

18. No inconsistencies were identified

(e) Effective implementation

19. Turkey has systems to ensure effective implementation of the CbC filing requirement which include a notification requirement and a penalty regime in the case of late, inaccurate or non-filing of CbC reports.

Conclusion

20. Turkey has legislation to impose and enforce a CbC filing requirement that meets all of the terms of reference, with the exception that:

- It is recommended that Turkey take steps to amend its legislation or otherwise bring the definition of Constituent Entity in line with the standard

- It is recommended that Turkey clarify that the annual consolidated group revenue threshold calculation rule applies in line with the OECD guidance on currency fluctuations in respect of an MNE Group whose Ultimate Parent Entity is located in a jurisdiction other than Turkey.

Part B: The exchange of information framework

(a) Exchange of information framework

21. As of 31 March 2020, Turkey has no bilateral relationships in place for the exchange of CbC reports. It is recommended that Turkey take steps to have qualifying competent authority agreements in effect with jurisdictions of the Inclusive Framework that meet the confidentiality, consistency and appropriate use conditions and with which Turkey has an international exchange of information agreement in effect that allows for the automatic exchange of tax information.

(b) Content of information exchanged

22. No changes were identified.

(c) Completeness of exchanges

23. No changes were identified.

(d) Timeliness of exchanges

24. No changes were identified.

(e) Temporary suspension of exchange or termination of QCAA

25. No changes were identified.

(f) Consultation with other Competent Authority before determining systemic failure or significant non-compliance

26. No changes were identified.

(g) Format for information exchange

27. No changes were identified

(h) Method for transmission

28. No changes were identified.

Conclusion

29. It is recommended that Turkey take steps to have QCAAs in effect with jurisdictions of the Inclusive Framework which meet the confidentiality, consistency and appropriate use prerequisites and with which Turkey has an international exchange of information agreement in effect that allows for the automatic exchange of tax information. This recommendation remains unchanged since the 2017/2018 peer review.

30. It is recommended that Turkey take steps to implement processes or written procedures to ensure that the exchange of information is conducted in a manner consistent with the terms of reference relating to the exchange of information framework ahead of its first exchanges of information. This recommendation remains unchanged since the 2018/2019 peer review.

Part C: Appropriate use

Appropriate use

31. No changes were identified.

Conclusion

32. It is recommended that Turkey take steps to ensure that the appropriate use condition is met ahead of its first exchanges of information. This recommendation remains unchanged since the 2018/2019 peer review.

Summary of recommendations on the implementation of Country-by-Country Reporting

Aspect of the implementation that should be improved		Recommendation for improvement
Part A	Domestic legal and administrative framework	It is recommended that Turkey take steps to amend its legislation or otherwise bring the definition of Constituent Entity in line with the standard It is recommended that Turkey clarify that the annual consolidated group revenue threshold calculation rule applies in line with the OECD guidance on currency fluctuations in respect of an MNE Group whose Ultimate Parent Entity is located in a jurisdiction other than Turkey.
Part B	Exchange of information framework	It is recommended that Turkey take steps to have qualifying competent authority agreements in effect with jurisdictions of the Inclusive Framework that meet the confidentiality, consistency and appropriate use conditions and with which Turkey has an international exchange of information agreement in effect that allows for the automatic exchange of tax information
Part B	Exchange of information framework	It is recommended that Turkey take steps to implement the necessary processes or written procedures to ensure that the exchange of information is conducted in a manner consistent with the terms of reference relating to the exchange of information framework.
Part C	Appropriate use	It is recommended that Turkey take steps to ensure that the appropriate use condition is met ahead of the first exchanges of information.

References

OECD (2019), *Country-by-Country Reporting – Compilation of Peer Review Reports (Phase 2): Inclusive Framework on BEPS: Action 13*, OECD/G20 Base Erosion and Profit Shifting Project, OECD Publishing, Paris, https://dx.doi.org/10.1787/f9bf1157-en. [1]

OECD (2018), *Country-by-Country Reporting – Compilation of Peer Review Reports (Phase 1): Inclusive Framework on BEPS: Action 13*, OECD/G20 Base Erosion and Profit Shifting Project, OECD Publishing, Paris, https://dx.doi.org/10.1787/9789264300057-en. [2]

OECD (2017), *Terms of reference for the conduct of peer review of the Action 13 minimum standard on country-by-country reporting*, OECD Publishing, https://www.oecd.org/tax/beps/beps-action-13-on-country-by-country-reporting-peer-review-documents.pdf. [3]

Turks and Caicos Islands

1. Turks and Caicos Islands was first reviewed during the 2018/2019 peer review. This report is supplementary to that previous report (OECD, 2018[2]).

2. The first filing obligation for a CbC report in the Turks and Caicos Islands applies to reporting fiscal years ending on or after 1 January 2020.

Summary of key findings

3. Turks and Caicos Islands meets all the terms of reference (OECD, 2017[3]) relating to the domestic legal and administrative framework for implementing the BEPS Action 13 minimum standard.

4. It is recommended that Turks and Caicos Islands take steps to implement processes or written procedures to ensure that the exchange of information is conducted in a manner consistent with the terms of reference relating to the exchange of information framework ahead of the first exchanges of information. This recommendation remains unchanged since the 2018/2019 peer review.

Part A: The domestic legal and administrative framework

5. Turks and Caicos Islands has laws in place to implement the BEPS Action 13 minimum standard.

(a) Parent entity filing obligation

6. No changes were identified.

(b) Scope and timing of parent entity filing

7. No changes were identified.

(c) Limitation on local filing obligation

8. No changes were identified.

(d) Limitation on local filing in case of surrogate filing

9. No changes were identified.

(e) Effective implementation

10. No changes were identified.

Conclusion

11. Turks and Caicos Islands meets all the terms of reference relating to the domestic legal and administrative framework.

Part B: The exchange of information framework

(a) Exchange of information framework

12. As of 31 March 2020, Turks and Caicos Islands has 51 bilateral relationships in place for the exchange of CbC reports including those activated under the CbC MCAA and under bilateral QCAAs. Within the context of its international exchange of information agreements that allow automatic exchange of information, Turks and Caicos Islands has taken steps to have qualifying competent authority agreements in effect with jurisdictions of the Inclusive Framework that meet the confidentiality, consistency and appropriate use conditions.[1] Regarding Turks and Caicos Islands' exchange of information framework, no inconsistencies with the terms of reference were identified.

(b) Content of information exchanged

13. No changes were identified.

(c) Completeness of exchanges

14. No changes were identified.

(d) Timeliness of exchanges

15. No changes were identified.

(e) Temporary suspension of exchange or termination of QCAA

16. No changes were identified.

(f) Consultation with other Competent Authority before determining systemic failure or significant non-compliance

17. No changes were identified.

(g) Format for information exchange

18. No changes were identified.

(h) Method for transmission

19. No changes were identified.

Conclusion

20. It is recommended that Turks and Caicos Islands take steps to implement processes or written procedures to ensure that the exchange of information is conducted in a manner consistent with the terms of reference relating to the exchange of information framework ahead of its first exchanges of information. This recommendation remains unchanged since the 2018/2019 peer review.

Part C: Appropriate use

Appropriate use

21. No changes were identified.

Conclusion

22. Turks and Caicos Islands is a non-reciprocal jurisdiction and, as such, will not receive CbC reports submitted to tax authorities in other jurisdictions, and will not apply local filing. It is therefore not necessary for this peer review evaluation to reach any conclusions with respect to Turks and Caicos Islands' compliance with paragraphs 11(a), (b), (c) and (d) and paragraph 12(a) of the terms of reference on appropriate use.

Summary of recommendations on the implementation of Country-by-Country Reporting

Aspect of the implementation that should be improved		Recommendation for improvement
Part A	Domestic legal and administrative framework	-
Part B	Exchange of information framework	It is recommended that Turks and Caicos Islands take steps to implement the necessary processes or written procedures to ensure that the exchange of information is conducted in a manner consistent with the terms of reference relating to the exchange of information framework.
Part C	Appropriate use	-

References

OECD (2018), *Country-by-Country Reporting – Compilation of Peer Review Reports (Phase 1): Inclusive Framework on BEPS: Action 13*, OECD/G20 Base Erosion and Profit Shifting Project, OECD Publishing, Paris, https://dx.doi.org/10.1787/9789264300057-en. [2]

OECD (2017), *Terms of reference for the conduct of peer review of the Action 13 minimum standard on country-by-country reporting*, OECD Publishing, https://www.oecd.org/tax/beps/beps-action-13-on-country-by-country-reporting-peer-review-documents.pdf. [3]

Note

[1] No inconsistency with the terms of reference will be identified where a QCAA is not in effect with one or more jurisdictions of the Inclusive Framework that meet the confidentiality, consistency and appropriate use conditions, but this is due to circumstances that are not under the control of the reviewed jurisdiction. This may include, for example, where the other jurisdiction intends to exchange CbC reports using the MCAA but it does not have the Convention in effect for the relevant fiscal period, or where the other jurisdiction has declined to have a QCAA in effect with the reviewed jurisdiction.

Ukraine

1. Ukraine was reviewed as part of the 2017/2018 and the 2018/2019 peer reviews. This report is supplementary to those previous reports (OECD, 2019[1]) (OECD, 2018[2]).

2. The first filing obligation for a CbC report in Ukraine commences in respect of fiscal periods commencing on or after 1 January 2021.

Summary of key findings

3. Ukraine's 2017/2018 peer review report included a recommendation that Ukraine take steps to implement legislation to impose a CbC filing requirement. Ukraine signed a law to implement the BEPS Action 13 minimum standard on the 21st of May 2020. It has not been possible to carry out a review of this legislation for this peer review. The recommendation for Ukraine to implement legislation is therefore removed and review of the legislation will take place next year.

4. It is recommended that Ukraine take steps to have QCAAs in effect with jurisdictions of the Inclusive Framework which meet the confidentiality, consistency and appropriate use prerequisites and with which Ukraine has an international exchange of information agreement in effect that allows for the automatic exchange of tax information. This recommendation remains unchanged since the 2017/2018 peer review.

5. It is recommended that Ukraine take steps to implement processes or written procedures to ensure that the exchange of information is conducted in a manner consistent with the terms of reference (OECD, 2017[3]) relating to the exchange of information framework ahead of the first exchanges of information. This recommendation remains unchanged since the 2018/2019 peer review.

6. It is recommended that Ukraine take steps to ensure that the appropriate use condition is met ahead of the first exchanges of information. This recommendation remains unchanged since the 2017/2018 peer review.

Part A: The domestic legal and administrative framework

7. Ukraine's 2017/2018 peer review report included a recommendation that Ukraine take steps to implement legislation to impose a CbC filing requirement. Ukraine signed a law to implement the BEPS Action 13 minimum standard on the 21st of May 2020. It has not been possible to carry out a review of this legislation for this peer review. The recommendation for Ukraine to implement legislation is therefore removed and review of the legislation will take place next year.

(a) Parent entity filing obligation

(b) Scope and timing of parent entity filing

(c) Limitation on local filing obligation

(d) Limitation on local filing in case of surrogate filing

(e) Effective implementation

Conclusion

8. Ukraine's 2017/2018 peer review report included a recommendation that Ukraine take steps to implement legislation to impose a CbC filing requirement. Ukraine signed a law to implement the BEPS Action 13 minimum standard on the 21st of May 2020. It has not been possible to carry out a review of this legislation for this peer review. The recommendation for Ukraine to implement legislation is therefore removed and review of the legislation will take place next year.

Part B: The exchange of information framework

(a) Exchange of information framework

9. As of 31 March 2020, Ukraine has no bilateral relationships in place for the exchange of CbC reports. It is recommended that Ukraine take steps to have qualifying competent authority agreements in effect with jurisdictions of the Inclusive Framework that meet the confidentiality, consistency and appropriate use conditions and with which Ukraine has an international exchange of information agreement in effect that allows for the automatic exchange of tax information. This recommendation remains unchanged since the 2017/2018 peer review.

(b) Content of information exchanged

10. No changes were identified.

(c) Completeness of exchanges

11. No changes were identified.

(d) Timeliness of exchanges

12. No changes were identified.

(e) Temporary suspension of exchange or termination of QCAA

13. No changes were identified.

(f) Consultation with other Competent Authority before determining systemic failure or significant non-compliance

14. No changes were identified.

(g) Format for information exchange

15. No changes were identified.

(h) Method for transmission

16. No changes were identified.

Conclusion

17. It is recommended that Ukraine take steps to have QCAAs in effect with jurisdictions of the Inclusive Framework which meet the confidentiality, consistency and appropriate use prerequisites and with which Ukraine has an international exchange of information agreement in effect that allows for the automatic exchange of tax information remains. This recommendation remains unchanged since the 2017/2018 peer review.

18. It is recommended that Ukraine take steps to implement processes or written procedures to ensure that the exchange of information is conducted in a manner consistent with the terms of reference relating to the exchange of information framework ahead of its first exchanges of information. This recommendation remains unchanged since the 2018/2019 peer review.

Part C: Appropriate use

Appropriate use

19. No changes were identified.

Conclusion

20. It is recommended that Ukraine take steps to ensure that the appropriate use condition is met ahead of its first exchanges of information. This recommendation remains unchanged since the 2017/2018 peer review.

Summary of recommendations on the implementation of Country-by-Country Reporting

Aspect of the implementation that should be improved		Recommendation for improvement
Part A	Domestic legal and administrative framework	A review of Ukraine's domestic legal and administrative framework will be undertaken as part of the next BEPS Action 13 peer review.
Part B	Exchange of information framework	It is recommended that Ukraine take steps to have QCAAs in effect with jurisdictions of the Inclusive Framework which meet the confidentiality, consistency and appropriate use prerequisites and with which it has an international exchange of information agreement in effect that allows for the automatic exchange of tax information.
Part B	Exchange of information framework	It is recommended that Ukraine take steps to implement the necessary processes or written procedures to ensure that the exchange of information is conducted in a manner consistent with the terms of reference relating to the exchange of information framework.
Part C	Appropriate use	It is recommended that Ukraine take steps to ensure that the appropriate use condition is met ahead of the first exchanges of information.

References

OECD (2019), *Country-by-Country Reporting – Compilation of Peer Review Reports (Phase 2): Inclusive Framework on BEPS: Action 13*, OECD/G20 Base Erosion and Profit Shifting Project, OECD Publishing, Paris, https://dx.doi.org/10.1787/f9bf1157-en. [1]

OECD (2018), *Country-by-Country Reporting – Compilation of Peer Review Reports (Phase 1): Inclusive Framework on BEPS: Action 13*, OECD/G20 Base Erosion and Profit Shifting Project, OECD Publishing, Paris, https://dx.doi.org/10.1787/9789264300057-en. [2]

OECD (2017), *Terms of reference for the conduct of peer review of the Action 13 minimum standard on country-by-country reporting*, OECD Publishing, https://www.oecd.org/tax/beps/beps-action-13-on-country-by-country-reporting-peer-review-documents.pdf. [3]

United Arab Emirates

1. The United Arab Emirates was first reviewed during the 2018/2019 peer review. This report is supplementary to that previous report (OECD, 2018[2]).

2. The filing obligation for a CbC report the UAE applies to reporting fiscal years commencing on or after 1 January 2019.

Summary of key findings

3. The UAE's implementation of the Action 13 minimum standard meets all applicable terms of reference (OECD, 2017[3]).

4. The UAE's 2018/2019 peer review included a recommendation that the UAE take steps to implement a domestic legal and administrative framework to impose and enforce CbC requirements as soon as possible. The UAE now has the primary law in place to impose and enforce CbC requirements and the recommendation with respect to domestic legal and administrative framework issued in the 2018/2019 peer review is removed.

5. The UAE's 2018/2019 peer review included a recommendation that the UAE take steps to have QCAAs in effect with jurisdictions of the Inclusive Framework which meet the confidentiality, consistency and appropriate use prerequisites and with which the UAE has an international exchange of information agreement in effect that allows for the automatic exchange of tax information. Relationships are now in place and this recommendation is removed.

6. The UAE's 2018/2019 peer review included a recommendation that the UAE take steps to implement processes or written procedures to ensure that the exchange of information is conducted in a manner consistent with the terms of reference (OECD, 2017[3]) relating to the exchange of information framework ahead of the first exchanges of information. This recommendation remains in place since the 2018/2019 peer review.

Part A: The domestic legal and administrative framework

7. The UAE has law in place to implement the BEPS Action 13 minimum standard, establishing the necessary requirements including the filing and reporting obligations.

(a) Parent entity filing obligation

8. The UAE has primary law which imposes a CbC filing obligation on Ultimate Parent Entities of MNE Groups which have a consolidated group revenue above a certain threshold, whereby all required Constituent Entities of the MNE Group are included in the CbC report and no entity is excluded from CbC Reporting other than permitted by the Action 13 report (OECD, 2015).

9. No inconsistencies were identified.

(b) Scope and timing of parent entity filing

10. The first filing obligation for a CbC report in the UAE commences in respect of fiscal years beginning on 1 January 2019 or later. The CbC report must be filed within 12 months of the last day of the fiscal year of the MNE Group.

11. No inconsistencies were identified.

(c) Limitation on local filing obligation

12. The UAE does not apply local filing.

(d) Limitation on local filing in case of surrogate filing

13. The UAE does not apply local filing.

(e) Effective implementation

14. The UAE has legal mechanisms in place to enforce compliance with the minimum standard: there are notification mechanisms in place that apply to the Ultimate Parent Entity. There are also penalties in place in relation to the filing of a CbC report: (i) penalties for failure to file a CbC report and late filing and (ii) penalties for inaccurate information.

Conclusion

15. The UAE's 2018/2019 peer review included a recommendation that the UAE take steps to implement a domestic legal and administrative framework to impose and enforce CbC requirements as soon as possible. The UAE now has the primary law in place to impose and enforce CbC requirements. As such, the recommendation with respect to domestic legal and administrative framework issued in the 2018/2019 peer review is removed. The UAE meets all the terms of reference relating to the domestic legal and administrative framework.

Part B: The exchange of information framework

(a) Exchange of information framework

16. The UAE's 2018/2019 peer review included a recommendation that the UAE take steps to have QCAAs in effect with jurisdictions of the Inclusive Framework which meet the confidentiality, consistency and appropriate use prerequisites and with which the UAE has an international exchange of information agreement in effect that allows for the automatic exchange of tax information. Relationships are now in place and this recommendation is removed.

17. As of 31 March 2020, UAE has 49 bilateral relationships in place for the exchange of CbC reports including those activated under the CbC MCAA. Within the context of its international exchange of information agreements that allow automatic exchange of information, the UAE has taken steps to have qualifying competent authority agreements in effect with jurisdictions of the Inclusive Framework that meet the confidentiality, consistency and appropriate use conditions. Regarding UAE's exchange of information framework, no inconsistencies with the terms of reference were identified.

(b) Content of information exchanged

18. No changes were identified.

(c) Completeness of exchanges

19. No changes were identified.

(d) Timeliness of exchanges

20. No changes were identified.

(e) Temporary suspension of exchange or termination of QCAA

21. No changes were identified.

(f) Consultation with other Competent Authority before determining systemic failure or significant non-compliance

22. No changes were identified.

(g) Format for information exchange

23. The UAE indicates that it intends to use the OECD XML Schema and User Guide (OECD, 2017[4]) for the international exchange of CbC reports.

(h) Method for transmission

24. The UAE indicates that it intends to use the Common Transmission System to exchange CbC reports.

Conclusion

25. The UAE's 2018/2019 peer report included a recommendation that UAE take steps to put QCAAs in effect with jurisdictions of the Inclusive Framework which meet the confidentiality, consistency and appropriate use prerequisites and with which UAE has an international exchange of information agreement in effect that allows for the automatic exchange of tax information. Relationships are now in place and this recommendation is removed.

26. It is recommended that UAE take steps to implement processes or written procedures to ensure that the exchange of information is conducted in a manner consistent with the terms of reference relating to the exchange of information framework ahead of its first exchanges of information. This recommendation remains in place since the 2018/2019 peer review.

Part C: Appropriate use

Appropriate use

27. No changes were identified.

Conclusion

28. The United Arab Emirates is a non-reciprocal jurisdiction and, as such, will not receive CbC reports submitted to tax authorities in other jurisdictions, and will not apply local filing. It is therefore not necessary for this peer review evaluation to reach any conclusions with respect to the United Arab Emirates' compliance with paragraphs 11(a), (b), (c) and (d) and paragraph 12(a) of the terms of reference on appropriate use.

Summary of recommendations on the implementation of Country-by-Country Reporting

Aspect of the implementation that should be improved		Recommendation for improvement
Part A	Domestic legal and administrative framework	-
Part B	Exchange of information framework	-
Part B	Exchange of information framework	It is recommended that the United Arab Emirates take steps to implement the necessary processes or written procedures to ensure that the exchange of information is conducted in a manner consistent with the terms of reference relating to the exchange of information framework.
Part C	Appropriate use	-

References

OECD (2018), *Country-by-Country Reporting – Compilation of Peer Review Reports (Phase 1): Inclusive Framework on BEPS: Action 13*, OECD/G20 Base Erosion and Profit Shifting Project, OECD Publishing, Paris, https://dx.doi.org/10.1787/9789264300057-en. [2]

OECD (2017), *Terms of reference for the conduct of peer review of the Action 13 minimum standard on country-by-country reporting*, OECD Publishing, https://www.oecd.org/tax/beps/beps-action-13-on-country-by-country-reporting-peer-review-documents.pdf. [3]

United Kingdom

1. The United Kingdom was reviewed as part of the 2017/2018 and the 2018/2019 peer reviews. This report is supplementary to those previous reports (OECD, 2019[1]) (OECD, 2018[2]). The first filing obligation for a CbC report in the United Kingdom applies to reporting fiscal years commencing on or after 1 January 2016.

Summary of key findings

2. The United Kingdom's implementation of the Action 13 minimum standard meets all applicable terms of reference (OECD, 2017[3]).

Part A: The domestic legal and administrative framework

3. The United Kingdom has primary and secondary laws to implement the BEPS Action 13 minimum standard, establishing the necessary requirements including the filing and reporting obligations.

(a) Parent entity filing obligation

4. No changes were identified.

(b) Scope and timing of parent entity filing

5. No changes were identified.

(c) Limitation on local filing obligation

6. No changes were identified. The United Kingdom's 2017/2018 peer review included monitoring points[1] that remain in place.

(d) Limitation on local filing in case of surrogate filing

7. No changes were identified.

(e) Effective implementation

8. No changes were identified.

Conclusion

9. The United Kingdom meets all the terms of reference relating to the domestic legal and administrative framework.

Part B: The exchange of information framework

(a) Exchange of information framework

10. As of 31 March 2020, the United Kingdom has 68 bilateral relationships, including those activated under the CbC MCAA, under bilateral CAAs and under the EU Council Directive (2016/881/EU). Within the context of its international exchange of information agreements that allow automatic exchange of

information, the United Kingdom has taken steps to have qualifying competent authority agreements in effect with jurisdictions of the Inclusive Framework that meet the confidentiality, consistency and appropriate use conditions and with which the United Kingdom has an international exchange of information agreement in effect that allows for the automatic exchange of tax information.[2] Regarding the United Kingdom's exchange of information framework, no inconsistencies with the terms of reference were identified[3].

(b) Content of information exchanged

11. No changes were identified.

(c) Completeness of exchanges

12. No changes were identified.

(d) Timeliness of exchanges

13. No changes were identified.

(e) Temporary suspension of exchange or termination of QCAA

14. No changes were identified.

(f) Consultation with other Competent Authority before determining systemic failure or significant non-compliance

15. No changes were identified.

(g) Format for information exchange

16. No changes were identified.

(h) Method for transmission

17. No changes were identified.

Conclusion

18. The United Kingdom meets all the terms of reference regarding the exchange of information.

Part C: Appropriate use

Appropriate use

19. No changes were identified.

Conclusion

20. The United Kingdom meets all the terms of reference relating to appropriate use of CbC reports.

Summary of recommendations on the implementation of Country-by-Country Reporting

Aspect of the implementation that should be improved		Recommendation for improvement
Part A	Domestic legal and administrative framework	-
Part B	Exchange of information framework	-
Part C	Appropriate use	-

References

OECD (2019), *Country-by-Country Reporting – Compilation of Peer Review Reports (Phase 2): Inclusive Framework on BEPS: Action 13*, OECD/G20 Base Erosion and Profit Shifting Project, OECD Publishing, Paris, https://dx.doi.org/10.1787/f9bf1157-en. [1]

OECD (2018), *Country-by-Country Reporting – Compilation of Peer Review Reports (Phase 1): Inclusive Framework on BEPS: Action 13*, OECD/G20 Base Erosion and Profit Shifting Project, OECD Publishing, Paris, https://dx.doi.org/10.1787/9789264300057-en. [2]

OECD (2017), *Terms of reference for the conduct of peer review of the Action 13 minimum standard on country-by-country reporting*, OECD Publishing, https://www.oecd.org/tax/beps/beps-action-13-on-country-by-country-reporting-peer-review-documents.pdf. [3]

Notes

[1] With respect to the conditions under which local filing may be required (paragraph 8 (c) iv. b) and c) of the terms of reference).

[2] No inconsistency with the terms of reference will be identified where a QCAA is not in effect with one or more jurisdictions of the Inclusive Framework that meet the confidentiality, consistency and appropriate use conditions, but this is due to circumstances that are not under the control of the reviewed jurisdiction. This may include, for example, where the other jurisdiction intends to exchange CbC reports using the MCAA but it does not have the Convention in effect for the relevant fiscal period, or where the other jurisdiction has declined to have a QCAA in effect with the reviewed jurisdiction

[3] No inconsistency with the terms of reference will be identified where a QCAA is not in effect with one or more jurisdictions of the Inclusive Framework that meet the confidentiality, consistency and appropriate use conditions, but this is due to circumstances that are not under the control of the reviewed jurisdiction. This may include, for example, where the other jurisdiction intends to exchange CbC reports using the MCAA but it does not have the Convention in effect for the relevant fiscal period, or where the other jurisdiction has declined to have a QCAA in effect with the reviewed jurisdiction

United States

1. The United States was reviewed as part of the 2017/2018 and the 2018/2019 peer reviews. This report is supplementary to those previous reports (OECD, 2019[1]) (OECD, 2018[2]).

2. The first filing obligation for a CbC report in the United States applies to reporting fiscal years commencing on or after 1 July 2016. The United States also allows its MNE groups to file a CbC report on a voluntary basis, for reporting fiscal years beginning between 1 January 2016 and 30 June 2016.

Summary of key findings

3. The United States implementation of the Action 13 minimum standard meets all applicable terms of reference (OECD, 2017[3]), except for the following:

- It is recommended that the United States ensure that the definitions of "revenue" for the purposes of applying the threshold and for completing Table 1 are consistent with the definition in the Action 13 minimum standard, as further clarified by OECD guidance. This recommendation remains unchanged since the 2017/2018 peer review.
- It is recommended that the United States' competent authority should continue to work actively towards signing bilateral competent authority arrangements with jurisdictions of the Inclusive Framework that meet the confidentiality, consistency and appropriate use conditions, and with which the United States has an agreement in effect that allows for the automatic exchange of information. This recommendation remains unchanged since the 2017/2018 peer review.

Part A: The domestic legal and administrative framework

4. The United States has laws in place to implement the BEPS Action 13 minimum standard.

(a) Parent entity filing obligation

5. No changes were identified.[1]

(b) Scope and timing of parent entity filing

6. It is recommended that the United States ensure that the definitions of "revenue" for the purposes of the threshold and for completing Table 1 are consistent with the definition in the Action 13 minimum standard as further clarified by OECD guidance. This recommendation remains in place since the 2017/2018 peer review.

(c) Limitation on local filing obligation

7. No changes were identified.

(d) Limitation on local filing in case of surrogate filing

8. No changes were identified.

(e) Effective implementation

9. No changes were identified.

Conclusion

10. It is recommended that the United States ensure that the definitions of "revenue" for the purposes of the threshold and for completing Table 1 are consistent with the definition in the Action 13 minimum standard as further clarified by OECD guidance. This recommendation remains in place since the 2017/2018 peer review.

Part B: The exchange of information framework

(a) Exchange of information framework

11. As at 31 March 2020, the United States has 44 bilateral relationships activated under bilateral QCAAs.[2] A number of additional bilateral arrangements are expected to be signed soon. While noting that some time is needed for bilateral negotiations the United States' competent authority should continue to work actively towards signing bilateral competent authority arrangements with jurisdictions of the Inclusive Framework that meet the confidentiality, consistency, and appropriate use conditions, and with which the United States has an agreement in effect that allows for the automatic exchange of information.

(b) Content of information exchanged

12. No changes were identified.

(c) Completeness of exchanges

13. No changes were identified.

(d) Timeliness of exchanges

14. The US reports that in certain limited circumstances some US taxpayers are authorized to file on paper and this has resulted in a number of reports being exchanged late. The US has implemented functionality to create files in XML Schema format from the paper-filed CbC reports within their CbC report processing capability. As this issue has already been addressed no recommendation is required.

(e) Temporary suspension of exchange or termination of QCAA

15. No changes were identified.

(f) Consultation with other Competent Authority before determining systemic failure or significant non-compliance

16. No changes were identified.

(g) Format for information exchange

17. No changes were identified.

(h) Method for transmission

18. No changes were identified.

Conclusion

19. It is recommended that the United States' competent authority should continue to work actively towards signing bilateral competent authority arrangements with jurisdictions of the Inclusive Framework that meet the confidentiality, consistency and appropriate use conditions, and with which the United States

has an agreement in effect that allows for the automatic exchange of information. This recommendation remains unchanged since the 2017/2018 peer review.

Part C: Appropriate use

Appropriate use

20. No changes were identified.

Conclusion

21. The United States meets all the terms of reference relating to appropriate use of CbC reports.

Summary of recommendations on the implementation of country-by-country reporting

Aspect of the implementation that should be improved		Recommendation for improvement
Part A	Domestic legal and administrative framework – limitation on local filing obligation	It is recommended that the United States ensure that the definitions of "revenue" for the purposes of applying the threshold and for completing Table 1 are consistent with the definition in the Action 13 minimum standard, as further clarified by OECD guidance.
Part B	Exchange of information framework	The United States competent authority should continue to work actively towards signing bilateral competent authority arrangements with jurisdictions of the Inclusive Framework that meet the confidentiality, consistency and appropriate use conditions and with which the United States has an agreement in effect that allows for the automatic exchange of information
Part C	Appropriate use	-

References

OECD (2019), *Country-by-Country Reporting – Compilation of Peer Review Reports (Phase 2): Inclusive Framework on BEPS: Action 13*, OECD/G20 Base Erosion and Profit Shifting Project, OECD Publishing, Paris, https://dx.doi.org/10.1787/f9bf1157-en. [1]

OECD (2018), *Country-by-Country Reporting – Compilation of Peer Review Reports (Phase 1): Inclusive Framework on BEPS: Action 13*, OECD/G20 Base Erosion and Profit Shifting Project, OECD Publishing, Paris, https://dx.doi.org/10.1787/9789264300057-en. [2]

OECD (2017), *Terms of reference for the conduct of peer review of the Action 13 minimum standard on country-by-country reporting*, OECD Publishing, https://www.oecd.org/tax/beps/beps-action-13-on-country-by-country-reporting-peer-review-documents.pdf. [3]

Notes

[1] The United States operates a modified filing requirement for MNEs which qualify as state security contractors. In light of the United States' explanations and the limited number of MNE groups that are likely to qualify for the specified national security contractor status, no recommendation is made, but use of

modified reporting will be monitored. This monitoring point remains in place since the 2018/2019 peer review.

[2] In addition, joint statements have been issued by the Competent Authorities of the United States and France and by the Competent Authorities of the United States and Germany expressing the intention to spontaneously exchange CbC reports for fiscal years of MNE groups commencing on or after January 1, 2016 and before January 1, 2019, while bilateral QCAAs are being negotiated.

Uruguay

1. Uruguay was reviewed as part of the 2017/2018 and the 2018/2019 peer reviews. This report is supplementary to those previous reports (OECD, 2019[1]) (OECD, 2018[2]).

2. The first filing obligation for a CbC report in Uruguay commences in respect of reporting fiscal years commencing on or after 1 January 2017.

Summary of key findings

3. Uruguay's implementation of the Action 13 minimum standard meets all applicable terms of reference (OECD, 2017[3]), except for the following:

- It is recommended that Uruguay amend its local filing conditions as they are wider than the circumstances when local filing may be required under the terms of reference. This recommendation remains unchanged since the 2017/2018 peer review.

Part A: The domestic legal and administrative framework

4. Uruguay's law in place to implement the BEPS Action 13 minimum standard.

(a) Parent entity filing obligation

5. No changes were identified.

(b) Scope and timing of parent entity filing

6. No changes were identified.

(c) Limitation on local filing obligation

7. The 2017/2018 peer review included a recommendation to amend its local filing conditions as they are wider than the circumstances when local filing may be required under paragraph 8(c) iv. a) b) and c) of the terms of reference.[1] This recommendation remains in place.

(d) Limitation on local filing in case of surrogate filing

8. No changes were identified.

(e) Effective implementation

9. No changes were identified.[2]

Conclusion

10. It is recommended that Uruguay amend its local filing conditions as they are wider than the circumstances when local filing may be required under the terms of reference. This recommendation remains unchanged since the 2017/2018 peer review.

Part B: The exchange of information framework

(a) Exchange of information framework

11. As of 31 March 2020 Uruguay has 63 bilateral relationships, including those activated under the CbC MCAA and under bilateral CAAs. Within the context of its international exchange of information agreements that allow automatic exchange of information, Uruguay has taken steps to have Qualifying Competent Authority agreements in effect with jurisdictions of the Inclusive Framework that meet the confidentiality, consistency and appropriate use conditions.[3]

(b) Content of information exchanged

12. No changes were identified.

(c) Completeness of exchanges

13. No changes were identified.

(d) Timeliness of exchanges

14. No changes were identified.

(e) Temporary suspension of exchange or termination of QCAA

15. No changes were identified.

(f) Consultation with other Competent Authority before determining systemic failure or significant non-compliance

16. No changes were identified.

(g) Format for information exchange

17. No changes were identified.

(h) Method for transmission

18. No changes were identified.

Conclusion

19. Uruguay meets all the terms of reference regarding the exchange of information.

Part C: Appropriate use

Appropriate use

20. No changes were identified.

Conclusion

21. Uruguay meets all the terms of reference relating to appropriate use of CbC reports.

Summary of recommendations on the implementation of Country-by-Country Reporting

Aspect of the implementation that should be improved		Recommendation for improvement
Part A	Domestic legal and administrative framework	It is recommended that Uruguay amend the conditions for local filing or otherwise take steps to ensure that local filing can only be required in the circumstances contained in the terms of reference.
Part B	Exchange of information framework	-
Part C	Appropriate use	-

References

OECD (2019), *Country-by-Country Reporting – Compilation of Peer Review Reports (Phase 2): Inclusive Framework on BEPS: Action 13*, OECD/G20 Base Erosion and Profit Shifting Project, OECD Publishing, Paris, https://dx.doi.org/10.1787/f9bf1157-en. [1]

OECD (2018), *Country-by-Country Reporting – Compilation of Peer Review Reports (Phase 1): Inclusive Framework on BEPS: Action 13*, OECD/G20 Base Erosion and Profit Shifting Project, OECD Publishing, Paris, https://dx.doi.org/10.1787/9789264300057-en. [2]

OECD (2017), *Terms of reference for the conduct of peer review of the Action 13 minimum standard on country-by-country reporting*, OECD Publishing, https://www.oecd.org/tax/beps/beps-action-13-on-country-by-country-reporting-peer-review-documents.pdf. [3]

Notes

[1] See fifth subparagraph, article 46 ter, Title 4 of the 1996 T.O.

[2] Uruguay's 2017/2018 peer review included a monitoring point relating to the absence of processes in place to take appropriate measures in case Uruguay is notified by another jurisdiction that an error may have led to incorrect or incomplete information reporting by a Reporting Entity or that there is non-compliance of a Reporting Entity with respect to its obligation to file a CbC report. This monitoring point remains in place.

[3] No inconsistency with the terms of reference will be identified where a QCAA is not in effect with one or more jurisdictions of the Inclusive Framework that meet the confidentiality, consistency and appropriate use conditions, but this is due to circumstances that are not under the control of the reviewed jurisdiction. This may include, for example, where the other jurisdiction intends to exchange CbC reports using the MCAA but it does not have the Convention in effect for the relevant fiscal period, or where the other jurisdiction has declined to have a QCAA in effect with the reviewed jurisdiction

Viet Nam

1. Viet Nam was first reviewed during the 2018/2019 peer review. This report is supplementary to that previous report (OECD, 2018[2]).

2. The filing obligation for a CbC report in Viet Nam applies to reporting fiscal years commencing on or after 1 May 2017.

Summary of key findings

3. Viet Nam's implementation of the Action 13 domestic legal and administrative framework meets all applicable terms of reference (OECD, 2017[3]), except that:

- It is recommended that Viet Nam take steps to amend its legislation or otherwise issue detailed definitions and requirements to bring it in line with the Action 13 minimum standard. This recommendation remains in place since the 2018/2019 peer review.
- It is recommended that Viet Nam take steps to amend its legislation or otherwise clarify that local filing in Viet Nam is only required in line with the minimum standard for Action 13. This recommendation remains in place since the 2018/2019 peer review.
- It is recommended that Viet Nam amend its legislation or otherwise take steps to ensure that enforcement provisions relating to effective implementation of filing requirement for the CbCR are provided for as required by the terms of reference as soon as possible. This recommendation remains in place since the 2018/2019 peer review.

4. It is recommended that Viet Nam take steps to have QCAAs in effect with jurisdictions of the Inclusive Framework which meet the confidentiality, consistency and appropriate use prerequisites and with which it has an international exchange of information agreement in effect that allows for the automatic exchange of tax information. This recommendation remains unchanged since the 2018/2019 peer review.

5. It is recommended that Viet Nam take steps to implement processes or written procedures to ensure that the exchange of information is conducted in a manner consistent with the terms of reference relating to the exchange of information framework as soon as possible. This recommendation remains unchanged since the 2018/2019 peer review.

6. It is recommended that Viet Nam take steps to ensure that the appropriate use condition is met as soon as possible. This recommendation remains unchanged since the 2018/2019 peer review.

Part A: The domestic legal and administrative framework

(a) Parent entity filing obligation

7. No changes were identified.

(b) Scope and timing of parent entity filing

8. No changes were identified.

(c) Limitation on local filing obligation

9. No changes were identified.

(d) Limitation on local filing in case of surrogate filing

10. No changes were identified.

(e) Effective implementation

11. No changes were identified.

Conclusion

12. It is recommended that Viet Nam take steps to amend its legislation or otherwise issue detailed definitions and requirements to bring it in line with the Action 13 minimum standard. This recommendation remains in place since the 2018/2019 peer review

13. It is recommended that Viet Nam take steps to amend its legislation to require local filing only as allowed under the terms of the minimum standard

14. It is recommended that Viet Nam take steps to implement a domestic legal and administrative framework to enforce and monitor effective implementation of reporting as soon as possible.

Part B: The exchange of information framework

(a) Exchange of information framework

15. As of 31 March 2020, Viet Nam has no bilateral relationships in place for the exchange of CbC reports. It is recommended that Viet Nam take steps to have qualifying competent authority agreements in effect with jurisdictions of the Inclusive Framework that meet the confidentiality, consistency and appropriate use conditions and with which Viet Nam has an international exchange of information agreement in effect that allows for the automatic exchange of tax information.

(b) Content of information exchanged

16. No changes were identified.

(c) Completeness of exchanges

17. No changes were identified.

(d) Timeliness of exchanges

18. No changes were identified.

(e) Temporary suspension of exchange or termination of QCAA

19. No changes were identified.

(f) Consultation with other Competent Authority before determining systemic failure or significant non-compliance

20. No changes were identified.

(g) Format for information exchange

21. No changes were identified.

(h) Method for transmission

22. No changes were identified.

Conclusion

23. It is recommended that Viet Nam take steps to have qualifying competent authority agreements in effect with jurisdictions of the Inclusive Framework that meet the confidentiality, consistency and appropriate use conditions and with which Viet Nam has an international exchange of information agreement in effect that allows for the automatic exchange of tax information. This recommendation remains unchanged since the 2018/2019 peer review.

24. It is recommended that Viet Nam take steps to implement processes or written procedures to ensure that the exchange of information is conducted in a manner consistent with the terms of reference relating to the exchange of information framework ahead of its first exchanges of information. This recommendation remains unchanged since the 2018/2019 peer review.

Part C: Appropriate use

Appropriate use

25. No changes were identified.

Conclusion

26. It is recommended that Viet Nam take steps to ensure that the appropriate use condition is met ahead of its first exchanges of information.

Summary of recommendations on the implementation of Country-by-Country Reporting

Aspect of the implementation that should be improved		Recommendation for improvement
Part A	Domestic legal and administrative framework	It is recommended that Viet Nam take steps to amend its legislation or otherwise issue detailed definitions and requirements to bring it in line with the Action 13 minimum standard
Part A	Domestic legal and administrative framework	It is recommended that Viet Nam take steps to amend its legislation or otherwise clarify that local filing in Viet Nam is only required in line with the minimum standard for Action13
Part A	Domestic legal and administrative framework	It is recommended that Viet Nam amend its legislation or otherwise take steps to ensure that enforcement provisions relating to the CbCR's effective implementation are provided for as required by the terms of reference as soon as possible.
Part B	Exchange of information framework	It is recommended that Viet Nam take steps to have qualifying competent authority agreements in effect with jurisdictions of the Inclusive Framework that meet the confidentiality, consistency and appropriate use conditions and with which Viet Nam has an international exchange of information agreement in effect that allows for the automatic exchange of tax information
Part B	Exchange of information framework	It is recommended that Viet Nam take steps to implement processes or written procedures to ensure that the exchange of information is conducted in a manner consistent with the terms of reference relating to the exchange of information framework ahead of the first exchanges of information.
Part C	Appropriate use	It is recommended that Viet Nam take steps to ensure that the appropriate use condition is met ahead of the first exchanges of information.

References

OECD (2018), *Country-by-Country Reporting – Compilation of Peer Review Reports (Phase 1): Inclusive Framework on BEPS: Action 13*, OECD/G20 Base Erosion and Profit Shifting Project, OECD Publishing, Paris, https://dx.doi.org/10.1787/9789264300057-en. [2]

OECD (2017), *Terms of reference for the conduct of peer review of the Action 13 minimum standard on country-by-country reporting*, OECD Publishing, https://www.oecd.org/tax/beps/beps-action-13-on-country-by-country-reporting-peer-review-documents.pdf. [3]

Zambia

1. Zambia was first reviewed during the 2018/2019 peer review. This report is supplementary to that previous report (OECD, 2018[2]).

2. There is no filing obligation for a CbC report in Zambia yet.

Summary of key findings

3. Zambia does not yet have legislation in place for implementing the BEPS Action 13 minimum standard.

4. It is recommended that Zambia take steps to implement a domestic legal and administrative framework to impose and enforce CbC reporting requirements as soon as possible.

5. It is recommended that Zambia take steps to have qualifying competent authority agreements in effect with jurisdictions of the Inclusive Framework that meet the confidentiality, consistency and appropriate use conditions and with which Zambia has an international exchange of information agreement in effect that allows for the automatic exchange of tax information.

6. It is recommended that Zambia take steps to implement processes or written procedures to ensure that the exchange of information is conducted in a manner consistent with the terms of reference (OECD, 2017[3]) relating to the exchange of information framework ahead of the first exchanges of information.

7. It is recommended that Zambia take steps to ensure that the appropriate use condition is met ahead of the first exchanges of information.

8. These recommendations remain in place from the 2018/2019 peer review.

Part A: The domestic legal and administrative framework

9. Zambia does not yet have legislation in place for implementing the BEPS Action 13 minimum standard.

(a) Parent entity filing obligation

(b) Scope and timing of parent entity filing

(c) Limitation on local filing obligation

(d) Limitation on local filing in case of surrogate filing

(e) Effective implementation

Conclusion

10. It is recommended that Zambia take steps to implement a domestic legal and administrative framework to impose and enforce CbC reporting requirements as soon as possible.

Part B: The exchange of information framework

(a) Exchange of information framework

11. As of 31 March 2020, Zambia has no bilateral relationships in place for the exchange of CbC reports. It is recommended that Zambia take steps to have qualifying competent authority agreements in effect with jurisdictions of the Inclusive Framework that meet the confidentiality, consistency and appropriate use conditions and with which Zambia has an international exchange of information agreement in effect that allows for the automatic exchange of tax information.

(b) Content of information exchanged

12. No changes were identified.

(c) Completeness of exchanges

13. No changes were identified.

(d) Timeliness of exchanges

14. No changes were identified.

(e) Temporary suspension of exchange or termination of QCAA

15. No changes were identified.

(f) Consultation with other Competent Authority before determining systemic failure or significant non-compliance

16. No changes were identified.

(g) Format for information exchange

17. No changes were identified.

(h) Method for transmission

18. No changes were identified.

Conclusion

19. It is recommended that Zambia take steps to have qualifying competent authority agreements in effect with jurisdictions of the Inclusive Framework that meet the confidentiality, consistency and appropriate use conditions and with which Zambia has an international exchange of information agreement in effect that allows for the automatic exchange of tax information. This recommendation remains unchanged since the 2018/2019 peer review.

20. It is recommended that Zambia take steps to implement processes or written procedures to ensure that the exchange of information is conducted in a manner consistent with the terms of reference relating to the exchange of information framework ahead of its first exchanges of information. This recommendation remains unchanged since the 2018/2019 peer review.

Part C: Appropriate use

Appropriate use

21. No changes were identified.

Conclusion

22. It is recommended that Zambia take steps to ensure that the appropriate use condition is met ahead of its first exchanges of information.

Summary of recommendations on the implementation of Country-by-Country Reporting

Aspect of the implementation that should be improved		Recommendation for improvement
Part A	Domestic legal and administrative framework	It is recommended that Zambia take steps to implement a domestic legal and administrative framework to impose and enforce CbC requirements as soon as possible.
Part B	Exchange of information framework	It is recommended that Zambia take steps to have qualifying competent authority agreements in effect with jurisdictions of the Inclusive Framework that meet the confidentiality, consistency and appropriate use conditions and with which Zambia has an international exchange of information agreement in effect that allows for the automatic exchange of tax information.
Part B	Exchange of information framework	It is recommended that Zambia take steps to implement the necessary processes or written procedures to ensure that the exchange of information is conducted in a manner consistent with the terms of reference relating to the exchange of information framework.
Part C	Appropriate use	It is recommended that Zambia take steps to ensure that the appropriate use condition is met ahead of the first exchanges of information.

References

OECD (2018), *Country-by-Country Reporting – Compilation of Peer Review Reports (Phase 1): Inclusive Framework on BEPS: Action 13*, OECD/G20 Base Erosion and Profit Shifting Project, OECD Publishing, Paris, https://dx.doi.org/10.1787/9789264300057-en. [2]

OECD (2017), *Terms of reference for the conduct of peer review of the Action 13 minimum standard on country-by-country reporting*, OECD Publishing, https://www.oecd.org/tax/beps/beps-action-13-on-country-by-country-reporting-peer-review-documents.pdf. [3]

Printed by Libri Plureos GmbH in Hamburg,
Germany